Clare Hollingworth's dramatic career ... the world heard from her that the Second World War was about to start, as she was reporting from the Polish border when German tanks invaded on September 1, 1939. She covered the Italian invasion of Greece, the war in the Western Desert and other key events. During the 1950s she spent much time in strife-torn Algeria where her bravery became proverbial. She covered fighting between India and Pakistan, and the Vietnam war. She has been the *Daily Telegraph* Correspondent in Peking and until recently the paper's Defence Correspondent. She now lectures at the University of Hong Kong and is a research worker at the Centre of Asian Studies.

By the same author

The Three Weeks' War In Poland
There's a German Just Behind Me
The Arabs and The West

CLARE HOLLINGWORTH

Mao

TRIAD PALADIN
GRAFTON BOOKS

LONDON GLASGOW
TORONTO SYDNEY AUCKLAND

Triad Paladin
Grafton Books
8 Grafton Street, London W1X 3LA

Published by Triad Paladin 1987

Triad Paperbacks Ltd is an imprint of
Chatto, Bodley Head & Jonathan Cape Ltd and
Grafton Books, A Division of the Collins Publishing Group

First published in Great Britain by
Jonathan Cape Ltd 1985

Copyright © Clare Hollingworth 1985

ISBN 0-586-08545-9

Printed and bound in Great Britain by
Collins, Glasgow

Set in Ehrhardt

Contents

Illustrations

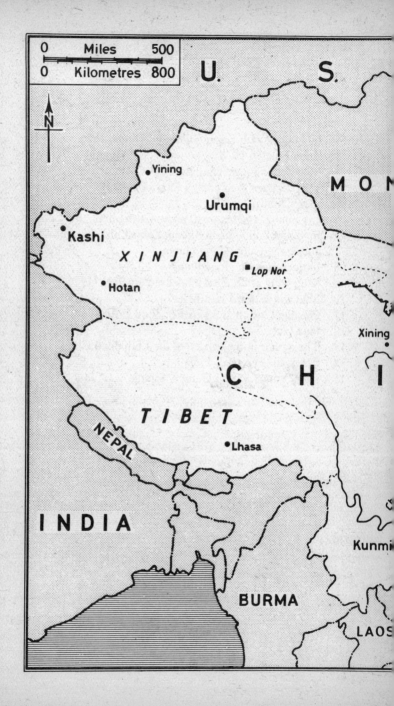

Preface

Scores of people are in prison today because they talked with journalists and diplomats, my Chinese friend said with a note of alarm in his voice. A round of arrests had followed the publication of a highly successful book by a foreign correspondent in 1982. My friend – an official – then expounded as essential to our talks what are known in London as 'Chatham House rules'. Members and visitors attending lectures there may use the information so long as the name of the speaker is not divulged.

Friendly contacts spoke bitterly of the everlasting fame some correspondents achieved after visiting Peking by betraying their acquaintances. In fact, most Chinese, then as now, are careful what they say to their 'round-eyed' contacts but there are rare occasions when political or personal pressures build up and they become indiscreet. Such a period occurred early in 1976 after the death of Premier Zhou Enlai in January and before the earthquake which heralded the end of the Chairman's long drawn out illness in September.

Men and women wanted to give foreigners the inside information about the second disgrace of Deng Xiaoping, which took place long before the Ching Ming demonstrations in Tiananmen Square on April 6th, when the crowds paid tribute to the late Premier and applauded Deng. Almost all my Chinese friends then believed the Gang of Four would take over on the Chairman's death, indeed, they said Jiang Qing was already using his 'chop' or seal which is as authoritative as a signature in China.

They claimed with truth that they wanted the world to know what an intelligent, far-sighted and diplomatic role had been played by the late Premier whose supporters were certain, they then feared, to follow Deng into oblivion or worse. Some people were frightened and I recall waiting in cold and dark places for contacts who failed to appear. But when we did eventually meet they frequently passed on sensational information, much of which has since been confirmed in the trial of the Gang of Four and elsewhere.

Certainly in 1976 fear unleashed tongues about the early close association between 'the traitor' Lin Biao and the Russians during the three and a half years he spent in Moscow in the early 1930s. Many believed their secret association had been maintained with minor plots organized until Lin's attempted coup failed in 1971. The conspirators believed the Russians would attack China in the north while they established a new capital in Nanjing and attacked from the south.

A picture taken by Jiang Qing showing the bald pate of Mao's 'chosen successor' disclosed to the Central Committee and the diplomatic corps that all was not well between them, for apart from mopping the sweat from his forehead, Lin never took off his army cap. Jiang Qing appeared as an unscrupulous, power-hungry woman, loathed by all those who had opposed the excesses of the Cultural Revolution.

Mao was obsessed in his later years by the ten men who led campaigns designed, he believed, to destroy his political and personal power and he constantly alluded to the 'ten bitter struggles on the question of our line' – the party line – which were, in fact, nothing but major disputes over policy and leadership.

Chinese characters have been romanized in this book in the pinyin way now used by the Chinese, with the exception of a few people and places better known to foreigners in their pre-pinyin forms such as Peking, Hong Kong, China's first President, Sun Yat-sen and Chiang Kai-shek.

Many people have helped with translations, suggestions for further research and the correction of manuscripts. In my early days in Peking the Ambassador, the late Sir John Addis, was extremely kind; so, indeed, were members of his staff. I also received enormous help from the late Ambassador David Bruce, the first Liaison Officer for the United States, his wife Evangeline and his successor, now the Vice President, George Bush. The Ambassadors of France, Canada, Australia, New Zealand, Algeria and Iran were always happy to exchange views, giving more than they received from me.

When I began work outside China, Elizabeth Wright and the staff of the Great Britain China Centre were most supportive and

Introduction: The Millennium before Mao

The Chinese established a literate civilization five or six centuries after the Egyptians, at roughly the same time as the Minoans flourished in Crete. Indeed, the Han Chinese were the first to produce a non-porous glaze for earthenware on the banks of the Yellow River. They also devised a calendar at about the same time as the Great Pyramid of Cheops was being constructed in the desert beside the Nile around 2500 B.C. But of all the river-valley civilizations of antiquity, China was unique in its geographical isolation.

The Chinese claim four thousand years of recorded history and long before China was united under one emperor in 222 B.C. they achieved a high level of culture and learning. The animal-drawn plough appeared in the fourth century B.C. and at the same time canals were constructed for internal trade and to keep the population 'occupied'. These canal works, in turn, led to irrigation schemes and caused vast areas to be brought under cultivation.

In military techniques iron was widely used a thousand years earlier than in Europe. The crossbow, too, was invented in China centuries ahead of the West.

One of the most remarkable Chinese scholars was Sun Tzu who wrote a series of essays on the art of war in the closing years of the sixth century B.C. Sun Tzu, who has had a profound influence throughout Chinese history, and on Japanese military thought, was the basic source of Mao Zedong's strategic theories. Sun Tzu's doctrine held that combat involves far more than the collision of armed men, that indeed the moral, intellectual and circumstantial elements of war are more important than the physical. He cautioned 'kings and commanders' not to place reliance on sheer military power.

He believed the most successful generals were those who never ordered an arrow to be shot into the air. Sun Tzu talks of 'inflation' as an inevitable accompaniment for military operations and outlines a theory of physiological warfare.

In his lifetime work was begun on the Great Wall as the small states constructed defensive walls against the nomads in the north. The first emperor of the Qin dynasty (221–206 B.C.) linked some of these fortifications into one continuous barrier running from the sea at Shanhaiguan westward to the bend in the Yellow River and then south-west to Lanzhou. The Han dynasty (206 B.C.–A.D. 220) extended the system as far west as Xinjiang Province to provide a base for military campaigns in central Asia and, more important, to protect Chinese settlers, their stores of grain and traffic on the old Silk Road. The latest and perhaps the greatest wall builders were the Ming emperors (1368–1644).

Another remarkable Chinese scholar, Confucius, who was born a little later than Sun Tzu in 552 B.C., has probably exerted more influence in China than any other single person. Exiled from his state of Lu (Shandong), he wandered around with a group of disciples conversing with feudal princes and trying to convert them to a philosophy of 'just and harmonious relations in society'. He preached respect for moral values, and especially for the head of the state and the family. When Confucius died his life was an apparent failure yet he has often been referred to as the uncrowned Emperor of China. His teachings continue to influence Chinese society, even in the twentieth century. Confucianism, it must be stressed, is a moral and political system. It largely ignores the distinctions between human and divine, lay and ecclesiastic or church and state.

Taoism ranks second only to Confucianism in its influence on Chinese thought. It began to develop shortly after Confucius died in 479 B.C. but it lacked a literate teacher until the third century B.C. when the legendary Lao Tzu wrote the Tao or Way – 'the soure of all being which governs all existence'. The central principle is 'wu wei' or 'do nothing' and with its appeal to get back to nature Taosim served as a counterbalance to Confucianism. Many educated Chinese through the ages have not found the two philosophies incompatible and officials were frequently Confucians in their offices while at home they became Taoist mystics intent on blending with nature. Taosim had little influence on matters of government but a profound effect on poetry and painting through-out the ages.

While European culture evolved and moved from Greece to

Rome and the West, China was isolated, surrounded by seas and 'barbarians'. Indeed, China remained virtually cut off from the rest of the world until Chinese silk was brought to Greece in about the second century B.C.

Some of the silk came by junk either to the Persian Gulf or the Red Sea via primitive trading stations in what is now Borneo or Rangoon. It was then carried overland either to Alexandria or one of the Turkish ports. But from the first century B.C. until the fall of the Roman Empire, silk was worn by all the fashionable women of that empire. A considerable proportion of trade goods and some scholarly travellers crossed Asia by land via northern Persia, through Afghanistan and the desert to Turfan, Lanzhou and Xi'an or, as a result of local conditions, by a variety of other routes, some to the south of the Himalayas.

The silk trade with Byzantium slumped in A.D. 552 when a monk or, more likely, a series of monks, artisans and merchants managed to smuggle silkworms out of China. The favourite legend is that a priest carried the cocoons inside a hollow crucifix, but these valuable creatures were also hidden in porcelain bowls and amongst the furs which found their way from China to Rome.

Before that time, Buddhism, developed from the teachings of Gautama, who lived in northern India at roughly the same period as Confucius, was brought into China first by merchants and then by monks along the silk route in the early years of the Christian era. Buddhist monasteries on the route provided shelter for travellers who used them to exchange goods or gold for the local currency. In addition the honest priests accepted treasures to store for travellers about to undertake dangerous journeys. Thus they are now described as the 'fathers' of international banking.

By the fourth century A.D. Buddhism played an active part in both the artistic and religious life of China, at first especially in the north and then spreading southwards. The eighth century was the great age of Buddhism in China. It satisfied the people's growing need for the hope of an afterlife while giving them pageantry in this world. In addition, the monks provided medical care and attention. Buddhism taught the equality of women which naturally encouraged the faith amongst the female population who had grown tired of the Confucian doctrine of respect with its concentration on the male head of the family.

Although Christians travelled the silk route, it was the Nestorians who came in from Syria via Persia during the sixth and seventh centuries who made many converts in the seventh and eighth centuries, as the steles in the museum in Xi'an testify. Christianity was virtually wiped out in 841-5 during a period of religious persecution.

Great advances in science and technology, including the construction of iron suspension bridges, which were introduced around A.D. 660, enabled the Tang dynasty (617-906) to expand. They subdued the whole of Manchuria together with Korea and Xinjiang and even penetrated Tibet, where the king 'welcomed' a Chinese wife.

Throughout Chinese history the emperor ruled by divine right. He was the 'Son of Heaven' who 'mounted the Dragon Chariot to be a guest on high' at his death. He commanded his ministers to propitiate the Spirits of the Air in times of drought or floods. And, on the whole, despite many exceptions over the centuries, he left his subjects to their worship of Buddhist deities and their adherence to Taoist tenets, or even Christian and Islamic practices, so long as they remained a matter of religion only.

Only one woman, the Empress Wu Hou, Wu Zetain, widow of a Tang emperor, assumed the title of 'Daughter of Heaven' and dominated the empire from A.D. 684 to 705. Chinese historians were traditionally anti-women; thus Hosea Morse wrote in 1907 that chroniclers vied with one another in heaping obloquy on her name.

Earlier in the second century B.C. the wife of the first emperor of the Han dynasty played an important role during his lifetime and the administration of his puppet son. Indeed, she controlled the empire, it is said, in much the same way as the famous Dowager Empress Cixi (Tsu-hsi) whose long period of power roughly coincided with the reign of Queen Victoria.

The Tangs were one of the few dynasties to welcome foreigners and their capital Chang-an – Xi'an today – became a meeting place of scholars from Arabia, Persia and Syria. The first Christians settled in Xi'an. There were, too, many foreign entertainers, such as Indian jugglers and horse and camel stunt riders. Indeed, in the eighth century over 4000 foreign families were in Xi'an.

In 845 the Court suddenly became alarmed that the vast number of monks might eventually challenge the very foundation of Chinese society for it was feared that too many men were escaping into the monasteries to avoid service in the army or bureaucracy. A major purge was mounted without warning and over 4500 temples were wantonly destroyed and 260,000 monks and nuns secularized overnight. Foreign settlers were expelled and visitors ordered home.

By far the most important discovery of the ninth century was the use of gunpowder, which was made around 850, although its first appearance on the battlefield was not until 919. The gunpowder was produced in the form of grenades or small bombs that were fired initially from trebuchets. Later it was developed for use with many different forms of projectiles. During the same period the Chinese also developed a weapons system unknown in the West – the arcuballistae which had the capability to release many arrows or bolts at one time and was made up of sets of crossbow springs mounted on a carriage.

Studies of the Chinese Classics, herbal medicine and mathematics also made sensational strides under the early Tangs. The Songs (960–1276), who took over after half a century of unrest, developed the cultivation of tea and improved techniques in the manufacture of porcelain. During this dynasty painting and literature flourished not only amongst the mandarins but also amongst the ever-growing number of merchants and the emerging bourgeoisie.

But the good ships and the grenades they had inherited did not prevent the Songs in their turn from being overthrown by the Mongols who took Peking in 1215 and, after the last Song prince was killed in a sea battle in 1279, established themselves as masters of all China. Indeed, the Mongols controlled an area which extended as far west as Budapest, as far east as Canton (now Guangzhou) and included Basra on the Persian Gulf. The roads of central Asia were then safer than they had been at any time before or since and scholars and merchants poured into China. Thus it was that the Venetian Marco Polo spent seventeen years as a court official.

Christians made a second attempt to penetrate the Middle Kingdom during the Ming dynasty which succeeded the Songs around 1368 and lasted until 1644, but the Franciscan friars achieved no more success than the Nestorian clergy six centuries earlier.

Although foreigners, and especially the famous Italian Jesuit Matteo Ricci, contributed enormously to Chinese scientific knowledge and culture, the secret societies, which had already become a traditional problem in China, launched a national cult that developed into a campaign to be rid of outside influences.

The movement was backed by other secret societies dedicated to the expulsion of the Mongols as Confucianism gradually gained ground once more and the Chinese gentry infiltrated back into the administration which, since the conquest, had been dominated by Mongols. In 1383 the Mings established their Imperial capital in Nanking (now Nanjing).

The new dynasty opened a period of maritime exploration, trade and conquest. Sixty-three ocean-going junks visited the Paracel and Spratly groups of islands, lagoons and other countries in the Western Pacific, South-east Asia and the Indian Ocean and brought back the kings of Palembang and Ceylon to offer homage. European traders then began to approach the Chinese coast: the Portuguese had settled in Macao around 1534 and the first English sailors arrived in 1637 at the end of the era. The Russians meanwhile failed in their efforts to make contact through Siberia which they were, however, slowly conquering. The Spaniards, who had already occupied parts of the Philippines, brought books to Guangzhou and established some trade as they introduced the Mexican silver dollar into Chinese commerce.

The British East India Company finally established a factory in Guangzhou, then the most prosperous Chinese port, in 1699. Almost a century later the brilliant and experienced Lord Macartney led a diplomatic mission to Peking in an effort to increase the already considerable volume of trade and to establish diplomatic relations with the celestial court. Although he was received four times by the 82-year-old emperor, Lord Macartney had no chance of real discussions with him. Further, the Chinese refused to allow the hot air balloon, which was one of the presents he brought, to ascend the atmosphere. The emperor's attitude was explained in a letter to George III which is well worth studying today.

Apart from explaining that it would be impossible to have foreign ambassadors living at his court and 'all possible facilities for trade have already been provided at Guangzhou', he added, 'Our dynasty's majestic virtue has penetrated into every country under heaven . . . We possess all things. I see no value in objects strange and ingenious and have no use for your country's manufactures.' The emperor wrote as though George III was a vassal. Macartney was baffled by the assumption of a power the Chinese did not possess but although his mission was technically a failure he brought back a great deal of information about China.

Trade expanded and after the Japanese opened their doors to foreigners it became increasingly difficult for the Chinese to keep Europeans at bay. The treaty following the Opium War in 1842 opened five ports to trade and Hong Kong island became a British colony. But the war introduced a century of humiliation for the Chinese from which they have yet to recover. The gunpowder they had invented for grenades and developed for fireworks in the thirteenth century was applied by foreigners to reduce their splendour to a charade.

The Ming dynasty is noted for its defences, paved highways, rock gardens, bridges, temples and shrines. In this period over five hundred towns were completely reconstructed. But the bureaucracy eventually became too large and powerful and in 1469 there were 80,000 military officers and over 100,000 civil servants. As a result of a power struggle between the eunuchs and the Confucian scholars the dynasty collapsed. Manchu aid was sought after the last Ming emperor committed suicide. Once in the capital nothing would remove them, so the Qing dynasty opened in 1644 and endured until a republic was established in 1911.

The Ming saw the opening up of the Chinese roads to foreign traders, the establishment of European-controlled ports and areas on the Chinese coast and the eventual build-up of anti-foreign movements and ever more powerful secret societies. Equally important, close on the heels of the explorers, conquerors and traders came the missionaries, many of whom made great contributions to the scientific, medical and cultural attainments of the huge bureaucracy.

A dramatic increase in population took place while the Ming dynasty occupied the Celestial Throne from an estimated 150 million in 1600 to around 300 million by 1727, and to over 425 million by 1850. This increase, in turn, led to a large emigration of the poor, especially from the coastal areas, to the Chinese settlements already established in Indo-China, Burma and the Philippines. Population was growing faster than production and this factor, together with the continual pressure of Europeans, exacerbated the expected opposition to the dynasty, which grew in the traditional manner. However, the situation eased when new crops, including maize and tobacco, were introduced to China, a system of state granaries was, once more, established and small-scale silk and porcelain industries multiplied.

The Russians, who had by this time conquered Siberia, and the Europeans and Japanese in the south were not the only threat to the Manchu court. New political ideas arising from the French Revolution influenced scholars and soldiers, as well as the ever growing bourgeoisie, and debates on the value of European science and technology, which was already being absorbed by Japan, divided the mandarins. Opposed to those who valued this new knowledge remained a large and influential group that believed China would be wise to avoid these 'barbarian' innovations.

The introduction of Christianity caused other problems that played a role, albeit an unfortunate one, in the Taiping Revolt, which arose when a village schoolmaster, Hong Xiuquan, who was one of the 'dog-eating' Hakkas of South China, together with a charcoal dealer, an out-of-work coolie and one rich landlord formed the 'Society of God Worshippers'. The group, which had much in common with the old secret societies of the Triad type, organized a religious movement designed to destroy idols and temples. The movement assumed strong political overtones and was quickly transformed into an open rebellion against the Manchus. By 1851 the rebels had taken over large areas of southern China and established their capital in Nanjing where Hong Xiuquan declared himself emperor or 'Heavenly Monarch'.

Although their attempt to penetrate the north and take over Peking failed, the rebels remained in control of the south until 1846 with a policy based on land reform and the equality and liberation of women, including the end of foot binding. As an anti-Manchu gesture the men cut off their queues (pigtails).

For a time the foreigners, consuls and traders alike, could not decide whether to back the revolt or the Peking regime. As the revolt spread, the British and French governmental advisers decided it would be a good moment to put pressure on the Manchu emperor and in 1860 a second joint Anglo-French military operation led to the burning of the Summer Palace in Peking. It ended with the signing of a treaty that opened eleven ports to foreigners and granted many privileges to foreign residents.

The Taiping Revolt, weakened by corruption, succumbed to the supporters of the emperor. But the fact that slaves were freed, women accepted, in theory, as equals and a flavour of a European way of life was introduced had a lasting effect on the population.

Despite the activities of hundreds of secret societies – mostly xenophobic in origin – many of the new middle-class Chinese were anxious to introduce western technology as the Japanese were doing. Some were especially keen to see European methods used in the development of the armaments industry. Others saw the economy growing but falling into foreign hands and, with the development of tea plantations and increased rice production, agriculture becoming specialized to the detriment of the small or cottage industries.

Efforts towards adopting western techniques were generally frustrated by the powerful Dowager Empress Cixi whose career in the Palace began in 1860 and ended with her death in 1908. For thirty-seven of these forty-eight years she ruled absolutely. After entering the palace as a junior concubine she realized her value as an intelligent adviser to the emperor because, unlike nearly all the women and a proportion of the men at court, she was literate. In addition, she had the good fortune to bear the emperor his only son.

Although her father was 'cashiered' for 'running away' during the Taiping Revolt, she gave the emperor excellent advice on the generals to send, who finally put it down. Westerners who met her praised her charm and culture but she was also extremely ambitious and blessed with enormous physical vitality.

In 1898, a handful of enlightened scholars had managed to persuade the emperor to adopt the non-political changes in the administration that had been introduced in Japan. The Dowager Empress did not approve of the proposed reforms, with the result that the emperor spent the rest of his life as a prisoner in the Imperial City while the men with progressive ideas who failed to escape were executed.

At the turn of the century many secret societies, dubbed 'Boxers' by Europeans, rose and laid siege to what was known as the 'Legation Quarter' in Peking where almost all the foreigners then lived. After fifty days they were relieved by an expeditionary force mounted by seven western powers and Japan. Cixi then cut her four-inch-long fingernails and fled to Xi'an.

China was required to pay a huge indemnity but from then, 1901, until the Revolution of 1911 foreign trade flourished. The whole state appeared to prosper. The Chinese Imperial Maritime Customs, which since 1861 had been in foreign hands, produced honest men as officials, more railways were constructed, many schools were opened by missionaries and others and even the Dowager Empress was forced to introduce a few reforms, which included the establishment of secondary schools.

Following the pattern of previous dynasties as they drew to a close, there was a period of growing warlordism as the power of the central government declined. Indeed, warlords who varied in their power and methods ruled in different parts of China. Generally, though not always, they paid lip-service to the support of the emperor. Many levied taxes that were collected by the village headman, who received his financial bonus as well as a special status and privileges. Some warlords commanded towns, others vast tracks of territory, and when groups of them formed an alliance, they could become extremely powerful. Many of the warlords were both corrupt and vicious.

Foreign companies had already installed telephone lines linking the main cities, coal-mines had been opened up and some heavy industrial plant such as machine-tool building enabled the Chinese to undertake rice husking and making 'cattle cake' for cows and pigs from soya beans, as well as match-making and paper manufacture. All this and the presence of thousands of foreigners in the Treaty Ports created an ever-increasing middle class, some of whom went to Japan or even Europe to finish their education.

It was from such a group of students that Dr Sun Yat-sen (1866–1925), China's first President, albeit only an acting one, collected thousands of followers who aimed at overthrowing the outmoded dynastic regime. Sun was the son of a peasant who received a reasonable basic education largely because he was a convert to Christianity. Frustrated by conditions in the Guangzhou area where he was born, Sun left for Honolulu where his elder brother was a farmer. Here Sun trained to become a doctor and while so doing he absorbed many liberal and progressive political ideas. On his return to China, Sun founded the 'Revive China' Society but this was too much for the local mandarins and he had to flee to Hong Kong and Macao where he practised medicine. Later he went to Japan and the United States where he preached an anti-Manchu doctrine. In London the Chinese Embassy attempted to kidnap him but failed.

Meanwhile Sun founded the 'United League' with even stronger anti-Manchu teachings which gained ground in China, as the central government was extremely weak following the death of the Dowager Empress in 1908. The revolution of October 10th, 1911 – known as the Double Ten Revolt – opened as the result of a grenade exploding by accident in Wuhan. The combination of the teaching of the United League and widespread discontent spread the movement. The Government's decision to nationalize the railways also played into the hands of the revolutionaries. Sun read of the revolt in a newspaper in the United States and hurried back to Shanghai as fast as possible along with crowds of other republicans and students.

Sun, unfortunately, lacked a powerful political base and he had no military one either. On his return he was elected provisional President of the government which established itself in Nanjing but he was forced to resign the following year in favour of Yuan Shikǎi (Yuan Shih-kai), a powerful warlord who, from time to time, had voiced reformist views. However, Yuan as President suppressed an independent movement in the Yangtze region and by 1915 was sufficiently confident to have himself declared emperor. But he died shortly afterwards, leaving a divided China which lapsed into a period of rule by warlords.

Meanwhile, Sun was able to establish a military government in Guangzhou but his base was always weak and he died in 1925. However, Sun's widow, Soong Ching Ling (Sung Qingling), remained a powerful though elderly figure in communist China until her death in June 1981. She was the sister of the widow of Chiang Kai-shek (Jiang Jieshi). Despite warlords and a great deal of banditry and widespread corruption, the war in Europe created a demand for food, especially eggs and flour, leather, edible oil and other basic materials, that more than compensated for the fall in demand for porcelain and silk.

Some towns and cities that were administered by their chamber of commerce achieved local tranquillity and prosperity in their isolation but there was, people claim, always an atmosphere of uncertainty about the future. However, many Chinese and English language newspapers sprang up, most of them reflecting the liberal democratic views of French and British thinkers.

Chiang Kai-shek (1887–1975) took over the Guomindang or Nationalist Party that had evolved from Sun's United League and he managed to reunite parts of China under his government in Nanjing. And, following the example of Sun, he received help and advice from the Soviet Union.

PART ONE
The Rise to Power

1
Birth of a Rebel

Chairman Mao Zedong was born on December 26th, 1893 during the dying phase of an empire that had ruled China for a millennium. His birthplace at Shaoshan in the Hunan Province of South China is still something of a national shrine, visited by hundreds of Chinese pilgrims and a few score foreigners each year. Mao's father built additional rooms to what was originally a small village house as he gradually raised himself from the position of a 'middle' peasant, employing one labourer, to a prosperous grain merchant. The site is enhanced by a charming lily pond at the front door where the youthful Mao learned to swim and the scene is flanked by green and wooded hills. Indeed, the setting is so strikingly picturesque that some cynical foreigners have, wrongly, doubted its authenticity.

At the height of the Chairman's personality cult, from the end of the Cultural Revolution in 1967 to his death, the village was 'the Bethlehem or Mecca of China' and hundreds of thousands flocked to the village where special postcards and souvenirs were sold. But Mao's childhood was far from idyllic for from the age of six his father made him work in the fields after school. Indeed, Mao's family background was the archetype of what he grew to hate and despise: that of a peasant or urban worker struggling hard to raise himself to the level of the petty bourgeois.

Mao's father was an ex-soldier who had received only two years' schooling, which, however, was just enough to enable him to keep his accounts. He appeared to have no religious beliefs although there are reports of him suddenly accepting the Buddhist faith after escaping the attentions of an angry lion. Mao's mother, who was completely illiterate, was a devout Buddhist and insisted on her family receiving religious instruction.

The group was not a happy one. Mao was the eldest of a family composed of three boys and one adopted girl. The children adored their mother but were frightened of and sometimes positively hated their strict and difficult father. Years later Mao told Edgar Snow, an American journalist who was one of the first Anglo-Saxons to penetrate the nationalist lines and visit Mao in Yenan, that although they had adequate food they never had eggs or meat to eat. The hired labourer was given one egg with his rice every week. This was because Mao's father sold much of the grain he cultivated to the nearby town.

In disputes between the two parents the children always stood solidly behind their mother who disapproved of any overt display of emotion, fuss or open rebellion claiming that this was not the Chinese way of behaviour. When there was a famine in the village Mao's mother gave grain to the poor peasants when her husband was not present. The food shortage gave Mao's father an opportunity to make considerable profits from selling all his surplus rice in the towns. Indeed, by the time Mao was thirteen his father's successful speculations in grain had made, Mao claimed, 'what was considered a considerable fortune in that village'.

Mao and his brothers attended the local primary school where he learned to repeat Confucian classics without much understanding of them. But his youthful education really came later, largely from reading newspapers and the novels of the period. He claimed he was deeply influenced by the historical novels *Water Margin* and *Romance of the Three Kingdoms*. In *Water Margin* a group of bandits rebel against a corrupt court and hold out on a mountain top. Mao is reported to have said that he disliked these classics in later years. One of the many campaigns which was launched in his name by the radicals now known as the 'Gang of Four' during the mid-1970s was against *Water Margin* on the grounds that the rebel leader, who operated in the manner of Robin Hood, robbing the rich in order to give to the poor, finally came to terms with the emperor. Indeed, after the second disgrace of Vice Premier Deng Xiaoping which followed the death of Premier Zhou Enlai in February 1976, Deng was attacked as a 'capitulationist' and compared with the hero/villain of *Water Margin*, Sung Chiang.

There were family disputes soon after the six-year-old Mao began to work in the fields because even at that age he wanted freedom to spend time swimming and talking with his friends. One evening after he had just learned to swim, in the middle of a dispute he scared his father by poising himself on a muddy, slightly inaccessible bank of the lily pond and threatening to throw himself in and drown unless his father gave way. This act had an immediate impact on Mao's father who feared most of all that he would have no one to work for him and look after him in old age and, also, though agnostic, that there would be no one to care for his tomb.

At the age of ten Mao ran away after being beaten both by his schoolteacher and his father. He recalled, to Edgar Snow, wandering aimlessly around in what he believed to be the general direction of the nearby market town until he was eventually found by a member of the family. Mao discovered, to his amazement, after this adventure that his father was 'more considerate' and that his teacher was 'more inclined towards moderation'. Mao's first act of rebellion was a success.

In 1906 when Mao was thirteen his father insisted that he leave the local school to devote all his attention and time to the land. However, Mao continued to read and together with the literate villagers he devoured political writings. These people included local disciples of Cheng Guanying who was then leader of a group of intellectuals urging the Chinese to develop themselves scientifically and modernize their economy. At the same time, Cheng's followers condemned the way foreigners treated the Chinese in Shanghai and other coastal cities as second-class citizens.

Mao claimed that reading books and political articles stimulated him to resume his studies and he left home a second time to join a friend who was an unemployed law student and had space for the enthusiastic Mao in his room. Although the experiment was not wholly successful, Mao managed, despite his father's opposition, to begin his studies at the advanced age of sixteen in the Dongshan modern higher primary school in Xiang (Hsiang), a few miles from home.

Here he learned something of the activities of the Dowager Empress Cixi and the vast corrupt bureaucracy in Peking that attempted vainly to unite a nation that was disintegrating, largely through the activities of the local governors and rising warlords as the Manchu dynasty drew towards its end. Difficult though it may be to believe, he learned of the death of the Dowager Empress in 1908 two years after it happened. Mao heard too of the political power of the secret societies of the period.

In 1910 a local famine caused a popular revolt that was brutally overcome and the heads of the ringleaders placed on spikes outside the town to serve as a lesson to others who might consider robbing the landlord's storehouses when hungry. Mao and his fellow students talked of little else for months and their sympathy was solidly with the rebels – so he told Edgar Snow. Soon after the disastrous revolt Mao and his friends fell under the influence of a pamphlet that mourned the occupation by Japan of the islands of Taiwan, Indo-China and Korea. Mao apparently forgot both the title and the name of the author but remembered the opening sentence years later when he was in Yenan and he quoted, 'Alas, China will be subjugated.' There can be little doubt that this helped to inspire the nationalist tendencies which never left him and later caused vast trouble in his relations with the Soviet Union.

During these informative years, too, Mao saw peasant women being beaten up by their husbands and having little or no voice in the management of thir own lives or those of their families. Indeed, Mao's father and mother betrothed him to a young woman in the village and this added to his fury that girls were treated like chattels and, if not actually sold into prostitution, as many of the female children of the poorer peasants were, married to someone for whom they had no affection. In fact, Mao's father arranged the marriage in order to obtain extra and free labour in his rice fields.

Mao apparently needed no further books to inspire him against the bitter injustices of the system. He formulated his ideas then and there on the necessity to liberate women – though he did not use this word until years later – claiming that 'it would be impossible for men to be free unless women were treated as their equals'. All his life Mao believed in the equality of women in the home as well as in public life. (But he did not put his convictions into practice latterly, because of troubles with his wife, Jiang Qing.) Doubtless, too, he was moved by the richer women of the town hobbling round with sticks because their feet had been bound in order to make them sexually attractive, and the wives of pretentious peasants – kulaks – who had bound feet and were forced to work in misery on the land when things got bad. At least the peasant women in Mao's native village did not suffer from this affliction of 'lily feet'. Because they had to work on the land their feet, as babies, were not bound. Mao also noted with interest that the women who had always worked and were too poor to have 'lily feet' did have more share in the family councils.

Mao only stayed at the Dongshan school for a year – perhaps because he did not get along well with the other students. To begin with he was six years older than they were and conspicuously tall and stocky, and further, he had not acquired (nor did he ever aspire to acquire) the rigid formal politeness of the land-owning and merchant classes. His fellow students thought him both arrogant and uncouth. He was all too conscious of the fact that he had only one decent suit and that he spent most of his time wearing patched clothes much too small for him.

A desire to see more of the world and leave the misery of the Dongshan school behind him inspired Mao to try his luck at entering the normal school at Changsha, the local county town, and to his surprise and delight he was accepted by the headmaster. Once there he began to enter into political discussions through which he learned of the Taiping Revolt, the destruction by Anglo-French forces of the Summer Palace, the Boxer Rebellion and the many and various promises of reforms made by the Dowager Empress.

Here Mao read the newspaper produced by the republican leader Sun Yat-sen. This apparently inspired him to write his own first political comments on a wall poster in the school. This form of expression based on tradition was then popular. It was later to become one of Mao's favourite political instruments in the Communist Party especially during the Cultural Revolution.

Despite Mao's anti-Manchu posture and what was for that isolated rural area his wide reading of republican and revolutionary newspapers, he, like thousands of others in China, was taken by surprise when the revolution did break out at the end of the summer of 1911. The 'Double Ten' rising – the tenth day of the tenth month – erupted in Wuhan and from there spread across the country gaining support from the impoverished peasants and the underpaid urban workers. The Manchu dynasty did not receive the help from the foreign powers they had expected and in January 1912, Sun Yat-sen, the Republican leader, was elected President of the new government, which had its headquarters in Nanjing.

Mao and his colleagues were naturally excited when they heard the news, indeed, Mao was on the point of leaving the town to join the republican forces in Wuhan when the movement spread to Changsha.

Mao witnessed what he claimed were 'bloody battles' at the gates of the town when the revolutionaries were reportedly held up for just long enough to enable the governor to escape through a carefully prepared hole in the back wall of the official residence. The 'battle' deeply impressed the future Chairman but a number of his critics claim that, like many young people watching armed conflict for the first time, he allowed his imagination to run away with him.

From the top of a hill where Mao had been watching the fighting he saw a banner stating that a republic had been established. This elated Mao and his companions and, in his excitement, Mao rushed off to join the republican army. He spent the next six months on garrison duty in the town learning, nonetheless, something of the inner workings of a military unit.

In the army Mao made friends with a miner and an engineer thus broadening his vision which had hitherto been largely devoted to the countryside. He spent more than half his pay on buying water from the professional carriers rather than lugging the buckets himself from the well to his quarters, for Mao then considered himself as an intellectual and above this type of labour. However, Mao achieved popularity in the barrack room by writing letters home on behalf of the many illiterate men. In his free time, Mao read all the local newspapers and talked endlessly on political issues with other soldiers. During these discussions it became clear to Mao that too often the Chinese political leaders were in the hands of warlords and the idea evolved in his mind that political power grows from the barrel of a gun.

At the end of six months Mao abandoned the army, claiming that the republic was already well established, and returned to the normal school to continue his studies, but he soon became dissatisfied with the routine and the rigid classical syllabuses and began to visit libraries to work on his own. He was restless and answered many newspaper advertisements to try to obtain special courses. He attended a commercial course but let this lapse after a month because English was the language of instruction and he could not understand enough to make it interesting or worthwhile. At this time, Mao began to take a special interest in the political ideas that had emerged in Europe during and after the French Revolution and which had been absorbed by Japanese students and travellers from the West. Almost all western ideas then came into China through Japan.

Mao was obsessed with the necessity for China to develop not only modern industry but an up-to-date and 'clean' bureaucracy. Like many young men of that period, and indeed from any period, his views were not entirely consistent. But he did not veer from a pasionate devotion to China and a deep interest in military leaders and the careers of great soldiers and statesmen. It was thus curious that despite his passion for reading descriptions of past battles, he appeared to take but little interest in the First World War then raging not only in Western Europe but in the Middle East – Western Asia according to Chinese jargon – which was well reported in the newspapers he read.

Nonetheless Mao began to stand out as a bright, intelligent, youthful leader among the other students of the town although he remained unkempt in appearance and disdainful of traditional manners. Mao was proud to relate that he came under the most important influence in his life at this time, during what corresponds roughly to the period of the First World War, in the shape of a professor of ethics, Yang Changzhi (Yang Changchih), who had studied in Japan, England and Germany. Later, much later, Mao was to marry his daughter, but Mao then had no time for flirtations or courtship.

All Mao's free time was taken up with unending political discussions and physical culture. He hardened his feet by walking around without shoes and even by climbing rocky cliffs bare-foot. During the winter he bathed in icy water and frequently went on what would now be called walking tours, dossing down for the night with the peasants and learning a great deal about their lives and the hardships they endured.

Mao's first published article (April 1917) was entitled 'A Study in Physical Culture' and in it he outlined a system of daily exercises which he said would strengthen both body and mind. 'The principal aim of physical education is military heroism,' he stressed. A sideline on life at this period was well illustrated when Mao was toughening himself mentally and physically for what he then expected would be a life devoted to teaching and local political activity. He became chief of the 'volunteer army' designed to defend the first normal school against attacks from the various military factions – warlords – who were then fighting among themselves in the province.

Mao was also secretary-general of the students' society which was fighting traditional educational methods and demanding that more western science be taught, together with European philosophy. The small town of Changsha reflected the effervescence taking place throughout China as students and intellectuals debated the political ideas that continued to arrive from Europe via Japan. Scores of small societies, secret as well as open, provided the framework in which the new ideas were circulated. Chinese liberals were everywhere proclaiming themselves free from 'old thoughts, old ethics, old values' as they propounded their belief in the freedom of the individual.

As a result of the Wilsonian philosophy of self-determination, which had been widely publicized in China, the intellectuals were profoundly shocked in May 1919 when the Peace Conference meeting at Versailles awarded Shandong, which had been a German sphere of influence before the First World War, to the Japanese, who had taken it over during the period of hostilities. Huge student demonstrations against the western powers and the Chinese delegation in Paris were organized in many cities. Thousands of telegrams were sent to Woodrow Wilson reminding him of his idealism and what he said about the rights of poor and weak nations.

Mass protests continued over a period of weeks and in Peking students burned the house of a pro-Japanese politician. When the police arrived most of the student agitators had already dispersed but they managed to arrest ten of the ringleaders. The immediate reponse was a general strike of students not only in the capital but in provincial universities as well. The strike then quickly spread to other provincial cities as shopkeepers, industrial workers and commercial establishments all over the country laid down their tools. A concerted boycott of Japanese goods followed and people stopped buying Japanese products or using Japanese steamers, whilst dock hands refused to off-load Japanese goods. Under enormous pressure from the general public the Peking regime was forced to release the students on May 4th. Thus May 4th became the name of a movement that had, already in effect, been influential throughout the country for some years.

In 1918, Mao, at the age of twenty-five, appeared to have the educational attainments of an intelligent student of the period of around seventeen. Despite his wide reading, he knew little or nothing about science, geography, economics or engineering. But the future Chairman had already realized he was a natural leader of men and developed the ambition to gain local political power. Mao at that time held views on life which were contradictory as they combined his conviction of personal superiority over the less well educated workers with a strong determination not to adopt the manners or the vocabulary of the mandarin. Mao was constantly looking for a political doctrine that would enable the miserable lives of the peasants to be improved. Nevertheless his strong nationalist tendencies did not prevent him from wanting to import foreign books and political philosophies as well as technical innovations.

2
Mao Becomes a Marxist

The Republican Revolution of October 10th, 1911 – the Double Ten Revolt – all too obviously failed to unite China, which remained divided by warring warlords and foreigners. Imperialist powers competed against one another, especially on the coast, to obtain ever-increasing political and territorial influence and trade. All the liberal-minded Chinese were shocked by the large bribes the European nations paid to individual warlords. The republican leader himself, Sun Yat-sen (whose widow Soong Ching Ling remained Vice Chairman of the National People's Congress, China's rubber stamp Parliament, until her death in 1981) lacked military backing and a power base.

Sun and his lieutenants had formed the Guomindang (KMT) or Nationalist Party, in the wake of the United League, which was based on 'The Three People's Principles – Nationalism, Democracy and the People's Livelihood' and stressed the need for land reform and some control of capital. The nationalist creed was aimed both at the foreigner and the Manchu dynasty, whilst the main objective of democracy was the establishment of some form of parliamentary system.

After the powerful warlord Yuan Shikǎi took over from Sun in March 1912 he moved the capital to Peking. Parliamentary elections were held – though one wonders how they were organized – and the Guomindang won 269 seats out of 596 in the lower house and 123 out of 274 in the upper chamber. But Yuan had by that time declared himself opposed to democracy and he outlawed the Guomindang in 1913 which caused Sun to flee to Japan. Sun attempted to reorganize the party from there but he was disillusioned by the lack of cohesion amongst his ranks in which assassinations and corruption ran rife.

Mao was aware of some of this history as he made his way from Changsha in the autumn of 1918 to Peking which he found, with justification, to be the charming and beautiful city of his dreams. He was in the capital largely because he had been working with groups of students who were leaving for Europe on the well-known 'Work/Study' programmes. Mao had at one point decided to go to France but a combination of circumstances compounded of lack of money and the fact that he was a really bad linguist caused him to drop out at the last moment. Officially, Mao gave as his reason a desire to learn something of his own country before going abroad.

Many of Mao's strongest supporters have since suggested he made the wrong decision and he and his colleagues who were trying to establish a new regime suffered from his ignorance of the world and how it was administered. Although Mao could claim that former leaders – emperors – never left China, they all lived and ruled before the days of the aeroplane, motor car and radio. Mao's two visits to Moscow did but little to increase his understanding of the western world and he died believing, as his ancestors had done, that Peking was the centre of civilization.

Shortly after his arrival in Peking Mao contacted his former teacher, Yang Changzhi, who was by then a professor at the university. He put Mao up for a time and helped him to obtain employment, in the university library, cleaning the rooms and keeping the books and papers tidy. But it enabled him to attend lectures when he felt so inclined.

The librarian, Li Dazhao, impressed Mao who had already read his articles in *New Youth* before going to Peking. The library became known as the 'Red Chamber' because it was the meeting place of people with left-wing inclinations. Mao was disappointed that the professors using the library were not as kind and helpful to him as Yang and Li had been. Indeed, Mao felt that when he registered the names of people who came to read newspapers, which was part of his job, they avoided getting into conversation with him. 'I didn't exist as a human being,' he moaned.

Mao was fortunate in meeting some anarchists outside the university and they introduced him to books by Kropotkin and Bakunin. It was a time when intellectuals and politicians were trying to size up the October Revolution and Mao heard many lengthy arguments on the subject in the library. Mao said before the Revolution the Chinese had not heard of Marx or Engels, both of whom, despite the dispute with the Soviet Union, are official heroes in China today.

Mao in his restless way joined a journalists' society and a Marxist study group where he spoke in favour of the peasants who then as now formed over 80 per cent of the population and were in dire need of 'liberation'. In later years Mao complained about his discomforts in Peking where he stayed in excessively crowded quarters. Seven or eight students shared a kang – a clay bed with a small fire under it in winter – and he had to warn the others before he turned over. However, Mao enjoyed much of his life in the capital despite all its frustrations and he fell deeply in love with the daughter of Professor Yang. They could not marry because his salary was totally inadequate to support a wife.

It was strange that so soon after becoming emotionally involved Mao should give up his job and make for Shanghai. This was at least in part due to his anxiety to meet and make new political contacts. There were initially two groups of Marxists – communists – forming in China at that time. Mao already knew the Peking group which was led by his 'protector' Li Dazhao, the librarian who had hailed the Bolshevik Revolution as a 'great and universal force' and compared it with the earlier revolution in France.

The group in Shanghai was led by Chen Duxiu, a classical scholar and a friend of Li Dazhao who had made a special study of Darwin and eighteenth-century French revolutionary literature. (When Edward Heath met Chairman Mao in Peking in 1974 he presented him with a first edition of Darwin and this caused the Chinese leader to recall his youthful studies in Peking.) Chen Duxiu at that time, like many others, believed that China's salvation must follow the line of western democracy. But he moved away from this idea on the grounds that democracy had been used as a tool 'to swindle mankind' in order to promote imperialist political power. Chen then moved towards the European Marxist view that emphasis should be placed on the urban worker whose progressive elements must of necessity spearhead the Marxist/Communist Movement and the coming revolution. Chen claimed, with reason that, 'The peasants are scattered and their forces are not easy to concentrate.' In addition, he said, their cultural level is low and their desires in life are simple and they 'easily tend towards conservatism'.

Thus two different interpretations of Marx were expounded in

China in the wake of the Russian Revolution and the May 4th Movement.

Although the university of Peking was noted for its free speech, political tensions mounted as a result of the discussions in the library and Li was eased out of his job because of pressure from conservative elements. After leaving the university Li devoted himself almost entirely to politics and his thoughts, like those of Mao, tended to dwell increasingly on the peasants and their unending problems with avaricious landlords and 'wicked' warlords. Li wrote, 'In economically backward China the peasants, who form more than 90 per cent of the population, must play an important role in the Revolution.'

Mao who met Chen several times during his visits to Peking and Shanghai, claimed 'He had influenced me more than anyone else.' Apparently they did not then dwell on whether or not workers or peasants should spearhead the Labour movement for Mao was especially keen to advocate equal rights for men and women together with his plans for the establishment of a representative government. The one point he invariably pressed in favour of the poor landless peasants was that, 'Unlike other classes of Chinese society, the women were forced to work for economic reasons.' 'Thus, they acquired a voice in the affairs of the family which was lacking in all other classes.'

In later years Mao said his final conversion to Marxism came gradually as a result of the Russian Revolution, details of which seemed only to sink slowly into his consciousness, perhaps because he was working hard and writing so much about local conditions in China. The accounts of events in Russia apparently appealed more to what Mao later dubbed his 'political consciousness' than Marx's written words.

Mao actually left Peking to see some students off to Europe on the Work/Study project from Shanghai. It seems typical of him at this period that he went to the station with insufficient money but friends came to his rescue and gave him both money and food for the journey.

The countryside – along the railway line – was buzzing with news about the Versailles Peace Conference and rumours were rife that the Chinese delegation had agreed to 'a Japanese presence in China' which appeared to be contrary to President Woodrow

Wilson's creed of 'self-determination'. In addition, those victorious European countries holding territorial concessions in China appeared reluctant to give them up. What a few months later became established as the May 4th Movement of 1919, as a result of a spontaneous series of student demonstrations, was already in being, indeed, it had been spreading across the coastal provinces for months.

Mao returned to his birthplace in Hunan after a brief stay in Shanghai where he made contact with the scores of young men and women who were about to leave on the Work/Study project. Back in Changsha he obtained a job as an assistant teacher but continued to devote all his spare time to politics. However, instead of the endless discussions in which he had indulged before going to Peking he now began to write articles for newspapers and magazines with frenzied enthusiasm.

Mao was actually travelling on May 4th when over five thousand students spontaneously demonstrated in Peking against the decision of the Versailles Peace Conference that Japan should acquire rights in Shandong Province. In Changsha he gradually became aware that the May 4th Movement was gaining power and making the government in Peking its main target. Indeed, members of the government were accused of being 'traitors' for having accepted the Japanese demands. A strike of students and lecturers was soon taken up by factories, offices and shops as a massive boycott of Japanese goods was organized. The Chinese love to name movements after dates and this unsponsored series of urban demonstrations spilled over and became an intellectual revolution as China grappled with new ideas coming in from the West. Many of the early members of the Communist Party emerged from the May 4th Movement.

Revolutionary activities

In Changsha where Mao was by now teaching he started various weekly political magazines – one of which was closed by the authorities. He confessed later that he frequently had to sit up all night writing the articles himself as the contributors so often failed him at the last moment, either from fear of becoming unpopular with the local warlord or the right-wing government, or from sheer laziness.

As a result of Mao's revolutionary writings and political activities especially in running a students' paper called *New Hunan* he was ultimately forced by the governor to leave the province. He went to Shanghai in December 1919 where he worked in a laundry. This break enabled him to renew his intimate relationship with Chen Duxiu and their talks led him further along the road to Marxism. By the summer of 1920, Mao said he 'had in theory and to some extent in action become a Marxist'.

Mao Zedong's conversion first to Marxist philosophy and then to communism as a means of practical implementation ended his youth which had been spent, in his words, in a quest for 'a means of bettering the lives of the people'. By 'people' he meant the peasantry. Since he was a peasant and the vast majority of the people he knew even in the towns had family roots on the land, it was natural that their sufferings and problems were uppermost in his mind. Further, Mao's contacts with town dwellers had been far from happy and, in general, he felt they despised him as 'a country bumpkin'. People always noted his clothes were old and 'rustic'. Indeed, one of the odd points he and Jiang Qing – his third wife – had in common when they first met in Yenan was their youthful sufferings – she in Shanghai and he in Peking – because they wore old suits that had been handed down to them from other members of the family. Doubtless, too, Mao's farmyard language and strong southern dialect did not endear him to the intellectuals who were using the library in which he worked or the schools in which he taught. Indeed, instead of trying to model himself on the city intellectuals, Mao, whilst thinking of himself privately as 'a cut above the rest', grew to retain his peasant ways and manners almost as a matter of pride.

For instance, long before Mao lived in a cave in Yenan – where the remark may have had point – he frequently shouted to those about to enter the room, 'Have a good fart before you come in,' and, at the end of any difficult discussion, even when Chairman, he normally suggested to companions who disagreed with him that they should 'go away and have a good bowel movement' when he was sure they would feel better and become more reasonable. And, long before he took any personal interest in women, Mao's comments to his colleagues on sexual matters were equally earthy. But despite his earthy approach, there was no doubting his intellect and gift for leadership. One of the few people still living who knew Mao at this time recalls that he 'had an air about him' and that he naturally assumed the leadership in any gathering not attended by such obvious superiors as Li Dazhao or Chen Duxiu.

Mao's father died, so too did Professor Yang Changzhi, but shortly after these sad events, in 1920, he was offered the post of headmaster at the normal school of Changsha and, for the first time in his life, Mao enjoyed a good salary. This enabled him to marry the daughter of his late professor, Yang Kaihui, with whom he had maintained an irregular correspondence. It is rather typical of the future chairman that the date of his marriage is unknown and there is a school of thought that suggests they never went through any formal ceremony but merely decided to live together.

Soon afterwards Bertrand Russell, who was spending a year teaching in China, visited Changsha and Mao heard him talk. His comments on 'the British aristocrat' were interesting for he said Russia favoured communism but was opposed to the dictatorship of the proletariat. Indeed, Russell stressed that there was no need for war or revolution – merely a change, through education, in the minds of the ruling class. Mao disagreed with this on the grounds that education required money and that was almost entirely in the hands of the capitalists.

Students of Chairman Mao's early writings claim that unlike many Marxists he wrote extremely little about capital and state finance. This apparent lack of interest in how states are administered in economic terms, could, in part, account for the mistakes Mao made later. They were certainly based on his refusal to go abroad and his total lack of education in these spheres. But despite the troubled times, caused largely by disputes between rival warlords, Mao seems to have spent what for him was a quiet year with his comely and intelligent new wife, as they both continued work in the various Marxist and other study groups he had helped establish.

Mao cleverly set up a bookshop in Changsha which sold publications with a strong left-wing bias and he persuaded the right-wing governor to open it. At the same time, he established a secret cell of young communists in the town.

Before the Chinese Communist Party was eventually founded, three main groups supporting the teaching of Karl Marx had already been established outside Peking and Shanghai. The first was in the industrial areas where labour leaders had been active, especially amongst the Chinese workers in foreign firms, in setting up labour unions. On the whole the left-wing industrial elements favoured what is now dubbed the Russian form of communism and advocated that socialism – for that was their avowed aim – could best be achieved through the revolutionary efforts of the urban workers. Some of the labour leaders were in close contact with a score of Russian agents Moscow had sent into China to promote, influence and report on Marxist activities there.

The second group stressed the hidden power of the peasants and comprised Mao and the small group of intellectuals he had gathered around his already dominating personality in Hunan. Constantly recalling the peasant uprisings of the past, Mao suggested that the harsh conditions imposed by the landlords would again render the peasants revolutionary material.

The third group of left-wing support, which developed later, was made up of students who returned from Europe after they had taken part in the 'Work/Study' scheme. Initially, Mao, as already stated, had helped to raise money for the project but decided not to go. The returned students included Zhou Enlai and his wife, Deng Yingchao (although she did not go to Europe with him), together with Deng Xiaoping, Li Lisan, and a much older former 'imperial' officer Zhu De, who was to become the 'Father of the Red Army'. In addition Zhou Enlai and other Chinese students had formed Chinese communist parties of their own in Paris and Berlin. Many of the students travelled widely in Western Europe before returning home, generally, via Moscow.

There were many wide grey areas between the three sectors. And it is a dangerous over-simplification to suggest that the group based on urban unions developed into 'capitalist roaders and pro-Russian revisionists' in later years. Undoubtedly, some of them took this path but the vast majority had the sense to keep their heads down and their mouths closed after the dramatic breach with Moscow in 1959 when the Russians refused to hand over the nuclear secrets they had promised.

Formation of the Chinese Communist Party

Sometime in 1920 the Comintern sent Gregory Voitinsky to China to act as a catalyst in the formation of a Chinese Communist Party. He made contact with Li Dazhao and Chen Duxiu as well as the handful of communist cells that had been established in several cities. This resulted in the calling of the so-called 1st Party Congress when twelve people met in a girls' school in the French Concession in Shanghai to form the new Chinese party. Although Li and Chen were not present, they were honoured as 'founder members' of the party. The congress was disturbed by the police and the Chinese concluded their business in a hired boat on a nearby lake pretending to be tourists. The Russian representatives did not accompany them.

Mao who was present returned to Hunan to establish a branch of the party there and during the following year he claimed he organized 'more than twenty trade unions in the province' including 'railway workers, municipal employees, printers and workers in the government mint'. Mao's activities also covered western Jiangxi where the important Anyuan mines are situated. Here he had two assistants who were to become extremely important in his life, Li Lisan and Liu Shaoqi (Liu Shao-chi) who had attended Mao's group before he studied in Moscow. Liu was to become a leader, Head of State and the Chairman's 'chosen successor' before his ultimate disgrace during the Cultural Revolution. He was rehabilitated after his death by Vice Premier Deng Xiaoping.

When Mao was organizing his study group for youthful Hunanese intellectuals he had advertised in a local paper for interested students. He told Edgar Snow in 1936 that he had three and a half replies. One came from Luo Zhanglong (Lo Chang-lung) and will be referred to later but the half reply was from 'a non-committed youth named Li Lisan' who, Mao claimed, 'listened to all' he had to say but went away and their 'friendship never developed'.

There was at times a curious vagueness about Mao that is typified in his disclosure of how he missed the 2nd Party Congress of the party which was called in Shanghai. 'I intended to attend', he said, 'but forgot the name of the place where it was to be held and, as I could not find any of the comrades, I missed it.' Soon after this Mao either resigned or was dismissed from his post as headmaster. His mother-in-law helped him financially but his presence in the area became hazardous after a new governor was appointed.

Mao did not miss the 3rd Party Congress which was held in Guangzhou in May 1923 when the vital decision was taken, as a result of pressure from Moscow, to co-operate with the Guomindang or Nationalist Party known as the KMT. Sun Yat-sen and the Nationalists had reorganized the KMT from Japan and established a republican administration in Guangzhou in 1921 with the blessing of a friendly warlord. At the time the central government in Peking had little power outside the immediate area of the capital, and the north of the country was largely administered by local warlords while foreign powers maintained order with small forces in some of the main ports such as Shanghai and Tianjin.

It is difficult to estimate the strength of the Communist Party at that time as none of the leaders has mentioned the number of members. But in fairness to the Russians they had sent into China some able organizers who concentrated on trade unions in the major cities of the south and east. Sun Yat-sen lacked a power base even in the south and he was pleased to receive representatives of the Comintern who from time to time gave him assistance in the form of military experts and political advisers. The formation of a Communist Party had acted as a catalyst in the re-organization and strengthening of the KMT.

Although Mao opposed the proposal for a united front with the Guomindang he was nonetheless elected for the first time as a member of the Central Committee of the Communist Party and he became head of the Organization Department which required that he live in Shanghai. In January 1924, when Mao attended the 1st Congress of the KMT as a delegate, he was giving lively support to Sun Yat-sen. Indeed, the hard work he accomplished in Shanghai for the KMT caused him at that time to be severely criticized by Li Lisan. In 1925, Li, then already one of the small Communist Party, criticized Mao again for the same reason.

From time to time Mao disappeared from the scene or was genuinely sick. Some of his supporters claimed he was ill as a result of the psychological problems caused through being a devoted communist and working hard for the KMT. About this time, in 1924/5, he entered into a series of disagreements with Chen Duxiu who, as the Communist Party 'Boss', was taking in Mao's view a 'Right opportunist line'.

Mao was not in Guangzhou when Sun Yat-sen died in 1925 and differences of opinion within the KMT grew to dangerous proportions. For a time shortly after this Mao was acting head of the KMT's Propaganda Department when he predictably stressed the need for the organization to concentrate on the peasantry. This was the reason Mao was put in charge of the Peasant Training Centre which can still be viewed by tourists in Guangzhou today.

The now famous Whampoa Military Academy was established by the KMT to train a professional officer corps to lead the Nationalist – or Revolutionary – Army and the man appointed as President was the then little known Chiang Kai-shek, who had taken part in the Revolution of 1911 and then been trained in Japan where his instructors had described him as 'brilliant'. Chiang's appointment was also influenced by the fact that he had married Song Meiling (Soong Mei-ling), sister of Sun Yat-sen's wife, and a member of one of the richest and most influential merchant banker families in Shanghai. Another point in Chiang's favour was that he had studied at first-hand in Moscow the Soviet military methods and their system of political indoctrination.

However, Chiang's deputy head in the Political Education Department of the military academy was the young communist Zhou Enlai, the future Premier, fresh from France and amongst the students in the fourth grade was Lin Biao, the future second 'chosen successor' to Chairman Mao. It is hardly surprising that grave disputes soon arose between the republican and the communist elements that were to continue overtly or secretly until 'liberation' in 1949 and the establishment of the People's Republic. Authority, which was based on money and arms, rested first on Stalin's representatives, then the KMT, which was financed by rich traders and landlords, and last and, at that time by far the least important, those Chinese who like Mao believed in a revolution supported by the peasants.

But despite these disagreements the general cry was to unify China and remove the divisions created by warlords and foreign interests. Sun died in 1925 before this had been accomplished but the nationalists eventually achieved this objective through what is now known as the 'Northern Expedition' of 1926–7 which opened as a joint KMT–communist effort but ended in bitterness and tragedy.

There can be no doubt that during his period as Director of the KMT-financed Peasant Movement Training Institute, Mao became even more convinced of the great power latent in the peasantry. 'I had not realized the degrees of class struggle amongst the peasants,' he said. In 1926 Mao was sent to inspect the peasant organization in five counties and the report he produced, 'On an Investigation into the Peasant Movement in Hunan', is famous for many reasons and is freely available to the world in volume 1 of Mao's official *Selected Works*. According to Mao, inter-provincial meetings attended by two Russian agents supported his recommendation for a widespread redistribution of land but the 5th Congress of the Communist Party in April/May 1927 rejected it. Mao's critics suggested that his 'grand claims' to have organized peasant associations in Hunan were 'greatly exaggerated'.

Mao was furious and, perhaps, took too little account of the political background for he was as yet inexperienced. Chiang Kai-shek had already led a 'counter-revolution' against the Communists in Shanghai and Wuhan but Chen Duxiu, whose hold on the party was failing, still claimed there was something to be gained from co-operation with the KMT and called for 'moderation and concessions'. Mao disclosed nearly a decade later to Edgar Snow that:

I was very dissatisfied with party policy then, especially its attitude towards the Peasant Movement. I think today over a decade later (1937) that had the Peasant Movement been more thoroughly organized and armed for a class struggle against the landlords, the Soviets or 'Mountain Tops' – the name given to communist guerrilla bases – would have had an earlier and far more powerful development throughout the entire country.

Early breakdown of co-operation with Chiang Kai-shek

The root of the trouble was that during the Northern Expedition intense competition developed between communist and KMT factions on who was to take control of the main cities. The greatest drama, indeed a bitter tragedy, took place in Shanghai where Zhou

Enlai had been sent at the last moment as Director of the Military Department. After intensive work with the labour unions, a successful strike of thousands of workers was organized for March 21st, when Chiang's troops were on the outskirts of the city, with the result that there was virtually no resistance and within a few days Shanghai was in the hands of the Northern Expedition Forces. However, less than a month after this brilliant piece of organization by Zhou, Chiang became apprehensive about the Communist Party and staged a 'bloody' counter-coup. Zhou escaped with his life but Zhao Shiyan (Chao Shin-yen), his second in command, was captured and executed with hundreds of other communist supporters. The bitterness never left Zhou Enlai, who spoke of it in 1974 during President Pompidou's visit to Shanghai, still with deep and bitter emotion.

It was in the atmosphere left by these events that the controversial 5th Party Congress (which failed to consider Mao's Hunan report) took place in April 1927. However, after Mao had left the congress in anger and disgust – pretending he was ill – he was only elected as an alternate member of the Central Committee. Liu Shaoqi, his friend, the trade union organizer from Hunan, was elected to the Central Committee for the first time while efforts were made to 'ease out' Chen Duxiu who was said to have run out of steam. Chen now heads the list of ten names of those men who opposed Mao, or, in Maoist communist jargon, 'The names of those who led the ten struggles between the two lines.'

The break with the KMT was finally made possible by the Nanchang Uprising of August 1st, 1927, which is now celebrated as the birthday of the Red Army. At an earlier meeting of the Politbureau Chen had proposed a complete break with the KMT on the grounds that they were attempting to assume control of the Revolution. 'The Communist Party must either abandon its leadership of the mass movement or break with the KMT altogether,' he said. He appealed publicly to Stalin's representative, Borodin, who apparently agreed with him but added, 'Moscow will never permit it.'

The Nanchang Uprising was one of the glorious failures of the Communist Party in its early days and has come to rank in the annals of China as a victory second only to the epic Long March.

By July 1927 the Communists had been dismissed from the left-orientated KMT organization in Wuhan and, in despair, they planned a coup in Nanchang. Ye Ding was the key military figure but other leaders included Zhou Enlai, Zhu De and He Long (Ho Lung), who commanded the 20th Army in Nanjing. The cream of the Chinese Communist Party appear to have been near the scene, including Zhang Guodao (Chang Kuo-tao, a founder member who later led an important 'mountain top' but quarrelled with Mao during the Long March and left the Communist Movement in 1938), Li Lisan (soon to become party leader), Nie Rongzhen (Nieh Jung-chen, the future 'father' of China's atom bomb), Liu Bocheng (Liu Po-ch'eng, a future 'Marshal') and Zhou Yichun (Chou I-chun, later to lose his life on an inspection tour in mysterious circumstances).

Immediately the city came under communist control and a twenty-five man revolutionary committee was established that included the sympathetic though then non-communist figure of Madame Sun Yat-sen. However, the urban masses did not rally to their support and, after five days in power, Ye Ding decided to withdraw rather than be encircled by KMT forces. While the rebel forces moved south towards Guangdong where in late September they held Shantou for a few days, Zhou Enlai became seriously ill and was evacuated on a small boat to Hong Kong with Ye Ding and Nie Rongzhen. They remained based in Hong Kong for a year or two while the fate of the Communist Party, according to Mao, reached 'a disastrous low'.

An 'emergency conference' was then called in Hankou on August 7th and, although Mao had already begun what has since been termed 'his years in the wilderness', he attended the meetings that deposed Chen Duxiu as leader, who may or may not have been allowed to remain in the party. Zhu Qiubai (Chu Chiu-pai), already a member of the Politbureau, was elected as secretary of the party leader – despite the fact that he was a sick man suffering from tuberculosis. Mao was again only elected an alternate member of the Central Committee. All hope of co-operation with the KMT was then given up. In Mao's own words, 'The KMT had already become the tool of imperialism and could not carry out the responsibilities of a democratic revolution.' 'The long open struggle for power now began,' he added.

Chen Duxiu thus became the first name on the list of ten men who challenged Mao's leadership. There were many others, some more important than those listed by Mao himself and almost all the men concerned have been accused of 'rightist' opportunism although Mao termed the first three on the list 'left opportunists'. They were Chen Duxiu, Zhu Qiubai and Li Lisan.

There is in the Chinese Communist Party a recognized right and left as there is in any western political movement. In simplistic terms, the left support extreme broadbrush radical movements such as 'World Revolution' in the international sphere together with giving moral approval to left-wing guerrillas and revolutionary parties. In the domestic sphere the left believe in the total abolition of private plots in agricultural communes and, perhaps even more important, overtime pay or any other material incentives. In making political appointments it is more important an administrator or army officer be 'red' than 'expert'. In other words they are working towards a state of 'true' communism where there will be no money and each will receive food, clothes and lodgings according to his needs.

The right wing for their part are pragmatists who see the benefits to be derived from 'material incentives' while paying lip-service to the philosophy of a people's war. They realize this will not be effective in many parts of China where the population is sparse. Thus they press for the re-arming and modernization of the People's Liberation Army, Navy and Air Force with nuclear and sophisticated conventional weapons.

There are other vital differences between right and left in China in culture and, especially, in the sphere of education where the left believe it is more important for students to have a well-developed political consciousness', to be 'red' rather than attain academic distinction. Meanwhile the rightists suggest students can be 'expert' as well as good members of the Communist Party.

But despite these clearly defined lines most people who have been expelled from the party or purged have been dubbed 'rightist' at one moment and 'leftist' at another. Generally, of course, those who initially believed in full co-operation with Moscow were called 'rightist opportunists', or Pro-Russian Revisionists. But this term of abuse was from time to time, and for no apparent reason, changed to 'leftist'. Chairman Mao's definition of what is right and left in the Communist Party had a peasant flavour. 'A baby takes nine months to form in its mother's body,' he said. 'If you try to force out the baby in seven months you are a leftist trying to rush ahead too quickly. But if you attempt to prevent the baby leaving its mother's womb after nine months then you are a rightist taking too long over everything.'

The failure of the Nanchang Uprising led to the period of Soviets or 'mountain tops'. (Mao was not the only youthful Chinese rebel who had been deeply impressed by the thirteenth-century traditional saga *Water Margin* translated by Pearl Buck as *All Men Are Brothers*.) In 1927 known and active communists had few choices open to them. They could work underground in Shanghai, Peking or one of the other cities, escape to Moscow or Hong Kong or collect what followers and arms they had and establish themselves on a 'mountain top'. 'Mountain tops' were generally chosen on the borders of two or three counties where no local authority was responsible for the security of the area. They benefited from the bandit tradition of falling between two or three administrative or police stools. The technique was obviously not new. Indeed, it was but one of the many military ideas Mao had acquired from reading the *Art of War* written around 500 B.C. by Sun Tzu, which was the first known treatise on the subject.

Mao was driven to his 'mountain top' partly by the failure of peasant uprisings in Hunan, a few months before the Nanchang Uprising. When talking with journalists in Yenan and the few heads of state he met in later years, Mao always insisted that a great opportunity had been missed by the Chinese Communist Party because Moscow failed to recognize the inherent power of the peasant.

While Mao was organizing the peasants for what became known as the Autumn Harvest Uprising, 'travelling between miners and the peasant guards' and his 'mountain top', he was captured by the KMT. In his own words, 'The Guomindang terror was then at its height and hundreds of suspected Reds were being shot.' Mao was ordered to be taken to a local military headquarters where he was to be killed. 'Borrowing several tens of dollars from a comrade, however, I attempted to bribe the escort to free me,' said Mao, 'for the ordinary soldiers were mercenaries with no special interest in seeing me killed.' However, the subaltern refused to permit this – there was, after all, a very high price on Mao's head – and Mao had no alternative but to make an escape.

Some two hundreds yards from the military headquarters Mao saw some high grass above a pond and broke loose. He said he remained in the same spot until sunset and the soldiers and peasants searching for him came near enough for him to touch them twice, but he escaped detection. After dark when the search was abandoned, Mao made his way across the mountains without shoes, saying his feet were badly bruised although he had walked many miles as a young man with bare feet in order to harden himself. During the night Mao met a peasant (again and again Mao met people who helped him when he was in difficulties). He must have had great charm, because the unnamed peasant gave Mao shelter and money that he used to buy 'shoes, an umbrella and some food'. This enabled him to return to safety.

The failure of the Autumn Uprising was in part due to the fact that Mao, who had inspired and sponsored the movement, was captured just before 'D' day which was September 9th. But there can be no question that the future chairman had gravely misjudged the enthusiasm and military capabilities of local peasants and the Anyuan coal-miners who made up what he called 'his four regiments'. Mao brought the operation to an end after a week and admitted that 'discipline was low, political training virtually non-existent' and, he added, 'there were many desertions'. Mao also admitted that the operation was not sanctioned by the Central Committee who, he claimed, 'reprimanded' him 'no less than three times and then expelled him from the party'. But like a few other statements made by Mao at this time, it might well be an exaggeration. There is, however, no doubt that he was then very much 'in the wilderness' of the Communist Party.

But what the communists now call the Second Revolutionary Civil War had opened and by the winter of 1927 Mao was established on the 'mountain top' at Jinggangshan (Ching Kang-shan) with the remnants of the four regiments together with two former warlords or bandit leaders who joined his unit, which was made up of about one thousand communist soldiers. Mao said while he was there the bandits behaved like good communists but after he left they reverted to banditry and were killed by the peasants who, by that time, had learned how to operate as guerrillas.

Mao's motley throng was saved, albeit temporarily from the KMT pressure by the arrival of Zhu De who had a military background which at that time made him invaluable as a commander in the field. In 1911 during the revolt in Kunming which brought down the Manchu authorities, Zhu had been an officer and in 1916 he took part first as a regimental commander and then as a brigadier in the campaign to thwart the restoration of the monarchy. In the years before 1920 Zhu was caught without knowing it, according to Agnes Smedley who knew him well, in 'warlordism' and he was fond of his many concubines as well as his pipes of opium. A series of coincidences combined with reading leftist books persuaded him to give up this type of life and he deliberately broke himself of the opium habit by travelling on a British ship in the Yangtze where none was available. After visits to France, Germany and Russia he returned to become a member of the Communist Party as the one man who had been trained as an officer and had first-hand experience of combat.

Zhu De and Mao made several attempts to contact one another again in the confused period after Zhu De's men helped Mao. Zhu had then marched from Nanchang south towards Guangdong and on to Shantou where his force was routed by Chiang Kai-shek's army. After this, however, Zhu De received some help from a KMT commander whom he had known many years earlier in Yunan. For this bit of collaboration Zhu was severely reprimanded by the Politbureau before he moved his troops to Yizhang (I-chang) in southern Hunan and established a new Soviet there.

Mao, who was having great difficulties in obtaining food at that point, in January 1928 abandoned Jinggangshan for a brief period to join Zhu De. Their strength was then further increased when another commander, Peng Dehuai (Peng Te-huai), who had a small group of radical guerrillas under his command, joined them from the north in the autumn of that year. Peng like Mao came from Hunan. But after Peng had returned to the Hunan Jiangxi border, Zhu and Mao were then estimated to have around 5000 men of whom only half were armed.

Quarrels with Moscow over peasants and urban workers

Although Zhu Qiubai, the new party leader, had volunteered to publish the full text of Mao's report on 'An Investigation into the Peasant Movement in Hunan' and even wrote an introduction to it, he was by nature orientated towards Moscow both as a scholar – he had translated Tolstoy into Chinese – and as a politician. Stalin, for reasons unknown, replaced his agent Borodin with a young Georgian, Besso Lominadze, and the party line changed abruptly and dramatically from one of urging a United Front of all sympathizers to ordering open urban and rural insurrections against the KMT. After the failure of the Autumn Harvest Uprising in which Liu Shaoqi, then a leader of labour unions, took part and the Canton Insurrection, which led to unbridled repression, Zhu Qiubai was charged with 'left opportunism' or putschism.

The 6th Party Congress which took place in June/July 1928 was held in Moscow, officially because it was then considered most unsafe for the leaders to gather in China but the real reason seems to have been Stalin's desire to gain a complete hold over the Chinese Communist Party. Zhu Qiubai was replaced as Secretary though he retained his membership of the Politbureau and the unknown man who took over allowed the real power to slip through his fingers and fall into the dynamic hands of Li Lisan. Zhu stayed on in Moscow where he gained prestige in the international Communist Movement as 'Strakhov', the Russian translation of his name, meaning 'fear'.

Meanwhile, from his secret underground headquarters in Shanghai, Li Lisan sent out a series of military orders that did not make much sense to the experienced Zhu De or, indeed, to Mao. Li Lisan wanted them to adopt 'strong aggressive tactics' and advance on Changsha and other towns. In the villages he urged a campaign of 'terror' designed to demoralize the gentry whilst a 'mighty offensive' by urban workers, which included uprisings and strikes, would paralyse the enemy in his base. Li Lisan was given to understand, or so he said, that substantial military assistance would come from Russia. He appeared genuinely to believe 'flank attacks' would take place in the north from Outer Mongolia and Manchuria backed by the USSR. Mao claimed, with reason, that Li grossly overestimated the military strength of the Chinese Red Army which was only just beginning to emerge as a disciplined force with a series of rules and slogans that the simple Red soldier could understand. The rules, unhappily, did not coincide with Li Lisan's orders.

The slogans again adopted by Mao and his supporters, basically from Sun Tzu, were:

1 When the enemy advances: we retreat.
2 When the enemy halts and encamps: we trouble them.
3 When the enemy seeks to avoid battle: we attack.
4 When the enemy retreats: we pursue.

These four directives were each contained in four simple Chinese characters whilst the eight orders on how the soldiers were to behave were made into Chinese marching songs:

1 Replace all doors – which had been used for sleeping on – when you leave a house.
2 Return and roll up the straw matting on which you sleep.
3 Be courteous and polite to the people and help them when you can.
4 Return all borrowed articles.
5 Replace all damaged articles. [This was virtually impossible.]
6 Be honest in all transactions with the peasants.
7 Pay for all articles purchased.
8 Be sanitary and, especially, establish latrines at a safe distance from people's dwellings.

According to Mao the last two orders came from Lin Biao, then an up-and-coming company commander.

Mao also complained that at irregular intervals he received contradictory and defeatist orders from Li's headquarters urging him to retreat to the border. He told visiting Americans in Yenan later that whenever the Red Army departed from their own slogans they failed in their objectives. He stressed that their forces were then small and stretched and their resources extremely limited, 'only by adopting skilful guerrilla tactics' could the scattered units which made up the Red Army hope to have any success in their struggle with the KMT fighting from 'vastly richer and superior bases', he said.

The Red Army under Zhu, Mao and Peng Dehuai, who had already emerged as a brilliant guerrilla leader and supported Mao on the main issues, but who was slightly under a cloud at the time for having an affair with the wife of a brother officer, sought to avoid 'positional warfare'. They adopted the tactics the Americans notably failed to achieve four decades later against the communists in Vietnam of 'consolidating' an area and gaining the mass support of the peasants before advancing. Li Lisan, like the Americans who wanted speedy results in the pacification campaigns, repeatedly urged Mao to advance far too quickly. Further, Li wanted to concentrate all their available arms in the hands of the Red Army who he believed could gradually absorb the partisans.

The Red Army had, according to Mao, planned a 'wavelike or tidal development' rather than an advance gained 'by leaps and jumps' without deep consolidation of the territory gained. These tactics had been developed from experience, but Li Lisan, who was powerful both in Moscow and in the underground movements of the cities, continued to demand action.

Whilst it is difficult to make any judgment on this particular 'grey' period of Communist development in which there are so many contradictory and self-serving reports, it does appear that Li was asking far too much when he ordered Peng Dehuai to join Zhu and Mao for a second attack on Changsha. The newly organized Red Army under Peng Dehuai did attack Changsha, the capital of Hunan where Mao had taught, but the success was fleeting and three days later nationalist troops retook the town and inflicted heavy losses on the rebels.

About this period Mao's wife, Yang Kaihui, who was still in Changsha, was captured. She was later executed, together with his sister, while other members of his family were held in prison by the KMT. It is curious that Mao left his wife behind apparently confident that she was quite safe. Yang Kaihui was told her life would be spared if she would disclose all she knew about Mao and his associates. This she refused to do with the result that she was executed in public outside the gates of Changsha in 1930. She was later to be immortalized in Mao's poems. But even before the execution Mao had begun living with the party worker He Zizhen (Ho Tzu-chen) who became his second wife.

There was an enormous 'dead or alive' price on Mao's head for in a curious way he had already become a myth. One day a plane flew over his old village and the peasants said it was Mao about to return 'home'. They warned the men who had been cultivating Mao's fields that Chiang would have to pay compensation for the trees he had felled and other damage.

In his secret headquarters Li Lisan considered it 'natural' that the Red Army led by Zhu De, Luo Zhanglong and Mao should come to the aid of the 'lagging' industrial workers' movement. Moscow had suggested to Li that now was the time to cash in on the 'New Revolutionary Wave' that the Russians said had been proclaimed as a result of the chronic world depression in 1929. Militarily, the Russians too were advising immediate action against Chiang Kai-shek whose leadership of the KMT was endangered by the northern warlords Yan Xi (Yen Hsi) and Feng Yuxiang (Feng Yu-hsiang) who had risen against him. Li, it was said later, had not informed them just how weak the Red Army was at that stage. Indeed, Peng Dehuai stated in Yenan that 1930 was the first year in which his force established any contact with the Central Committee led by Li Lisan.

The guerrilla leaders were also under constant local pressure. But Li stressed they 'stubbornly adhered to the military concept of guerrilla warfare in opposition to the expansion of the Red Army'. He frequently pressed them to 'discard the outmoded guerrilla tactics of the past and make a fundamental change' in order to be able to undertake positional warfare tactics. Li, wrongly as it turned out, claimed in innumerable despatches to the guerrilla leaders that when they were ready to mount an attack on an urban area the masses had told him 'whenever the insurrection comes, notify us, we will come'.

In fact, the masses everywhere failed to rally to the support of the urban leaders. Thus it was hardly surprising that Mao, Zhu and Peng became increasingly sceptical of Li's boasts. At one point they made a move to sacrifice Li as they had Chen but, instead, sent Zhou in to chastise him.

In 1930 Mao claimed 'Li Lisanism' had been overcome in the Red Army but although this was not quite true, his influence, in some measure due to Peng Dehuai's support for Zhu and Mao, was on the wane.

By the end of that year, Chiang, with about one hundred thousand armed men, mounted the first of five KMT extermination campaigns. These were organized on the advice of the able German

General von Falkenhausen, whose mission had replaced the Russian military advisers with Chiang Kai-shek. Mao said later that the Red Army could then mobilize about 40,000 men, soldiers and partisans. Despite the disparity in numbers, by admitting the enemy troops 'deeply into territory held by the Red Army' and carrying out sudden and concentrated attacks on isolated KMT units, the enemy was eventually defeated or, at least, made to withdraw. 'Our tactics were', Mao said, 'swift concentration and swift dispersal.' Basically Mao attributed the victory – if such it could be called – to the 'liquidation' of the Li Lisan line. A second extermination campaign four months later was equally unsuccessful. However, Mao, despite the shadow hanging over Li and his policy, was still far from the leadership, and he was not authorized by the Politbureau to deal with military matters. Indeed, Mao himself said that from October 1932 until the opening of the Long March in 1934 he devoted his time 'almost exclusively' to administrative work with the Soviet Government leaving the military command to Zhu and others.

The Japanese take over Manchuria

In 1931 other more important political and military distractions appeared for Moscow and Chiang's government in Nanjing when the Japanese invaded Manchuria. The Soviet Union formally declared war on the Japanese though there was little anyone could do as Soviet China was virtually encircled by the KMT. Indeed, had there been a chance of military action it is unlikely Moscow would then have declared war. The long-term Moscow line, if they had one, appeared to be to get China first united and then attempt to check the Japanese, who had annexed Korea in 1910. The Russians encouraged a Manchurian and a Mongolian Autonomous Movement in order to gain hold of these mineral-rich areas. A famous Japanese proverb circulating in China at that time indicates the military mood in Tokyo. 'To conquer the world it is necessary first to conquer China and to conquer China it is necessary first to conquer Manchuria and Mongolia.'

Tokyo's military authorities, perhaps unknown to their Government, had set 1932 as the target date for the occupation of

Manchuria but the Guangdong Army there would not wait and a series of incidents played into Japanese hands. Although Tokyo urged restraint the explosion of a bomb, causing minimal damage to Mukden station, in September 1931, provided the necessary excuse for the army to go ahead and they quickly occupied Changchun, Andong (Antung), Yingkou and Jilin (Kirin). Five months later, the same province was under Japanese control but it was not until the following January that the isolationist President of the United States, Herbert Hoover, announced the USA would not go to war. To 'legitimize the naked aggression the Japanese created the puppet state of Manchukuo'. However, the League of Nations Commission led by the acting Viceroy of India, Lord Lytton, was not deceived by the façade and condemned Japan as an aggressor.

The end of Li Lisanism

Li Lisan finally lost influence because he overestimated the military strength of the Red Army and even more so the 'revolutionary factors' or strength in the national political scene. He became especially resented by the labour unions because his aggressive tactics had evoked such stern counter-measures from the KMT. Indeed, officials claimed that the rank and file workers had even grown afraid to join the unions. Nonetheless efforts at the Third Plenum of the Central Committee in 1930 to overthrow Li failed though he was later called to Moscow where he remained in exile for some years. Stalin had by that time realized that Li lacked the authority to implement Moscow's policy of building the Chinese Communist Party on the urban trade unions. In China today Li is perhaps the best known of all the men who challenged Mao in the early days. Stalin then replaced him with Pavel Mif, former Chancellor of the Sun Yat-sen University in China, in an effort to settle the inter-party strife. He was accompanied by a group of former Chinese students who had become known as the '28 Bolsheviks'.

For a brief spell after Li Lisan departed, and before a Fourth Party Plenum was called and Wang Ming took over, Luo Zhanglong was the Party Secretary and hundreds of communists recognized him as their leader. But during a dispute at the Fourth Plenum held in Shanghai in January 1931, Luo walked out of the meeting in a fit of temper and would not, or did not, return as this would have lost him too much face. However, it did lose him his important position in the party and enabled Wang Ming and the '28 Bolsheviks', with whom he had already quarrelled, to charge him with 'obstructing the party' by refusing to comply with its policy. Further, they dubbed Luo 'undemocratic' before voting that he be expelled from the party. It is interesting to note that the expulsion was referred to the Comintern and approval given to it some six months later.

Mao was not actively engaged in the meeting where Luo was trying to initiate a party policy based largely on labour unions and opposing or standing between the '28 Bolsheviks' and the Soviets. Indeed, after his expulsion Luo attempted to set up a separate party leadership based on the unions and independent of the returned students and the Soviets. Luo's attempts met with some success until the British police in Shanghai arrested him and a group of his supporters and handed them over to the KMT. Most of them were executed but Luo escaped to Hong Kong and later returned to work in disguise for a brief period in the party. He fled a second time to Hong Kong but died years later in one of Ho Chi Minh's prisons in Hanoi.

Mao placed Luo fourth in his infamous list and accused him of leading a 'handful of splinters' who 'later became real rightists and degenerated into counter-revolutionaries'. Some of Luo's intimate supporters were later accused of working for Chiang Kai-shek's intelligence service. But Mao was personally hurt and affronted that the man who had answered his newspaper advertisement for 'youths who were hardened, determined and ready to make sacrifices for their country' should in Mao's own words 'have joined the Communist Party and betrayed it'. Zhu Qiubai was the only man on the infamous list to whom Mao accorded apotheosis, perhaps because he was killed during the Long March. Luo Zhanglong remains a traitor for ever in the annals of the Chinese communist regime.

Fortunately for Mao and Zhu they were then isolated 'on their mountain top' from these major disputes which threatened the very existence of the Party. Li Lisan – so far as 'Mr Wang', the

Chinese man in the street, is concerned – was directly replaced by Wang Ming, leader of the returned students or '28 Bolsheviks'. Certainly Wang Ming finally triumphed over Li Lisan and his ideas and proposed a new anti-Japanese united front policy. Although Wang Ming was so strongly backed by Moscow it was not easy for him to assert his authority over the Red armies in the hinterland.

Wang Ming was an excellent speaker whose real name was Zhen Shaoyu (Chen Shao-yu). He first attracted attention at the 6th National Congress of the Chinese Communist Party in Moscow in 1928 as an outstanding interpreter. After secret work inside China, he emerged as the leader of the Russian-returned students – the '28 Bolsheviks' – in 1929 in Shanghai. Although Wang Ming shared Li Lisan's opposition to Mao's guerrilla tactics he nonetheless caused many additional complications for Li during the later days of his leadership.

Mao, sensing the desperation and divisions within the Politbureau, boldly invited all its members to attend the 'First All-China Congress of the Soviet' which he said would be held in Ruijin on November 7th, 1931. The '28 Bolsheviks' arrived in a condescending mood with the intention not of supporting Mao's Soviet but of chastising him personally. Although Mao repeated this account to many visitors, his opponents claim that at this critical point in the power struggle the Politbureau arrived en masse in Ruijin supported by the Comintern military adviser, Li De (Li Te), with the sole intention of discrediting and replacing Mao. After all, Mao had already been accused by the party of 'opportunist pragmatism' as well as 'general ideological poverty' and condemned for his failure to adopt a strong 'class and mass line'. However, Mao and his men were in good spirits having survived the first two KMT extermination campaigns.

Mao's personality dominated the congress and in an obvious power struggle only three returned students, including the absent Wang Ming, were elected to the Central Executive Committee of the now All-China Government.

Mao scored an impressive victory largely because he had established his Soviet or 'mountain top' with the full support of the local peasants. In addition, he had a party and government apparatus of his own and, perhaps most important of all, an independent military force that operated from a secure base. However, Mao remained an outsider and was not as he had hoped co-opted into the Politbureau because differences between him and the returned students were too fundamental. Indeed the '28 Bolsheviks', despite Mao's successes in mobile guerrilla tactics, were still demanding that he introduce 'positional' warfare. On the difficult issue of the increasing threat from Japan, Mao said he was willing to take part in a United Front. The Politbureau, however, rejected military co-operation with what they termed 'reformist groups' and urged that the Red Army be rapidly expanded in order that it would fulfil its 'sublime duty' in 'safeguarding the Soviet Union against imperialist attacks'.

Chiang Kai-shek's third extermination campaign in July 1931 had been cut short by the Japanese invasion of Manchuria and, much more alarming, the opening of a second front in Shanghai early in 1932. However, Chiang, worried by the gains the 'Soviets' – guerrillas – were making, decided it was not feasible to wage an effective war against the Japanese until he had quelled the 'Reds'. This was also the view held by his German advisers. The Tang-ku Truce signed in May 1933 with the Japanese provided the opportunity for the fifth extermination campaign which was launched by Chiang the following October with seven hundred thousand men – or so it was said. Chiang adopted what he called a 'strategically offensive but tactically defensive posture', relying on encircling the Reds in the 'mountain tops' and starving them out. Nationalist troops constructed fortresses and pillboxes around the Red areas while the peasants were promised 'rural reconstruction' by Chiang who claimed the problem was 70 per cent political – communist – and only 30 per cent military.

The Politbureau, led by the '28 Bolsheviks', made a truly disastrous decision in not going to the military aid of the Fujian (Fukien) rebels who had established a 'mountain top' in Fuzhou (Foochow) the previous November. Mao did attempt to work out some sort of co-operation not only to help his comrades but also to force the nationalists to fight on two fronts. Left to their own devices the nationalists overran the Fujian base in January leaving Mao and Zhu to take the full force of their campaign.

Beset externally by Chiang and with the returned students trying to destroy him from within, Mao's situation was critical and it is something of a miracle that he survived. For a period his personal authority was seriously diminished and for the first time efforts inspired by Moscow were made to 'kick him upstairs' and turn him into a powerless figurehead. Similar efforts were to recur on many occasions during Mao's long life. Moscow barred Mao from party meetings and for some months, if not actually under house arrest, Mao was living under a heavy political cloud. But as Mao himself observed,

Revolution is not a tea party, or writing an essay, or painting a picture, or doing embroidery; it cannot be so refined, so leisurely and gentle, so temperate, kind, restrained and magnanimous ... A revolution is an insurrection, an act of violence by which one class overthrows another.

The opening of the Long March

Mao was prepared, and he used such authority as he had to plan the escape from the 'Soviet Republic' that had been a rebel base in one form or another for seven years. It was *later* suggested that the communists wanted to leave Jiangxi also in order to be able to play a role in the fight against the Japanese. But, in fact, the break-out from Ruijin in the middle of October, which was not easy, was solely to escape from the nationalists.

Some hundred thousand men, quite rightly, left their wives, the sick and the wounded behind them. It is assumed many of the wounded died while the women were absorbed into the local population and many of them remarried after their husbands had failed to communicate with them for a year or two. Mao himself left two children with the peasants but took his second wife, He Zizhen, who was again pregnant, along with him. (The children were never heard of again.)

The regular troops were burdened not only by every piece of artillery they had ever captured but also by heavy machinery which they had dismantled in the hope of setting it up again when their as yet unknown destination was reached. The roads were reminiscent of the tracks through the Rocky Mountains around Pike's Peak when the Americans threw their precious furniture out of the covered wagons in the late nineteenth century in order to make the journey to the west coast. The Chinese route was littered with bits of machinery and weapons for, unfortunately, there were few horses and virtually no other transport.

Mao commanded one of the main columns for it seemed that, in the crisis which had enveloped Ruijin as Chiang's troops closed in on them, he had regained some of his former authority. After a short battle at Haienfeng, which took them successfully through the nationalist encirclement, the men plodded along at the rate of about 25 miles a day or night. Not only was Chiang's army blessed with artillery, trucks and armoured cars, they had aircraft that harassed the Red columns when they exposed themselves by marching during the day. The fight for the crossing of the Xiang River lasted a week and cost the Red Army just over half its strength for many men decided the going was too hard and deserted during the night marches. Until they reached Zunyi (Tsunyi) in northern Guizhou in January 1935, the '28 Bolsheviks' dominated the army and party and as they moved westward the morale, never high, dropped to a dangerous level.

It is universally accepted that Zunyi marked the vital turning point in Mao's career as it firmly established his complete control of the party. Once in the relative safety of Zunyi, Mao demanded a meeting of an enlarged Politbureau – naturally to include himself – and opened it with a strong attack on the '28 Bolsheviks' and their followers for having failed to support the Fujian Revolt and their wrong and stupid decision in ordering positional warfare. Supported by Zhou Enlai, who up to that time had been loyal to the '28 Bolsheviks', he defeated those returned students who wanted to march towards Xinjiang and establish themselves near to the Russian heartland. Mao was elected to the newly created post of Chairman of the Politbureau and he and Zhou decided together that the March should head north to Shaanxi (Shensi) province. Zhou, who until then had been Chief Political Officer, gave way to Mao's leadership.

In order to deceive the nationalist forces who chased the Red Army relentlessly many detours were made and deception plans devised in efforts to enable the 'Red Army' to cross the Yangtze River. They made it appear they were making for Lengkai, one of the few navigable points in the upper Yangtze. Chiang ordered an enveloping movement and the removal and burning of all boats from the southern bank of the river. However, the Reds suddenly changed direction after a nationalist pilot had reported they were building a bamboo bridge that would take at least a week to complete. After a series of forced marches and wearing captured KMT uniforms, a battalion of Red soldiers descended upon the only other possible small town that possessed a ferry – Zhou Bing (Chou Ping) Fort – in Yunnan Province where they entered quietly at dusk and disarmed the garrison. They 'persuaded' a nationalist guard to call for boats because here they had not been burned. Across the river a second garrison which was found to be playing mah-jong was easily overcome and the entire Red Army was transported over the Yangtze during a period of nine days without loss of life. Once over the river they destroyed the boats thereby forcing the nationalists to make a detour to the nearest crossing point.

The March continued through Sichuan Province where it was faced with an even more formidable obstacle in the form of snowy mountain terrain and the fast-running Dadu River. Indeed, the crossing of that river and the capture of the famous chain iron suspension bridge at Luding, followed by the city itself, was the most remarkable achievement of the whole Long March and involved great deeds of heroism and fortitude. When it was discovered crossing by boat was far too slow and would enable the nationalists to encircle them, the Red Army initiated a series of forced marches to reach Luding, the only suspension bridge across the river. Despite the fact that the wooden planks covering the chain iron bridge had been removed, volunteers crossed the bridge under heavy machine-gun fire and overcame the guard. Scores of men dropped into the river after they were wounded. For those who waited, victory was life, defeat certain death.

Once across the Dadu the Red Army was no longer harassed by Chiang's forces but the natural obstacles remained tremendous. Indeed, losses were still grave in the uninhabited grassland where there was nothing to eat and in passing through regions used by non-Chinese warlike tribes – the Lolos. Only 8000 men continued the journey across the Minshan and Liuban ranges to the relative safety of Shaanxi. During the march a critical dispute arose between Mao and Zhang Guodao who had been chief party leader in the Oyuwan Soviet after 1931, about their final destination. The two had already clashed on what type of tactics the guerrilla forces would employ. After two conferences when no agreement was reached, Zhang moved westward, towards Russia, taking Zhu De with him and Mao marched on towards the north – to Shaanxi. There has never been a satisfactory explanation of why Zhu did not stay with Mao but the reason, given decades later in Peking, was that Zhu was actually having talks with Zhang and their forces were cut off from those of Mao, rendering his return impossible. However, Zhang's forces suffered dreadful hardships and heavy losses and when he finally joined Mao in Yenan he was in no position to challenge his leadership.

The Long March was in reality in the tactical sense a lengthy retreat marked by one disaster after another with losses in personnel reaching about 90 per cent of the initial force. But it has become the great military epic of the century and Mao always referred to it as 'a great psychological victory for communism'. 'If his men could survive that they could survive anything,' he said. The core of its participants formed a cohesive leadership that remained largely intact for the next three decades. Deng Xiaoping took part together with Chen Xilian (Chen Hsi-lien) who commanded the Peking Military Region during Mao's last years and Ye Jianying (Yeh Chien-ying), who took charge of the Defence Ministry after Lin Biao's attempted coup. Li Xiannian, the Party's financial wizard, Yang Yong (Yang Yung) who commanded first Peking and then Xinjiang, Nie Rongzhen, the father of China's atom bomb, as well as the future 'notorious traitors' Liu Shaoqi and Lin Biao, were all involved.

One of the few politically active women on the Long March was Deng Yingchao, the wife of Zhou Enlai. He was extremely sick at times during the March and had to be carried on a stretcher over many hundreds of the 6000 miles the marchers covered. In the Nanzu (Nantzu) territories the tribal queen, who had implacable hatred for all Chinese, threatened to boil alive anyone who helped the marchers. Unable to obtain food by capturing it, the Red Army was at times forced to make war in order to obtain a few cattle. Mao said, 'To obtain one sheep cost the life of one man.' However, Mao certainly overstated the case when he said the vegetable crops in the high altitude and rarefied atmosphere near Tibet grew to be five or six times their normal size and one turnip would 'feed fifteen men'!

Nonetheless, Mao's 'statistical recapitulation' which he made in Yenan is worth repeating. There was on average, he said, almost one skirmish a day somewhere along the line while fifteen days were devoted to major pitched battles. Out of a total of 368 days en route, 230 were consumed by day marches and 18 by night marches. (From the conversation and writings of survivors I would have thought there were many more night marches.) One hundred days were spent at halts many of which were also devoted to skirmishes. The Red Army is reputed to have crossed eighteen mountain ranges, five of which are perennially snow-capped, and they crossed twenty-four rivers, occupied sixty-two cities or towns and eluded ten different unfriendly provincial warlords as well as the nationalist troops.

The cadres (men of officer rank whether civil, military or Communist Party) once safely in Yenan were able to construct safe cave dwellings in the soft loess (sandstone) that formed the steep hillsides and within a few months all the permanent staff were so housed. The cave homes developed into what tourists can see today: two rooms carved out of the hillside. One in the case of Mao and Zhou, was used as an office, and the second inner sanctum as a bedroom. A mosquito net was a great luxury and rice paper over the lattice 'windows' a status symbol.

The local population was suffering from lack of organization and neglect by the communists who had established a base there in the early 1920s but had made little effort to set up a local administration. Admittedly, there were problems and the standard of living was far lower than in south-eastern China. When Deng Yingchao had solved the basic sanitary problems, she began to organize a campaign against the prevalent disease from which she as well as many others had suffered, tuberculosis. She then started propaganda to prevent the binding of girls' feet and the sale of young children – especially girls.

While on the Long March Mao and Zhou, together with Wang Ming and Zhang Guodao, had been elected to the Executive Committee of the Seventh Comintern Congress which took place in August 1935. A policy of a united front against fascism had been adopted largely as a result of the European communists' growing fear of Nazi Germany and Mussolini's Italy. But Russia's fear of a Japanese invasion of Mongolia also rendered the Kremlin far more amenable to compromise with the powerful KMT forces than they had been earlier in the decade. The Chinese communists remained the 'poor cousins'.

3
Yenan

A haven for thought and experiment

Life in the security of Yenan gradually developed a social and political pattern that cemented Mao's position as the leader. When Zhang Guodao and Zhu De arrived with their battered half-starved band they, metaphorically, touched their forelocks to Mao, who was clever enough to treat them well. Small incidents assumed great importance amongst the members of the isolated community and Mao's bowel movements were a constant subject of conversation – the change of diet from rice to millet on top of the hardships of the March had caused him and many others to suffer from chronic constipation – so that after a bowel movement people would congratulate him. This may seem laughable but there can be no doubt that many of the Long Marchers, at the opening of the Yenan period, suffered because they had to eat millet instead of rice and meat, and from the shortage of fruit and vegetables. However, they did manage to obtain tobacco of a sort (which they later grew) and Mao's cave became thick with smoke from home-rolled cigarettes as the leader discussed immediate and long-term problems. The feeling of safety Yenan engendered (the walled town of Poan was surrounded by mountains) enabled Mao frequently to talk until three or four in the morning and sleep until noon which to him was a great luxury.

Edgar Snow, who, as already stated, was one of the first western reporters to penetrate to Yenan in July 1935, had no doubt that Mao was very much the 'boss' and he obtained the only first-hand biography authorized by the Chairman. It appeared in *Red Star over China* two years later and represents a remarkable stroke of fortune for Snow since Mao and all the Chinese communist leaders always expressed serious reservations about disclosing details of their past lives. Maybe, initially, they did not want their fellow comrades to know that they had relatives who were landowners, merchants or bankers but the tradition grew and it is now considered almost bad form to disclose details of personal background, education or career. 'Self-advertisement' was the phrase used in Peking for such disclosures when Mao was alive and active. Snow recalled that while he was taking down the details of the Chairman's life through an interpreter, Mao's wife, He Zizhen, came in from the kitchen where she was 'preparing a dish of apricots', to listen to what her husband had to say as much of the information was quite new to her. She was frequently sick. She gave birth to a son during the Long March and appeared never to recover from this ordeal. Although she had been an enthusiastic party member and worker before she married Mao, she took no part in the urban social and administrative activities organized by Deng Yingchao.

Some months after Snow arrived in Yenan the famous Xi'an Incident in December 1936 still further complicated political issues with the nationalists. The story of what happened has never been fully disclosed, but Chiang Kai-shek was kidnapped at six one morning from the hot springs about an hour's journey from Xi'an. Rare visitors – I was one – are shown the small room in which he had bedded down with a concubine together with the small back window through which he escaped, leaving behind his clothes and false teeth, up a steep mountain-side at the back of the spa. But the climb was too much for the ageing Chiang and his more agile captors soon caught up with him. The report I was given in Peking forty years after the event suggested long before the kidnapping a few of Chiang's units had been influenced by 'Red' propaganda stressing the advantages of a United Front. Indeed, leaflets had been infiltrated by Zhou Enlai's organization into the nationalist forces asking 'Why are Chinese soldiers fighting Chinese?' But, perhaps more important, while the Japanese were forever encroaching on Chinese territory in the north, two well-trained and equipped divisions near the communists in Yenan, led by generals Zhang Xueliang (Chang Hsueh-liang, 'The Young Marshal') and Yang Huchang, had become lukewarm in their support for Chiang on the grounds that their guns should more properly be turned against the 'foreign invader'. Zhou Enlai established secret contacts with the two generals in June 1936 which gradually led to regular meetings between them. They then began to discuss the establishment of a United Front to fight the Japanese. They also agreed, naturally again in secret, to notify one another of any military movements or planned attacks.

When Chiang visited Xi'an, General Zhang put forward his views quite openly on a United Front which were brusquely rejected by Chiang who, shortly afterwards, decided to deploy the two divisions that apeared to support collaboration with the 'Reds' further south. When the generalissimo returned to Xi'an to discuss details of the projected troop movements and a new campaign he hoped to launch against the communists, he was kidnapped. Mao was extremely anxious to have Chiang put on trial in Yenan but Moscow was deeply opposed to this action. The world was shocked by the news that Chiang was a prisoner of the 'Reds' and he and the KMT – Nationalists – lost a great deal of 'face'. Moscow's authority was demonstrated by the fact that they pressed Zhou Enlai and Ye Jianying (Yeh Chien-ying), later to be Defence Minister, to go to Xi'an immediately to negotiate Chiang's release on the grounds that they 'wanted to preserve him as a leader'. Mme Chiang Kai-shek, the sister of the distinguished pro-communist widow of Dr Sun Yat-sen, Soong Ching Ling, arrived to negotiate with Zhou Enlai and, doubtless, to ensure that the concubine was no longer around. Although the essential points of the communist demands for a United Front were conceded by Chiang no written agreement was reached under pressure from Moscow. The nationalist – KMT – forces ceased to attack the communists. But Premier Zhou said years later that Chiang did not keep the other agreements on joint military co-operation against the Japanese.

General Zhang 'quixotically' accompanied his erstwhile prisoner back to Nanjing where he was immediately arrested. Later he was tried and sentenced to ten years' imprisonment. Before the KMT left the mainland he was transferred to Taiwan and after he was released from prison he was kept under house arrest. Indeed, according to his brother who commented on a recent film made of the incident, he is still 'confined to his home'.

Mao, when not actually talking, sat back and thought as he burned his candles late into the night. He attempted to tidy up articles on political and military issues he had already written and to draft new 'thoughts'. When a new article was written whether on party organization or tactics to be employed against the Japanese he would try it out first on a handful of senior comrades and then in the form of a lecture to a large audience.

Mao's wife, He Zizhen, bore him another son in Yenan before leaving for medical treatment in Xi'an and then Moscow. She was obviously suffering from what is now dubbed a nervous breakdown caused by the arrival of the starlet Jiang Qing from Shanghai, who was slim 'with beautiful and clever eyes' and a determined manner. Deng Yingchao (Mme Zhou Enlai) went to Xi'an in an effort to persuade He Zizhen to return rather than go to Moscow for further treatment. But she said through her tears that all was over between Mao and herself and, that being the case, it was best to go as far away as possible.

There are many different stories of how Jiang Qing first met the Chairman but a Chinese woman in Yenan at the time told me it was at a lecture. Jiang Qing was protected from the moment of her arrival by the influential security chief, Kang Sheng, who had visited Moscow before meeting with Wang Ming in Xinjiang. It was through his influence that Jiang Qing obtained a job as a filing clerk in Mao's confidential inner military office. Apart from the fact that both Jiang Qing and Kang Sheng came from Shandong they appeared to have little in common and Kang's critics hint that he was merely attempting to use Jiang Qing to advance his own interests with the Chairman. However, Kang remained firmly loyal to Jiang Qing long after they left Yenan, indeed, throughout his life. But in the early days in Yenan, Jiang Qing, who bore Mao a daughter soon after they were married, was grateful for any support she could get. The older generation of women such as Deng Yingchao were from a different social background, well educated and travelled and also experienced in organizing political movements amongst women. Spouses then, as now in China, were not invited to meals or to take part in discussions because they were wives or husbands; they were entertained in their own right as specialists in a given subject or not at all.

There was tremendous opposition in the Politbureau to Mao's marriage with Jiang on the grounds that He Zizhen had been a good party worker and had borne Mao five children, in addition to becoming extremely ill during the Long March. The women in Yenan feared this second-class film star might become too influential with the Chairman who was obviously infatuated with her.

Thus the senior comrades agreed to the marriage only on condition that Jiang Qing played no political role. Indeed, Jiang Qing rarely appeared with Mao in Yenan except when people called at their cave. Even members of the Russian mission said she was charming though she hardly opened her mouth and seemed always anxious to please Mao. However, she did go to the Saturday night 'hops' that were a great feature of social life in Yenan. The Chairman waltzed clumsily and attempted to fox-trot in an inexpert manner, but with spirit, while she was a graceful ballroom dancer; so, too, was Zhou Enlai.

It is odd that after the harmless pleasure the communists then derived from ballroom dancing it should have been forbidden in China after the Cultural Revolution. Before that upheaval, there were tea dances on the well-sprung floor of the ballroom at the Peking Hotel and from time to time Zhou Enlai, coming away from his barber, would allow himself a quarter of an hour to spin round the ballroom before returning to his office. In the early 1970s not only was ballroom dancing dubbed 'decadent' but the Diplomatic Service Bureau which provides foreign residents with domestic help ordered waitresses and others to 'withdraw' from any residence where ballroom dancing was taking place. This was changed only slowly after the downfall of the 'Gang of Four'. Ballroom dancing was introduced into the International Club in Peking and no longer frowned on in diplomatic houses until the end of November 1981 when a notice suddenly appeared at the club announcing there would be no further ballroom dancing. Although comparatively few Chinese were involved, officials suggested there had been too much 'hanky-panky' going on in the corridors in which diplomats from the Third World were implicated.

In Yenan, Mao actually taught young people to play mah-jong which was also a proscribed pastime in Peking in the 1970s. No one has ever provided a satisfactory explanation for these sudden changes in Mao's standards of behaviour. Some hints were put out that it encouraged gambling – to which the Chinese worker was, and still is, addicted – but the pastime was not totally forbidden. However, I frequently heard the hotel staff playing mah-jong in empty rooms near to mine. But, again, in Yenan one American visitor recalls teaching the comrades to play gin rummy and how quickly and skilfully they progressed to poker.

Yenan was later described by the Chairman as a 'golden period'. After a year, when free of the mundane military and political decisions, he undertook a serious study of the writings of Marx and Lenin. Indeed, between 1938 and 1940, as Stuart Schram points out, Mao's own works fall into two categories, 'the first concerned primarily with the military aspects of the war and the second with political questions' – current and long-term problems. Mao produced a small volume dealing with the day-to-day conduct of guerrilla warfare primarily for the use of the 'Red Army'. He later discussed the place of guerrilla warfare in the anti-Japanese struggle and only then did he deal in concrete terms with the day-to-day strategy of war.

Mao was helped if not actually inspired in his writings by the arrival of Chen Boda (Po-ta) who had reached Yenan in 1937. This former professor, journalist and underground political worker does not seem to have made a special mark on the Chairman until about 1940. Chen Boda, who was then called 'a rising theoretician', became the Chairman's Political Secretary and devoted almost all his time to assisting Mao with his political speeches and essays. In addition, he wrote clever and critical reports for the communist press on the occasional 'Fascist tendencies' of Chiang Kai-shek and the 'wrong line' still being taken by Wang Ming and some of the '28 Bolsheviks'. For with the return of Wang Ming to China in 1937 after six years in Moscow the power and authority of the pro-Russian elements increased significantly. Wang Ming had an interview with Stalin just before he left Moscow. According to Jiang Qing, Wang Ming registered 'formal' protests on behalf of the Comintern against the land reform policies Mao had been advocating. However, Jiang Qing's biographer, Roxane Witke, suggests that 'the polemics were less pointed in her own mind than the personal antagonism and Wang Ming's tiresome presence in the community of leading comrades'. Jiang Qing stressed the Chairman's good nature and said he 'acted magnanimously and even came to his [Wang Ming's] rescue at dangerous moments'. As an example Jiang Qing claimed that during the 7th Party Congress of 1945, which was held near their home, 'not one of the delegates' would vote for the election of Wang Ming to the Central

Committee. 'Only after the Chairman prevailed upon them was he elected,' Jiang Qing said. He was, however, given the forty-third place and his deputy the forty-fourth and last. In her days as an actress in Shanghai, Jiang Qing had suffered at the hands of some of Wang Ming's pro-Russian supporters and, doubtless, this accounted in part for her venom. Mao, in fact, proposed Wang Ming as a Central Committee member as a result of Russian pressure.

It is worthy of note that the three people then working in or around Mao's office were to the left of centre, his security director, Kang Sheng, Chen Boda and Jiang Qing, all of whom became leading members of the small group which nearly twenty years later was to organize the Cultural Revolution.

One of the more important people in Yenan was Dr George Hatem, known as Ma Haide, an American-trained medical doctor of Lebanese descent, who found his way to the Yenan base in 1937 because of his political convictions. There he rendered disinterested assistance both as a doctor and, at times, a high level interpreter. He married a beautiful Chinese woman and has a son now in his late thirties who does not speak English. Like so many of the foreigners who have worked for the Chinese for years he has little to do with non-Chinese residents. But I was fortunate to meet him, by accident, in Hainan. Still extremely active and capable of giving a glowing account of what the Chinese were doing today in their hospitals, he impressed those few foreigners who met him. Indeed, only one of the scores of foreigners who had worked for years as a translator for the Chinese had regular meetings with me during 1973-6. He was American and extremely knowledgeable. He helped me in my attempts to understand the then current party line. Many of the other British and Americans living in Peking and working for the Chinese Government were downright rude when approached at public functions.

It is interesting, too, that in the Yenan days foreigners could easily marry Chinese. Today this is virtually impossible. During 1975 a Chinese fell in love with a British student who appeared to be a convinced Marxist/Leninist. They appealed for permission to marry. He was immediately sent to an unknown commune 'hundreds of miles away from Peking' and she left for home. Even in November 1981 a Chinese intellectual, Li Shuang, was arrested and sent to a labour camp for two years' 're-education' for having an affair with her French fiancé who was a diplomat. (She was released before completing her sentence and allowed to leave for Paris as a result of pressure from the French Government.) No male correspondent is ever given a female interpreter and my own (female) was only able to obtain permission to have one meal with me in six months on the grounds, I suppose, that I might have influenced her with my bourgeois ideas. Since the downfall of the Gang of Four this too has changed. But the pendulum still swings.

After the Xi'an Incident, Zhou Enlai became Mao's number one trouble-shooter while his distinguished wife, Deng Ying-chao, remained in Yenan and kept him well informed. Zhou shuttled in the early days between Nanjing and Yenan and later Chongqing, which became Chiang Kai-shek's wartime capital. Zhou invariably returned to Yenan to lead negotiations with important missions whether from Moscow or Washington and gradually adopted the unofficial role of a powerful adviser and reliable deputy to the Chairman. His knowledge of the world was useful to Mao as were his natural good manners and diplomatic approaches to problems.

The years spent in Yenan not only gave Mao and his supporters time to think about the type of communism they would introduce should they ever attain power in China but it also provided opportunities to try out their economic and social projects. In Yenan the necessity for self-sufficiency was all too apparent. Li Xiannian (Li Hsien-nien) who was to become one of Peking's leading specialists in economic affairs had led guerrilla units in the Oyuwan Soviet or 'mountain top' in the late 1920s and early 1930s which was second only to the group led by Mao and Zhou in Jiangxi. Li took part in the Long March and although 'he did not study in a university or receive any kind of higher education', according to Mao, he became the Chairman's number one practical financial adviser. He introduced a local currency and by dint of stern rationing and 'political consciousness', which would be called public spirit in the West, everyone was reasonably well fed and warmly if inelegantly clothed and shod. Opium was unobtainable, which was important, and, although it was said that scores of soldiers had joined the Red Army in order to get away from their wives, the population was sexually fairly well behaved and there were few cases of soldiers attempting to rape the local girls.

One of the most far-reaching developments borne in from Yenan was in the cultural sphere. The left-wing intellectuals who came mostly from Shanghai were, according to the American journalist Harrison Forman, who wrote after a visit to Yenan, 'as far from the [Chinese] peasant folklore' of the soldiers 'as James Joyce is from Confucius'. Further, they did tend to despise the ignorant peasants who, in turn, had no time for the urban high-brows who continued to write poetry, novels and to paint pictures solely for their own pleasure. Mao, according to people with him in Yenan, was then shifting from one phase of leadership to another: from a youthful revolutionary and guerrilla leader to a more mature 'military strategist and political theorist', which left him free to discuss the arts. It is certain he was prompted in this by Jiang Qing. After a series of discussions and debates with the left-wing intellectuals, Mao wrote his now famous report called 'Talks at the Yenan Forum on Literature and Art'.

Mao then accused writers and artists of standing aloof from the masses and 'leading empty lives' with the result that they were 'unfamiliar' with the language of the people. During the discussions on which his report was based Mao confessed that in his youth he had felt it undignified to carry luggage and added that he did not mind wearing second-hand clothes of intellectuals but 'would not put on' the second-hand clothes of peasants, believing them to be dirty. This warmed many hearts to him. Mao suggested that the men from the 'garrets' of Shanghai were not all good communists and their writings were often too bourgeois. Works should now be written for the masses, Mao insisted, and 'heroes' with 'nowhere to go' had little place in revolutionary literature. Many of the Chairman's ideas were still confused but his main objective was to lead discussions that would enable the old feudal types of literature to be gradually dropped in favour of an as yet untried form of revolutionary art. 'All the dark forces harming the masses of the people must be exposed.' This was the fundamental task of revolutionary artists and writers, the Chairman claimed. These words doubtless paved the way for the revolutionary ballets and films produced by his wife, Jiang Qing, who acted as his secretary throughout the talks on the now famous forum. It is interesting that the Chairman arrived at the forum for the first of his talks 'in a small car' – the Chairman's status symbol – according to eye-witnesses and, although it was raining, hundreds sat outside the overcrowded hall as he outlined the means by which he hoped to ensure that literature and art could be made to serve the revolutionary cause. Art, Mao believed, could be employed 'for uniting and educating the people as well as for attacking and destroying the enemy'.

During the lengthy discussions in the forum, many supporters of Wang Ming 'stood up' to Mao. They were especially opposed to his warning that 'burning satire and freezing irony', which were perfected, Mao claimed, when the emperors had denied free speech, were inappropriate under the new regime. Another person to stand up to the Chairman was the famous feminist and novelist, Ding Ling (Ting Ling), who was fighting against the party's campaign to achieve absolute control over literature and art, which Mao was advocating. Ding Ling was a leading egalitarian and she criticized the communist leadership for failing to carry out the lofty ideals they preached, citing the inequality of women in Yenan as an example. After the talks in the forum a movement was launched against Ding Ling, who was soon afterwards quietly removed from her post as editor of the literary page of the *Liberation Daily*, and the job given to her arch-rival.

Although Ding Ling's downfall was not to be completed for many years to come, she made an enemy of Jiang Qing perhaps because although she had herself married she scorned the institution as such and considered sexual equality as essential in a well-conducted communist society. In addition, she ridiculed Mao's claim to have revolutionized the position of women. Ding Ling deplored the life led by the wives of members of the Politbureau – including Jiang Qing though not by name – and suggested 'male chauvinism still reigned supreme'. However, Ding Ling did admit that the situation of women in Yenan was better than elsewhere in China. Ding Ling re-emerged during the 'Hundred Flowers' campaign for a short time before disappearing from public view to become a cleaner at the office of the Writers' Association, which changed its name from time to time. But she was firmly rehabilitated and allowed to travel after the fall of the 'Gang of Four', in 1976.

Some elderly Chinese cadres (officials) now claim that while

Chairman Mao was concentrating his political efforts on eliminating the influence of the 'Capitulationists' led by Wang Ming, and artists with independent ideas, one of his most successful and faithful generals, Lin Biao, had been building up contacts with the Russians that were to be useful to him over twenty years later when he attempted a coup d'état against the ageing Mao. Lin distinguished himself as commander of the 115th Division of the 8th Route Army in combat with the Japanese in 1937, but in 1938 he was severely wounded in action, and in December, although the American journalist Haldore Hanson reported that he had fully recovered by the autumn, he left for Moscow, officially 'for medical treatment'. While he was in the Soviet Union, Lin lectured on the war in China and wrote articles for the Russian press and there are reports that he took part in the defences of Leningrad and Stalingrad before returning the Yenan via Xi'an in February 1942. Few knew what Lin was doing during the three years he spent in and around Moscow but it is certain he learned to speak Russian fluently as well as to read and write what is a difficult language for the Chinese. Lin was already beginning to develop the habit of not washing his body with soap because he thought it both bad luck and unhealthy to remove the natural oils from the skin. Whilst an unwashed general in Yenan had passed almost unnoticed, in the heated rooms of Moscow Lin's friends became aware of an odour they put down to 'being Chinese' or they made excuses that it had something to do with his health.

The nationalists and doubtless Zhou Enlai too became conscious of his strange practice when Chairman Mao sent him to Chongqing to assist Zhou in his unending talks with Chiang Kai-shek. Although Lin was not such a good diplomat or negotiator as Zhou he took over his role as Mao's representative when the future Premier was away. It is reported that Lin got on well with junior American officers and foreign representatives, especially those interested in military matters. After his return to Yenan, Lin gradually resumed a military role before making a second trip to the Soviet Union for undisclosed reasons. It is now understood he reported to the Russians on the difficulties the communists were experiencing with the nationalists both at the conference table and in the field and the urgent need for Russia to supply arms to the Red Army. Lin's contacts were so good he succeeded in obtaining much needed small arms and mines which had been 'held up' by the Russians for months. In 1944, back in Yenan, Lin was elected for the first time to the Central Committee of the Chinese Communist Party. By the end of 1945 Lin had 100,000 troops under his command and was, inaccurately, frequently referred to as the Commander of the Red Army in Manchuria after the Japanese surrender.

Mao prepares for the end of the Second World War

Mao began to prepare for the end of the Second World War as early as 1942 when he said with foresight that the Battle of Stalingrad had sealed Hitler's doom, adding that this development would have a direct effect on the Far East where the headaches of Japanese fascism would grow until 'it descends into its grave'. The Chairman was well aware that the Japanese were indirectly doing the Chinese communists a good turn by keeping his Russian allies out of Manchuria and forcing Chiang Kai-shek to make his capital in Chongqing. But Mao knew too the nationalists were making active preparations to take over the country when the defeated Japanese withdrew. The communists for their part believed this could best be done through obtaining the sympathy and confidence of the peasants on the ground. So far as arms were concerned Mao did not anticipate any generous gesture from the Russians. The Red Army was therefore being trained in tactics that included fighting with weapons captured from the enemy.

During the spring of 1945 while preparing for the 7th Party Congress, which was held later that year, Mao strengthened his own position as leader by persuading the Central Committee of the party to adopt resolutions dealing with the errors to the left and right that had been committed by his opponents to date: Chen Duxiu, Zhu Qiubai, Li Lisan and Luo Zhanglong. Wang Ming was not mentioned by name but the party only gained in strength and vigour, the resolution suggested, after the Zunyi Conference, when it was implied the Chairman provided 'the correct' leadership. At the Conference itself all the members of the former pro-Russian group were dropped from the Politbureau. Further, Mao's opening address 'On Coalition Government' strongly indicated that he was preparing for an all-out struggle with the nationalists for control of China once the Japanese were defeated.

On August 6th the Americans dropped the first nuclear bomb on Hiroshima without prior warning to their Russian allies. Two days later the Russians invaded Manchuria with an army of over 1½ million men and declared war on Japan without informing the United States of their intentions. The Russians managed to occupy almost all Manchuria and North Korea whilst the Americans took over South Korea. After the Japanese surrender an agreement was signed between Russia and the nationalist Chinese who obtained a share in the running of the railways but real power rested with Moscow.

Later in the year Mao somewhat softened his attitude to the nationalists under tough American pressure and in August he went to meet Chiang Kai-shek for the first time in twenty years. Members of the Russian Mission had informed Mao that Stalin would not 'interfere' in the internal affairs of China although he publicly dubbed Mao's policy as 'adventurous' and it was feared in Moscow, according to a Tass correspondent, that it would 'generate a situation fraught with world conflict'. In the Russian view this 'adventurism' was embodied in the list of demands Mao took with him to his meeting with Chiang. First, Mao wanted 'recognition' of the 'Government elected by the people' – the Joint Committee of Liberated Areas – in Yenen and elsewhere. Second, he insisted that communist representatives should receive the surrender of the Japanese troops in the area they controlled. In addition, Mao demanded the immediate release of political prisoners and the severe punishment of traitors. His last demand was the establishment of a democratic coalition government.

The opening banquets in Chongqing were civil enough but it was apparent to onlookers that the two Chinese leaders were unlikely to reach a lasting agreement. Talks between Mao and Chiang, however, lasted for over six weeks, from late August until October 11th, when some tentative agreements on the outstanding issues between the two sides were reached. Zhou Enlai remained in Chongqing to continue negotiations and early in January a ceasefire agreement was signed and a Committee of Three, the American General George C. Marshall, Zhou Enlai and the nationalist General Chang Chung, was set up. Assisted by Dong

Biwu and his wife, Zhou spent 1946 bogged down in negotiations with the Americans and the nationalists and he left Chongqing with them when they moved the capital back to Nanjing in the spring. In Peking, Ye Jianying, later to become Defence Minister, in the mid-1970s, was head of a large communist team in the tripartite executive. Truces were frequently broken and it was apparent the country was heading towards a civil war when Zhou finally left Nanjing, despite appeals from General Marshall, for Yenan. A few months later the communists denounced the American efforts to obtain a truce as a subterfuge to provide time and aid to the nationalists. After the breakdown of the ceasefire agreement signed in January 1946, the nationalists concentrated on holding the cities and the railway lines whilst Mao continued to increase his strength by organizing the peasant armies in the countryside. Lin Biao's army moved into Manchuria with relative ease despite the fact that Chiang's main strength there was his fire power.

As the Japanese pulled out civil war flared up throughout the country and the communists prepared to leave Yenan in two groups for long-term security reasons. Few then guessed that within two years they would be establishing a government in Peking. Jiang Qing and others have described the air-raids on Yenan that finally persuaded them to evacuate the base. Deng Yingchao (Mme Zhou Enlai), who was going to work in a city, took the Chairman's daughter Li Na with her while Mao and Jiang left on horseback later. Both seemed to enjoy the opening of this new March and in the beginning, at least, they devoted a great deal of time to eating and mixing with the peasants in the villages in which they encamped. It was Jiang Qing's job to pass on to the Chairman what was being said about them and the nationalists as they travelled from one village to another, using assumed names for political reasons. Zhou and Ren Bishi also accompanied Mao on this new Long March. Towards the end of the first year, as the nationalists broke down, the communists began to suffer from lack of sleep. Indeed, Zhou collapsed from exhaustion, his nose bleeding. Mao then insisted that the stretcher that had been brought for his use should be sent instead to Zhou who refused it. Naturally, the capture of Mao's headquarters by the nationalists in March 1947 achieved global publicity but it was in fact an empty victory.

Despite the difficult problems of communication, Mao remained technically in overall charge of military operations during the first few months after leaving Yenan but, late in 1947, as the communist generals became more and more successful, he began to concentrate on domestic policies for the areas that had already been 'liberated' based on the experiences of Yenan. By April 1948 Mao was able to establish a temporary base at Pingshan in West Hebei where he remained until he moved to Peking. It was here he contemplated the difficult task of transferring power from the countryside to the cities and he continually warned the victorious armies against 'arrogance' when they occupied urban areas.

Mao was anxious to hear progress reports from Manchuria where, following the military victory, Lin Biao had pressed south leaving Gao Gang (Kao Kang) in charge. Gao had established the Shaanxi guerrilla base prior to the arrival of Mao at the end of the Long March in 1935. Mao had spoken of him in the most flattering terms saying that,

The outside cadres [officials] must certainly be somewhat inferior to local cadres in their detailed knowledge of the conditions and their relations with the masses. Take my example. I came to northern Shaanxi five or six years ago and yet I cannot compare with comrades like Gao Gang in my knowledge of conditions here or my relations with people of this region.

Later during the 1948/9 period Gao was elevated from the post of Deputy Political Commissar of the North-east Military Region under Lin Biao to be Commander as well as Secretary of the North-east Bureau. Thus he became the overall military commander as well as the 'boss' of the Communist Party and the Chief State Administrator. It was in this capacity he went to Moscow in 1949 where he negotiated a twelve-month barter agreement that provided for Manchuria to send soya beans, vegetable oils and grain to the Soviet Union in exchange for Russian industrial equipment, petrol, trucks, textiles, paper and medicines. It has since been pointed out that the agreement was most significant because it was concluded before the People's Republic had been officially inaugurated in 1949 and it was thus the first contract between Moscow and a Chinese communist governmental organ signed while the Soviet Union still had diplomatic relations with the nationalists. It was too the first region of China under complete communist control, Gao Gang thus providing for the second time a secure base from which the Red Army could operate and the civilian communist authorities experiment with land reform and the functioning of state-owned industries.

On the nationalist side Chiang Kai-shek became over-confident and claimed the civil war would be over in a few months. In the beginning he was of course successful but by mid-1947 the situation changed. In Manchuria Lin Biao's army inflicted heavy losses on the best troops Chiang possessed, which were foolishly deployed there. This spelled, in the words of the American General Barr, 'the beginning of the end', for the morale of the nationalists suffered a dramatic fall after the appalling loss of over 450,000 troops. Chen Yi, later to become Foreign Minister, occupied Shandong while Lin Biao's armies, freed from Manchuria, formed a pincer movement against Peking and Tianjin. The order of battle written by the nationalist General Fu Zuoyu was stolen from his headquarters in Tianjin by a communist agent, causing him eventually to surrender. Chiang Kai-shek was forced to resign for a short period and his deputy, still hoping to hold the southern half of China, attempted to negotiate with the communists, but Mao, who had played no major role in the fighting, spurned all offers as victory was so clearly in sight. It was significant that Liu Shaoqi wanted to settle for a communist north leaving Chiang in control of the south. Moscow, too, strongly favoured this safer option but Mao remained adamant.

Although the Chairman was suffering from fatigue and even admitted to 'beginning to feel his age' during the later part of the journey from Yenan to Peking, he had the supreme satisfaction of knowing that he had made the grade as the unchallenged leader. The period in Yenan – especially the later years – had enabled him to rehearse the part he was going to play as the first communist Emperor/President of China. He gained enormous prestige with the Central Committee from rightly assessing that it would be stupid to settle for a communist state in the southern half of China and leave the north to the nationalists, as Stalin and the 'capitulationists' had advised, especially when Gao Gang and the communists were in control of Manchuria. From Pingshan in West Hebei the Chairman, aided by Jiang Qing, who was the only woman in his party, discussed land reform in the liberated areas and Manchuria together with the vital problem of shifting the focus of power from the countryside to the cities.

At the celebration of the twenty-eighth anniversary of the founding of the Communist Party on June 30th, 1949 the Chairman announced that his new government, when established in Peking, would 'lean to one side', that of the Soviet Union, and in domestic affairs the 'enemy' – the landlord class – would either be transformed or crushed. At the same time he warned members of the Central Committee against becoming 'arrogant' when they entered the cities.

Long before the whole of China was in communist hands Mao confidently made arrangements with the men who had fought with him for the past decade to form the government for the next. None dared argue with him for at that time he appeared as the brilliant if obstinate 'Red Emperor' who had risen from the farm to the throne as a result of his own efforts. None wished to topple him, despite the fact that the Russians, who were outwardly congratulating Mao, were by no means pleased that he had become so much the undisputed leader of Communist China.

4

Rebel to Ruler

The establishment of the People's Republic

Chairman Mao Zedong frequently told his intimate Chinese friends that no sensation would ever surpass the one of joint comradely militant pride and achievement he felt when proclaiming the People's Republic of China on October 1st, 1949 in Tiananmen Square before tens of thousands of cheering people. But he also admitted that his troubles were only then beginning, for the state the Communists took over was chronically run down as a result of hostilities against the Japanese and the civil wars. The Chairman was, of course, surounded by the band of trusted comrades who had accompanied him on the Long March and joined him in Yenan. Unhappily, almost all the press photographs taken during the ceremony are no longer available, nor, indeed, are the valuable postage stamps that carried an engraving of the scene. Sales were initially stopped during the Cultural Revolution after the purge of Mao's 'chosen successor', Liu Shaoqi, but stocks were all destroyed 'on orders from the Central Committee of the Chinese Communist Party', following the attempted coup d'état of Lin Biao, the Chairman's second 'chosen successor', in 1971.

The transformation from rebel to ruler for Mao and his associates had been eased by the experience they had acquired both in the field of diplomacy and in civil administration during the decade they had spent in Yenan, but they faced formidable problems. For instance the nationalists had removed what foreign currency there was in the state coffers, just as they had taken to Taiwan scores of trains loaded with treasures from Peking and other museums. Agricultural production had dropped drastically because the peasants were away fighting, and industrial output was pathetic. In an effort to get people back to the paddy fields and the factories, the communists stressed the Chinese nationalist and 'United Front' side of their policies and, indeed, produced a number of distinguished non-communist politicians to support their claims. But it would not be enough to restore normality and the pragmatic new Premier, Zhou Enlai, had to persuade Chairman Mao that however hard the peasants worked China would need extra rice and wheat in order to feed the 'liberated' population and that it would be essential to import industrial machinery and certain types of weapons from the Soviet Union.

The Chairman and his Premier were by then living in elegant little pavilions – bungalows – beside the lake in Zhongnanhai in the western sector of the Imperial City and now opposite the Great Hall of the People, which was built during the 'Great Leap Forward'. They frequently talked far into the night long after other members of the Politbureau, who occupied similar dwellings nearby, had gone to bed. In the days immediately after 1949, although there were security guards on the gates, the Chinese were permitted to wander inside Zhongananhai to have a look around. The Premier was generally to be seen through the window of his office while the Chairman frequently walked smartly from one government department to another without an escort.

While Chairman Mao and Premier Zhou were setting up the party and state machinery in Peking, the Regional Military Commanders 'enjoyed unprecedented power'. The country was divided into six vast regions governed by military and administrative committees. During 1950 many of the regional leaders went to Peking to occupy key positions, especially on the Military Affairs Commission. This has since been described as, 'appearing to combine most of the functions of the Secretary of State for Defence and the Chiefs of Staff'. In any case, it was the highest military decision-making body and remains so to this day.

By the beginning of 1950 Regional Military Commanders were rightly using their troops in many capacities according to local requirements. First they tackled the problem of insurgency, generally effectively; then they used the troops to educate the peasantry in the Maoist form of communism. Soldiers were naturally employed to rebuild vital bridges and construct roads as well as to repair railway lines and ports. Those forces which were least effective in combat were naturally the first to be deactivated. In Xinjiang the majority of the 1st Field Army was redesigned as the Production and Construction Army and was assigned the task of developing the vast untapped agricultural and mineral resources.

Somewhat naturally, modernization and training for contemporary warfare were low on the table of priorities.

The economic situation grew critical as winter approached and Premier Zhou, who was also Foreign Minister at that time, contacted the Russian diplomatic mission in Peking to arrange for the Chairman to make his first trip abroad, to Moscow, with a begging bowl in his hands. Mao had earlier announced his 'lean to one side policy' but again stressed, 'The Chinese people must lean either to the side of imperialism or to the side of socialism ... There can be no exception ... There can be no sitting on the fence nor third path.' Chairman Mao's visit to Moscow – accompanied by Chen Boda – resulted in the formation of the Moscow–Peking Axis which was formally established on February 14th, 1950. Stalin agreed to the military alliance as part of the Treaty of Friendship and Alliance and granted some £100 million in credits to China together with a promise of Russian experts to assist in the modernization of industry and the Red Army. Shortly after his return to Peking the Chairman said that obtaining aid from the Russians was more difficult than 'getting raw meat out of the mouth of a tiger'. Mao had hoped for 'cash' as well as credits.

However, back in Peking, Mao talked also publicly of the 'lasting, unbreakable and invincible alliance' with the Soviet Union while Liu Shaoqi, who was senior to Premier Zhou in the Communist Party hierarchy, announced the detailed plans. Indeed, despite their own urgent requirements and those of Eastern Europe after the end of the Second World War, the Russians were quick to send over 4000 military experts to the Army and about half that number respectively to the Air Force and Navy. Some 5000 administrators and specialists came into China to assist in industrial enterprises, railways, docks, coal mines and the ultimate production of nuclear weapons. By February 1954, when Khrushchev and Bulganin visited China, the Russians had agreed to participate in the construction of 160 major production units such as the building of dams, establishment of an arms industry and machine-tool factories. The Russians also encouraged the Chinese to play a major diplomatic role in Asian affairs, but beneath the outward show of cordiality, major problems soon arose between the two powers. The Chinese developed inherent nationalist tendencies in their efforts to achieve world power status and they insisted on stressing the role of the peasantry. 'Our form of communism is very different from that of the Soviet Union,' Chinese officials frequently claimed in the early 1950s.'

The opening of the Korean War in June 1950, so soon after the foundation of the state, had the effect of slowly binding the whole nation together. At the beginning the Chinese feared the Americans were going to attack them as they noted the increased presence of the 7th Fleet especially in patrolling the Taiwan Straits. Nonetheless, the Chinese warned Washington that they would regard any movement north of the 38th parallel in Korea as a hostile act. Peking was, of course, desperately concerned about China's industrial hinterland in Manchuria which was dangerously near the firing line.

Many experts now believe that Mao was not averse to entering the Korean War for other reasons. Although none of Mao's generals had tried to establish themselves as warlords, he sometimes feared they might do so. Korea gave him an opportunity to disrupt the potentially dangerous internal allocations of political military power by the massive despatch of combat forces to the north-east. Further, administrators and commanders were able to use this 'foreign threat' to force through internal reforms and to call for 'sacrifices' on the part of the population. The Korean War, too, had the additional and unfortunate diplomatic disadvantage of driving a still greater wedge between the United States and the People's Republic and binding the Chinese, reluctantly, closer to the Soviet Union.

In the political and industrial fields, too, there were troubles and purges that ultimately led to the downfall and suicide of Gao Gang, the seventh man on the list of those who opposed Chairman Mao. Gao's end was to make a deep impression on Mao personally and a marked dent in the party hierarchy. For this efficient administrator had played a major role in the development of the Shaanxi base which had provided a haven for Mao at the end of the Long March. Gao's rise to become the Supreme Military Commander in Manchuria happened during the winter of 1948/9 when the other generals either moved south with Lin Biao or assumed political roles at the Chairman's headquarters at Pingshan in West Hebei or later in Peking. Gao was the only man after the establishment of the Six Military Regions who held all four key posts – army, party, administration and economic – and, in his case, dealt with the Russians who had rights on both the railways and the port of Luta (Dairen). In any case Gao 'took over' Manchuria and personally negotiated a one-year barter agreement with the Russians, sending soya beans to the Soviet Union in exchange for urgently required industrial equipment, trucks, petroleum, textiles and medicines. Although the Russians had stripped Manchuria of much of its plant, it still remained the most industrialized area of China and later Gao made successful efforts to get the wheels turning to provide military equipment for the 'volunteers' fighting in Korea in 1950 shortly after liberation. Manchuria, too, later served as the logistic base for Chinese troops entering Korea during the war and Gao was so successful in this, and other tasks, that he was awarded the 'accolade reserved for the very few' of 'one of Chairman Mao's close comrades in arms'. Furthermore, as the 'boss' of the first 'liberated' territory Gao had tested land reform in addition to his industrial efforts. In November 1952, he was called to Peking as a member of the ruling Politbureau to lead the new State Planning Commission about to draft the first Five Year Plan, but he retained his position as Chairman of the Northeast Administrative Committee.

Although Gao's contacts with the Russians were extremely good, accusations were made that he was working in league with Beria – the much-hated head of Stalin's Secret Police – but these suggestions are not totally discounted. Although there is no hard evidence to support the theory, a handful of Gao's friends who survived the purge claim Gao was merely 'invited' by Beria to send reports on the activities of the White Russians working on the railways in Manchuria, which were in the process of having their tracks changed to the standard gauge of the Soviet Union. One of Gao's former associates claimed that when Gao was in Moscow in 1949 Stalin proposed that he should support a proposal to make Manchuria an independent state closely allied to the Soviet Union, indeed, in the same position as Mongolia is today. Gao reportedly turned down the proposition so curtly that Stalin was personally offended and gradually allowed it to be leaked to Chairman Mao that the proposal had been made. This was Stalin's way of getting his own back for Gao's lack of enthusiasm but it is still difficult to understand his motive. Chairman Mao was apparently angry because Gao had not informed him of Stalin's proposal. This may well have sparked off the dangerous rift between Mao and Gao who already had serious differences on party, economic and industrial issues which had been building up for some months.

Another report mentioned by one of Gao's former supporters was that although his contacts with the Russians were good, Stalin, in some curious and treacherous manner, indicated to Mao that his relations with Gao were too close to be all that healthy for the Chairman. However, there can be no doubt that Gao was deeply impressed by the work of the Russian experts in Manchuria and he repeatedly suggested that Moscow's methods of administering heavy industry were far more efficient than those advocated by the Chinese communists. Indeed, Gao strongly advocated the 'one-man management' of factories as opposed to the various forms of collective leadership then being tried out in China. 'A committee cannot run a large industrial enterprise,' Gao said as he continued to stress the vital importance of concentrating state resources on the development of heavy industry. Gao's last major report was delivered to the Central Committee in September 1950 and in it he advocated greater concentration on heavy industry.

Gao's downfall can be dated from January 20th, 1954 – the thirtieth anniversary of Lenin's death. Differences with the Chairman had been mounting for a year or more on basic economic strategy – how much to allocate to heavy industry – together with methods of state administration and, perhaps the most important, control of party apparatus. Gao had stated publicly that he thought it 'absurd' that party secretaries should be supreme and have the right to dismiss leaders of industry.

In a manner that was to become a tradition amongst Chinese communists, a series of articles critical of Gao's methods but not naming him appeared in the press. At the same time Liu Shaoqi demanded a return to collective leadership, besides castigating 'certain high ranking cadres' (officers) who had grown to regard the region in which they worked as 'their personal property or independent kingdom'. A year was to elapse from the time the articles began to appear until Gao was given a serious official warning and then purged. The final indictment stated that Gao had attempted to take over the post of Secretary General of the party from Deng Xiaoping and rather than admit his guilt he had 'committed suicide as an ultimate expression of his betrayal of the party'. In addition to Gao's 'alleged accomplice' Rao Shushi (Jao Shu-shih), who as a member of the Central Committee was a national figure, seven other well-known men were expelled from the party for their activities in the 'anti-party block'. Further, many thousands of unnamed supporters and scores of ranking army, state and party cadres were also dismissed or demoted within weeks of his fall.

In the early 1970s, the Chinese were outspoken about Gao's alleged sins and he was said to have attempted to set up a semi-autonomous region in Manchuria closely allied to the Soviet Union, or, even worse, to have been a traitor in league with Moscow. What is clear is that Gao was keen to establish an efficient administration of the vital industrial plants in the north-east and to this end he was willing to jettison collective management and to introduce material and other incentives to increase production. No serious evidence has been produced that makes Gao a traitor. But there is evidence to confirm a sudden personality clash with Mao, which may in part have resulted from the fact that after the inauguration of the People's Republic, Mao grew less willing to hear views opposed to his own. Gone were the days when in his cave in Yenan he encouraged people to criticize his speeches and put up ideas of their own. The corrupting influence of power was beginning to be noted by those around him. Apparently, only Premier Zhou Enlai, Liu Shaoqi and Deng Xiaoping were allowed to criticize him freely, according to a member of the Politbureau.

'Let a hundred flowers bloom'

By the time the first Five Year Plan was due for implementation in 1953 the population of the People's Republic had witnessed a series of political campaigns that varied from 'Resist America – Aid Korea' to one on the marriage law and a dozen minor ones designed to improve hygiene and public health. However, there was a good deal of suppressed unrest amongst the intellectuals in China, especially amongst the non-communist parties supporting the Government, that was doubtless inspired by the Hungarian uprising of 1956 and Khrushchev's secret speech revealing the excesses of Stalin. Somehow or other texts of this – both true and false – were circulating amongst the elite.

Mao and the Government began slowly to move away from the highly centralized, technocratic, heavy-industry orientated Russian style of economic administration to branch out on their own. Mao's speech on the 'Ten Great Relationships' demonstrated an awareness of what was happening and the many complex problems the Government were facing, especially those arising from the ever-increasing gap between those who worked in urban industrial plants and rural agriculture. Mao suggested, indeed insisted, the masses should be allowed to continue 'letting off steam' partly to avert any possibility of a Hungarian-type resolution but also to ferret out the real critics of the regime. The Chairman then issued his famous slogan 'Let a hundred flowers bloom and a hundred schools of thought contend'. Many members of non-communist organizations that supported the 'United Front' saw this as the moment to say just what they wanted about the communist regime and its leaders. Intellectuals, especially, rushed to their brushes to write bitter satirical and critical articles mainly on their want of freedom, the dearth of foreign books and the lack of equal opportunities for women.

One of the most interesting features was the stance taken by Ding Ling, a school friend of Mao's first wife and a true egalitarian and shining symbol of female independence in a revolutionary situation. Ding Ling became extremely vocal after the thought reform to which she had been subjected as a result of her independent stance in Yenan. Though later she was, as already stated, drastically degraded to become the charwoman for the Writers' Union, Ding Ling was rehabilitated a second time early in 1978 and now enjoys influence and great prestige in literary circles. Similar though less severe forms of punishment were meted out to other intellectuals who were too frank in their criticism. Not only Liu Shaoqi and Deng Xiaoping but the Chairman himself was stunned, indeed downright alarmed, by the intensity of the spontaneous criticism that suddenly erupted throughout the nation. Mao was then pressed by the entire Politbureau to terminate the campaign with speed. This he did before either he or his colleagues had been too badly hurt. But the 'hundred flowers' campaign did indicate to the leaders that there were millions of Chinese who longed for more physical and cultural freedom than the Communist Party could then afford to permit.

Despite criticism from Gao and others about methods, the Chinese leaders were nonetheless encouraged by their domestic achievements during the first few years of independence, although claims to have 'conquered' inflation, which was running at between 30 and 40 per cent in less than two years, may well have been exaggerated. However, the introduction of work points, based each week on the current price of five commodities – rice, oil, coal, flour and cotton cloth – enabled prices to be controlled as the amount of paper money in circulation was drastically reduced. Agricultural production, said in 1949 to be 70 per cent below the pre-war figure, was stimulated through land reform. Indeed, by 1952 an agrarian revolution had been completed. 700 million mou (one mou = one-sixth of an acre) had been redistributed to 300 million peasants. In heavily populated and productive areas of the south and south-east the peasants received only one mou which rose to two mou in central China, three mou in the north and as much as seven in Manchuria. Immediately the distribution had been effected, the Government began to drive towards collectivization with the object again of increasing production and preventing the emergence of a new kulak class.

One of the darker periods of the Chinese Revolution was the manner in which the landlords and rich peasants were treated during the initial land distribution. According to a Chinese communist estimate, some 5 million people were 'tried' either by their former tenants or the authorities. There were atrocities and executions but it is impossible to estimate how many. Premier Zhou said he believed 2 million people died or were executed although foreign observers who were in China at the time put the figure higher – at from 3 to 4 million. This land transfer was followed by bitter disappointment on the part of thousands of peasants who, having achieved their life-long dream of owning a plot of land, found they could not cultivate it because they lacked the necessary agricultural implements, unless they joined an agricultural co-operative.

In 1952, the People's Republic claimed that industrial production had increased by 77.5 per cent since 'liberation' in 1949. As a result, after several false starts a Five Year Plan was introduced in

1953, but lack of machinery, inexperience, the purge of Gao and a dearth of statistics delayed its real implementation for two years. Until 1956 genuine, even spectacular advances were made and although the pace then slowed down, the First Five Year Plan was still reported to have fulfilled the original targets. The Chinese released far more statistics at that time than they did after the close-down caused by the Cultural Revolution in 1976, until around 1980. They claimed that steel production had reached 5.2 million tons annually, iron 5.8 million tons, and coal production 122 million tons. This success caused the Government to introduce a far more ambitious Five Year Plan. But hardly had the details of this new plan been circulated down to the grass roots for comment before Chairman Mao, to the horror and surprise even of some members of the Politbureau, launched his 'Great Leap Forward' in a feverish effort to expand the already over-heated economy and to move from agricultural co-operatives towards People's Communes.

Students, officials and highly skilled technicians were urged to take part in industrial production and by the autumn of 1958 nearly 600,000 back-yard furnaces had sprung up all over the country. Later it was disclosed that although production had surpassed that of 1957 by 65 per cent – which was certainly an exaggeration – 3 million of the 11 million tons of steel produced was pronounced 'unfit for industrial purposes'. A back-yard furnace just could not replace a modern steel mill. Further, many of the spades and other basic agricultural implements had thoughtlessly been thrown into the furnaces on the grounds they would no longer be required. This caused a chronic shortage of agricultural tools. The ploughs to be driven by tractors, which the optimists had expected to be on hand, were not manufactured and, indeed, in many parts of China today the peasants are still ploughing with horses, mules and even teams of men.

The establishment of the agricultural commune was attempted far too soon with insufficient preparation and pressed forward much too quickly. Many peasants who had just begun to accept the co-operatives revolted against further socialization. Chairman Mao paid personal visits to an area where up to thirty co-operatives were amalgamating into a People's Commune to encourage the whole nation to press ahead with the movement.

It was at the time of establishing the agricultural communes that Chairman Mao had his first prolonged and bitter dispute with Liu Shaoqi. None outside the Standing Committee of the ruling Politbureau was aware of the major differences of opinion that had developed between the Chairman and his chosen successor. In Liu's opinion the Chairman was endangering the progress achieved by the communists since they came to power through his attempts to rush ahead with the transformation of collective farms into communes. And even more harmful to the new state were the Chairman's 'wild' efforts to set up industrial plants in back yards. Premier Zhou Enlai acted, as he did so often, as the great mediator and, as a result of his efforts, the relationship between Mao and his most important colleague in the party was restored. But from that time Mao is known to have harboured reservations in his relations with Liu. Before the Long March the two men had held widely different views on how socialism should be achieved, Liu favouring the Russian line of working through the urban workers and trade unions whilst Mao, of course, believed in the power of the peasants.

Later I was to note young men and women – including my own male interpreter – standing in front of a picture of Chairman Mao with an air of respectful admiration as though they were about to genuflect. The old people on the communes recalled the good advice about farming Mao had given them during his visit as a result of his upbringing on the land. A few had well-worn photographs of themselves, in a group with the obviously beloved leader, which were great personal treasures.

These visits by Mao, which became widespread, served to stimulate the commune movement. Although Mao taught that the state was more important than the family, the commune allowed married people to continue their life together with their children while the unmarried were put into separate hostels and provided with communal meals. The Chairman, despite the obvious pleasure he personally derived from female company and sex, seriously considered breaking up the family on communes and having husbands and wives live apart. Mao also then believed the family as an institution had almost outlived its usefulness and was likely to disappear over the next few thousand years. Many people were thus extremely relieved because there had been serious reports that married couples were to be parted, except for holidays. The 25,000 people who made up the average commune had their own shops, schools, hospitals, old people's homes and some form of light industry. The leadership that administered the commune was, in theory, elected by the members who later during the Cultural Revolution took the title of Revolutionary Committee. From five to eight hours each week was devoted to 'study' or political indoctrination and in most communes, as the team worked in the fields, loudspeakers relayed revolutionary music and speeches.

The workers were allowed to retain small private plots in many communes on which they could keep pigs – Mao had said that every pig was a natural fertilizer factory – chickens and grow a few vegetables for the family. If there were any surplus, the produce could then be sold on the local market. Thus members of communes near large cities such as Peking, Shanghai, or even Xi'an did well out of their private plots, which remained a major bone of contention in the state until Deng re-assumed power in 1977. The radicals claimed they should be abolished and many communes made moves towards this end by using the communal tractors to plough up all the private plots. At first they promised the former 'owners' could cultivate them but they were gradually absorbed into the communal lands. Other pragmatic Revolutionary Committees allowed the private plot system to continue.

In addition to private plots, families living in communes were generally allowed to build and 'own' their house. Families saved to purchase the necessary materials and friends and relations supplied their labour free with the result that a four-roomed house of two storeys could be built for about £400. I recall my driver – most foreigners have to have drivers in China – requesting special days off to help his father build a house on the commune because he 'would inherit' it. The same driver was a demon for overtime pay and, although he spent much of every day sitting or sleeping in a room the *Daily Telegraph* was forced to provide for his use, he logged up every half hour of overtime with glee. When I pointed to long 'rolls of honour' outside factories giving the names of those radicals who refused to accept overtime pay, my driver would reply, not caring who heard, that he was not that kind of fool – and he said this in 1973–6 at the height of radical power.

There were, to be fair, some truly spectacular achievements in the 'Great Leap Forward' including the building of the Great Hall of the People – an enormous structure covering eleven acres which was constructed in eight months. The Great Hall on the western side of Tiananmen Square is a concentration of many official government buildings. Premier Zhou had his office suite on the third floor of the south-eastern wing where the lights often burned until three or four in the morning. All major official banquets are given in the Great Hall and 6000 people can eat there in elegant comfort. There is, in addition, a huge assembly hall, with a platform that alone seats over a hundred, where the Party Congress and the National People's Congresses are held. This is also used as a theatre. Every province of China is represented by a large reception room decorated in regional style and there are spacious quarters where Chairman Mao and Jiang Qing lived for a time after Lin Biao's attempt on the Chairman's life. Naturally, there are rooms for guards and the security services as well as the permanent kitchen staff.

It is interesting to note that the kitchen and the military band which plays at receptions in the Great Hall know as soon as the Foreign Ministry of any planned foreign visit, months ahead of the diplomatic corps or the press. This enables the cook to learn to prepare a dish from the country of the visitor, in advance, and for the band to learn the national anthem.

Mao responsible for the fall in the nation's morale

The lowering of morale on a national basis in the immediate aftermath of the formation of the state in 1949 was nowhere more pronounced than in the defence forces, which, unlike the Chinese, many foreign observers still regard as the most important of their three power bases. (The others are, of course, the Communist Party and the state bureaucracy.) But the depression amongst both officers and men arose from a new concentration of problems which had been endemic in some sections of the Red Army since the People's Republic was established in 1949.

In 1950 as some 5 million guerrilla fighters, highly skilled in the conduct of irregular warfare, were about to be transformed and streamlined into an army capable of maintaining power in the contemporary era, Chairman Mao and his colleagues in the Politbureau decided it was necessary to intervene in the Korean War. The sprawling force of irregulars were already divided according to the Six Military Regions. North of the Yangtze River the army had generally subdued nationalist resistance and indoctrinated the population with socialism. They had, in addition, established a form of local administration largely controlled by them. In the south and west of the new united China these operations were taking place long after the People's Republic was established. There was still little communication between one region and another and central control was often difficult to enforce. Indeed, it was only the army's almost mystic but robust loyalty to Chairman Mao, and the general reshuffle caused by the Korean War, that then, as later, prevented the establishment of any 'Red Warlordism'. However, the Chairman and Liu, noting the enormous power of the army commanders and the loyalty that had been built up between them and their subordinates, with whom they had sometimes been serving for twenty years, thought a unifying 'national' war against an imperialist outsider could only have a healthy effect.

There is no doubt, too, that the Chinese leadership feared American forces in Korea might, one day, without warning, overrun the country and, in view of the ill-defined frontier between China and Korea, occupy a 'slice' of Chinese soil as well as taking control of one or more vital ports. Any foot of what the Chinese deemed to be 'their' soil would, if occupied by the United States, have resulted in a dangerous loss of face for the new regime. Chairman Mao also hoped that co-operation with the Russians over Korea would ensure Moscow's support when the time came for him to launch an attack on Taiwan. Indeed, the long-term impact of the Korean War on China's defence forces can hardly be overstated.

Initially, the People's Volunteers crossed the Yalu River under the command of the highly experienced soldier, Marshal Peng Dehuai, late in October. He and, indeed, the Military Affairs Commission (MAC) which then combined the duties of the Chiefs of Staff, were all too well aware that the force lacked artillery, transport, communications equipment and back-up. Peng attempted to overcome the weakness by 'engulfing the enemy in a human mass'. This was the reasoning, if such it can be called, behind the concept of the 'human sea' tactics. In the first rounds they worked perhaps because Peng was a robust outgoing commander who shared the hardships of the men in the field, eating the same rations, smoking the same cigarettes and venturing further forward with them into combat than his staff considered wise or even sensible.

Waves of Chinese 'volunteers' attacked in the first stages and drove back the United Nations forces despite the fact that one in five or six of the Chinese soldiers, at the opening of the campaign, carried no arms other than a staff and was detailed to pick up the rifle of the first dead comrade he saw. Weaknesses in the Chinese system were all too apparent, for the force lacked logistic support: they were using arms captured from the Japanese or the nationalists during the civil war and fresh supplies of the correct type of ammunition for small arms were rarely available. Medical supplies, too, were totally inadequate and rations often short. One Chinese prisoner stated that over 8000 'volunteers' died of cold or exposure in addition to those killed or wounded in action. Indeed, Maoist ideology was 'no match for the terrifying reality of United Nations firepower and the indifference of South Korean villagers to the Chinese commissars' communist sermons', one neutral Swedish military expert wrote.

The United Nations – largely American – forces soon learned to absorb the first Chinese attack and they counter-attacked so successfully that by the late winter of 1951, the Chinese Army in Korea was on the brink of collapse. Although the Government in Peking was by that time producing their own small arms and ammunition, the supply was almost worthless from a military viewpoint. Thus, in order to prevent the fall of the North Korean regime, the Russians suddenly came to the rescue of the Chinese and released large quantities of weapons and equipment. The aid was not only instrumental in causing a military stalemate, but it served as the vital springboard for bringing the Chinese defence forces into the era of modern conventional warfare. The Chinese Army, which had suffered from American air attacks, realized the urgent need to establish a modern air force of their own; so, too, did Chairman Mao, whose son, An Ying (by his first wife Yang Kaihui) was killed during an American air raid on Chinese military headquarters. Marshal Peng insisted that the Chairman's 'volunteer' son should not be exposed to the dangers of the front line and retained him in what he believed to be the safety of his own GHQ. Peng claimed during his subsequent quarrels with the Chairman that 'Mao never forgave me for the loss of his son.'

Marshal Peng, who was a popular commander, later described the first eight months of the Korean War as 'horrific', when battles were raging up and down the narrow peninsula between the Chinese and American troops. From the stalemate that followed the introduction of the Russian weapons and equipment until the armistice of July 1952, Peng never had fewer than 700,000 men under his command and these he naturally trained in conventional warfare. There was little time for political indoctrination and the importance of the political commissars, who were attached to every unit of battalion size, continued to diminish.

It is important to add that although the Russians did not give the Chinese their latest weaponry – indeed, they tended to hand over tanks, artillery and equipment that were already being phased out of the Soviet forces – what they received inspired the Chinese commanders and men with a taste for conventional equipment as opposed to the concept of a people's war. The latter, which had been so successful throughout the period of the war with Japan and the civil wars, was based on the Chairman's philosophy that men are more important than weapons and wars are won by the political will and determination of the soldier. This philosophy, after the People's Republic was established, made virtue out of necessity and had much to be said for it, and still has in an undeveloped country where steel is scarce and heavy industrial plant extremely limited. In addition, it fitted perfectly into the international posture of the new China which was entirely defensive. China, Chairman Mao stressed repeatedly, would never attack anyone and they would only use offensive measures if they were driven to it, in order to re-unite their own people. This has developed over the years into a well-defined policy and Peking's armed forces are entirely geared to a defensive role, but they reserve the right to re-occupy areas they claim are Chinese such as Taiwan, the Paracel Islands – which they took over at the end of the war in Vietnam – and the Spratly Group in the South China Sea where many remains and coins of the Ming dynasty have been found.

Towards a modern defence force

However, although the Chairman himself declared more than once there was a need for a modern army, he was genuinely ambivalent in his attitude and constantly harped back to the strategic as well as tactical advantages of the people's war philosophy long after China had become a nuclear power. In 1951 the Central Committee called for a 'study on how to transform the People's Army', which was admittedly backward, into 'a superior, modernized revolutionary force'. And in 1953 Chairman Mao said that 'in order to prevent imperialist invasion the air force and navy must have completely mechanized armaments', adding, 'What we now need is a large number of people who are grasping and utilizing modern science and technology.'

Indeed, for years after the Chinese had a nuclear deterrent – much as they disliked the phrase – because of their completely outdated conventional equipment that would have been useless in combat with the Russians, they were forced back to the people's war concept. 'Should the Russians launch a nuclear attack and destroy every Chinese city there will still be over a hundred million Chinese to carry on,' the Chairman said. Indeed, this argument was used to encourage the construction of thousands of air-raid shelters. But in the 1950s the modernization of the Chinese Army proceeded steadily as Russian experts instructed Chinese officers in the use of the weapons they were providing and the organizational backing and installations it was necessary to set up to support a modern land force.

In addition to the 1½ million men who had served in Korea, the elite of the Chinese force had secured some training in Yenan, where the guerrillas had set up a variety of training establishments including one for artillery officers although they admitted they had but few guns. But although doctors, signallers, engineers and gunners were trained together with infantry, tank and horse cavalry officers, they all devoted about one-third of their time to political indoctrination. After the Korean War, commanders were to grow impatient with the amount of time 'wasted' in so-called 'political studies' which they felt could have been more usefully devoted to learning how to fire a rifle, drive a truck, man a telephone exchange or fulfil some other fundamental tasks that men bred in the countryside had not always acquired. At this period, the power of the political commissars waned still further as they were no longer given all orders to countersign. Indeed, some political commissars complained they were unable to obtain the necessary transport to follow their units on manoeuvres, to which the commanders replied that they should learn to march like the men.

Much has been made of conscription in China but, in fact, as almost all labour is directed, it means very little. During the Korean War and the following few years some 3 million people were demobilized. Naturally, the movement was gradual and a unit which was or looked like being unsatisfactory in the field was put on guard duty before it was finally disbanded. Despite the heavy casualties incurred in Korea, a fact that gradually leaked out to the broad masses, there was tremendous competition from both men and women to get into the armed services. For in the armed forces one learned a trade and, after serving with the People's Liberation Army (PLA), people had a far better chance of being sent to work in a factory rather than on a remote agricultural commune in an inhospitable climate.

One immediate effect of the introduction of conscription and the establishment of a regular army was the downgrading of the People's Militia which, in the mid-1950s, during the high tide of Russian-orientated modernization, fell into relative oblivion and little or no publicity was given to its activities. After the first signs of unofficial disappointment with the Russians were noted, items began to reappear in the *People's Daily* commenting on militia activities in the countryside, and this gradually led to a campaign to 'make every man or woman a soldier'. Despite outspoken disapproval from the senior ranks of the PLA some 220 million people were stated in the late 1950s to be members of various types of militia. It is fair to add that, then as now, there were probably some 5 million members of the armed militia, together with key agricultural communes who had some specialized, albeit very short, military training in communications, the use of ack-ack guns or anti-tank weapons. Another 15–20 million basic militia were trained in guerrilla and anti-insurgent activities, again in communes whose locations have some tactical importance but especially those within a few hundred miles of the Manchurian section of the Sino-Soviet border. These people could all drill and use a rifle –

some of them an automatic one. Further, they devoted anything from one to four weeks annually to military training. Nonetheless millions of the militia could be compared with the poorest section of the British Home Guards in 1940. The leaders may have had some military training twenty to thirty years earlier but in the mid-1950s as, indeed, today they were generally unarmed. The morale of the People's Militia was often high because its members genuinely believed they were carrying out Chairman Mao's guidance, in that a nuclear attack by the imperialists could not kill all the Chinese and the People's Militia could and would resist any army that attempted to occupy China.

Marshal Peng returned to Peking late in July 1952 to a hero's welcome. He had, at that moment, enormous influence, too, with the Politbureau whose meetings he had in the past so rarely been free to attend. He was determined after the bitter lessons of the Korean War to professionalize the PLA with the help of the 1000 Russian military advisers who were already in China. Soviet drill manuals together with their concepts of military organization were translated and handed down to the grass roots of the army. Further, after Korea Peng insisted that the air force and navy which had been neglected should be included in the 'modernization, organizational and training drive'. The Marshal ordered the formation of a civil defence system that would, in the first instance, provide vital protection to government offices, radio and communications centres, railways and roads against what was considered the ever-growing nuclear threat posed by the United States. This, Peking rightly believed, would raise the moral of the civilian members of the administration. Peng then supervised in 1954 the organization of the country into eleven Military Regions each with a marshal or (full four-star) general in command. The powerful Defence Ministry in Peking 'did not discourage' the marshals from obtaining what industrial help they could obtain locally. This naturally caused acute dissatisfaction amongst party officials about the proportion of heavy industrial products finding their way directly to the defence forces, together with trackers, trucks and much-needed 'buckets, wire and pipes', later mentioned, in anger, by party leaders.

Many soldiers assumed the line of their Russian instructors and became openly scornful of the back-yard furnaces and other by-products of the Great Leap Forward which they dubbed a great waste of effort. Indeed, scores of new officers, though generally members of the Communist Party, were not hard-core communists. The creation of ten field-marshals and the introduction of elaborate Russian-style uniforms had done little to assuage the discontent of the officer class who, according to the radical wing of the party, were no longer living, eating and suffering with their men but demanding a privileged existence. It is interesting that Marshal Peng was frequently excluded from this widespread criticism.

There had been strains in the Sino-Soviet friendship from the beginning, as Stalin was angered by Mao's obstinate refusal to adopt the Russian form of communism. He feared China's influence on left-wing parties in Africa and Asia and, basically, he mistrusted Mao. The Chairman, for his part, never forgot that Stalin had failed more than once to inform him of projected military and political actions he proposed to take that would have provided Peking with an opportunity to attack the nationalist forces in the early days and later the government in Taiwan. Indeed, Mao was displeased by Moscow's retention of diplomatic links with the nationalists until the last moment when they left Guangzhou for Taiwan. On the political side too he was offended that the Chinese Communist Party had not been invited to join the Cominform which was established as successor to the Comintern in 1947. But until Stalin's death in 1952 there were, according to one member of the Central Committee, 'strains and disagreements, even minor disputes, but no out and out rows'.

One of Mao's objects in launching the Great Leap Forward was a desire, even though a stupid one, to overtake the Russians in the production field. What is odd is that the Russians were unnecessarily concerned that he might succeed. Both Moscow and Peking attempted to keep their differences of opinion hidden from the 'imperialists' although Peking used Albania, then a European satellite, to attack Moscow.

Peng was concerned if not downright alarmed by the growing gulf between Russia and China as he and all the professional soldiers believed it was more important to be 'expert' than 'red' and they were apprehensive that a major dispute would influence Mao to revert to what was termed the 'pure' people's war concept of defence, if Moscow continued to refuse 'sharing' nuclear know-how as Stalin had promised.

In 1959 Khrushchev went to Peking to demand that a 'joint control' be established to assume command of China's nuclear establishment as well as the Chinese Navy. Mao refused with characteristic bluntness and vigour. This must have impressed Khrushchev who responded by offering more industrial assistance together with additional vehicles and machine tools for new factor-ies. Khrushchev was apparently staking a great deal on reaching a nuclear agreement with the United States but this may not have been known or fully understood at the time by the Chairman. Basically, Moscow was reluctant to supply or to promise sample nuclear devices because they feared Chairman Mao might enter into some 'adventurism' over Taiwan. And with the Americans already entrenched in Korea, supported by excellent naval bases in Japan and the Philippines, the Russian High Command was nervous of being dragged into a conflict in the Far East, especially at a time when they knew all the equipment, from ballistic nuclear weapons down to automatic rifles, was generally inferior to that of the United States. Despite discouragement from Moscow, Mao continued throughout 1958 to dwell on the Jinmen–Mazu (Que-moy–Matsu) Straits crisis whenever he met a Russian. To add to the tensions that grew between the two major communist powers, Chairman Mao began to challenge Khrushchev's leadership of the World Communist Movement.

Sino-Soviet dispute

Marshal Peng Dehuai, as acting Chairman of the party's Military Affairs Commission (MAC) which as already stated combines the functions of Minister of Defence and the Joint Chiefs of Staff, suddenly found himself in the centre of a gigantic dispute between Mao and Khrushchev. In 1957, as the Military Chief and Politbu-reau member, he had accompanied the Chairman to Moscow to attend the fortieth anniversary of the Russian Revolution. After the formal celebrations were over, Peng led a large and important delegation of Chinese commanders to discuss joint Sino-Soviet strategy in the wake of the launching of Russia's first satellite and the testing of an intercontinental ballistic missile (ICBM), which had taken both China and the West by surprise. After 'summit' meetings with the military chiefs of Warsaw Pact countries, Peng made a lengthy tour of Russian military installations and returned home via Khabarovsk and Vladivostok which was noteworthy as so few Chinese had ever been permitted to visit, let alone view the military installations of these nearby cities.

During the tour the Russians promised Peng massive practical support in the modernization of the defence forces but when he returned to Peking he was obviously disappointed and it appears they had renegued on their pledges. Thus shortly after his return, Peng made a speech that suggested his negotiations in Moscow had been 'less than satisfactory' and China would be forced to rely on its own industrial base as a 'prerequisite for strong defence'. It should be noted that the speech was delivered in January 1958 when the Great Leap Forward, with its stress on self-reliance, was just getting into its stride. After a two-month-long meeting of the MAC, which finally terminated in July, Peking launched a powerful propaganda campaign geared to the 'liberation' of Taiwan. Moscow believed this to be extremely dangerous – 'a folly' – because there was intense United States naval activity in the Taiwan Straits at the time.

But despite these setbacks Mao was in no mood to make long-term concessions to the Soviet Union for he was still living in the after-glow of what even today his admirers regard as his 'finest hour'. This is pinpointed as the 8th Party Congress which took place in September 1956 after a lapse of eleven years. Mao was then re-elected as the party Chairman and he received 'scores of seemingly unending ovations from the delegates'. The congress noted with satisfaction that internal and external peace had been achieved in the new state of over 6000 million people while, in addition, industry and agriculture were going forward satisfactorily and the world was moving towards full diplomatic recognition. Indeed, there was what was later described as 'a universal spirit of optimism' amongst the leading members of the party. But all references to Mao's 'thoughts' were omitted from the new party constitution drafted by Liu Shaoqi.

This euphoric atmosphere was soon dispelled by setbacks that arose as a result of the campaign to 'Let a hundred flowers bloom and a hundred thoughts contend' which was followed by the more dramatic and disastrous Great Leap Forward. But Chairman Mao, who so often in the past had been quick and sensitive to note the change of mood amongst the masses, appeared at that moment to have lost his touch and, despite reports from friends in the Politbureau, failed to realize how much his popularity had slumped.

By the time Marshal Peng was invited to lead a goodwill military delegation to Moscow and the Warsaw Pact countries in April 1959, discontent had already penetrated into the ranks of the army, which, after all, was largely made up of peasants. Soldiers did not enjoy having senior officers, including generals, serving with them in the ranks and sharing their canteens and sleeping quarters as well as entertainment and other facilities. They were aware that Mao had insisted the officers spend up to three months living with their men, but they rightly assumed no officer would wish to share their discomforts for more than a day or so.

The Marshal had a multitude of personal friends as well as professional contacts in the Russian Military Command arising from his service in Manchuria, the Korean War and the many visits exchanged between senior officers. These contacts were used to imply he was pro-Russian by Mao when their quarrels began.

The Marshal and his goodwill delegation arrived in Poland at the time Foreign Ministers of the Warsaw Pact countries were about to meet, and the East European Ministers gathered there made no secret of what they thought about the stupidity and wastage of the Great Leap Forward. At the same time the staff officers there criticized Mao's much-publicized ideas that it was better to be 'red' than 'expert' and 'the folly' of threatening to attack Taiwan. Indeed, the Warsaw Pact Command was truly frightened that they might be dragged into a war in the Far East.

Although Khrushchev had been concerned earlier about the possible success of the Great Leap when it was first launched he was now, he informed Peng, when he met him after the Warsaw Pact meeting in Tirana, the capital of Albania, veering towards anxiety about the future of his communist neighbour. Relations between Moscow and Peking were already strained and early in 1959 the Russians had deliberately delayed some of the much-needed machine tool equipment for the armament factories they had built near Xi'an. This was in addition to their failure to 'share' nuclear secrets and know-how. The climax of the Tirana meeting was a denunciation by Khrushchev of the waste of time, material and energy the Great Leap had caused combined with severe criticism of the amount of time Chinese soldiers were devoting to political indoctrination, farm and construction work when they should have been training in the use of their new Russian arms and equipment. Doubtless, Peng felt much of the Russian criticism was justified and he told the Russian leader that he had already reduced the amount of time the soldiers were spending on studying the thoughts of Chairman Mao. Peng outlined the Chinese Maoist policy of 'self-reliance' when Khrushchev pressed him to accept closer co-operation with the Warsaw Pact countries in the military sphere in return for increased aid. Further, Khrushchev raised yet again the question of the establishment of a joint command which the Chairman had turned down so angrily at their last meeting. The forthright Marshal Peng, in his private conversations with Khrushchev, let it be known that in his view the Chairman was making some grave mistakes. But Peng's friends on the Central Committee in later years stressed that he was never disloyal to Mao, indeed, one claimed that 'this would have been out of keeping with his nature.'

Khrushchev urged Peng to write to Mao from Tirana and make all the points he had raised. Peng then drafted a letter and discussed it in detail with the Russian leader before the final draft was despatched to Peking. It is believed that one of the officers in Peng's mission, doubtless in the hope of personal advancement, leaked this information to an acquaintance of his who was then working on the Chairman's personal staff. Peng's main points, which he stressed to the General Staff on his return to Peking, after stopping over in Moscow for talks with the Russian Defence Minister, Malinovsky, and a second meeting with Khrushchev, were that it was worth making some concessions to the Soviet Union in order to maintain the military and civilian equipment so urgently required by the defence forces together with the help of over 6000 Russian experts.

While Peng was abroad he was re-appointed Defence Minister by the 2nd National People's Congress, which met in April 1959, as well as third-ranking Vice Premier, while at the same time he replaced the veteran Zhu De as the Vice Chairman of the National Defence Council.

Unhappily for Peng what then appeared to be the final rupture between Moscow and Peking took place on June 20th, a week after his return to Peking. He was nonetheless dismayed when a junior – the Deputy Director of the Political Department – Xiao Hua (Hsiao Hua), delivered the report on the results of the goodwill mission Peng had led to a mass meeting of senior officers despite the fact Peng was publicly billed as the speaker. Doubtless encouraged by all he had heard and seen on his trip as well as by his own regional commanders and general staff, Peng stressed in private the need for 'inter-dependence amongst socialist states', rather than the 'go it alone policy in a spirit of self-reliance' as Chairman Mao urged. At that time the steam engendered by the Great Leap Forward was already running down amongst the masses who began to see the low quality of goods which were being produced by the back-yard furnaces. Encouraged by all he heard, Peng had the temerity to challenge the wisdom of Chairman Mao's vision of a people's war and a mass mobilization of the People's Militia at the Lushan Conference in August 1959 where he criticized the 'Great Leap Forward' as 'petty bourgeois fanaticism'. Many senior officers supported Peng and suggested that self-reliance in the military sphere would render China extremely vulnerable to the nuclear might of the United States, especially if the Russians succeeded in their efforts to move towards a détente with Washington.

Mao may well have been jealous of Peng's enormous popularity with the armed forces for he was in a sensitive mood having been criticized in private by members of the Politbureau for having launched the Great Leap. Further, Mao had been obliged to relinquish the post of Chairman of the People's Republic, which was the equivalent of Head of State, to Liu Shaoqi. However, despite the fall in his personal popularity and authority, Mao was determined to get rid of Peng for what he called 'anti-party' activities and he was replaced by Lin Biao at the end of September. But unlike others who were purged by Mao, Peng was free to wander around Peking and he even attended an official funeral in 1960. His name has not been deleted from official records nor from the history of the People's Republic of China. Chairman Mao even referred to him in his selected works as 'comrade' but other chances were made to give less praise and prominence to his successful activities as a military commander. One authority stated that Chinese authors writing on the Chinese Communist Movement during Mao's lifetime were not expected to mention Peng 'any more than is necessary' and added that the Marshal's name has been left out of the official account of his exploits in Shaanxi in 1936. Peng was rehabilitated in 1979.

Through a clash of personalities and differing views of how relations with the Soviet Union should be maintained, China lost a first-class defence chief, much to the chagrin of the army, which caused a still further drop in the popularity of the Chairman. After being placed on the list of those who had 'taken the wrong line' – purged – Peng was very bitter but stuck to his views about the defence policy China should adopt. The Chairman, for his part, was deeply offended by Peng's references to his policies as 'petty bourgeois fanaticism' – a phrase that was later to be used against him by Khrushchev during the Cultural Revolution.

While Mao concentrated on the defence forces as he initiated Lin Biao into the job of Minister, the super-pragmatist Liu Shaoqi was gradually dismantling various measures Mao had inspired and built up during the Great Leap. There was no doubt that Mao's popularity was sinking dangerously and, although he survived Peng's attack, he was aware that at least one-third of army officers sympathized with Peng's views which he dubbed as 'pro-Russian revisionist'. It is, however, likely that this name was inspired by the radicals, and the now disgraced 'Gang of Four', led by Jiang Qing and the Security Chief, Kang Sheng, were bringing him reports from the grass roots that were, as he had instructed, 'the truth and not what I might wish to hear'.

5

The Power Struggle between Liu and Mao

After the dismissal of Peng Dehuai the stage was set for what Chairman Mao Zedong dubbed an intensification of the 'struggle between two lines'. In more direct language, this meant a power struggle between Mao, who wanted to 'prevent the revolution from dying out', and his heir apparent, Liu Shaoqi, whose chief aim was the restoration of stability and a revival of the economy in both the countryside and urban areas after the catastrophes of the Great Leap Forward. The Chairman was angered that he could do little to halt what he saw as Liu's dangerous political moves to the right. Material incentives – private plots in agricultural communes and overtime pay in industry – were being used and over-used in Mao's view to increase production. The Chairman felt extremely frustrated for, after being the acknowledged leader of the Communist Party since 1935, he found by 1960 he had virtually no access to the media as it was under the control of Liu and the party, and few of his speeches were published.

Mao was clever enough, when he realized Peng had become a minor national hero, not only in the army but amongst the broad masses, to admit he had made mistakes, even 'bad mistakes', and he conceded that the price the nation had had to pay for the Great Leap experiment was 'too high'. But whether or not the broad masses knew of the Chairman's confessions, his critics in both the party and the state bureaucracy became more vocal and bolder.

While Mao's supporters blamed bad weather for the poor harvest, Liu Shaoqi claimed that a survey of peasants indicated that natural calamities were responsible for a mere 30 per cent of their difficulties whilst 'man-made factors' accounted for some 70 per cent. Liu's task to restore production was made more difficult by the fact that when the ultimate breach with the Soviet Union took place in July 1960 and Soviet aid was abruptly terminated, the 1390 Russian technical advisers and technicians then working inside China were recalled and took their blueprints with them. However, after 1958 Liu Shaoqi gradually assumed more and more power, and by 1962 he appeared to have brought the country's economy almost back to normality. Certainly the nation was well on the way to recovery and even modest progress. Chairman Mao had meanwhile experienced two years or more of self-imposed semi-retirement during which he tended to concentrate his attention on Lin Biao and the political indoctrination of the defence forces that led ultimately to the abolition of ranks; but that was not until the spring of 1965.

Liu Shaoqi as Head of State was anxious to see a gradual termination of Chairman Mao's personal, charismatic type of leadership and, with the support of the Secretary General of the party, Deng Xiaoping, he made efforts to gain control of the party machine. This was not easy for, despite Mao's loss of popularity amongst the bureaucrats and senior party cadres, the Chairman was still deeply loved and revered, almost worshipped at grass roots level. Although Liu lacked the strong and engaging personality of the Chairman, this dour, rather colourless man was nonetheless clever and accepted by his colleagues in government and on the Central Committee as 'practical, thorough and assiduous'. Liu was well aware that he lacked the magnetic charm of the Chairman and, according to his wife, he felt he was under a serious handicap because he could not openly oppose Mao.

Outwardly the Chairman appeared to be at the apex of his glory during and immediately after the 8th Party Congress in 1956. For since the 7th Party Congress had met in Yenan in April 1945, the Chinese people had been 'liberated' and united into a single communist state. Mao was the unique and undisputed leader who had established the People's Republic and then conducted the nation through a series of reforms in both agriculture and industry that had enabled them to recover from the trauma of civil war. However, the delegates at the congress were aware that all references to Chairman Mao and his thoughts had been deleted from the constitution, under the influence of Liu Shaoqi, it is now known. Only a handful of senior officials then realized the gravity of the life and death struggle for power just beginning to take shape virtually before their eyes. Few noticed this because in the past Liu had appeared so much the Chairman's 'éminence grise' or 'yes man' who, until the time of the Great Leap Forward, had implemented Mao's wishes and decrees.

The Chairman was already fully aware of Liu's ambitions and state of mind even before he had, in Mao's own words, attempted to transform him into a Buddha on a shelf – an effort that forced Mao to stand down as Head of State. Further, the publication of Liu's book, *How to Be a Good Communist*, which was brought up to date and re-issued in August 1962, angered Mao. Indeed, the Chairman then said, in private, that the book advocated a 'bourgeois' revisionist, political programme and he later called it publicly a 'poisonous weed'. The Chairman told Edgar Snow and others years later that this caused him to begin to take counter-measures against what he dubbed as 'the adverse wind'. Mao began the Socialist Education Movement without at first any clearer definition of its aims other than that the participants should study his 'thoughts' and how they related to the four areas of politics, the economy, ideology and organization. Initially, the movement was confined to those districts where little resistance was anticipated as well as rural areas where the relaxations coming after the Great Leap Forward had caused laziness and corruption or the return of small landlordism.

The Chairman urged at the same time that students from the urban areas be sent to work in the fields as a demonstration of classlessness and unity and they should, while attempting to achieve the maximum production work, 'strive' towards the creation of a classless society. Shortly after the Socialist Education Movement opened there were purges of leading philosophers, including Feng Yilan, together with less well known academics, journalists, cartoonists and dramatists. All were accused of sowing seeds of 'traditionalism', or 'revisionism' and following the 'capitalist road'. Many of them were sent to toil in the paddy fields and as they were unorganized and lacked influential leadership, there was but little resistance. At the Tenth Plenum of the Central Committee, which met in August and September 1962, Mao had succeeded in halting – at least on paper – any further concessions being made in the agricultural socialization programme. At the same meeting the Chairman also sponsored a resolution that stressed the urgent need to guarantee that 'revolutionary successors' were cultivated amongst the more youthful members of the party. After this meeting, which from Mao's viewpoint was successful, he dispensed with any further large formal party gatherings for around four years.

Mao gives his attention to the military

Mao had chosen Lin Biao as Defence Minister in an all too obvious attempt to negate Liu's growing power, for he believed he could count on Lin's absolute loyalty despite a background many leaders would have viewed with deep suspicion. Lin had, in fact, far more good contacts in the Soviet Union than Peng, the man he replaced at the Defence Ministry. Further Lin, who had been a first-class soldier throughout much of the civil war, made it his business to flatter the Chairman outrageously in public and whenever possible at meetings of the Politbureau and other gatherings of Ministers. On becoming Defence Minister he had overtly dropped the interest he had once shown in what Mao called 'positional warfare' and, unhesitatingly, accepted what was often claimed as the Chairman's concept of a people's war with all the supporting ideology including that it is better for soldiers to be 'red' than technically proficient in their handling of weapons. In fact, Mao actually said early in 1966 soldiers should 'advance along the Red *and* Expert Road'.

While Peng had urged soldiers to train in order that they could fire their rifles effectively in combat, Lin ordered commanders (officers) to make way for around 20,000 new political commissars to promote the 'thoughts' of the Chairman. Lin Biao, who like his predecessor was acting Chairman of the Military Affairs Commission as well as Defence Minister, claimed that 'great good' had come as a result of sending over 120,000 commanders to work as soldiers at the grass roots with units that were not always their own. This had been one of the Chairman's ideas Peng had deplored. Almost Lin's first act on taking over the Ministry was to open a campaign to urge the PLA 'to march ahead under the Red Flag of the party's general line and Mao Zedong's military thinking'. Indeed, Lin's stress on the 'human factor' being more important in war than weaponry caused serious tensions to develop between the Ministry and professional soldiers in the field. But, to be fair, from time to time Lin did stress that 'although politics came first the complexities of modern weaponry require that more time be devoted to normal military training than to political thinking'.

Some Chinese military observers now claim that Lin Biao accepted with some reluctance the Chairman's orders to put politics first and training military personnel second during his first few years at the Defence Ministry. Whatever Lin's thoughts may then have been they are now hard to ascertain, but there can be no doubt that he was a strong advocate of building up the nuclear force in order that China might become a great military power. Lin knew how outdated China's conventional weapons were in comparison with those of the United States, and how chronically short they were of ammunition and spare parts since the split with the Soviet Union.

Lin shared with the Chairman a fear that the Vietnamese War might 'spill over' into China and did his best to obviate this by making some changes in deployment, increasing the number of troops in the South-eastern Military Region. The Chairman urgently needed the full backing of the army in 'the struggle between the two lines' with Liu Shaoqi. For Mao was ever mindful of one of his earliest 'thoughts', that 'political power grows out of the barrel of a gun'. He had noted this was how the warlords achieved influence and authority in his youth. Later Mao changed the slogan to 'Political power grows out of the barrel of a gun but the gun must be under command of the party'. However much Mao stressed in later years that the gun must be under the command of the party, this never altered the basic concept. While Liu and Deng were, in Mao's eyes, trying to undo all his revolutionary work within the party, they had at that time but limited influence with the defence forces. Meanwhile, in what Mao recognized as the opening stages of the struggle, Mao gave Lin all the help and support he could because he felt he would ultimately need the unconditional goodwill of the army, which, with its nationwide organization, had far more 'clout' than either the party or the state bureaucracy. The Chairman may have been moved by Lin's flattery.

Lin's position, however, appears to have been, at best, unconsolidated when he took over the Defence Ministry. After all, he had twice left the forces, once during a six-year period from 1939 to

1945 when he was either recuperating in Moscow or negotiating with the nationalists in Chongqing and again after a serious illness in 1952. Many thought he was then on the verge of death. But whatever the reason Lin was again absent from the armed forces for nearly seven years. Some of the top-ranking officers were amazed by Lin's appointment because there were some little-known, curious episodes in his past that suggested he had not always been so loyal to the Chairman as he now pretended to be.

Indeed, initially Lin had been elected to the Politbureau in 1952 but degraded shortly afterwards because of his intimate contacts with Gao Gang in Manchuria, in what was called the 'anti-party alliance', which led to Gao's purge and suicide (already discussed). Somehow through many painstaking outward and private displays of loyalty to the Chairman, Lin was deemed to be 'clean' and readmitted to the ruling Politbureau in April 1955 when Deng Xiaoping was elected for the first time. Mao chose Lin as the Defence Minister for what he thought were his qualities of latent obedience inherent in a soldier and few realized he had ever been thrown out of the Politbureau.

Lin's position in the PLA was, however, far weaker than was generally thought by the broad masses. Most civilians based their judgment on the fact that he had been an outstandingly successful commander of the 4th Field Army which in 1950 numbered a million men. But the so-called Linist faction in the army was really based on the original 100,000 men of this famous force who served initially in Manchuria. Over 600,000 men were later recruited there in readiness for the war in China proper but they were not necessarily keen admirers of the general whose early victories they had not shared.

The attitude of Premier Zhou Enlai during what were called 'the difficult early sixties' is hard to define. He observed there were serious economic problems which Liu and Deng were trying to help him solve. Zhou's verbal directives to the bureaucracy at the time were to assist the party to restore order. But the Premier never deviated from his robust loyalty to the Chairman in public and he therefore supported his line, although at times with reluctance, so far as opposing material incentives was concerned.

During the period both Liu as Head of State and Premier Zhou travelled abroad a good deal and greeted many foreign delegations visiting China. Mao tended to sulk on the sidelines, from time to time receiving the odd celebrity and making a rare visit to an agricultural commune where he was invariably treated as a god/ emperor. Both he and Liu saw the struggle between their two policies gain momentum as the 1960s advanced. Mao firmly believed the Revolution was seriously endangered and would ultimately be overthrown as the French and Russian Revolutions had been in their differing ways. In a cool, calculated manner, late in 1964 Mao called for an overhaul of the party that was to be called a 'Cultural Revolution'. Mao was irritated by Liu Shaoqi and Deng Xiaoping who showed but little interest in the study and application of his 'thoughts'. They were being pursued by the PLA with far more zeal than the broad masses. Between 1962 and 1964 the Socialist Education Movement had achieved far less than the Chairman had hoped in urban areas.

Thus at a small meeting of 'certain members of the Central Committee' held in 1965, which was called an unofficial conference, Mao urged that there should be a 'Cultural Revolution'. To make the necessary plans, he proposed that a group of five 'leading comrades' be set up to organize the projected campaign and to the surprise and delight of Liu and his friends he put forward the names of four of his principal antagonists who were strong supporters of Liu. It was, in fact, a cunning and clever move as the fifth member was the old Security Chief and Politbureau member, Kang Sheng, who would naturally report all that transpired unofficially back to the Chairman. Mao wanted to enlarge the Socialist Education Movement and transform it into a Cultural Revolution providing leaders who had some clout in order that it could operate on a nationwide basis. Indeed, the Chairman was especially anxious that the movement should begin to operate in the urban areas. For during the early 1960s Mao had been unable to do much to halt the ever-increasing control of the party Liu was achieving with Deng's help. This irked Mao who had thought Liu's able assistant, Deng, was one of 'his men'. Dissatisfied, too, by the conventional necessity of living amongst his 'enemies' in Zhongnanhai, the attractive western section of the former Imperial City, which housed members of the Politbureau in Peking, Mao spent long periods in the country.

The drama was without doubt heightened by the attitude of the wives of the leading characters who, at that time, with the possible exception of Deng Yingchao (Mme Zhou Enlai), all disliked the Chairman's wife, Jiang Qing, and were extremely resentful of her political power. When the Chairman first met Jiang in Yenan, there had been strong opposition to their marriage which was only finally agreed to by the Politbureau on condition she played no political role. In the eyes of Wang Guangmei, Liu's fifth wife, who was herself good-looking and well educated, Jiang was an ignorant, scheming, second-rate actress who had unfortunately caught the eye of the Chairman. Ye Qun (Yey Chun), Lin Biao's wife, who acted as the Minister's private and confidential secretary in their home, also found her 'difficult'.

It is important to note that from the moment the Chairman allowed Jiang to play a political role, their personal relationship changed. Further, although there is much evidence to the contrary, it is possible that Jiang's sicknesses were psychological rather than physical. Certainly, after the Chairman started to use her in a public political role little more was heard of the tuberculosis, intestinal troubles and skin complaints from which she had previously suffered. Jiang was sent to Moscow four times for medical treatment and her fears and apprehensions increased with every visit. Although she was initially invited to lunch with Stalin, she recalled all too vividly that Mao's second wife was also sent to Moscow for treatment and, when this was said to fail, back to a mental home in a remote part of China. Jiang was disturbed that the Chairman did not visit her when he attended the fortieth anniversary of the Russian Revolution in Moscow in November 1957 at a time when she was having treatment in hospital in that city.

Jiang herself later admitted that by 1960 political power had taken the place in her life which was once concerned with her marriage and sex. No longer was she apprehensive of the Chairman's good-looking interpreters, with whom he enjoyed cordial relations, or jealous of his secretary or nurse as she had been in the past. Jiang established her own small suite of private offices beside those of the Chairman in their joint bungalow and here she kept a special basket in which to throw marked papers and books she thought might be of special interest to him. At small political gatherings Jiang treated the Chairman with great respect if not downright deference and only rarely did he contradict her in front of other members of the Central Committee for making some statement he felt stupid or wrong. Her political ideas were radical, perhaps out of conviction, but certainly her enemies, especially in the cultural sphere, were to the right. She had lacked the opportunity in her youth but now Jiang made an enormous effort, encouraged by the Chairman, Chen Boda and Kang Sheng, to read basic communist literature and to educate herself in Marxism. Unhappily for Jiang, her well-publicized weaknesses were similar to those of her enemies in that she loved clothes, good food and 'capitalist' films.

The Chairman ponders

During the early summer of 1965, Chairman Mao Zedong decided the time had come for him to take stock, think and then draw up plans and general guidelines for major future political actions. He had a great advantage over national leaders in the West – with the possible exception of General de Gaulle – in that he had the opportunity to get away from his desk in Peking, where he was bothered by Ministers and senior party officials, and retreat with a small personal staff and Jiang Qing to the countryside.

Thus the Chairman and Jiang Qing took up their residence in a charming villa, once the proud possession of a banker, on the steep hillside above Hangzhou. Although, in theory, the villa was open to any member of the Politbureau the Chairman was left alone to enjoy the view and the refreshing breezes in the early morning and evening coming from the Western Lake. An additional attraction was a little-used major airfield with a long runway nearby that could facilitate the Chairman's speedy transport in an emergency to Shanghai or Peking. But the travelling was mostly done by Jiang who had by this time become invaluable to the Chairman both as a reporter on what people were thinking and saying and as a political adviser. The site was conveniently near to Shanghai, where Jiang had established close contacts with powerful radical elements in the party and people in the cultural sphere.

In the same retreat the previous year, Mao had been told that the peasants were still talking about the disasters that followed the

Great Leap Forward. Although conditions on the land were currently tolerable, wise members of agricultural communes were taking a variety of steps to prevent a recurrence of their former troubles. Many had increased the size of their private plots and were doing a lively business in selling their produce in the open market in the cities. Indeed, some were producing luxuries – flowers and exotic fruits – for what the Chairman called a 'black' market. In his view many peasants were gradually transforming themselves into small capitalists and spending their money on buying extra comforts such as mattresses – a luxury the Chairman firmly refused – together with chests and chairs while in the agricultural communes members were building additional rooms to their homes.

In support of their actions, the commune members told the Chairman's visiting representatives that the Secretary General of the Communist Party, Deng Xiaoping, had recently stated in what is now a famous sentence, 'Private farming is "all right" as long as it raises production, just as it does not matter whether a cat is black or white so long as it is a good mouser.' Mao, who had done so much to push Deng forward in the party because of his drive and ability, was shaken by what he heard. But he was even more saddened and shocked when it was reported back to Mao that Liu Shaoqi was making a tour of the countryside in order to drum up support for his own policies, which Mao thought were rightist. Everywhere Liu told officials that 'all possible means should be used to contribute to increase the productive enthusiasm of the peasants'. This gave a loud 'all-clear' for further material incentives, and when questioned about these Liu repeatedly stated, 'the problem of capitalist tendencies appearing is not so horrible'.

That sentence sealed Liu's permanent downfall in Mao's mind according to Jiang Qing. He was further dismayed by reports of other rightist tendencies coming from a variety of visitors. Senior party officials had established special superior schools for their children and car pools in their offices, while they enjoyed better housing together with gadgets such as radios and tape-recorders that were not on sale in the open market.

The Chairman also heard the opposition's views from his youthful nephew, Mao Yuanxin (Mao Yuan-hsin), who came to visit him and told him of the frustrations experienced by students and young people who saw the state and party being administered by men and women they referred to as 'Long Marchers', people, in any case, in their late sixties and seventies. These elderly party veterans, Mao's youthful visitors claimed, had lost all their 'revolutionary enthusiasm'. They reported to the Chairman, too, the renewed stress in universities and technical training institutions on being technically 'expert' rather than 'red'.

The explosion of China's first nuclear device in 1964 had encouraged scientists and university professors in general to reaffirm their belief that academic courses should not be cut down and interspersed with work on the land as many radicals had advocated. In addition, most universities, feeling that they were backed by Liu Shaoqi, took the opportunity to remind their more revolutionary elements that students who were admitted on the basis of their scholarly achievements rather than their political ideology were more likely to contribute to the scientific advance of the nation. For it was obvious that technocrats would be needed in the nuclear age.

When all this seeped through to the Chairman it confirmed his worst fears as it hurt and depressed him. He stressed to more than one of his visitors – one of whom informed me – that many great inventors and 'thinkers' such as Watt and Edison came from working-class families. Franklin, who discovered electric power, the Chairman said, had been a newspaper boy and Jesus had had no formal education, but worked in his father's carpenter's shop. The Chairman felt an urgent requirement for the education system especially to be re-established on what he believed to be the 'correct line'. It was in the universities and senior schools he hoped to find his revolutionary successors.

The more Mao pondered on the current political scene the more he realized he had insufficient power in the party to change the policy or, indeed, to challenge or repel the chief architect of the 'rightist line'. After all, Liu Shaoqi was still the Head of State and Mao's 'chosen successor'. The Chairman went through days of uncertainty and gloom because he felt he was not one hundred per cent sure of the backing of the bureaucracy, despite the fact that Premier Zhou Enlai had been extremely loyal throughout the sixteen years since the founding of the People's Republic while he had built up the machinery of state he administered so successfully.

But the Chairman feared Premier Zhou might choose law and order and conditions that favoured productivity rather than a new political upheaval Mao felt was essential to retain power. Mao also feared that Premier Zhou, although no longer Foreign Secretary, was anxious that China should show an orderly face to the outside world, which the periodic upheavals Mao planned would disturb.

It is not quite clear whether Mao was completely taken in by Lin Biao's outward show of loyalty, for evidence is still coming to light of the two-faced game Lin as Defence Minister was playing at this time. Indeed, Mao was initially concerned by Lin Biao's opposition in 1963, in the Central Committee and elsewhere, to 'China's patriotic move away from the Soviet Union'. Lin told the committee that the anti-Soviet revisionist line in the military sphere was premature and stressed that China should not have taken such a firm and independent stand against Russia until she had firmly established herself as a nuclear power. Further, he expressed great support for the policy that there should be no firm stand – against Russia – until nuclear weapons were thoroughly mastered by the PLA. Lin Biao said China should have accepted Khrushchev's terms for the supply of 'specimen' nuclear weapons. And Lin knew this meant the establishment of a 'joint command' for the defence forces of the two communist powers, with the ultimate control of China's nuclear weapons, and perhaps even the war machine, in Moscow's hands.

Initially, the projected joint command was explained by the Russians in terms used by Washington and London. For example, in the case of nuclear weapons supplied to Britain by the United States there is a 'two key system' to ensure that the missile cannot be fired without both British and American consent. But although Russian and Chinese scientists were working secretly together on nuclear projects up to 1966, it soon transpired that the Russians wanted a far greater control over the Chinese nuclear force than the Americans have over the British one, in or outside NATO. Furthermore, Khrushchev was obviously trying to extend Russia's authority to the conventional forces on the grounds that the Soviet Union supplied many of the weapons and all the technology. Various Chinese magazines, including *Hong Qi* – *Red Flag* – actually hinted that Lin's 'over-indulgence in the importance of nuclear weapons' had led him to believe that China should 'serve' the

Soviet Union which 'had by then firmly established itself as a superpower with nuclear sophistications'. Such ideas constituted 'traitorous thinking' on Lin's part, observers claimed at the time.

It has been suggested by a senior Chinese officer that Lin excused himself to the Chairman by saying that the armed forces were already so torn between being 'red and technically expert' that he made a series of such statements in an effort to gain the personal support of the commanders. Certainly, it was true that the commanders were growing ever more disgruntled by the aftermath of Russia's withdrawal of military assistance. There was an acute shortage of spare parts and ammunition especially for the artillery Moscow had delivered during the late 1960s. The Chief of Staff, Luo Ruiqing (Lo Jui-ching), later to be dismissed, indeed purged, was openly critical of Lin Biao's orders to devote more time to reading the thoughts of Chairman Mao than to weapon training. He, too, was critical in private of the breach with Moscow.

What is certain is that, by whatever means he used, Chairman Mao acquired the full support of Lin Biao in his determination to change the policy of the party and if necessary to 'get rid' of Liu Shaoqi. Mao's totally unfounded doubts about the attitude of Premier Zhou Enlai gave him the feeling that he had no real power base outside the army. But even if he had had the Premier's support, without that of the defence forces it would have been almost worthless in the struggle against Liu and the party.

While the Chairman was in Hangzhou, he was visited several times by Lin Biao who stayed in a nearby villa and the two men discussed the theme of Lin's now famous article 'Long Live the Victory of the People's War'. This caused a flap amongst intelligence services attempting to interpret Chinese policy in the United States and Europe when it was published by the *People's Daily* on the twentieth anniversary of the Japanese defeat. Lin opened in the long-winded manner the Chinese normally use with a careful analysis of the tactics Mao had employed during the war of resistance against Japan. Mao had established rural bases of the Red Army that gradually assumed control of vast areas of the countryside with the willing co-operation of the peasants. Thus the communists were able to encircle and finally to destroy the enemy in the city. These tactics, which had been so successful in China, Lin now advocated be universally adopted. Thus in the global terms he named, the cities of the world are, metaphorically speaking, North America and Western Europe, whilst the rural areas are Asia, Africa and Latin America. In the Third World these oppressed nations were struggling against imperialism. Lin forecast that world revolution would ultimately follow the Chinese pattern and the 'cities' would gradually be encircled by 'the rural areas'.

Naturally this article also caused a flurry among diplomats in Peking, who feared that not only were the Chinese once more reverting to open military and moral support for revolutionary movements in distant Africa but also that they would be likely to do far more to help the South Vietnamese as well as other rebel groups in North India, Thailand, Burma, Cambodia, to name but a few. Although Chairman Mao had little experience of the world outside China and tended to leave the details of foreign policy in the competent hands of Premier Zhou Enlai and the Foreign Ministry specialists, he nonetheless frequently mulled over China's future position on the international scene and the leadership of the communist world that he wanted, so much, to take over from the Soviet Union.

While relations with the Soviet Union deteriorated almost every month, the second superpower, the United States, was fighting a war in Vietnam and engaged in combat activities, including bombing, far too near to the Chinese frontier for Mao's comfort. Indeed, some senior officers professed to believe there was a real threat of an American invasion. To relieve the situation Liu Shaoqi proposed to the Politbureau that they should send a delegation to the 23rd Party Conference in Moscow and attempt to repair Sino-Soviet relations. Chairman Mao was apprehensive that this would result in China being dragged into the Vietnam War as had happened in Korea, for he feared above all else being dependent once more on the Soviet Union; nor did the Chairman see any chance of coming to terms with the United States while they were waging a war on the Asian mainland and using Taiwan – an integral part of China in communist eyes – as a rear base for their operations. The Chinese General Staff claimed, with reason, to be alarmed at the possible danger of fighting a war on two fronts. So, indeed, was Mao but concluded that the most dangerous enemies were the ones inside China and the continuation of the two external threats would help to unite the nation. As Washington had already realized, they had bitten off more than they could chew in Vietnam and there were no plans to harass China, but the Chinese could hardly be expected to believe this at the time.

The opening salvoes of the Cultural Revolution

Mao and Jiang Qing returned to Peking in September 1965 and Mao, as Chairman of the Central Committee, called meetings of the Standing Committee and the Politbureau. Refreshed by his long holiday and frequent swims in the Western Lake, Mao began by attacking the revisionist education policy which Liu Shaoqi and the other leaders were following. Then, with encouragement from Jiang, whose main interest was still in the cultural sphere, he appealed for renewed efforts to 'criticize bourgeois reactionary thinking especially in art and literature'. The Chairman pointed specifically to the play written some four years earlier by Wu Han, a well-known historian and author, entitled *Hai Jui Dismissed from Office*. The drama referred to an honest official of the Ming dynasty who had the unusual courage to criticize the emperor with the result that he was dismissed and unjustly punished. This form of satirical drama is traditional in China and everyone in the capital knew that the play was really aimed at the Chairman himself for having dismissed his former Minister of Defence, Marshal Peng Dehuai. Further, the play could not have been produced in Peking without the blessing of the Mayor, Peng Zhen, who was also a member of the Politbureau. The play was, therefore, a disguised attack on Mao himself.

Mao realized at the same time there was a strong and open movement in the party to have Peng, if not reinstated, at least appointed to some new, high-level job. Mao was for his part still virtually unable to make his voice heard as the press remained generally under the control of Liu Shaoqi. However, a series of national propaganda campaigns had been launched by Lin Biao and supported by Premier Zhou Enlai such as 'Learn from the PLA' which had a twofold objective. Soldiers would help peasants with the harvest and in construction of difficult bridges and terraces on the agricultural communes while passing on the thoughts of the

Chairman. There were other movements that lasted on and off for years – one was 'Learn from Dazhai', the model agricultural commune that received considerable capital funds from the state to assist in their elaborate building projects while, it was later disclosed, falsifying some of their high production figures. 'Learn from Daqing', the twin industrial campaign, referred to China's major oil field and was based on fact. The production, with outdated equipment, especially in the sphere of water injection to aid the extraction of oil there, was, and still is, truly remarkable.

Lin Biao produced a small red-covered book of selected quotations from Chairman Mao's thoughts designed to be carried by soldiers in their pockets and to ensure not only that they studied them but quoted the slogans correctly. Lin wrote the preface and soldiers received their copies as they came off the printing presses. This later became famous as the 'Little Red Book'. But there were problems with the civilian distribution as Liu Shaoqi's *How to Be a Good Communist* was still in the place of honour in the centre in every bookshop window as well as filling the shelves inside.

Mao was impressed by the manner in which Lin Biao was building up various sectors of the People's Militia. Millions of men and women with some previous experience in the armed forces were being organized and trained – generally without weapons – to take part in any new people's war or disturbances that might arise. Lin was also paving the way for the formation of the youthful Red Guards.

The Chairman, despite the pessimistic attitude of the peasants, received reports of the improved economic situation in the country, for by 1965 China was free of debt and both grain and industrial production appeared to have recovered from the aftermath of the Great Leap Forward and to have reached their 1958 levels.

Poisonous weeds

During a long and acrimonious meeting of the Politbureau in the late summer of 1965, Mao sent Jiang Qing to Shanghai where she was already on good terms with the only important party member, Zhang Chunqiao (Chang Ch'un-ch'iao) who had already openly opposed 'the revisionist line' of the local parties. Zhang, in turn, put her in touch with a writer, Yao Wenyuan (Yao Wen-yuan), who although young had made a reputation as a critical journalist. This resulted in an article appearing in a Shanghai newspaper, *Wen Hui Bao*, on November 10th in which Yao dubbed the play *Hai Jui Dismissed from Office* 'a poisonous weed' – already a favourite communist term of abuse – produced by 'bourgeois elements opposed to the dictatorship of the proletariat'. These accusations in Chinese eyes also included the Mayor of Peking, who was the immediate superior of the author and a 'leader' of the bourgeois elements opposing the Maoist line.

The Mayor, Peng Zhen, had been warned of Yao Wenyuan's activities but had taken no action. Like Deng Xiaoping a decade later he had been extremely cool towards Jiang's projects when she was first attempting to introduce revolutionary themes into Peking operas. Indeed, the Mayor claimed it was impossible to sell tickets to revolutionary operas. (Deng said later that he did not mind Jiang producing the operas so long as he did not have to watch them.) Peng's immediate reaction was to order that the *People's Daily* did not reprint the Shanghai article but he was later persuaded to reverse this decision. However, Peng requested that there should be an editor's note expressing the view that the criticism was artistic rather than political and other writers would, at a later date, add their own views.

The Chairman, predictably, again became miserable living in Zhongnanhai, Peking, amongst people with some of whom his relations were strained, so he decided to move back to Hangzhou. But before doing so and to dispel any possible rumours of his death or ill health he took the unusual step of inviting some 30–40 'foreign friends' to Shanghai to dine with him to celebrate the eightieth birthday of one of his old-time foreign supporters, Anna Louise Strong. Many of them worked as translators or writers for the Foreign Language Press or in the Foreign Language Institute of the Government. Although only two amongst the British or American 'foreign friends' ever had the courtesy to pass the time of day with foreign diplomats or journalists, the word that the Chairman was in 'fine fettle' soon got around. This was important because Mao disappeared this time for five months, which was the longest period between 1949 and his death that he failed to attend any public function or receive official guests.

Too abrupt a change

Kang Sheng emerged somewhat naturally as the only man to take Mao's side after Peng Zhen had misguidedly reactivated the Group of Five, which had been initially formed by the Chairman to 'guide a Cultural Revolution for workers and to purify art and literature'. Indeed, the five senior party officials had rarely, if ever, met until suddenly called by Peng to prepare a report repeating his contention that Wu Han's play with its scarcely veiled attack on the Chairman should, nonetheless, be treated as a cultural issue.

Peng's report, which later became known as the 'February Outline Report', claimed that Wu Han and others should be allowed the same freedom the Chairman himself accorded to writers during the early period when 'a hundred flowers' had bloomed in 1956/7. Kang Sheng, known to be a staunch Maoist, was apparently not invited to the meetings that drew up the report. A copy was given to Liu Shaoqi and Peng Zhen went to Hangzhou to see the Chairman but did not show Mao the actual document, which he released in Peking a few days later, saying it had the Chairman's 'chop' or seal of approval on it. Kang Sheng, then in Peking, spent hours on the telephone with Jiang Qing, for the Chairman was already hard of hearing, with the result that Mao, always a master of rousing and earthy phrases, began drafting his reply.

Meanwhile, Liu and his wife made plans to spend three or four weeks on a state visit to Pakistan, Afghanistan and Burma in late March. Again Kang Sheng, who, in addition to being the Security Chief, had become the party's foremost representative for contacts with foreign communist parties, found out what they were doing and reported to the Chairman. Liu and his wife over-optimistically believed that 'the row' about the play would have blown over by the time they returned. Moreover, they were leaving behind them the administrative wizard Deng, who they trusted to prepare for a 'showdown' with Mao should one become inevitable.

Premier Zhou Enlai made a private unpublicized visit to the Chairman in Hangzhou in late January 1966 doubtless to discuss the many intrigues that, together with plots and counter-plots, were taking place in the early weeks of that year. For it is inconceivable (to me) that the curious but nonetheless true reports had not reached Premier Zhou's ears.

Jiang Qing's radical friend from Shanghai, Zhang Chunqiao, who was deputy leader of the new Cultural Revolution Group, earlier that month had called a leading student from Peking University, Kuai Dafu, to his room at Zhongnanhai, site of the Party Centre and State Council as well as the residence of senior members of the Politbureau. He then directed Kuai to discredit both Liu Shaoqi and Deng Xiaoping. Zhang stressed to Kuai Dafu that, 'Those two in the Central Committee who put forward the reactionary bourgeois line have not yet surrendered.' He advised Kuai to get hold of other youthful 'revolutionary fighters' and 'make their – Liu and Deng's – names stink', adding 'flog the cur that has fallen into the water'. As a result of this conversation Kuai felt flattered, he said, because Zhang had 'put all his cards on the table' and shown a special trust 'in me'. Kuai quickly roused other friends to help organize a demonstration. A small group of students then paraded through the streets shouting 'Down with Liu Shaoqi' and 'Down with Deng Xiaoping' and, according to foreigners living in Peking at the time, they plastered some buildings in the city centre with posters and distributed leaflets emphasizing the same theme.

Even worse, Lin Biao, who was after all Defence Minister, slandered Deng Xiaoping by accusing him of being a 'member of a sinister gang' as well as 'an anti-party element' and 'a Khrushchev-type person'. In addition, he accused Deng of having 'fleets' which at that period was almost a code word in China for private armies bent on overthrowing the regime in power. It became one later.

Another bizarre statement was made by Kang Sheng, Security Chief, as early as the summer of 1966 when he accused Marshal He Long 'of secretly deploying troops in readiness to stage a February Mutiny'. He Long, a Long Marcher who had figured prominently in the conquest of both north and south-west China, was by this time a Vice Premier and an important member of the MAC as well as being a member of the ruling Politbureau.

These three, Zhang, Lin and Kang, were all on intimate political terms with Jiang Qing and there is reason to believe that she gave them the necessary orders or at least inspired them to act. It is likely that then, as on other occasions, she claimed to be acting in the name of the Chairman and this may have been true. As Lin frequently saw Mao he could so easily have questioned him about such an order. Kang Sheng also had easy access to the Chairman.

After Premier Zhou's visit to Hangzhou, the Chairman's response to the February Outline Report was finalized. This foreshadowed the Cultural Revolution by stating that China was heading towards an 'arduous, complex and long-term struggle' designed to eliminate 'the dictatorship of the black line': in other words those members of the Politbureau and Central Committee who had opposed Chairman Mao. 'Black', in general, in Chinese communist terms, referred to wicked people or collaborators with the 'bourgeois capitalist roaders in power'. Believing he could count on the army, and now knowing Premier Zhou Enlai was indubitably on his side, the Chairman then launched an attack on the Peking party and Peng Zhen by name two days or so after Liu had left the country. Mao then demanded that the editor and the committee that ran the *People's Daily* should be dismissed, together with the senior staff of Xinhua, the official Chinese news agency.

During Liu's absence abroad in March and early April 1966 Deng Xiaoping presided over a meeting of the party Secretariat that was attended by Zhou Enlai, Kang Sheng and Chen Boda, who it will be recalled had been the Chairman's political secretary and speech writer before becoming the leading party theologian and a member of the Politbureau. Kang convinced Deng that Peng Zhen had made mistakes in opposing Chairman Mao and Kang then reported back to Mao. The Chairman quickly called a meeting of the Standing Committee of the Politbureau which on April 16th agreed to dissolve and disband the Group of Five that was organizing the Cultural Revolution.

When Liu returned from his trip four days later the cool welcome accorded him at Peking airport indicated that his troubles with the Chairman were not over and he soon learned, to his surprise, that Deng and Zhou had both cast their votes against Peng despite the fact that they knew how heavily he, Liu, relied on Peng for party work in the capital and the surrounding areas.

Newspapers and magazines now generally under Mao's control reinforced their attacks on Peng and on May 6th, 1966 the *Liberation Army Daily* (which is not sold to foreigners) went further in a leading article by saying that Yao Wenyuan's criticism of *Hai*

Jui Dismissed from Office was far more serious than 'a mere scholar's rebellion' but a part of a 'life and death struggle'. The paper said some people – Peng and his friends – had 'resisted the leadership of the party and committed anti-party and anti-social crimes because they wanted to have a trial of strength with the proletariat'. The armed forces, the article claimed, did not 'live in a vacuum' and all the comrades would 'take part in this great struggle' holding high the banner of Mao Zedong thought in order 'to carry the great socialist cultural revolution through to the end'. Odd references to Peng, who had 'defended the production of bad films', suggested that Jiang Qing had seen the article before publication and added a few sentences, if not, as many people at the time believed, actually drafted it jointly with Lin Biao.

Mao, who rarely bothered about details, but preferred to deal with broad issues and campaign directives, leaving the organization to others, was biding his time. He repeated his wartime slogan that 'a man can only eat a meal a bite at a time and in the same way enemy forces could only be destroyed one by one'. He realized that, if he attacked too many personal enemies at the same time as Peng, the opposition would mount and combine, thus becoming too strong for him to tackle. While he was in the capital on a visit he looked around the suburbs and confirmed with his own eyes reports Jiang Qing had made to him about the decadence that was setting in with the ever-increasing number of senior party cadres using big cars not only for official business but for the journey to the office and back home. He observed, too, disapprovingly that the furniture in government offices was 'shiny and new' and 'looked bourgeois' while many cinemas were still showing old and traditional, non-revolutionary films. Indeed, Mao saw the Chinese Communist Party was falling, or indeed, had already fallen, into the same bad ways as the Russians and was forming a new elite – an executive class – that wore leather shoes, instead of the felt slippers of the workers, acquired better housing, more books and good radio sets although they still donned the Mao jackets and trousers like everyone else. This all provided the Chairman with the extra incentive and determination he knew he would require to take the steps necessary to launch a major political upheaval. After calling 'an enlarged' meeting of the Politbureau, in which the additional members ensured his majority, the Chairman dismissed

Peng and the five-man cultural group. He then formed a new one which included Jiang Qing, Chen Boda and Kang Sheng to guide the activities of the Cultural Revolution. The Chairman also issued a directive that caused disquiet among members of the Central Committee, for he claimed (in almost the identical words he used a decade later) that representatives of the bourgeoisie had 'sneaked' into the higher ranks of the party, the state bureaucracy and the army. Their object, the Chairman stressed, was to transform the dictatorship of the proletariat into a dictatorship of the bourgeoisie. 'Some of them we have seen through,' Mao said, but 'others not' and there were 'still people like Khrushchev nestling in our midst'.

The Central Commitee also issued two circulars with instructions that they were to be passed down to party leaders at county level. (A Chinese county varies in size on roughly the same pattern as English counties.) The first was about Peng Zhen, Politbureau member and Mayor of Peking, and the second about (General) Luo Ruiqing, who was still Chief of Staff under Lin Biao. In it Luo was accused of 'using the bourgeois line to oppose the proletarian military line'. The meaning of this was clear at the time for, as already said, Luo disagreed with Lin's view that it was more important for soldiers to study the thoughts of Chairman Mao than to become efficient shots on the rifle range. Further, Luo believed that it was imperative that the 3 million strong PLA should be rearmed with modern conventional weapons. He disagreed with Lin's ideas on a people's war and claimed that the Ministry of Defence had not learned from the Chinese experiences in Korea. Luo, the circular stated, had been ordered to undertake a personal self-criticism as a result of his wrong thinking and he had then attempted to commit suicide. This, the Central Committee claimed, was a cowardly way out and Luo was thus formally deprived of his post and expelled from the party. (I talked with him when he re-appeared with many rehabilitees in July 1975 looking extremely fit.)

During the discussions that took place while the circulars were being drafted, Chairman Mao displayed an all-too-human dislike of Yang Shangkun (Yang Shang-k'un), a party official who had made tape-recordings of the Chairman's instructions during the meetings of the Central Committee without his specific authorization. The Chinese are extremely sensitive about tape-recorders and no one (except top Chinese officials) is allowed to carry one into the Great Hall of the People. Normally speeches are perfected and retaped before their release. The records of Mao had somehow or other been replayed to outside audiences and Kang Sheng had heard about them. They were played and retaped by diplomats at the International Club. Yang's case was that expert shorthand writers could not cope with the Chairman's well-known and strong Hunanese accent, coupled with his use of earthy peasant words and lack of resonance in his voice. The elliptical style he adopted so often during meetings provided another difficulty. (Later in life the Chairman's niece, Wang Hairong, a Vice Minister at the Foreign Ministry, had the unenviable task of translating the Chairman's nods and grunts as well as his four-letter words into Mandarin Chinese when he received distinguished guests while another interpreter, generally Nancy Tang if English were required, would then translate into the language of the visitor.)

Chairman Mao did not want all his colourful abuse of colleagues and use of farmyard words to be circulated too far beyond the inner circles of the party. (He may have been wrong because the literal translations of his off-the-cuff comments are frequently impressive for their originality and freshness.)

Lin's account of a phoney coup d'état

When Lin Biao addressed the enlarged Politbureau meeting in secret on May 18th he passed from sombre to dramatic terms. The intelligence staff of the PLA, he claimed, had discovered that some members of the Central Committee had been engaged in underground counter-revolutionary activities and, to add to the serious charge, he named people who had been working with Peng Shen and Luo Ruiqing. Chairman Mao Zedong 'had not slept for many days', Lin stressed, as he had been forced to devote all his time to preventing a coup d'état. This was quite untrue according to a member of the Central Committee who met Mao at this time. Indeed, the coup d'état may well have been a figment of Lin's imagination as no one else has ever spoken of it. But he did announce that troops, obviously specially selected from 8341 Brigade – the brigade that, from Yenan days, was responsible for the personal safety of Chairman Mao and the Politbureau – had been sent to key and sensitive places such as radio stations, telephone exchanges, police posts and government offices in Peking. Lin also announced that two senior officers had been dismissed, which naturally paved the way for the introduction of 'his' men into these important vacancies. The episode was almost forgotten by most members of the Politbureau until 1971. (See Chapter 12.) The test for entry into 8341 Brigade was personal loyalty to Mao.

By this time party organizations at 'county' levels were beginning to receive and study the circulars about Peng Zhen and Luo Ruiqing and many of them expressed concern that the Chairman had been out of sight for so long. The cadres (officials) appear to have been dispirited and somewhat confused, fearing quite rightly that all was not well amongst the leadership.

Meanwhile, Mao's efforts were beginning to take effect at a higher level and from about June 1966 onwards Liu Shaoqi appears finally to have lost political control of the vital official party newspaper, the *People's Daily*. Further – as the inevitable purges of Peng Zhen and Luo Ruiqing took place – (Marshal) Ye Jianying, who had helped Mao to handle the Luo affair, was promoted in the party hierarchy, that is, he rose in the so-called 'pecking order' of the Politbureau. Ye was, too, an old friend of Premier Zhou.

After Peng Zhen's fall, because the Chairman was back in Hangzhou, Liu Shaoqi again assumed responsibility for the organization of the Cultural Revolution. He sent 'work teams' made up of stalwart party members as 'troubleshooters' to schools, government offices, factories and agricultural communes in what was termed a 'rectification campaign'. The idea was basically to increase the authority of the party in the trade unions, women's organizations and youth groups. But Mao, with the assistance of Kang Sheng, Jiang Qing and Chen Boda, now serving on the new Group of Five to sponsor the Cultural Revolution, did all in his power to negate Liu's efforts.

The first of a series of crises which led to the opening of the real Cultural Revolution occurred on May 23rd when Nie Yuanzi (Nieh Yuan-tzu), a lecturer in philosophy in Peking University, put up her now famous 'big character poster' denouncing the Deputy Director of the department in charge of the university together with the President of the university and the First Secretary of the Communist Party in Peking. Nie, an acquaintance of Jiang Qing, was already well known as a 'red'. She had run into many difficulties with the scholastic authorities as a result of her political zeal and she had already seen the circulars damning Peng and Luo and others for 'taking the capitalist road'.

Part of the text is worthy of reproduction:

Why are you so afraid of big character posters? This is a life and death class struggle to counter the Black Gang that launched frenzied attacks against the party, socialism and the thoughts of Chairman Mao Zedong. It is the best style of military mass activity to hold meetings and put up big character posters. But you 'lead' the masses by telling them not to hold meetings and not to put up posters ... by doing so you have suppressed the mass revolution, banned it and opposed it. We absolutely won't allow you to get away with this.

As with so many translations from Chinese to English the official rather stilted version still has a ring of the original language in it. The poster also urged all revolutionaries to break down 'the controls of the university and rise up in the struggle to wipe out ghosts and monsters and all Khrushchev-type revisionists'.

The weather was good at the time and not only students but hundreds of thousands of Chinese responded to the call. Within hours of the appearance of this poster at Peking University a foreigner loyal to the communist cause, who was then working as a translator for the Chinese Government, said some thousands were written and he admits that team leaders were saying, 'Anything goes, the most important object is to get the discussion going'; 'Do not wait until you have cast-iron evidence'; 'If you feel someone needs criticizing then criticize'; 'We'll sort out the truth later on.' Naturally, the party veterans were alarmed by what appeared to be anarchy and the so-called 'work teams' under Liu's influence made vigorous efforts to keep the numbers of posters to a minimum and their contents as innocuous as possible. But neither the work teams nor the cadres made an impact until Liu called a party meeting where Deng Xiaoping, the party General Secretary, this time supported Liu by saying the current poster efforts had gone too far and were taking on strong overtones that were not against revisionism but against the party and socialism too. The decision to 'counter-attack the attackers' apparently delighted the party officials and what has since been described by radical elements as the fifty days of 'white terror' from June 10th to July 31st was launched.

Mao was still in Hangzhou watching anxiously as old party hands in some areas seemed gradually to quench the enthusiasm of the masses on whom he had always counted. Soldiers had already established good contacts with many schools and universities during a campaign – 'learn from the PLA how to be self-sufficient and study Mao Zedong's thought' – to gain further influence in these institutions and, doubtless, in readiness to help them to form Red Guard units. But the whole situation was so confused that foreign ambassadors were openly bewildered and admitted that they did not know what was happening. This bewilderment also applied to many senior provincial members of the Chinese Communist Party who have since told me that they kept 'their heads down and their mouths closed'. In other words they decided to be as inconspicuous as possible until they were able to understand what the trouble was all about.

A decade later what had seemed to be a clear division between Liu, supported by party veterans, and the militant leftists from the top down to grass root levels did not then appear as a correct analysis of the scene. Indeed, it was far more complicated. Meanwhile, Liu used the work groups to go to government offices, universities and schools where there was trouble in order to protect the party organization. Frequently, the work teams were mistaken by the leftists for their supporters when they arrived, but they soon discovered their mistake when they said no more posters or demonstrations would be permitted. In many places the dispute was based on clashes of personality, when local party leaders had attempted to use the political scene as a means of ridding themselves of rivals who frequently held views similar to their own. In other areas the clash was a plain power struggle between groups of people with identical views, those in power and those out, or the 'haves' and the 'have nots'. Relics of this dispute still disturbed Chinese cities as late as 1976 (see later chapters).

Thanks to the practice the Chinese had, and indeed still have, of employing solitary English speakers as teachers in provincial towns, the position in five or six cities was well documented and even more so by the Red Guards themselves. Excitement grew and in some cases troubles blew up in provincial universities immediately after Peking radio broadcast the text of Nie Yuanzi's poster. Some university campuses were described as looking similar to Speakers' Corner at Hyde Park on a Sunday morning with students standing on stools or steps shouting their denunciation of the professors for such activities as 'luxurious living' and 'counterrevolutionary activities'. The living quarters of teachers were often ransacked and 'bourgeois books', including in one case a complete and rare set of Chaucer and Shakespeare, were burned whilst furniture was destroyed just for kicks. A few days later in many colleges and senior middle schools the teachers chosen as targets were made to walk round wearing dunces' caps proclaiming their crimes. Students naturally enjoyed getting away from the daily routine and the prospect of examinations. It was fun, too, for them to demonstrate in the delightful weather many regions of China enjoy in the early summer. The Chairman then gave their activities fresh vigour with his new slogan, 'To rebel against reactionaries is justified' whilst the Peking press urged students 'to sweep away freaks and monsters'.

Work teams

But there was frequently a nasty, seamy side to the period when the work teams sponsored by Liu and the Central Committee and backed by the local party machines entered the institutions. The students who had written the posters themselves became the object of even more unpleasant persecution than the professors had experienced a few weeks earlier. Liu Shaoqi, who realized the party veterans with the work teams were the shock troops fighting to preserve the authority of the Communist Party, naturally turned a blind eye to the excesses of his supporters. Indeed, Liu sent his wife Wang Guangmei as part of the work team to Qinghua University in Peking where she caused deep offence by arranging that the teenage children of party leaders were given key jobs on the grounds they were 'absolutely reliable'. Although this did not endear her to the students they appeared at that stage too bored or frightened to oppose her. She was to regret her actions later.

In Xi'an, in central China on the Yellow River, the once beautiful, ancient capital that houses the finest museum and the oldest university in China, the events were watched by an English teacher. When the work team arrived in the university they devoted their attention almost exclusively to a high-spirited girl named Wang Yongting (Wang Yung-ting) who had written some twenty big character posters attacking the authorities. The work team then ordered other students to write posters accusing Wang of being 'an enemy of the people'. She was, in addition, described as a 'witch' and a 'drowning dog'. The work team then 'arrested' her and forced her to write a series of confessions. But this was not enough and Wang was put on public display for some hours in what was called an 'animal exhibition'. Wang's personal possessions were taken away while seven students were detailed to 'guard' her until a trial could be arranged. Wang committed suicide by jumping from the window of the room in which she was held prisoner.

In Shanghai, later famous as a revolutionary city and within a short flight from the Chairman's base at Hangzhou, the old party veterans were said to have gone through the motions of organizing a Cultural Revolution campaign while, in fact, they did everything in their power to keep the students under control. The First Secretary of the Municipal Party Committee, Cao Diqiu (Ts'ao Ti-chiu), took a limited initiative in sponsoring Mao's initial drive but, at the same time, he warned the party that it was dangerous to 'wave red flags as a cover for an attack on the Red Flag' and added that he would take action against party members who did this. The work teams in Shanghai were reported to be particularly repressive and threatening.

There are two quite distinct schools of thought about Chairman Mao's policy during this period. A majority believed he could not lose. If the work teams sponsored by Liu and the party veterans suppressed the students, as they generally did, the radicals could complain that the masses in educational establishments were not being allowed to air their views. If, on the other hand, the work teams allowed the students full freedom to criticize, demonstrate and indeed revolt against the authorities they would soon get out of hand. Liu again could be criticized for not maintaining order. Nonetheless many Chinese and foreign observers at the time believed Mao was playing with fire and could easily have lost and been kicked upstairs as a powerless Head of State or, in Chairman Mao's own words, as 'a Buddha on a shelf', as Liu Shaoqi had initially planned.

Certainly, Chairman Mao knew that his majority on the Central Committee was indeed a narrow one – if it existed at all – hence his tendency to call 'enlarged meetings of the Politbureau' to which he added his own supporters. Living as he did in Hangzhou it must have been difficult for him to know just what was happening throughout the country, in spite of the careful reports he received from Jiang Qing and Kang Sheng. The uncertainty added to the Chairman's worries about the succession. For although there is no doubt that his basic aim in launching the Cultural Revolution was 'to keep revolution going', at the time Mao frequently talked to his visitors about the succession struggle, as for example when he received Deng Yingchao (Mme Zhou Enlai) who had been a member of the Central Committee in her own right for over twenty years. (Doubtless Deng called when Jiang Qing and her revolutionary friends were away as there was by this time no political love lost between the two women.)

The Chairman took particular interest in the way the struggle had evolved after Stalin's death and he wished, above all, to avoid such a state of affairs in China. Mao was also still bitter in his conversations about the ever-growing size of both the state and party bureaucracy and the privileges they enjoyed. Doubtless he wanted Deng Yingchao to pass this on to her husband, Premier Zhou, for China was, Mao feared, already developing the elite class he so deplored in the Soviet Union.

But before taking the final decision to return to Peking and leave his safe political base in Hangzhou, the Chairman spent nearly a week in discussions with his Defence Minister, Lin Biao. There was no doubt, Lin claimed, that the army was solidly one hundred per cent behind Chairman Mao. (Later events revealed that this was far from correct but it is important that the Chairman believed it to be so at the time.) Lin praised the work young cadres had done on a nationwide basis in rallying teenagers to support the Chairman. The soldiers who had been employed in the campaign had gone on to indoctrinate youth with the ideas that resulted in the formation of the Red Guards. In addition, Kang Sheng used the network of secret agents he controlled to co-operate with the militia and the defence forces in undertaking the initial work to set up the essential framework for the establishment of the Red Guards. But these were details passed over by the Chairman while he concentrated on the power struggle and a dramatic way to make a political comeback.

From the time he dined with 'foreign friends' in Peking on November 26th, 1965 until July the following year outsiders had little idea of his whereabouts. A picture of Mao did appear in the *People's Daily* in June; he is shown with a visiting Albanian and is flanked by Deng and Zhou, which proved that he was still alive but did not indicate where he was living. Reports that he was suffering from a variety of diseases from cancer to tuberculosis circulated abroad and were widely believed.

PART TWO
The Cultural Revolution

6

Mao's Yangtze Swim

On July 16th, 1966 the Chairman turned the spotlight of world propaganda on to himself as he plunged into the Yangtze River at Wuhan and crossed at least part of the river in the midst of groups of cheering young swimmers televised and photographed from accompanying boats. Mao looked extremely fit and, although he lacked the style of many of the young men and women swimming with him, for a man of seventy-two he made remarkable progress in the water. It is likely, however, that he took advantage of well-known fast currents to cover much of the 5 to 6 miles it was claimed he swam in sixty-five minutes. While the exploit was reported in the Chinese press in terms Europeans generally regard as absurd, because of the flowery language and exaggerations, there is no doubt that Mao made the point that he was still vigorous in his eighth decade. Although most foreigners were then sceptical about the Chairman having actually crossed the river, they recognized that he had appeared in robust health. The pictures issued by the New China News Agency, Xinhua, silenced the sceptics.

The Chairman returned to Peking two days later and called an enlarged meeting of the Central Committee. He then attacked Liu Shaoqi and Deng Xiaoping for the behaviour of the work teams in attempting to suppress revolution. The 'big bugs' of the party, the Chairman stressed, remained in their offices rather than visit places where disturbances were taking place. He vented his wrath against the new government and party offices with large staffs that Liu and Deng had set up, saying, 'I am alone here and I am doing quite well . . . we did not have such mammoth offices in the past and we made out.' The work teams formed by the party were, Mao claimed, frustrating the efforts of the students to express themselves. Let them air their views, Mao urged, adding, why should we be nervous and afraid of a few big character posters and reactionary slogans? But Mao added, perhaps as a sop to Liu, that it 'does the leftists no harm to be beaten up from time to time'. The Chairman's theme song on that day was, 'Unless you help kindle the flames of revolution you will assuredly be consumed by its fires.' (A typical Mao saying, designed for the Central Committee, but one that could not afterwards be used as a slogan as most of his theme songs were at that time.)

Jiang Qing in her own forthright manner later disclosed what the Chairman had told the committee members: 'You are too impatient, claiming the situation is confused or even beyond control'; 'The broad masses have made no mistakes'; 'Let them continue for a few months'; and 'If you think they are confused we can then take decisions when they have agitated – let off steam – to their hearts' content.' The Chairman also blamed those men who had been running the party in Peking during the past six months for the political confusions that had grown up there.

Both Liu and Deng were aware of the formation, still in embryonic form, of the Red Guards which they, somewhat naturally, viewed with apprehension, if not downright alarm. As a result of Mao's outbursts, the work teams were ordered to withdraw from almost all educational institutions. A boost to the projected Red Guard Movement was given by Mao when he sent a warm letter of support to the Red Guards of the middle school attached to Qinghua University in Peking, who claimed to have formed the first Red Guard unit.

The PLA and People's Militia trained groups of teenagers in schools and universities to form Red Guard units which were designed, before they went wild, to operate as militant, albeit junior members of the party to promote the teachings of the Chairman. Mao also expressed the hope to his radical friends that they might throw up some new youthful leaders.

On August 5th, 1966 the Chairman disclosed his intention to get rid of Liu and perhaps Deng too by putting up a big character poster of his own. Under the stirring title of 'Bombard the Headquarters' Mao indicated that the headquarters concerned were none other than those of the party itself. 'Some leading comrades from central down to the local party level have ... enforced a bourgeois dictatorship and struck down the stirring movement of the Great Cultural Revolution of the proletariat,' he wrote. 'They have ... suppressed revolutionaries, stifled opinions that differed from their own, imposed a white terror and felt very pleased with themselves ... how poisonous!' This was the only poster Mao ever wrote under his own name after becoming Chairman of the Communist Party. Immediately it appeared to those people in Peking who were 'politically aware', that is, actively engaged in party policy, that a vital power struggle was in progress. They guessed accurately that it had something to do with the recent campaigns and counter-campaigns in the universities and schools. Groups of men and women collected outside the party headquarters (they were fortunate to know the location of the building, for even party officials professed not to know this in the 1973–6 period). Chairman Mao, going out into the street, told the crowd, 'You should be concerned about the national crisis and you should carry out the Great Cultural Revolution to the last.' Few people, however, knew what he really meant.

At another enlarged meeting again of the Central Committee at the same period, the Liu faction complained that not only had the hall been packed with Mao's supporters but also that these outsiders rendered free speech impossible. Liu claimed, too, that Mao had violated his own creed of 'democratic centralism' in order to get his own way. Democratic centralism was Mao's form of ascertaining the views of the people – the 'broad masses' in his jargon. Policies considered by the Central Committee, on anything from foreign policy to the acceptable size of private plots, were passed down to party officials at regional, then county levels before reaching the grass roots for consideration. Comments and constructive observations were then passed back through the same channels to the Central Committee. Sometimes uninspired ideas were thrown up from the grass roots. Once, however, a decision had been taken and announced by the Central Committee no further discussion was allowed.

The meeting Mao called nonetheless ended as an official plenum which crossed the 't's' on all the decisions the Chairman had taken and the dismissals he had called for during the past four years. The Committee also endorsed his resolution on his foreign policy, which was critical of the Soviet Union. But even more important, the plenum adopted a sixteen-point communiqué evaluating the Cultural Revolution as it had progressed up to that point and setting down the policies for its future evolution. The document, which became known as the 'Sixteen Point Decision', was broadcast

over Peking radio. The first point re-established the aims of the
Cultural Revolution, which Liu's work teams had managed to
confuse. The targets were named as 'people in authority taking
the capitalist road' together with 'certain academic and cultural
authorities who continue to propagate bourgeois ideology'.

The second point emphasized the faith (of the party) in young
people who, in the month of May, had displayed their revolutionary
zeal by putting up big character posters and organizing political
debates. Point three stated that the outcome of the Cultural
Revolution will be determined by the ability of the leaders of the
party to arouse the masses boldly. Point four stressed that it was
up to the masses to liberate themselves and warned the cadres that
the masses can be relied upon and that they should not fear
disturbances. Point five asserted that more than 95 per cent of
officials and more than 95 per cent of the masses were against
rightists and revisionists (this had been the Chairman's figure since
the end of the Great Leap Forward). Point six indicated that
reason and not physical violence should be used in the current
struggle. Point seven was a clear condemnation of the work teams
sponsored by Liu Shaoqi. No action is to be taken in future against
students and school children 'because of problems that arise from
the movement' unless there is clear-cut evidence of crimes being
committed in which case the culprit should be handed over to the
authorities in accordance with the law. These were the most
important points. Neither the names of Liu Shaoqi nor Deng
Xiaoping were mentioned, possibly because the nature of the
leaders' errors had not yet been clearly defined.

The Red Guards

By a brilliant feat of organization, for which Defence Minister Lin
Biao was largely responsible, the 90-acre square in the centre of
Peking, Tiananmen, was filled with orderly rows of teenagers
wearing blue uniforms with red armbands before dawn on August
18th, 1966 and, with dramatic effect, as the sun rose in the east
casting its first rays on the famous pre-revolutionary red building
of the Gate of Heavenly Peace, Chairman Mao appeared on the
upper balcony. The boys and girls who had been singing and

shivering for much of the night burst into a gigantic cheer that turned into a roar. Mao was wearing the olive-green uniform of a soldier with his cap pulled down on his forehead. Behind and above the Chairman was his picture, gigantically enlarged. Other buildings carried slogans: 'May Chairman Mao Live 10,000 Years' (a classical wish in China for all emperors); 'Long Live the People's Republic'; and, long since out of fashion, 'Workers of the World Unite'. Huge pictures of Marx, Engels, Stalin, Lenin and Sun Yat-sen were erected in front of the modern Great Hall of the People on the west side of the square and the whole area was ablaze with thousands of red flags.

The Chairman left the speeches to others, waving his hand from time to time to the enthusiastic crowd and, at given moments, which were televised and filmed, mixing with the youngsters. He 'exchanged revolutionary experiences' with one group and later in the day allowed a pretty girl to fasten a Red Guard armband to his uniform. By accepting the armband Mao gave the full weight of his authority to the new Red Guard Movement. While doing this the Chairman suggested that the girl should change her name from Pingping (meaning graceful gentleness) to Yawu (desire to be warlike). The great weakness of the event was the ineffectiveness of the main speaker, Lin Biao, who read his text in what was universally described at the time as a 'thin uneasy voice'. Despite the fact that he had just achieved his life's ambition in acquiring the accolade of Chairman Mao's 'closest comrade in arms', in addition to having displaced Liu Shaoqi as the number two man in the Communist Party hierarchy, he nonetheless looked nervous and ill at ease.

In his speech Lin praised the Chairman in an unreal and extravagant manner and, in terms he was afterwards to regret, as 'the genius of world revolution'. (Mao objected to this almost immediately.) Lin called for the sweeping away of 'old things' and the striking down of all 'followers of the capitalist road'. Liu Shaoqi, who remained Head of State and had had only recently learned of his official demotion from second to eighth place in the hierarchy, was, on the film of the event, wandering round the back of the platform unsmiling, uncomfortable and obviously unhappy.

The man who may well have most disliked the whole spectacular parade, Premier Zhou Enlai, looked completely at ease, wearing an open-necked short-sleeved bush jacket on that hot August day and not the long blue-sleeved Mao tunic used by the other members of the Politbureau. Zhou appeared, like a good television actor, to be taking an interest in everything that was happening in the square below him. In his speech Zhou repeated, in milder terms, Lin's praise of Chairman Mao and greeted the crowd, begging the students in Peking to act as good hosts to the thousands who had travelled to the capital from the provinces.

Nie Yuanzi, the radical professor who had pasted up the first poster at the university, concentrated her speech on attacking bourgeois customs and habits, while Chen Boda – named as leader of Chairman Mao's revolutionary group – presided over the giant assembly.

After the rally the emotions of the Red Guards were at fever pitch. New slogans appeared quoting Chairman Mao saying that 'destruction must come before construction'. Chen Boda urged Red Guard leaders 'to be ready to fight' and many groups began to implement Chairman Mao's directive to eradicate old ideas, old culture and old customs by visiting newspaper and government offices on what at first seemed like a tour of inspection. The Red Guards complained if there were any pictures on the walls other than portraits of Chairman Mao and promptly destroyed photographs of wives and children that some officials had misguidedly placed under the glass tops of their desks. As success went to the heads of the Red Guards they ordered government officials to shave off their moustaches or cut their hair. Indeed, their behaviour deteriorated rapidly and soon Red Guards were entering office buildings without ceremony and searching through the private possessions of officials for bourgeois books, cosmetics, western music or pictures. Officials believed to be the grandsons or granddaughters of landlords or rich merchants had a specially hard time. There could be little doubt that Chairman Mao was aware of what was happening within a few hundred yards of his home and office in Zhongnanhai. Indeed, this enclosure behind nine foot high walls, which includes two lakes with numerous clumps of weeping willow trees and pavilions, was one of the few places never forcibly entered by the Red Guards.

After dealing with government offices, the Red Guards turned their attention to shops and restaurants. The neon lights were pulled down in the main shopping street of Wangfuching from establishments selling silks, fur coats and other goods the Red Guards classed as luxuries. Hairdressers were warned not to give European-type or elaborate cuts and styles and even restaurants were ordered to 'simplify' their menus. The thousands of Red Guards out 'exchanging revolutionary experiences', frequently the euphemism for a good gossip and sight-seeing tour, wanted cheap noodle soup rather than expensive Peking duck.

Commission shops (really second-hand shops which still exist in every city of China today) were raided for 'old' or 'fancy' objects which were promptly destroyed. The scene deteriorated still further when Red Guards began to force their way into flats and living quarters. Calls to the police brought no help. The invasion of important government offices was stopped – to be resumed at a later stage in the Cultural Revolution – after bands of Red Guards took files from which they extracted both personal and secret information that they quickly used on big character posters and in their own newspapers. One foreign diplomat found classified Chinese documents 'blowing about the street' and some found their way to Hong Kong where they were sold.

Premier Zhou Enlai was later applauded for averting a complete breakdown of the administration during this early difficult period. There were reports, which have since been confirmed, that the Chairman reached some form of secret and unofficial agreement with his Premier not then known even to other members of the Politbureau. While Mao was urging the Red Guards and others to create even greater chaos in order to get rid of party veterans, the canny old Chairman knew that food must be produced, not to mention coal and oil, in order to avoid anarchy. And Mao knew, too, that the only man with the necessary administrative experience coupled with the required ability and charm to get on with all sorts and conditions of people was Zhou.

At first Premier Zhou disliked and indeed mistrusted the whole project concerning the formation of the Red Guards but he doubtless also saw that the political tide was moving more in favour of Mao and the radicals than towards Liu Shaoqi, his friend, Deng Xiaoping and the moderates. Zhou agreed to attend rallies on condition that the Red Guards would be prevented from disturbing agricultural and industrial production. Further, that 'certain institutions of learning', such as those where Chinese nuclear scientists are trained and senior PLA training establishments, would not be disturbed or molested. They were, in any case, well away from the main cities.

Agricultural communes near to big cities and provincial railway stations were certainly bothered by Red Guard units demanding food and lodgings but, on the whole, the Cultural Revolution made comparatively little impact on their productive capacity at this stage. There were major problems in the transportation system, not unnaturally, as millions of Red Guards swanned around the country. This caused a reduction in essential freight traffic by almost 10 per cent. The Red Guards even hijacked a train bound for Vietnam that was loaded with Russian arms. It was at this point Premier Zhou made one of his many interventions with the Chairman and persuaded him it was time the Red Guards went back to their homes in order that food for domestic consumption and products for export might be transported around the country. Before that moment arrived seven more gigantic rallies took place in Peking. At the second one Lin Biao congratulated the Red Guards on their efforts to 'wash away the sludge and filth from the old society'. He repeated his warnings about the bourgeois and revisionist leaders who had 'wormed their way' into high positions in the party. At the third rally Lin returned to the Chairman's poster 'Bombard the Headquarters' and used this as his main theme.

Red Guard units were being formed around this time in almost every sizeable town, indeed sometimes there were three or four different units competing with one another to obtain recruits and fist fighting between rival gangs frequently took place. Some factions stole arms from army camps and used them against their rivals. Students were killed and, most unusual in China, a handful of girls raped in the disorders. Hooliganism developed and not only were towns quite literally painted red by the teenagers but the decorations and the statues in hundreds of beautiful old temples were destroyed. Since then the temples have remained closed, although much restoration work is now in progress. Some celebrated people were molested, including the distinguished elderly Vice Chairman of the National People's Congress, Madame Soong

Ching Ling, the widow of China's first President, Sun Yat-sen. Although a sister of Madame Chiang Kai-shek, she threw her lot in with the communists although she only joined the party on her deathbed in 1981. Her bourgeois style of life – she changed for dinner every evening – attracted the attention of the Red Guards. Premier Zhou later apologized to her and admitted there were, perhaps, too many cases of hooliganism.

However, no apologies were forthcoming after hooligans entered the Sacred Heart convent smashing religious relics and badly beating up the elderly nuns who had remained in China as much needed teachers of foreign languages at schools attended by the children of diplomats. Many thousands of people were so scared they destroyed their own possessions before the Red Guards could get near them. Caged birds, goldfish bowls and potted plants were considered specially bourgeois and several people have told how they killed their birds and destroyed plants before the Red Guards discovered they owned such damning objects. Others broke old gramophone records and smashed their western musical instruments such as violins and guitars as these were repugnant to youthful Red Guard enthusiasts. Fear grew so great that people in Guangzhou, who over the years had collected a number of foreign objects from Hong Kong, burned their imported blankets and other presents given to them by relatives. For Red Guards frequently entered flats in Guangzhou and seized all foreign things, seriously molesting the owners afterwards.

Diplomats were shocked when seemingly innocent people were attacked. Neither the police, nor even the army, responded to calls for help; nor did the defence forces make efforts to maintain order, indeed, Premier Zhou Enlai admitted years later that the armed forces were then under orders not to interfere with Red Guard activities. However, it is difficult to believe that the big character poster claiming that Premier Zhou declared 'killing was understandable' was true, for Zhou's period of approved murders was limited to the secret work he did in Shanghai in the early days of the civil war and liberation. Even Chairman Mao, since the mid 1950s, when the Party was well and truly established, had been opposed to executions on the grounds that 'you cannot cut off a man's head as though it were a stick of celery'.

First efforts to dampen radical enthusiasm

In an effort to dampen Red Guard activities during the autumn, Lin Biao reminded them that the main targets of their attacks 'must be those within the party who were following the capitalist road'. Many party leaders in Peking and the provinces were coming under attack from the Red Guards. Evidence of the power struggle taking place in the Politbureau and amongst the leadership, which was first disclosed by Chairman Mao's poster 'Bombard the Headquarters', was revealed on October 17th when large posters appeared in Peking urging the population 'to defend Chairman Mao to the last'. (It is interesting to note that identically worded posters appeared in Peking after Vice Premier Deng Xiaoping's second disgrace in April 1976.) On the following day slogans for the mammoth Red Guard rally were changed three times and reports began to circulate that a new and dangerous power struggle was in progress and the outcome uncertain. The millions who attended the rally were disappointed because instead of the normal speeches and adulation of the Chairman, the party leaders merely drove through Tiananmen Square and the rally was dismissed. At a meeting in the evening Premier Zhou, doing his usual job of appeasement through tact and charm, attempted to explain the absence of speakers by saying that Jiang Qing was unwell and Lin Biao had not had time to prepare his speech.

Lin's repeated accusations to senior party members, including Premier Zhou, that Liu Shaoqi and Deng were 'plotting' a coup were then impossible to explain. Some members of the Central Committee believe Lin knew the Chairman's ultimate aim was to get rid of Liu and Deng but with as much popular support as possible. And Lin, personally, was anxious to bring the Red Guard revolt to a speedy end as this was putting an enormous strain on the armed forces as well as denying them transport. Lin's enemies, even before he organized his own coup in 1971, said he believed Liu and Deng were unbeatable because, although Zhou had thrown in his lot with the Chairman, Zhou was still operating in his typical diplomatic manner as a go-between and moderate. Certainly Zhou and Kang Sheng, the Maoist head of the secret security, both stated after investigations that the plot report was utterly unfounded.

The coup accusations certainly rebounded on the Chairman's 'closest comrade in arms' and Lin, either of his own free will or at the request of the Chairman, dropped out of the national limelight for the next five months. Meanwhile, as a result of some backstage negotiations, Deng, who up to that moment had been obstinate, made his first self-criticism and admitted that both he and Liu had from time to time taken a 'bourgeois reactionary line'. But after this Liu and Deng both continued to attend mass rallies as members of the Politbureau. The Cultural Revolution group that had been loosely under party control now became a separate organization. Chen Boda became the Director with Jiang Qing as his deputy and her old supporter Kang Sheng as adviser together with Zhang Chunqiao from Shanghai, who with Yao Wenyuan had assisted Mao to arrange for the publication of the article criticizing the play *Hai Jui Dismissed from Office*. This had touched off the Cultural Revolution Movement.

The new Cultural Revolution Group moved into premises in the same building as the important MAC. Although Premier Zhou Enlai himself had admitted that travel was a good thing in August, public statements made by moderates in the Chinese Communist Party gradually veered towards reducing the number of Red Guards who came to Peking, ostensibly and officially, to be received by Chairman Mao before returning to their home towns to form Red Guard units in them. Between August and November over 11 million young men and women came to the capital.

In addition, units of the Red Guards were travelling round the countryside visiting warm springs, centres of tourism or the 'sacred places of communism' such as Chairman Mao's birthplace at Shaoshan. The strain on the railway system became too great and during the last big rallies in Peking on November 25th and 26th the Red Guards were told that they would be 'the last of the year and no more would be held' 'until the warm days of spring 1967'.

Further, the authorities warned the Red Guards that they must leave Peking by December 20th for after that free travel and free food would no longer be available. The political commissars of the PLA, who had been co-operating with the Red Guards, were ordered to see the Red Guards to the trains and then return to their units. Later Chairman Mao, one must guess, reproached by Premier Zhou on the confusion in the transportation system, admitted the disastrous turmoil he had created. The Chairman is reported to have said disarmingly at a meeting of an enlarged Politbureau, 'I cannot blame you if you have complaints against me.' He also admitted his surprise and astonishment at the violent impact caused by his personal directives to the Red Guards. The Chairman's defence was that errors were unavoidable and although he did not deny that many mistakes had been made, especially by himself, with the result that people had died, nonetheless, Mao claimed, it had taken twenty-eight years to bring the Communist Party to its present strength and the Cultural Revolution was only in its fifth month. The Chairman stressed that in his view 'experience could only be gained after five years' but he did not explain the magic of the five-year span. Nor did he expound upon his reasons for having said earlier that 'a few months of disturbances' would not be a bad thing.

About this time Chairman Mao again left Peking for Hangzhou and Jiang Qing, acting on his orders, assumed a leading role in the public direction of the Cultural Revolution. As a former actress, she already had presence and she quickly developed an attractive platform manner that delighted her youthful audiences despite the fact her cracks were generally harsh and at someone else's expense. The official Director of the Cultural Revolution Group, Chen Boda, was a brilliant writer and, indeed, had been Mao's amanuensis for years, but was such a poor speaker that Jiang was frequently the main performer at rallies.

Somewhat naturally Jiang Qing turned her attention to the cultural sphere. She was already 'adviser' to the PLA on culture and in a series of rallies she severely criticized those who had been in charge of the Peking Opera which had been producing traditional shows as well as western type films, ballets and concerts. Many of her old enemies in the cultural sphere from Shanghai were dismissed and replaced by people who wanted to introduce revolutionary themes into all entertainments. Heroes and heroines must, Jiang Qing stressed, represent the masses – workers, peasants and soldiers – not emperors and mandarins as in the past. Indeed, the new look in entertainment was extended to conjuring, acrobatics, puppet shows and all forms of ballet and dancing. Western music of all kinds too was dubbed 'bourgeois' and decadent. At the same time flirtatious scenes were cut from all productions and the sex element virtually eliminated. This is not easy to explain in view of Chairman Mao's own sexy language and the fact that he had had three wives and enjoyed the company of pretty and vicacious women throughout his adult life. The period of extreme sexual austerity coincided with this period of the Cultural Revolution when millions of youthful Red Guards were still touring the countryside. Considering the gigantic numbers involved there were comparatively few love affairs that resulted in pregnancy.

Although Jiang Qing was not at that time a member of the Politbureau, having dealt with the 'bad elements' in show business she then turned her attention to the party leadership.

Early in December the Red Guards arrested Peng Zhen (Politbureau member and Mayor of Peking) in the middle of the night and a few days later they picked up the former Director of Propaganda, Lu Dingyi (Lu Ting-yi), who had displeased Jiang Qing, and the disgraced Chief of Staff, Luo Ruiqing, together with Yang Shangkun (Yang Shang-k'un), known as one of the '28 Bolesheviks', and other senior officials. A week or so later the former Defence Minister, Marshal Peng Dehuai, already under house arrest, was flown to Peking in a military aircraft. All these arrests took place after the Central Committee had issued a stern instruction obviously aimed at the Red Guards forbidding unauthorized arrests, torture, or the illegal detention of people. Anyone engaged in such unlawful activities would, the order stated, be dealt with in full conformity with the law. It is now known that this instruction was inspired by Premier Zhou who was by this time deeply concerned by the unruly behaviour of the Red Guards in the capital. Chen Boda and Jiang Qing did not even bother to attend that meeting of the Central Committee. However, Jiang Qing did issue a somewhat similar instruction that the Red Guards should not use force or coercion. But there remains a grave suspicion that even if she did not inspire the arrests it was her organization directing the Cultural Revolution that arranged for the military aircraft to transport the former Defence Minister Peng Dehuai from Chengdu to the capital.

Public trials by the masses

As a result of these arrests one of the most shaming incidents of the Cultural Revolution took place in the Workers' Stadium on

December 12th, 1966 when Peng Zhen, Luo Ruiqing, and Yang Shangkun were subjected to a public 'trial' by 10,000 Red Guards. According to communist Chinese eye-witnesses they were already physically frail but whether from mild torture, fear, shortage of food or a combination of all three was not stated. Luo, who was one of the last men to be rehabilitated by Premier Zhou Enlai and Vice Premier Deng Xiaoping in 1975, appeared in the stadium with his leg in plaster, perhaps to confirm the report that he had attempted to commit suicide by jumping from his prison window rather than face a trial by the Red Guards. But the main object was to make these men lose face so dramatically and completely that there could – so Jiang then thought, erroneously, as it turned out – be no comeback.

They were made to apologize to the masses and bow their heads in shame and to plead for forgiveness. The crowd enjoyed the spectacle of the mighty fallen and spat, jeered, pointed and abused. Communists sometimes suggest in China today that 'face' is no longer important but they are deceiving themselves. I have seen senior officials remain with bowed heads for weeks after losing face by being mildly reprimanded by Premier Zhou in front of foreigners.

Had the group directing the Cultural Revolution decided to allow these men to die or had them executed the crowd would have missed a free entertainment and the men might have become martyrs. Without face they could do or say nothing, or so it was thought. In all probability they earned their daily bowl of rice in the manner of all 'enemies of the people' who if not in prison are generally engaged in the dirtiest and most unpleasing tasks, such as collecting or transporting human excreta. In one or more of these cases, Premier Zhou Enlai intervened to seek more agreeable treatment on the grounds that these men were old and sick. In any event, they were not in the countryside for long. Although Chairman Mao may not have been able to prevent this and other humiliating scenes from taking place, he was kept extremely well informed of day-to-day events and he could easily have issued a private message to the group responsible for the organization of the Cultural Revolution to 'cool it'.

Premier Zhou Enlai naturally remained in Peking generally working through much of the night in his office on the third floor of the Great Hall of the People. In the day Zhou devoted his time to ensuring that the administrative machine did not break down altogether under the strain of the disturbances caused by the Red Guards. The Premier, too, made many attempts to influence the Red Guard leaders towards a more moderate policy but it was not easy even for him. Around the turn of the year there was some evidence to suggest that the group around Chairman Mao was still almost equally divided on the basic issue of whether Liu Shaoqi and Deng Xiaoping should remain in their high positions in the state and party or be dismissed. But this did not suit the Red Guards who could not gain access to Zhongnanhai where the Chairman and Chinese leaders lived behind their high pre-revolutionary red wall guarded by a first-class infantry brigade housed in several nearby barracks. Thus Liu and Deng, or any other members of the Politbureau not under arrest who were likely to be attacked by the Red Guards, had merely to stay at home and sit it out.

Maddened by their inability to talk with or molest Liu and his wife, one of the Red Guard units trapped Wang Guangmei (Mme Liu) by sending a false message claiming that her stepdaughter was badly injured and her signature was required at the hospital before a very necessary operation could be performed. Wang was then virtually ambushed and taken to Qinghua University where it will be recalled she had previously ventured as a leader of one of the work teams. After more than eight hours of fierce interrogation Wang was made to confess before a kangaroo court that she had indulged in bourgeois habits together with her husband who was, of course, still Head of State. Wang promised to send the students further reports exposing the 'reactionary line' taken by her husband. There is, however, no evidence that she ever did this and the whole incident must have produced a profound shock, as doubtless it was meant to do, in the Liu camp.

While Mao was urging the Red Guards 'to bombard the headquarters' and cause general havoc in the party hierarchy, it is only fair to admit that he had a case of sorts. Many of the party officials had formed themselves into an elite society enjoying a higher standard of living than the masses not only in Peking but in many provincial and county headquarters. Indeed, there seemed at that time every likelihood that China would follow in the steps of the Russian Communist Party in this respect. Although Chairman Mao was influenced by Jiang Qing in her diatribes against Liu's wife for wearing smart clothes and jewellery on a state visit to Indonesia, Mao also wanted to break up and destroy the new elite class that was forming. Further, Mao admitted that in the period immediately before Liberation people had been admitted to membership of the Communist Party en masse without going through the normal period of instruction; thus many of them were really 'revisionists' at heart. In addition, outside Peking up to one-third of the Chinese administration at a low level was still in the hands of clerks and others who had served Chiang Kai-shek and the Guomindang. Although these old clerks were in fact far too cowardly and timid, like most Chinese bureaucrats, to take any initiative, they would, it must be assumed, have rallied to any anti-communist invader. But it was well recognized that any such move was already in the realms of fantasy. Communism in China was and is there to stay though what form it will take in the future is impossible to forecast. Whilst it was reasonable for Chairman Mao's viewpoint to want to break up these two quite different groups, in the state and party, it is impossible to envisage who would have replaced them. And in fact the party leaders were in deep trouble after the Cultural Revolution when so many of the high-ranking cadres had been purged. The inefficiency in the bureaucracy accounted later for Premier Zhou's determination not only to rehabilitate Vice Premier Deng but also many former officers from the state, army and party.

7

Shanghai, Radical City

Peking and Shanghai became the pace-setters for the Cultural Revolution, although the prelude to action was lengthy in Shanghai because the First Secretary of the Party Committee, Cai Diqiu and his deputy, Zhen Peixian (Chen Pei-h'sien), were both stubborn and well-entrenched supporters of Liu Shaoqi. Further, Zhen had somewhat tactlessly suggested that Chairman Mao at seventy-two was 'getting too old and should take a rest'.

On the purely practical level the Shanghai Party Committee had printed and distributed over 400,000 copies of Liu Shaoqi's book on *How to Be a Good Communist*. These still clogged bookshops and left but little space in the soldier's kitbag for the 'Little Red Book' of Chairman Mao's thoughts which, with a preface by Lin Biao, had been rolling off the presses by the million since just before the first Red Guard rallies were held in Peking. (Over 83 million copies were eventually printed according to the official Chinese News Agency, Xinhua.) The only senior cadre in Shanghai to take a strong Maoist line already in 1965 was Zhang Chunqiao who was spending much of his time organizing the Cultural Revolution on a national basis in Peking. The rebel movement in Shanghai University and to a lesser degree in the factories was inspired by Nie Yuanzi, the woman who was to put up the first poster in Peking. She arrived in the autumn of 1966 with a maximum of publicity and stayed at the Peace Hotel. In addition, those undergraduates and senior school children who had attended Red Guard rallies in Peking in 1966 were anxious to establish units in their home town. The phrase 'exchange revolutionary experiences' was extremely fashionable and this took up hours of the Red Guards' working day. Nie Yuanzi transformed the Peace Hotel for a few days into a Red Guard meeting ground and publicity centre. Standing on the bund it remains a perfect example of art nouveau where Noel Coward in the early 1920s had written *Private Lives*. Until 1974 there was an old white-gloved English-speaking lift boy who remembered Noel Coward and the glorious days of the 'Palm Court's Jazz band'.

Wang Hongwen (Wang Hung-wen), later to become third man in the party 'pecking order' after Chairman Mao and Premier Zhou at the 10th Party Congress in August 1973, was already making a name for himself as a strong supporter of the Cultural Revolution at the No 17 textile mill. By November 1966 Shanghai Workers' Revolutionary Rebel General Headquarters was established and a public rally organized. Over 40,000 people gathered in the main square and listened to highly inflammatory speeches until nine in the evening when a delegation went off to see the 'reactionary' Mayor, Cao Diqiu. While he kept them waiting in an effort to dampen their ardour and spirits, the rebels decided to send a delegation to Peking to consult the party leadership. The train was, however, held up on the instructions of the Mayor when only twenty minutes from Shanghai Station at Anting. Here the workers' delegates were urged, indeed ordered, to go home but they sat passively singing revolutionary songs in the train and reading the 'Little Red Book' until Zhang Chunqiao arrived ten hours later in Shanghai having travelled in a special aircraft from Peking.

As a member of the group in charge of the Cultural Revolution Zhang Chunqiao was able to negotiate almost all their demands, making their journey to Peking unnecessary. Further, Zhang announced the recognition of the Workers' Revolutionary General Headquarters (WGHQ) as an official revolutionary organization. Big character posters publicized the workers' viewpoint; so, too, did hastily printed leaflets that were thrown into the crowded streets of Shanghai from passing military lorries. Outwardly the Mayor put a good face on the unexpected turn of events but in what was termed by the radicals 'an incredible act of perfidy' he ordered the public security bureau to list as 'counter revolutionaries' some fifteen leaders from the No 17 textile mill, including Wang Hongwen. By mid-December there were two distinct powers in Shanghai, the Workers' Revolutionary General Headquarters on one side and the Shanghai City Administration co-operating with the Party Committee on the other. Seeing their powers slipping away and a danger of riots, the City Mayor, Cao Diqiu, and his associates appealed to Peking for support.

Troubles and demonstrations spread to the docks where foreign

ships were kept waiting as there was no labour available for off-
loading cargoes. Peasants began to talk of holding up supplies of
food to the city until prices were arranged that satisfied them.
Admittedly, contract or casual workers both in factories and on the
docks had a raw deal for they earned far less than permanent
employees in factories and received no medical benefits or pensions
– they were sent back penniless to their villages when they grew
old. When the casual workers held a series of demonstrations,
much to their surprise their demands were met. Some dock
workers were given back pay in an effort to gain their sympathy
while others were offered large bonuses and a handsome increase
in their weekly wages.

The stores of Shanghai were soon denuded of all consumer
goods by what was termed 'economism', or the material benefits
the municipality was handing out to keep the peace. But these
extra wages, 'sugar-coated bullets' as they were already known, did
not prevent the gradual breakdown in the authority of the Mayor
as the very life of the city was threatened by strikes in the power
station, railways and water supply.

What later became known as the 'January storm' in Shanghai
opened on January 3rd, 1967 when the WGHQ took over the
Liberation Daily and threw out the 'capitalist roaders', the supporters of the Mayor who had been editing and printing it. On the
following day the paper carried 'a message to all the Shanghai
people'. In it the WGHQ described the grave situation in the city
and called on 'all revolutionaries to rebuff the evil wind of
economism'. At the same time they were urged to keep production
going, in order to frustrate the plots of the Mayor and reactionary
elements who had been running the city.

Many activists in Shanghai had read Marx's work on the Paris
Commune which was available in Chinese; the party's ideological
monthly *Red Flag* had carried a sympathetic article on the Commune in the previous year by its editor, Chen Boda, who was by
this time chief of the Cultural Revolution Group in Peking. As a
result of the *Red Flag* article and renewed publicity on the subject in
Shanghai, plant after plant was taken over by workers. Meanwhile at
the request of Zhang detachments of the army took up positions to
guard the radio station, power plants, docks, bridges and banks
against saboteurs. (Marx had criticized the communards in Paris

for not having seized the banks.) It was a classical revolutionary takeover with Zhang Chunqiao and Yao Wenyuan directing operations while Wang Hongwen was in the forefront of the 'battle'.

Three million people reportedly attended a mass rally on January 6th, 1967 that overthrew the Party Committee and municipal authorities and deposed Cao Diqiu as Mayor. Five days later the Central Committee of the party and the State Council in Peking sent messages recognizing the new revolutionary authorities in Shanghai. Further, the group organizing the Cultural Revolution issued two new slogans: 'Learn from the experiences of the revolutionary groups in Shanghai' and 'Cast away illusions and prepare for struggle'. On January 16th Chairman Mao formally approved the WGHQ seizure of power.

It is extremely difficult for many Anglo-Saxons to understand that tens of thousands of people actually returned their bonuses as well as overtime pay, although there was no legal or moral obligation to do so. It shows that there existed among the youthful Chinese many who really believed in equality. Maoists, however, claim that everyone from factory manager to cleaner should earn the same wages, 'each according to his needs' until money can finally be abolished after world revolution has taken place.

Thousands of young people who had already been sent – directed – to work in the barren countryside used this period to return home to the bright lights and political excitements of Shanghai. Eye-witnesses report tens of thousands of people milling round the streets throughout the day with frequent fist fights between rival groups of young people who had little to do but scream their support for Chairman Mao. Zhang issued warnings on the maintenance of order. He also cautioned the rebels against 'petty bourgeois anarchism', ultra democracy and self-interest. Indeed, when some students at Fudan University kidnapped three writers and held them in the college grounds, a small armed unit of the PLA went in to rescue them. What had been glorious revolution one month caused them to be dubbed 'ultra-leftists' in the next. This frequently happened during the Cultural Revolution and, indeed, after it.

During this early period of 1967 the establishment of a Shanghai People's Commune was seriously planned. It was finally decided that the ruling body should be elected by the thirty-eight organizations that formed the WGHQ, each one having the right to elect two members. The organizers, who had taken over from the Mayor, were keen to revive this revolutionary form of city control and began to organize the new administration. Yet another mammoth rally was organized and in February the formation of the Shanghai People's Commune was formally announced. The long-winded declaration stated 'the former Shanghai Municipal Party Committee and Municipal Council have been smashed! All power belongs to the Shanghai People's Commune!' The chief sponsors, Zhang Chunqiao and Yao Wenyuan, attended the rally and it was assumed that the Central Committee of the party had blessed the project which was to 'practise democratic centralism', which, as has already been explained, was taught by Chairman Mao.

Soon after the commune began to function Zhang and Yao were 'ordered' by Chairman Mao to go to see him in Peking immediately. It soon became strangely apparent that Chairman Mao deeply disapproved of the whole project and finally convinced the two Shanghai radical leaders that it was a big mistake. As a result of Mao's interference the commune was renamed 'The Shanghai Revolutionary Committee' on February 14th.

Mao turns against the commune

What had changed the Chairman's mind will always remain something of a mystery because the reasons he gave were not the ones that would normally be important to him. He told Zhang and Yao that the establishment of a Shanghai People's Commune would create a series of problems and he doubted whether they had thought them all out. Then, thinking aloud, the Chairman said, 'If the whole of China were to set up People's Communes, should the People's Republic of China change its name to the People's Communes of China?' 'Would others recognize us?' Mao asked, having rarely shown such concern about diplomatic gestures. 'Maybe the Soviet Union would not recognize us,' Mao said, 'but Britain and France would. And what should *we* do about our ambassadors in various countries?'

The Chairman then told Zhang and Yao that scores of places

had applied to establish People's Communes but the Central Committee had issued a document saying no place outside Shanghai might do this. At the same time, Mao urgently advised the Shanghai leaders 'to make a change' and transform the commune into a Revolutionary Committee or City Committee. 'Communes are too weak when it comes to suppressing counter-revolution,' Mao claimed – maybe this was his real reason for opposing the commune project. Mao told his niece years later that what he most disliked about the communes was the free elections, for the Chairman's group could have been outvoted by either the right or the left. 'Think of the danger if this were to spread over the whole country,' he said, revealingly.

Mao insisted that all major decisions must be taken by 'the Centre', which meant they were under his guidance. He could not bear any kind of separatist organization that could take important decisions not under the direction of the Politbureau. The Chairman also gave new instructions about slogans: 'Do not say in future "Overthrow the diehards who persist in following the revolutionary line," but "Overthrow those in authority taking the capitalist road."' Chairman Mao also ordered the Shanghai representatives to cease using a quotation 'The world is ours', which was extremely popular. Mao added that he could not remember using it although he had done so in 1920 and, even later, when speaking to young people – 'The world is ours; but most of all it is yours.'

Throughout January there were factional clashes in many parts of China including Nanchang, Guangzhou, Xi'an and even the remote areas of Xinjiang in the extreme north-west near to where China's nuclear installations and missile sites are located. In Peking, Red Guards demonstrated against the Soviet Embassy for nearly a week, hanging stuffed effigies of Brezhnev and Kosygin from trees in the street just outside the gates and with loudspeakers denouncing the 'revisionist renegades of the international communist movement'. Wall posters multiplied in the capital where, with the exception of Lin Biao and the Chairman himself, no Chinese leaders were immune from Red Guard attacks.

Meanwhile, Jiang Qing, after considerable pressure had been exerted by Premier Zhou, personally admonished the radicals for their attacks on the Foreign Minister, Chen Yi, who had reportedly confessed his mistakes. She and other radical leaders, however, were then attacked themselves in wall posters by 'ultra-leftists' in February and March in Peking. Mao admitted in 1970, to visitors in Peking, that the factional battles had been fierce and he deplored the lack of discipline on the part of the Red Guards. But the Chairman, with his keen sense of the political scene, realized that he together with Chen Boda and the group running the Cultural Revolution had virtually lost control of its direction. There can be no doubt that he was deeply concerned, for a year or two earlier he had said that if the people and the army did not follow him, he would start all over again as a guerrilla on a mountain top and fight his way back to power.

One observer at the time said China resembled a spastic whose limbs were unresponsive to its brain. As a result, the Chairman began taking practical steps in an effort to bring the Red Guards to heel while he still had Liu Shaoqi and Deng Xiaoping to deal with. After consultations with Lin Biao, Chairman Mao publicly instructed military commanders to go to the aid of his radical followers when they were 'assailed' by 'counter-revolutionaries'. While this order might sound reasonable to the Chairman, perhaps even to Lin Biao, it was quite impossible for a military commander, say, in Guangzhou or Urumqi to know which of the Red Guard units were really radical for they all operated under the name of Chairman Mao. Further, there was and indeed still is a tendency in the defence forces to oppose those elements that threaten the stability of the area in which they are based. But in general they did initially support the Red Guards. At the same time a series of admonitions from Peking went out urging the radicals to restrain themselves and Zhou Enlai openly castigated an assembly of Red Guards for their chaotic and arrogant conduct, claiming that many people who might otherwise have been won over to the Maoist cause had been alienated and that it was 'better to conquer the hearts of adversaries' than to 'scratch their skins'.

By March 30th, 1967 Lin Biao stated that some thirty infantry divisions – nearly 400,000 men – were deployed in maintaining China's essential services. In theory, they guarded radio stations and permitted broadcasts only of reports and statements that had already been 'blessed' by Peking. Similar rules were said to apply to provincial newspapers. But the troops' main tasks were obviously to guard airports, power plants, stations, water works, docks and roads.

However, by late March 1967 correspondents in Peking did report a more relaxed mood but this was apparently short-lived, for in April more kangeroo courts were established and Liu Shaoqi's wife was for the second time subjected to unpleasant treatment at the hands of Red Guard students. Soon after this the Red Guards opened a second and more determined campaign against the Foreign Minister, Chen Yi, and the staff of his Ministry which was a veiled, disguised attack on Premier Zhou Enlai. At first the Minister raised no serious objections and answered questions from the Red Guards but when young men beat up officials trying to protect secret files, he complained to Premier Zhou. The Red Guards handed the Premier an ultimatum demanding that Chen Yi and the two vice ministers, Ji Pengfei (Chi P'eng-fei) and Qiao Guanhua (Chi'ao Kuan-hua), be dismissed and arraigned before a Red Guard court. When the Premier rejected this ultimatum the Red Guards pasted up unpleasant posters about them and staged a second raid on the Ministry on 29th May.

It must be stressed that in spite of the chaos reported by correspondents and visitors, life still appears to have continued much along normal lines in a majority of the people's agricultural communes. There were, of course, notices posted up in praise of the Cultural Revolution and, in accordance with the cult of personality that Lin Biao and the PLA was sponsoring, there were scores of large pictures of the Chairman around and certainly hundreds more statues. But the agricultural workers appeared to be largely divorced from the political turbulence of the cities.

Despite the fact that so many troops were deployed to protect the railways and essential services, there were frequent breakdowns. The incident that alarmed Premier Zhou was the Red Guards' carefully planned 'capture' of a freight train carrying Russian small arms to Vietnam. The Red Guard unit afterwards confessed that they were 'tired' of manufacturing their own hand-grenades and mines. As a result of the widespread activities of Red Guards on the railways, there was a chronic shortage of oil and coal in many areas. Food shortages in the disrupted cities however were comparatively rare considering the chaos that existed in so many regions.

A speech made by Jiang Qing in April has special significance in view of the increasing political importance she assumed a decade later when the Chairman became daily more frail. Whether Jiang was attempting to establish herself as the only true interpreter of the Chairman's words at his request no one really knew, but her enemies claim the idea was hers. In several lengthy addresses, including one to the MAC, she introduced herself by saying that she and Chairman Mao 'lived together' and although there were many things she did not know, her place as his most intimate associate enabled her to 'interpret his thoughts'. The sum total of the speech was to tell the senior officers that they must respect the Red Guards. They must also get out of their barracks and offices to mix with the humble people in order to help them in the construction of a revolutionary power structure to replace the former party administration.

Clashes causing wounds, even deaths, were again reported from many Chinese cities throughout the early summer. In Yunnan where tempers rise quickly in the heat, 300 people were reported killed and over 1000 wounded – perhaps an exaggeration – in a street battle in Kunming. Scores of other incidents, though not involving so much loss of life, were reported as conditions in the cities continued to deteriorate. Foreign visitors to many cities outside Peking spoke of civil war, or conditions approaching civil war, in the late spring and early summer of 1967.

Some of the older members of the Politbureau have since told the odd distinguished visitor of the efforts Premier Zhou made to persuade Chairman Mao to order the Red Guards back to their universities, schools and places of work. Apparently Mao believed the young people would ultimately produce a group of leaders with the ideas he wanted to see supported by the next generation. Basically these were the endorsement of his form of communism combined with a strong streak of Chinese nationalism. Mao was extremely apprehensive that the Russians, who had been to so much trouble to influence the Chinese Communist Party in its infancy, would again penetrate its ranks through the youth. Indeed, Mao had been deeply shocked by the manner in which thousands of men and women who claimed to be convinced Marxists had accepted material incentives whether in the form of private plots or overtime pay. This brought him back to his initial objective that Liu Shaoqi and Deng Xiaoping were amongst the capital roaders and must be expelled from the party before he ordered the Red Guards to behave themselves.

8

The Wuhan Incident

Throughout the Cultural Revolution witnesses – especially foreign ones – frequently saw events through the eyes of the particular group they supported. In the capital, Peking, there were enough foreigners to sift out something that approached the truth. In the provinces, except for the early reports of the language teachers, who were not emotionally involved with either the Red Guards or the party veterans, detailed accounts of events contain important differences. This is especially true of the so-called Wuhan incident which marked a crisis point in the Cultural Revolution.

Wuhan was important for several reasons for it stands on the Yangtze (indeed it is where the Chairman swam the Yangtze) and the port can accommodate ocean-going vessels. Further, it is situated on the main railway line from north to south – Peking to Guangzhou – where the river is bridged and connected by a second railway line with the north-west. There are also good roads constructed to the north and south and along both banks of the Yangtze River. It is a major industrial centre and houses one of the most important military headquarters in the country. As a result of the excellent communications and nearby army training grounds, the region is used for the deployment and exercising of troops not under the operational orders of the regional commanders.

Despite the confused conditions throughout the country and the factional fighting in many towns at this time, Peking endorsed claims by Red Guards and other radical elements to overthrow the party leaders and disband their organization only in Shanghai and in the provinces of Heilongjiang, Shaanxi, Shandong and Guizhou where revolutionary committees were already established.

In Wuhan, Chen Zaidao (Ch'en Tsai-tao), who commanded the Military Region, claimed that he had attempted to collaborate with the Red Guards but this had proved to be impossible as 'they had struggled against us', he said. The authorities in Peking were concerned when the Henan military district, under Chen's command, flared up as rival Red Guard and party factions fought one another in the streets. The army by the order of April 6th, 1967 was forbidden to use force, but they did, with difficulty, restore some measure of order. The Cultural Revolution Group in Peking suggested that Chen had backed the wrong group when intense labour troubles flared up in Wuhan itself.

Basically two strong groups were fighting for control of this strategically important city. The first, known as the 'Million Heroes', claimed to have a membership of around one and a quarter million who confronted the Wuhan Workers' General Headquarters (WGHQ). The Million Heroes were strongly supported by the units of the PLA and they had, too, the indirect blessing of Chen who asserted, perhaps wrongly, that they were 'left'. The workers, who were composed of Red Guard units, thought otherwise. After many street confrontations, the two groups clashed on the Yangtze Bridge when several people were killed. The situation appeared so critical that Premier Zhou Enlai made one of his rare visits outside Peking to use his famous skill and tact in easing the tensions and persuading the two parties to become reconciled. The Premier could not remain for long away from his desk, and so requested Xie Fuchi (Hsieh Fu-ch'ih), the Minister of Public Security, and Wang Li, propaganda chief to the group organizing the Cultural Revolution, to follow him in Wuhan to back up the general agreement he had achieved with more detailed resolutions. The two men had just successfully concluded a similar task between the two rival factions in Kunming where as already reported 300 people had been killed.

However, when they arrived in the city of Wuhan on July 14th, over 2400 factories were either closed or working part-time and the mammoth Wuhan iron and steel works and all its subsidiaries were shut. The Minister spoke with Premier Zhou by telephone and surveyed the scene before calling a meeting on July 18th of divisional commanders – two-star generals and above in Anglo-Saxon terms – to discuss the situation. Xie informed the gathered generals that they were wrong in supporting the Million Heroes. He then refused to allow the political commissar of 8201 Unit to make a statement with the result that the commissar and others stormed out of the room. At dawn on the following sweltering July day members of the Million Heroes, wearing helmets and armed with clubs, knives and spears, were carried by army trucks to tactical points around the city, airport and railway station where they were backed by 8201 Unit in armoured cars. Thousands of big character posters had been pasted up overnight saying 'Down with Wang and Xie Fuchi'. The guest house where the two men had spent the night was surrounded and Wang was taken off. After being severely manhandled he was eventually smuggled to safety and later flown back to Peking with a broken arm. While the Ministers were being held as prisoners the Million Heroes were launching attacks on the buildings of all the organizations in the city that had opposed their assumption of power.

Peking was informed of the crisis and there were reports which were never officially confirmed that Premier Zhou returned to Wuhan in his private plane but the pilot was warned of a plot to ambush him when he was about to land. However, Premier Zhou arranged to move two or three divisions of paratroops, then under the Central Command, into Wuhan city to restore order and Chairman Mao issued a lengthy and, for him, unexciting order that the turbulence must be brought to an end. Chairman Mao's word appears to have carried sufficient weight and prestige to terminate the factional fighting. Rarely did Mao interfere in such a personal manner and thanks to his enormous prestige and to the fact that the 'broad masses' in Wuhan did know it was the Chairman speaking, and not one of his minions using the famous name, order was restored.

Mao's message was broadcast over hundreds of loudspeakers, which are set up in all Chinese cities, so there was little chance of anyone being unaware of what was happening. But as a safety precaution, sailors, from a naval vessel that had earlier been rushed to Wuhan, stood in the streets handing out leaflets containing the Chairman's statement to all passers-by. Shortly after the violence ceased another message was broadcast, this time in the name of the Government, the Central Committee, the Military Command and the Director of the Cultural Revolution that gave full support to the WGHQ which had been 'wrongfully tagged as counter-revolutionary'. The military leaders were, rightly, accused of supporting the Million Heroes, together with distorting facts and misleading the masses. In addition the commanders were accused of 'resorting to barbaric fantastic methods, assaulting and kidnapping people, even going so far as to attack physically emissaries of the party leadership'.

The order called for the immediate disarming of the Million Heroes and, after stressing the victory for the WGHQ, urged those who had been misled to return to the Maoist line. Chen was flown to Peking and Zeng Siyu (Tseng Szu-yü), the deputy commander from Manchuria, was appointed commander in his place. A week later 90 per cent of the factories were reopened and the city was reported to have a calm atmosphere despite the odd sign of past skirmishes. Wuhan, it is fair to add, has frequently been in the forefront of labour disputes and factional troubles; indeed, it is still the flashpoint of political and industrial unrest in central China.

An airport reception was arranged for Xie Fuchi and Wang Li on their official return to Peking. The Cultural Revolution Group used the incident to whip up enthusiasm and at a rally on July 25th in Tiananmen Square the speakers called for fresh efforts to 'strike down' Chairman Mao's enemies together with a warning that the Cultural Revolution would be subverted unless defended 'with blood and life', while the *People's Daily* portrayed Mao's enemies as 'rats running across the street', calling 'Kill them, kill them'.

The Red Guards were in fact beginning to flag and the organizers used the Wuhan incident in an effort to invigorate them. However, people who met the Chairman during this period claim that in his most open and sober moments, despite his great personal success in the Wuhan incident, he feared he had lost in the power struggle. For the two sides – the moderates in the party and the army and the radicals supporting Mao – were as he saw it evenly divided. In order to obtain a clear and absolutely certain majority, Chairman Mao would have liked to rally the peasants on whom he had always based his appeal and political philosophy. But, in the Chairman's view there was, alas, none against whom they could rise. They had already successfully revolted against the landlords and, Mao felt, they could hardly be encouraged to rebel against the men and women who were running the People's Communes – although in a very few cases they actually did this. It is odd that the Chairman had what amounted to a blind spot about this as the men and women running the agricultural communes were party veterans, similar people to those running the factories and other urban workers.

What kept the radicals in the ascendancy was, without doubt, the genuine love, adoration and respect in which the Chinese people held Chairman Mao.

The cult of Mao's personality, which he afterwards admitted went much too far, was necessary to the well-being of many peasants who had been robbed of their Buddhist gods and badly needed a new figurehead they could worship. Further, in comparison with other leaders including Liu Shaoqi, and Lin Biao, the Chairman, even at seventy-two, was the only person with enormous personality and charisma, in the same category as that of General de Gaulle. The latter I once witnessed walk into a violent and hostile Arab crowd in Tlemcen in inland Algeria. Towering above the tribesmen, de Gaulle signalled for silence and within ten minutes they were fighting to kiss his hand. Mao had even greater personality and, in addition, he endeared himself to those who worked with him every day by his charm and willingness to admit small mistakes. For Mao, it is said by his critics, only admitted 'small' mistakes and certainly there are many crucial ones he never acknowledged. But he did agree, in private, that he was responsible for the chaos arising from the Great Leap Forward.

Mao's insistence on foreign 555 cigarettes and his love of hot peppery food from Hunan Province where he was born became something special because they were his. Until his death the Chairman could rely on the fanatical support of the majority of the young people, whose lives are generally dull and prescribed in China. They were not allowed to indulge in the mildest kind of flirtation and it was frowned upon for a couple to visit a park on Sunday unless they were officially engaged. Thus they looked for their excitement in politics and wanted not only sporadic political upheavals, so dear to the Chairman's heart, but also a steady march towards true communism in China, which they stressed must be followed in correct Marxist fashion by world revolution.

In Wuhan, the PLA for the first and only time took a political decision not in accord with Peking. But this demonstrated to Mao that the army, which he believed to be anything from 70 to 95 per cent loyal to him, could not be used automatically in support of radical policies. It was noted, too, that Premier Zhou, who many thought was then bitterly opposed to the Red Guard, organized the initial agreement and when this broke down virtually pressed the Chairman to order a return to tranquillity while at the same time sending in reliable troops – the paras. Indeed, Premier Zhou Enlai, who was fighting hard for his own survival at this time, informed Chairman Mao, the Central Committee, and the Cultural Revolution Group, that unless they immediately undertook to do all in their power to calm the 'ultras' and extremists he, Zhou, would find his offices surrounded. The information contained in the Premier's files of secret documents would then be used by the Red Guard for big character posters.

Neither Chairmao Mao nor his wife, Jiang Qing, had reason to welcome this possibility for they had sent many private memoranda to Zhou that were not intended for any other eyes and would, indeed, cause monstrous reactions amongst the Red Guards if they were published. One particular example was that while Deng Xiaoping had been accused, rightly or wrongly, by the Red Guards of using military aircraft to get a good bridge four in the evening, at the time the Chairman had used military aircraft for daily communications with Jiang Qing and the Cultural Revolution Group when he was in Hangzhou. She also used military aircraft for picking up flowers and dessert fruit from south China when the winter diet in Peking was repetitive and the state was entertaining important people. The Chairman was thus once more frustrated in his efforts to allow the Red Guards and the extremists to rid him of Liu Shaoqi and all the old veterans who supported his political views. This irritated him, according to members of his staff, because Wuhan had introduced these doubts about the PLA despite all their slogans and outward show of loyalty to him. In fact, the cult of personality had its grave disadvantages for not only could the red flag be used against the red flag but Maoists were everywhere being used against Maoists.

9

The Cultural Revolution Reaches Hong Kong

The population of Hong Kong followed the Cultural Revolution as it developed through lengthy reports on the front page of the local press. Some concern was shown during the troubles experienced in Macao in December 1966 but none in the colony minded the increasing number of people who ran communist-controlled shops, banks, schools, trade unions and newspapers who wore large red Mao badges. The calm the colony had enjoyed was suddenly broken when labour troubles occurred in an artificial flower factory in Kowloon early in May 1967. Tese – Cantonese – police dealt with the crowds and the idle mischief-makers who joined in. Violence spread on the following day to other parts of Kowloon, but no one was killed (except a small boy on a balcony, possibly by a stone thrown from above) during three days of rioting. The police used nothing stronger than tear gas and a harmless American-made projectile that is fired at the crowd and ricochets to hit the demonstrators harmlessly on the shins. Party leaders, however, driving large cars, made their way to Government House on the following days to protest against police brutality. Their notes were accepted by an ADC and the crowd sang songs and shouted communist slogans whilst hundreds waved their 'Little Red Books'. The groups marched or drove up from the assembly area near the Bank of China in the centre of Hong Kong and for days Government House became an isolated and noisy abode.

While the demonstrations were taking place, schoolboy formations of Red Guards were busy transforming the back rooms of schools, offices and shops into work rooms for the production of home-made grenades and other simple weapons aided by a handful of youthful leaders who had secretly penetrated the colony from Guangzhou. The demonstrations grew noticeably tougher and rioting took place as the police forced the crowds down the hill each day after handing in their petitions to Government House. New and violently anti-British posters appeared on walls and the police who were making a cordon round Government House were attacked while youthful members of the crowd shouted slogans urging them to shoot their officers. The ringleaders were Chinese journalists, photographers and others working for local communist newspapers, as well as men and women working for Xinhua, the official Chinese news agency.

On May 15th, the British Chargé d'Affaires in Peking, Mr Donald Hobson, was called to the Foreign Ministry to receive a statement that armed troops and police had been 'turned loose' on 'bare-handed workers' and students, and large-scale 'sanguinary atrocities' had been committed in Hong Kong. This, the protest claimed, was all part of the British Government's scheme of collusion with the United States against China, a reference to the fact that American servicemen fighting in South Vietnam used Hong Kong for rest and relaxation. In addition, the British authorities in Hong Kong were, the Chinese claimed, stepping up hostile measures in a vain attempt to exclude the influence of the Cultural Revolution which 'they mortally feared and hated'. The Chinese demanded the immediate release of all those arrested including workers, journalists and cameramen. The British were warned of the 'grave consequences' that would follow if their demands were not met. Then, in the typical Chinese fashion of that time, the note was immediately released by Xinhua.

Further demonstrations were organized in Hong Kong in which youthful Red Guards did their best to provoke the police. More arrests were made by the British authorities and a curfew imposed. This was followed by yet another rash of violent anti-British posters and a transport strike. Fortunately, the strike tended to irritate the vast majority of the population of Hong Kong, who were forced to walk to work, and when the communists attempted to prevent the sale of foodstuffs they completely failed in their efforts. All this was surprising in view of the fact that there were at the time rumours – strong rumours – in the British colony that the Chinese were about to take over Hong Kong. This had, after all, been a somewhat vague, long-term objective of the Communist Party since the People's Republic was founded in 1949. And from the purely military point of view there was nothing to stop them. But the colony then provided China with $600,000,000 United States (approximately £250,000,000) worth of foreign exchange annually. This was over one-third of their total requirements and as it was used to pay for vital grain imports, even the radicals on the organization committee of the Cultural Revolution advocated restraint.

However, this did not extend to calling off demonstrations immediately. Indeed, soon after the British Government declared its support for the Hong Kong authorities the Revolutionary Committee in Shanghai issued an order insisting on the immediate closure of the British Consulate there and the withdrawal of the Consul, Peter Hewitt, and his assistants within twenty-four hours. (It has not since been re-opened.) On the way out Hewitt was vilely treated by Red Guards who spat at him as they kicked him in the stomach and daubed him with glue. About the same time communist supporters in the Portuguese colony of Macao forced the British Consul there to stand for seven hours in the hot sun as they reviled him.

Years later I was able to confirm the report of a Chinese refugee who had been a Red Guard leader and said that Premier Zhou Enlai had strongly opposed the violence in Hong Kong and in this he was supported by Defence Minister Lin Biao. But the Cultural Revolution Group led by Jiang Qing had secretly sent into Hong Kong a score or so of trained Red Guards to instruct those who had already formed themselves into units at various schools.

The violence continued in the colony throughout June and July at the time when, unhappily, the experienced Foreign Minister, Chen Yi, was temporarily thrown out of his office by the extremist Yao Dengshen who had been welcomed as a hero on his return to Peking after being expelled from Indonesia. Kang Sheng, too, gave Yao Dengshen powerful, although covert, support. Thus the agitators in Hong Kong had strong backing from the extremists in Peking for Yao was one of the leaders of the ultra-leftist May 16th Group, better known as the 516 Group which took its title from a directive issued by Chairman Mao. (When written in Chinese style the month is stated before the day.)

While Yao was in charge of the Ministry many embassies in Peking were attacked, beginning with the Burmese who, allegedly, refused to allow the Chinese living in Burma to wear Mao badges. Two Japanese communists were manhandled at Peking airport and there were demonstrations outside the Indian, Mongolian and

Russian Embassies in Peking whilst the leader of an Italian trade mission was prevented from leaving his office.

A kangaroo court was set up to 'try' a Russian who, quite accidentally, broke a glass in a restaurant. The French Ambassador was the target of an abusive shouting match and even the North Vietnamese and North Koreans were insulted by extremists. Foreigners who worked for the Chinese Government, and who wanted to demonstrate that they were far more revolutionary and devoted to Chairman Mao than the Chinese themselves, were all too frequently leading extremist groups, and many Anglo-Saxons were to be found in the 516 Group which was later dubbed as 'ultra-leftist' by the Chinese Communist Party and Government.

The ordeal of Anthony Grey

On August 18th Red Guards entered the house in the centre of Peking where Anthony Grey, Reuters correspondent, had been placed under house arrest in retaliation for the journalist who had been imprisoned in Hong Kong on charges of violence and disturbing the peace. The gang wrecked the furniture in Reuters' flat and office and hanged Grey's pet cat before they glued pre-written posters on his back and put him through what amounted to torture, called the 'jet plane treatment'. Grey was forced to kneel and bend forward while his arms were jerked back behind him. He was not allowed to move and he could see his face reflected in a pool of sweat on the ground. His guards made no effort to protect him. The following day there were demonstrations against the Embassy of Ceylon and on August 21st against Kenya.

On August 22nd large crowds collected outside the British Embassy as the Chargé d'Affaires, Donald Hobson, with a staff of eighteen men and five women, was waiting for the expiry of the 48-hour deadline mentioned in a Chinese note about the release of people in Hong Kong. Chinese troops lined up in front of the main gate, giving the impression that they were there to protect the diplomats inside from the crowds in the street who were shouting abusive slogans, setting up loudspeakers in trees and carrying violently xenophobic posters. As darkness fell one Red Guard unit brought up floodlights whilst another organized the crowd to sing revolutionary songs. At around 10.30 P.M. they burst into the embassy compound – the soldiers stepping aside to let them pass – and began burning the cars, which were parked near the swimming pool, before they entered the building. They then broke windows, destroyed furniture and started fires inside the embassy with the aid of petrol they carried in with them.

Donald Hobson and his staff had taken refuge in the strongroom which housed the archives and ciphers on the ground floor of the building to the left of the entrance, but they were driven out as the smoke poured in through the ventilating shafts. Later Donald Hobson wrote to his wife a description of what happened.

I opened the door and was first out followed by the others. There were perhaps 5000 people in the courtyard. Immediately I was beaten black and blue with blows. Whoever could lay hands on me hit me with everything they had got. The women, in a fury, threw themselves on me and tried to knock me out with batons. They dragged me by the hair and wanted to strangle me with my tie. I really do not know how I finally found myself a little further away in front of a door where all of a sudden a hand seized me by the arm. Someone shouted at me in Chinese 'Come this way'. He dragged me running towards the Indian Embassy [at the back of the British Embassy] where he hid me behind the entrance door.

I was stunned by the blows I had received in the head, more or less unconscious and bleeding like a pig.

Some of the women sought refuge in the Albanian Embassy opposite but the Albanians shut the iron gates in their faces and jeered at them as they were manhandled and abused by the crowds. Two girls did, however, manage to gain sanctuary in the Finnish Embassy. All the staff were made to bow to a picture of Chairman Mao whilst being spat upon and kicked. What is truly horrible is that a diplomat told me there were born Britishers in the assaulting crowds one of whom, a ringleader, from a 'very good family', was last seen jumping up and down in her handmade brogue shoes on a picture of the Queen.

Messages relayed to the crowd over the loudspeakers in the name of Jiang Qing and Chen Boda ordered them to disperse. But these did nothing to halt their fury around the embassy, nor did a later order from Premier Zhou Enlai have any effect. In the early hours of the morning the violence gradually abated and a second message was broadcast to the Red Guards and the 516 Group ordering them in the name of Premier Zhou 'to go home and stay there'.

The excesses of late August provided Premier Zhou with an excuse to regain control of the Foreign Ministry. For at this time, too, the Cambodian Head of State, Prince Nordon Sihanouk, always a favourite with Peking, threatened to withdraw the embassy staff and sever diplomatic relations with China on the grounds that it was no longer physically safe to remain in Peking where public security had broken down. Premier Zhou went to Chairman Mao who was as usual outside Peking and told him that China would not only lose face in the world, especially the communist world, if diplomats were abused and their lives endangered. Further, businessmen would no longer visit China and in this imperfect world, the Premier stressed, China was still dependent on the importation of food and other raw materials as well as technology.

Vital discussions between Chairman Mao and Premier Zhou Enlai

This vital but unrecorded interview between Chairman Mao Zedong and Premier Zhou Enlai, which could so easily have spelt the end of Premier Zhou's outstanding career, took place after the attack on the British Embassy and before August 30th. Although the two men had been extremely close to one another since the Long March of 1934/5, there had been many disagreements on policy in which Premier Zhou had frequently managed to persuade the Chairman to modify or drop some of his wilder revolutionary schemes. But their relations were at this moment severely strained. Premier Zhou was chronically over-tired, largely because of the nights he had devoted to dealing with problems arising from disturbances that had taken place in various provinces. Now he, the Premier, was being personally attacked by the 516 Group and by some of the Red Guards. His name was coupled on big character posters with those of the enemies, Liu Shaoqi and Deng Xiaoping. One night at this critical time a small party of Red Guards actually managed to penetrate into Premier Zhou's office in the Great Hall of the People demanding to see his files. The Premier's charm and force of personality persuaded them to leave without looking at the files but only after forty-eight hours of intermittent discussion. In addition to his other worries Premier Zhou was deeply concerned about the army. Despite the influence of Lin Biao, who like the Chairman was away from Peking, Zhou detected signs that the 'leftist' political commissars were getting the upper hand in many units. The ultra-leftist 516 Group were well away to the left of the radical group led by Jiang Qing and others in the Politbureau. Indeed, the 516 Group wanted to establish true communism overnight, abolish money and lend massive support to world revolution. Their theories were later partially put into practice in Cambodia by the Pol Pot regime. The ultra rightists in China were generally those who saw some virtue in the form of communism adopted by the Soviet Union and were dubbed pro-Russian revisionists.

The Premier apparently came away from his visit to the Chairman uncertain whether he had made his points or not. For Mao continued to stress that Liu Shaoqi and other 'capitalist roaders' were still around. As Mao's main object had been to get rid of Liu Shaoqi and other 'pro-Russian revisionists' when he launched the Cultural Revolution, he was naturally reluctant to get rid of the radical elements who were in his view still needed to complete the aim of overthrowing Liu Shaoqi. These youthful radical elements who wanted to introduce 'true communism' were the very people the Premier wanted to throw into prison or send to agricultural communes hundreds of miles from the capital.

What is now known is that Zhou threatened to resign as Premier and withdraw from the Standing Committee of the Politbureau. This was the only occasion on which he ever uttered such a threat to Mao. All the Chairman then asked was that Premier Zhou would continue 'to do his best' while he, Mao, remained in the country for a few days to think things over. Acting entirely on his own initiative, Premier Zhou then ordered some of the more violent armed extremists to be rounded up in Peking and he sent strong messages to the demonstrators in Hong Kong to 'cool it'.

But other unfortunate unforeseen results followed the British Embassy incident. The staff of the Chinese Embassy in London became tense, apprehensive and nervous. They had been informed they could not travel outside London without prior notice and many of the senior diplomats were, they claimed, followed when walking around London. A few trifling excuses caused the staff one morning to dash out of the embassy carrying their 'Little Red Books' in what developed into the 'Battle of Portland Place'. This was, in fact, a political demonstration organized by diplomats.

In Peking, Chinese officials, confused and alarmed perhaps by what diplomats would say when they left the People's Republic, refused exit visas to the families of British, Dutch and Indonesian diplomats. The general chaos and unwillingness of officials to take responsibility also played a role, as the Chinese were in a most uncooperative mood. There was, too, so much muddle in the bureaucracy that it is possible there was no one authorized to take responsibility for issuing exit visas to British diplomats. At the time, the British Embassy could not make any direct contact with any senior official or Minister. Despite Premier Zhou's concern about the violence and activities of the Red Guards, Chinese officials remained obstructive in their dealings with British diplomats, claiming that correspondents and journalists working for Xinhua (the New China News Agency) were still being illegally detained in Hong Kong. Perhaps because the British authorities in Hong Kong refused permission for the Chinese to establish a consulate or a representative, this role had been assumed unofficially by Xinhua. (By 1980 Xinhua had leased a huge building overlooking the Happy Valley Race Course which had been built as a hotel. They entertained the Government here and, in addition to journalistic activities, after the establishment of the Special Economic Zones – SEZ – they opened a visa office in 1981 in the same block.)

Another reason, since mentioned by communist sympathizers, for not permitting exit visas was that what was left of the Government wanted to prevent the appearance in the world's press of eye-witness accounts of incidents that would indicate that China was on the verge of civil war or, in any case, a country in which there was no public security.

Premier Zhou's main worry then was what he later referred to as 'the near state of anarchy' throughout the country. In almost every city the radicals and moderates seemed to be almost equally divided. The radicals themselves were frequently divided into two or more groups both loudly operating in the name of Chairman Mao and frequently coming to blows, fighting one another in the streets with batons, old bits of furniture and swords, not to mention rifles and machine-guns.

Mysterious actions and orders increased the unrest and uncertainty. For example, a telephone call from an unknown person in Peking warned all the large cities that a 'capitalist restoration' was about to be staged, and that they must fight to the last 'for Chairman Mao and the party'. Chairman Mao wisely remained outside the capital, at times in Behtaiho, at others in Shanghai or Hangzhou, or, it was stated, on a tour of inspection in the Yangtze River area. Lin Biao, too, was still away much of the time. Premier Zhou alone remained in the capital and during this period his relationship with Lin Biao deteriorated sharply. For Zhou thought the Minister of Defence would have been in a better position to exercise control over the armed forces from his headquarters in Peking.

The attention of the Red Guards and the older extremist groups who operated with them was then drawn to the army. A campaign was launched by Lin Biao and Jiang Qing to 'drag out the handful of capitalist roaders in the Army'. Premier Zhou Enlai feared this seriously threatened the overall unity of the armed forces for a week or two. Although the campaign, in fact, never really got off the ground and the slogan was dropped from big character posters after a few days, it caused deep apprehension amongst the senior commanders and in the Defence Ministry.

10

Mao Takes Action against Red Guard Leaders

By the summer of 1967 those few foreigners remaining in Peking reported that the inhabitants of the capital were growing desperately tired of the Cultural Revolution, and the Cultural Revolution Group which was still supposedly running it was in a state of political eclipse. This was confirmed by the fact that the journal, *Red Flag*, that had become its theoretical house organ, was under heavy attack. The monthly magazine had become important as it had replaced the party as the channel for the dissemination of 'the correct political line' from the top – the Cultural Group or the Central Committee – to the cadres at the grass roots. But it was too militant for the PLA and many of its readers. In spite of efforts by Jiang Qing and Chen Boda to protect them, many of the staff of *Red Flag* were arrested in November 1967 after the last issue of the magazine for some time to come was published. Jiang Qing who was, according to Premier Zhou Enlai, suffering from mental exhaustion then went off to recuperate in Hangzhou.

Chairman Mao realized that there was little or no enthusiasm for the Cultural Revolution amongst the bulk of the people after over a year and a half of demonstrations and activity. In an attempt to arouse new interest Mao made subtle changes in the ultimate targets the Cultural Revolution was hoping to achieve. Instead of searching for 'capitalist roaders *within* the party' the Chairman attempted to turn the attention of the over-enthusiastic Red Guard leaders and the bored public to landlords, capitalists and counter-revolutionaries *outside* the party. The Chairman was also concerned by the manner in which the PLA was substituting itself for the constituted authority as provincial leaders while the nation painfully hammered out the provisions for the establishment of new revolutionary committees at provincial, city and local levels.

Once again, the situation was confused. Jiang Qing returned to Peking but even she, supported as she now was by the Premier, could inject no new life into the Cultural Revolution Group. The military had meanwhile become so arrogant in the capital that the commander of the Peking garrison, Fu Chongbi (Fu Ch'ung-pi), supported by a truck load of armed soldiers, attempted to arrest a member of her staff. This Jiang Qing was able to prevent only through personal intervention. Premier Zhou's statements that the Cultural Revolution Group and especially Jiang Qing had given no encouragement to the now disgraced May 16th Group of ultra leftists went unbelieved and unheeded by the PLA and the general public. A rash of new big character posters appeared reflecting the accusations and counter-accusations being made not only by the student Red Guards but senior army officers and members of the Central Committee.

In yet another effort to give direction and new life to the Cultural Revolution, Kang Sheng, as State Security Chief, revealed some startling indictments of China's top leaders at a meeting in Peking in the early months of 1968. Liu Shaoqi, he said, had been 'arrested four times'. First, he had 'surrendered to the Guomindang in Hunan in 1925, then to Wang Qingwei [a nationalist warlord] in Wuhan in 1925 and to Chiang Kai-shek in 1936'. Wang Guangmei, Liu's wife, was, Kang said, 'a diehard secret agent for the United States, Japan and the Guomindang who had sneaked into our organization'. Kang claimed that Luo Ruiqing, the former Chief of Staff, was a secret agent who had never even joined the Communist Party, Peng Zhen, the former Mayor of Peking, was 'a renegade' and Peng Dehuai, a former Defence Minister, 'a traitor'. At the end of this tirade Jiang Qing shouted, 'Down with Deng Xiaoping,' whose name had not been mentioned, and Kang who was always known at this period as 'the Venerable Kang', replied, 'Deng Xiaoping is a deserter. It is necessary to expose him continuously.' The intense dislike shown by Jiang Qing and her associates for Deng must, in part, account for his second disgrace nearly a decade later.

But Kang's sensational revelations aroused no new enthusiasm, though various organizations marched dutifully through the streets of Peking behind a band and a mass of red flags supporting his denunciation. Although foreign correspondents described the scene in the city as listless, inside the university there were four or five armed camps or fortresses in which each of the rival Red Guard factions had made their headquarters. Armed now with automatic weapons as well as rifles – one group even boasted a makeshift tank – the fanatics fought and actually killed one another at irregular intervals. It was from these fortresses that the revolutionary cliques and groups set out each day with their loudspeaker vans, drums and cymbals to demonstrate, to harangue the crowds and paste up new big character posters.

It is most unlikely that Chairman Mao ever ventured disguised into the dangerous campuses, though there were reports he had done so, but he was kept well – amazingly well – informed on the activities of the Red Guard leaders and rivals who came to be known as the 'Young Generals'. Jiang Qing arranged that he was given copies of all the significant political posters that appeared on the campus. Early in 1968 the Cultural Revolution Group and government departments were inundated by thousands of complaints about the noise of the loudspeakers, which the fanatics frequently kept going until the small hours of the morning. Jiang Qing and other members of the Politbureau must themselves have suffered from the sleeplessness that exhausted members of the diplomatic corps and, more important, the workers in Peking.

Slowly the Chairman came to the conclusion during the early summer that the youthful leaders in whom he had put so much faith had let him down. They were not, he decided, of the calibre to be considered for the succession. The Chairman was forced to take action after he received reports from agents in the campus that the Red Guard 'Generals' were hatching a somewhat childish plot to set up a new National Red Guard organization designed to take over all the radio stations. And, if this was successful, they discussed their dream of establishing a National Red Guard authority throughout China. Although the idea of such action by the Red Guards, without the support of their adult and influential leaders, such as Chen Boda and Jiang Qing, was a pipe-dream, the youthful plotters had a handful of friends amongst the political commissars in the army as well as the press. Despite its naïvety it was a project the Chairman wanted to kill before it was born. Without apparently mentioning the plot, but in a depressed and disappointed mood, Mao announced the time had come to put an end to the fighting on the campuses which originated between the Earth and Heaven sectors. He was given strong support by Premier Zhou Enlai.

A few unarmed soldiers who had been sent to the campus failed to make any impression on the Red Guards. Thus, in the early weeks of July, Mao sent into the universities the massive 'Workers' Mao Zedong Thought Propaganda Teams' which had been formed initially to combat Liu Shaoqi's influence and factionalism. One foreigner wrote that 'a sudden blissful silence settled over the city' and for the first time in two years the noise of the loudspeakers ceased. The workers insisted that the students go to bed at ten o'clock. The Red Guard 'Generals' protested vigorously against the workers whom they called 'invaders' and claimed they were sent by the 'Black Hand' or anti-Maoist forces. But the workers made it clear, as more and more of them arrived, not only that they had authority but they were there to stay as long as the various factions were attempting to fight one another.

At Qinghua University the student 'General', the charismatic leader Kuai Dafu of the Jinggangshan Group, opened fire on the workers. (The Group was named after the mountain top where Chairman Mao had resisted the nationalist forces before the beginning of the Long March in 1934.) Five unarmed workers were killed and over fifty seriously injured by fire from Second World War sub-machine guns. This was crisis point. Chairman Mao sent for the student leaders to tell them he had decided to end the fighting and chaos and also their activities. Most residents of Peking thought he should have acted earlier – much earlier.

A few hours after the summons the Chairman was waiting to receive the 'Young Generals' in one of the smaller reception rooms in the Great Hall of the People with Premier Zhou Enlai and Defence Minister Lin Biao on either side. In the background were the Cultural Revolution Group, Chen Boda, Jiang Qing, Kang Sheng, Xie Fuchi, Yao Wenyuan, Ye Qun (Ye Ch'ün, Mme Lin Biao) and the new Army Chief of Staff, Huang Yongsheng (Huang Yung-sheng).

Nie Yuanzi, the professor who put up the first big character poster, who had risen to be Vice Chairman of the Peking Revolutionary Committee, led the group. She was followed by three 'commanders of the antagonistic student armies', Dan Houlan, a militant from the Peking Normal School, then Han Aiqing (Han Ai-ching), the extremist leader of the Aviation Institute's Red Flag, and Wang Dabin (Wang Ta-pin), who commanded the Aviation

Institute's Red Guards and was titular head of the Peking Earth armies, who brought up the rear.

The Chairman immediately noted that Kuai Dafu was not present and was told that he was engaged in a fight to capture the Black Hand who had sent the workers to the campus. 'But I am the Black Hand,' Chairman Mao almost shouted with the same sense of drama that inspired him to swim the Yangtze at the age of seventy-two. Mao went on to say, 'I sent the workers of the Xinhua Printing Plant, the General Knitwear Mill and the Central Police Department to the University telling them to deal firmly with the fighting there.' When the young leaders murmured in self-defence that 'they were in fact being oppressed and suppressed by the workers', the Chairman repeated, 'The Black Hand is none other than I.'

Mao then outlined to the student leaders how he and the Central Committee – although it is unlikely he had consulted the Central Committee – had decided to deal with the fighting and unrest. He claimed that of more than fifty institutions of higher learning in Peking, there had only been severe fighting in half a dozen establishments. Indeed, the Chairman stressed with frequent nods of support from Premier Zhou and Lin Biao that they had come to the conclusion the situation was completely out of hand, the young leaders had disappointed them and unless they themselves ceased the factional fighting a well-armed unit of the PLA would be ordered to take over. 'For two years you young people engaged in the struggle – criticism – transformation that is embodied in our Cultural Revolution,' he said. 'But today you are no longer struggling or criticizing and there has been no visible transformation.' Further, the Chairman complained that they had allowed the struggle to develop into 'a localized armed combat'. This, Mao claimed, had caused serious reactions amongst the people, who were not happy, indeed, neither the workers, peasants nor even the 'students in your schools' were happy about the situation. The Chairman revealed not only that he knew all there was to know about the 'armed combat' between the various groups of Red Guards but he also quoted the texts of many of the big character posters pasted up on the campus as each of the 'Generals' was reprimanded in turn.

Mao referred to Nie Yuanzi as 'Old Buddha', the nickname she

1 *(Above)* Jiang Qing (second from left) with Edgar Snow (second from right), the first Western journalist to visit Mao in Yenan, and Indian medical friends, 1939

2 *(Right)* Zhou Enlai in European clothes outside his office in Shanghai in 1928

3 Mao Zedong inspecting the People's Liberation Army shortly after independence in 1949

4 The declaration of the People's Republic, October 1949. Mao and Liu Shaoqi

5 *(Left)* Peng Dehuai, former Minister of Defence, whose opposition to Mao's Great Leap Forward caused his ultimate disgrace despite a distinguished past as a commander in the Red Army and Korea

6 *(Below)* Liu Shaoqi and his wife, Wang Guangmei, 1961, in Heilongjiang Province. Liu, formerly Head of State, was purged in the Cultural Revolution and died in prison. His wife survived and is now politically active again

7 *(Above)* During the Cultural Revolution Jiang Qing appears at the Gate of Heavenly Peace with Kang Sheng (to her right), Zhou Enlai, Lin Biao, and her husband, Mao Zedong

8 *(Below left)* Disturbances in Hong Kong – demonstrators wave their 'Little Red Books' on 18 August, 1966 at the height of the Cultural Revolution

9 *(Below right)* Jiang Qing at Da Zhai model agricultural commune, *c.*1976

10 *(Top)* Mao with Edward Heath, during his highly successful visit to China as Leader of the Opposition
11 *(Above)* President Nixon and Premier Zhou Enlai, in Peking, 1972

12 *(Above)* Hua Guofeng, Chairman of the Chinese Communist Party after the death of Mao and the fall of the Gang of Four

13 *(Right)* The author examines the arms of young Militia men in the Forbidden City

14 *(Above)* Chen Boda, Mao's speech writer and political adviser from the Yenan days until his disgrace, on trial in 1980

15 *(Below)* Deng Yingchao and Deng Xiaoping at the Fifth National Women's Congress, 1983. Premier Zhou's wife retains close personal and political ties with Deng Xiaoping

acquired in her faction, which suggested she was not universally loved. The Dowager Empress Cixi was always known as 'Old Buddha' and she and Nie sound like pretty similar characters. The Chairman then talked of education and examinations in which he had no faith. During his dissertation he is reported to have said that he had never read a book on military strategy. But this was surely untrue for Mao based his own successful form of guerrilla warfare on the works of the ancient China strategist Sun Tzu, the first known person to write exclusively on military affairs. The Chairman hinted that the Red Guards had themselves become a major problem rather than a means of solving larger national issues. He repeated the accounts of student violence, torture and forced confessions he had heard. Then Mao chastised the Red Guards for their factional deadlock and the manner in which they had treated the soldiers and workers who had gone to the university to restore order. Mao admitted that he, personally, was not without guilt for in his 'Report on the Investigation of the Peasant Movement in Hunan' he had written about 'parading people on the street in dunces' hats' as the peasants had done at the height of the May 4th Movement in 1919. Mao then summed up by outlining some of the problems that had arisen during the Cultural Revolution. Referring to the disturbing factionalism that had developed he discussed the 'fundamental issue of what political form [of government] would evolve out of their experiences with the class struggle'. Mao dwelt on the type of socialism that had already been established in China, and asked, 'Where do you think we go from here?' He admitted this presented a greater problem than fighting a war.

One student leader, Han Aiqing, refused to allow the Chairman to leave this vital subject without further questions on the development of factionalism in the Maoist camp. Unhappily the Chairman did not produce a satisfactory answer for there is no way, as Christians well know to their cost, of preventing believers from presenting differing interpretations of the leader's doctrinaire statements. Jiang Qing's tone throughout the meeting was bitter towards all young 'Generals' who had let her down so badly. After several especially scornful remarks to Han Aiqing the Chairman begged Jiang Qing not to criticize him and, after saying, 'You always blame others and never yourself,' added musingly, 'His [Han Aiqing's] character is something like mine when I was young.' This exchange is of special interest because it is one of the rare reports of the Chairman and his wife having a slight difference of opinion in public before 1974. Some observers believe she was angry and ill at ease because she feared the dissolution of the Red Guard Movement might well spell the end of her own political career. Fortunately for Jiang Qing this was not the case though she must have experienced many uncomfortable moments then and in the following year, 1969, when her chief associate in the Cultural Revolution Group, Chen Boda, who had also been the Chairman's speech writer and faithful secretary, fell into disgrace.

At meetings of the Central Committee, I have been told, in the days before the autumn of 1973 when Mao took the chair in person, Jiang Qing treated him with the greatest respect as though she were no more to him than an acquaintance and a fellow member of the committee. On those few occasions when I have seen her, or heard her speak, she has adopted an almost deferential attitude when mentioning Mao's name.

Before the meeting broke up the Chairman told the 'Generals' that he expected them to come to terms with the opposing factions as soon as possible and then to 'disperse'. He hoped, Mao said, that the students – that let out Nie Yuanzi who was already a lecturer when she wrote the famous poster – would set a good example to other Red Guards by going to the countryside 'to learn from the peasants'. This was not what the 'Generals' had expected after having, at least in their own view, played an active, indeed, leading role in national politics. But, after all, they had to obey the directives of Chairman Mao and here he was giving them in person. Naturally, Mao added that the 'Generals' had some learning and experience to convey to the peasants. But the prospect of going to live in a bad climate on, say, the Mongolian or Russian frontier where, in addition, there were no intellectuals, no libraries, indeed, no proper lavatories, did not appeal to the young leaders after their heady experiences in the capital. Chairman Mao told the youthful leaders that for the first time in his life he was using a tape-recorder so that they could not misquote him as they had so frequently in the past.

Nonetheless the 'Generals' were honoured to have seen and talked with Chairman Mao and the men and women whom he had now so obviously chosen as his immediate successors. First there was the Defence Minister, Lin Biao, and then Premier Zhou, both of whom were veterans of the 'Long March' and whose age had been so much criticized by the Red Guards. Then came the 'younger' element represented by people the Red Guard had once thought to be their allies, Chen Boda and Jiang Qing, both approaching sixty, while Kang Sheng was well over sixty. The only youthful person present was Yao Wenyuan, then forty-four who, despite his record of having triggered off the Cultural Revolution through his criticism of the play *Hai Jui Dismissed from Office* remained disappointingly silent, if not downright sullen, throughout the proceedings.

The 'Young Generals' well knew this spelled the end of the Cultural Revolution, so far as Red Guard activities were concerned, but they all made one last desperate effort the day after Mao had seen them to overcome the workers and their other opponents, claiming that Chairman Mao supported *their* political faction despite the tape. However, the crowds to whom they appealed were as uninterested and apathetic as the workers were opposed to their activities. A few days later the workers, assisted by soldiers from a nearby unit of the PLA, dismantled the elaborate fortifications the leaders of each faction had gradually constructed on the campus. Later army lorries were seen carrying away scores of sub-machine guns and hundreds of good old-fashioned .303 rifles of First World War vintage.

The fighting amongst various factions of the Red Guards was not confined to the capital, indeed, many eye-witnesses claimed it was far more serious in Guangzhou and there was prolonged violence in Harbin. There was trouble, too, in Kunming and Xi'an and widespread clashes in Anshan where steel production was delayed. Indeed, as late as 1968 there was an 8–10 per cent decline in freight transported by rail owing to Red Guard activities in commandeering trains. Few cities escaped the dangerous confrontations between groups of youthful extremists, all of whom claimed to be supporters of Chairman Mao. What is more serious is that the quarrels that arose between rival gangs during this period of the Cultural Revolution were, in many cases, only patched up superficially and flared up again at unexpected intervals.

Even the authority of Chairman Mao could not suppress the

nationwide activities of the Red Guards overnight and he and Premier Zhou Enlai were forced increasingly to rely on the PLA to restore order. They were strongly supported by the urban 'broad masses' who, after nearly two years of non-stop demonstrations and months of real disturbances, wanted nothing more than an end to overt political activity. There was, however, strange and contradictory as it may sound, some difficulty in convincing the population that the Cultural Revolution was over in all but name, for the rank and file had become so accustomed to making at least a show of taking part in the all too frequent demonstrations.

In an attempt further to stem Red Guard activity, Premier Zhou addressed a mass meeting early in September in Tiananmen Square in which he announced, 'The whole country is now red.' After 'repeated struggles over the past twenty months we have finally smashed the plot of the handful of top party persons in authority taking the capitalist road', the Premier said. He drew laughter and applause from his tired audience when he referred to the enemy agents and traitors headed by China's Khrushchev (Liu Shaoqi) who 'had attempted to restore capitalism'. The young people in the square were urged by the Premier 'to go to the grass roots level . . . to settle in the mountainous areas and the country-side and take part in physical work in factories, mines and villages'. For their part the Red Guards would have greatly preferred to hear one of the speeches leaders made during the early part of the Cultural Revolution that provided them with an excuse to go on the rampage.

Jiang Qing spoke after the Premier. Addressing a mass rally for the last time she attempted to soothe the visibly hurt feelings of the students by stressing the 'tremendous contributions' the Red Guards had made 'at the initial and middle stages of the Revol-ution'. Jiang Qing then recommended the young people to accept the leadership of the working class. Finally, she appealed to all workers to 'protect the young Red Guard fighters, help and educate them'. An American, Nancy Dall Milton, who was on the spot, wrote, 'These improvised remarks were the last echo of an appointed committee – the Cultural Group – which, at one time, hoped to achieve power that was second to none.'

A handful of the Red Guards committed suicide rather than face oblivion and hard work in the countryside, for there is little doubt power had gone to their heads in the real sense and Kuai Dafu was not the only one showing signs of madness. Parents who had disapproved of their children's activities accepted them once more into their homes and many of them made efforts to prevent their offspring being sent away.

11

The 9th Party Congress

The Soviet Union paradoxically ensured the unity and success of the 9th Party Congress, which had taken so long to prepare, by launching an attack across the Ussuri River in March. Premier Zhou Enlai had already expressed more concern than the Defence Minister, Lin Biao, about the massive build-up of Russian troops along the northern border. He feared that Moscow might be mounting incidents in this remote region of eastern Siberia as an excuse for a major attack on the rich industrial areas of Manchuria. The Russians had, after all, occupied Czechoslovakia the previous August. It was, according to official Chinese sources, the fifty-seventh border incident over Chenbao Island and the Premier also feared it would not have been 'blown up' by the Russians without some sinister motive. This small island is fifty miles from the nearest village and has no military or economic significance. But it is situated in the middle of the river, though slightly on the Chinese side, and, according to the Treaty of Aigun signed in 1858, the border line was to be drawn along the middle of the river. There are people who believe that Lin Biao knew all about the Russian plans to cause the incident and, indeed, supported them because he rightly believed such an attack would unite the delegates to the 9th Party Congress behind him. This was, indeed, what happened.

Premier Zhou also wanted the congress to take place in order to put an end to the militant period of the Cultural Revolution, to announce that Liu Shaoqi was no longer Head of State and, most important of all, to give direction to the new provincial Revolutionary Committees, which had been so difficult to establish but were urgently required to get down to the business of administering the country. The Premier wanted to devote himself to foreign affairs which he was unable to discuss with any ease at meetings of the Politbureau either before or indeed immediately after the 9th Party Congress. Alarmed by the ever-increasing military power of the Soviet Union, the Premier was anxious to pick up several olive branches Washington had thrown in his path, but he well knew that Lin Biao believed it was better to be allied with an abrasive socialist state than a friendly 'Imperialist'.

In addition, Chairman Mao Zedong and Premier Zhou were both, for somewhat different reasons, anxious to 'consolidate' the so-called 'fruits' of the Cultural Revolution and hold the 9th Party Congress. The Chairman wanted to see the new party structure firmly established without Liu and his provincial henchmen but, owing to the tremendous problems encountered in setting up the new Shanghai Revolutionary Committee, Mao gave up the idea of reorganizing the party from the grass roots upwards.

Throughout 1968 there were still frequent clashes taking place between former Red Guards, who resisted their orders to 'volunteer' to go to the countryside, and the army that required the Premier's attention. Hangzhou provides a typical example of the problem. It had been so secure a resort that the Chairman could relax there with a small bodyguard in the early days of the Cultural Revolution. The group that assumed power with the support of the army at the end of the period of violence expressed similar views to those of the people who had been thrown into opposition. The situation in the beauty spot became extremely tense and it was rendered all the more bewildering because there were no outstanding personalities leading the rival factions. Indeed, it was a barely concealed question of haves and have nots that blew up again and again and continued long after the 9th Party Congress.

Thanks to the efforts of the PLA order was slowly restored. In Guangzhou many extremists were arrested and some forty people were executed after a series of public trials. Widespread violence and disturbances were gradually brought under control by the army. This was the result of relentless pressure from Peking and the introduction of new methods of surveillance designed to note the activities of former extremists. In Guangzhou, for example, Little Red Sentinels – young schoolboys – reported not only on members of their own family but also aunts, uncles and any neighbours near enough for them to observe. Indeed, this type of surveillance, though generally not undertaken by children, was introduced throughout urban China and served not only to ensure that the authorities knew about the political activities of individuals but also their sexual habits. In the early 1970s if a young woman who normally reached her dormitory after work around 7 P.M. was half an hour late she was required to give an explanation of where she had been and what she had been doing.

Once order was restored, the PLA, again under pressure from Peking, began the work of establishing the Revolutionary Committees. Initially they received but little help from the party, those few stalwarts who attempted to obey the instructions from the senior cadres were thwarted in their attempt to hold branch meetings by the wide differences of opinion on what the party line should be. Indeed, in many urban areas, despite the fact that some millions of former Red Guards had been sent down to the countryside, the radicals were still strong and most unwilling to co-operate with the older party members, and especially those who had been rehabilitated towards the end of the Cultural Revolution. 'The triple alliance', as it was called, of youth, middle age and old was uneasy and the antagonism between the former Red Guards and party veterans remained strong. The result was that in many places the Revolutionary Committees, which should have contained, in theory, representatives of the 'new' – Red Guards – together with old party members and the armed forces, were largely made up of senior soldiers, who assumed a local party role, together with a thin sprinkling of young former Red Guards and veteran party officials.

During 1969, 'inside' people – members of the Central Committee of the Chinese Communist Party and Ministers – were aware that something – they did not quite know what – was wrong. For articles appeared which condemned the theory of 'having more than one centre' or 'many masters' and 'every group wants to become a nuclear power'. It is now known that these articles were personally inspired by Premier Zhou, who had insufficient time to write them himself, and that Lin Biao and Chen Boda were targets. Indeed, the fact that when at last all the Revolutionary Committees were elected, the Congress was timed twelve and a half years after the 8th Party Congress instead of the statutory five suggested something was badly wrong.

Premier Zhou may too have suspected Lin had some secret contacts with Moscow – because during the run-up to the 9th Party Congress he received reports from his intimate friend the former Chief of Staff of the PLA, Ye Jianying (later to become

Defence Minister), as well as other old trusties in the armed forces, that Chen Boda had been observed visiting military units where he whipped up political support for himself and Lin Biao. It can be safely assumed the Premier passed this information on to Chairman Mao and Deng Yingchao, his wife, but few other people.

Officially, the congress was designed to sum up the results of the Cultural Revolution, to adopt a new party constitution and, most important of all, to elect a new leadership. The way for this was paved by the completion – at long last – of the formation of Provincial Revolutionary Committees. Their establishment had taken two years longer than Premier Zhou had envisaged. The record number of delegates, 1512, resulted from the difficulty of the various Revolutionary Committees, the revived mass organizations and provincial party organizations in agreeing to any one person as their representative. Thus, many delegates were frequently chosen because they were innocuous and had no strong political feelings but had demonstrated their devotion to the party or state, such as 'model' industrial or farm workers. Indeed, over two-thirds of the delegates were wearing the olive-green uniforms of the PLA.

Chairman Mao opened the proceedings with a condemnation of Liu Shaoqi as the arch 'scab', 'traitor' and 'capitalist roader', but his speech was by way of introduction to the main report which was given by Lin Biao and took two hours and ten minutes to read. Lin and Mao appeared to the delegations to be on 'extremely good terms' and pictures taken then would confirm this impression. One delegate told me he felt they were 'at one' to judge by the way they exchanged glances and enjoyed private jokes about the reactions of the delegates. Certainly, although we now know all was not well between Mao and his second 'chosen successor' at that time, Mao needed Lin and the army and Lin needed Mao. Lin's speech, which was initially drafted by Chen Boda and drastically revised by both Chairman Mao and Premier Zhou, received a standing ovation. Almost every other paragraph of the script, which he delivered in a soft, hesitant voice, stumbling at times, contained praise for Chairman Mao. He urged that the Cultural Revolution should continue and repeated Mao's new slogan urging 'The whole party, the whole nation to unite to win still greater victories'. On foreign policy, Lin repeated Mao's words on imperialists being 'paper tigers' and expressed strong condemnation of both the United States and the Soviet Union.

The work of the congress to elect the new leadership – the Central Committee – then began and lasted for twenty-one days and indicated the wide breadth of disagreement between the three rival factions, which, as always in China, tended to overlap at various points. Certainly Lin and the armed forces were in the ascendancy and the handful of former youthful heroes of the Cultural Revolution found it extremely difficult to get a hearing. But despite the tremendous show of amity that Mao and Lin put on, Premier Zhou still retained a great deal of clout not only with Mao himself but also with a majority of regional commanders in the army. Indeed, Zhou could count on the staunch support of Ye Jianying, a former Chief of Staff of the PLA, the veteran Zhu De, who had been Commander in Chief of the PLA and his old friend and financial expert, Li Xiannian, together with at least two important regional commanders, Chen Xilian (Chen Hsi-lien) then in Shenyang and Xu Shiyu (Hsu Shih-yu) in Nanjing. One delegate told me that as the congress wore on Lin became progressively more tired-looking and frail while his speech became hesitant and at times inaudible. His 'meekness' was in marked contrast with Chairman Mao's self-confidence and robust posture.

As always, Lin overdid the praise he 'poured over the Chairman', according to one of the delegates. Mao Zedong's thought was described as the theoretical basis for the party and the country in an era when imperialism was heading for total collapse and socialism advancing to worldwide victory. Liu Shaoqi, it will be recalled, had upset the Chairman by cutting out all references to his thoughts from the party constitution. To those of us who visited China shortly after the congress, officials then stressed that it marked the end of the militant phase of the Cultural Revolution but this view was later changed. The Central Committee elected by the congress was not as radical or as youthful as many veteran party members feared. Indeed, the average age was sixty-one as opposed to fifty-six in the outgoing committee. Well over half the members came from the armed forces while the number of cadres (civil officials) went down from nearly 60 per cent to 31 per cent which meant a considerable rise in the number of 'model workers' and representatives of mass organizations, who invariably cheered the last speaker no matter what he had said. There were, too, far fewer former Red Guards than had been envisaged. The Groups represented were the Regional Military Commanders Xu Shiyu, Chen Xilian and Li Desheng (Li Te-sheng) as well as a Central Military Group headed by Lin Biao together with Huang Yong-sheng (Huang Yung-sheng), Chief of Staff, who was also a Regional Military Commander, and Wu Faxian (Wu Fa-hsien), Air Force Commander. Ye Jianying (Yeh Chien-ying), a former Marshal and Vice Chairman of the MAC, was a supporter of the State Administration Group led by Premier Zhou Enlai and Li Xiannian, the Finance Minister. The Radical Group was led by Mao himself and supported by Chen Boda, Kang Sheng and Jiang Qing, together with the 'Shanghai radicals', Yao Wenyuan and Zhang Chunqiao. The old party veterans like Zhu De played no real role but generally gave their support to the Premier.

Only the 'inside' people – members of the Politbureau, Ministers, certain regional commanders and party leaders – realized that the 9th Party Congress was not the magnificent personal triumph for Lin Biao that China and the world assumed. He had, of course, realized his ambition to be 'recognized' as Mao's 'chosen successor' and this fact had been written into the constitution which had to be studied by everyone from party members down to schoolchildren during their bi-weekly periods of political indoctrination. But the congress had revealed Lin's weaknesses as a political figure and the delegates were talking about his hesitant speeches, curious personal habits and total lack of charm. Much of this must already have been known to the older delegates who recalled Lin's failure in the diplomatic world when he was the communist representative to the Guomindang Government in Chongqing during 1942/3.

On the purely military front many of the senior officers who had been purged during the Cultural Revolution were, at one time or another, serving under Lin and were considered 'his' men. Indeed, the congress, according to Steve Chin (the leading Sinologist at Hong Kong University), disclosed the 'weak structure' of Lin's faction. Mao, however, was expected to remedy this situation by giving Lin Biao more military and political power as the official 'successor'. Certainly, despite the criticism it was generally believed that, given Mao's wholehearted backing, after a decade at the

Ministry of Defence, Lin would be able to stand on his own feet. Lin complained to his intimate associates that he had not always been able to appoint and dismiss commanders as he wished because Mao remained Chairman of the powerful MAC throughout the Cultural Revolution. Indeed, Lin claimed that almost all important documents, even military directives, were personally signed by the Chairman. Naturally Lin could put his own men into any positions other than, say, the top twenty-five when they became vacant. In fact, Lin was later accused of putting far too many of his own men into positions as they became vacant.

It was not then realized how much Lin Biao had come to rely on the advice of Chen Boda in his dealings with the state and the party. Chen was happy to assume this role as chief adviser and liaison officer for, although he was still number four in the party pecking order, Chen lacked a power base, and was apprehensive that he might lose face if not power. But acting as Lin's front man in his dealings with the Chairman, Premier Zhou and the radicals helped him to retain at least the semblance of his former authority.

12

Final Purge of Liu

The fact that the Communist Party was smashed at every level was even more serious for the nation than the lethargy and boredom of the urban population. The ruling Politbureau, which had been responsible for the policy of both the state and party since the formation of the People's Republic in 1949, had virtually ceased to operate by the end of 1967. Indeed, after the Cultural Revolution Group headed by Chen Boda had assumed the political leadership, the Politbureau rarely met. From the regional level down to the humble factory committee there were virtually no effective parties operating. The trade union movement, the Women's Federation and the Young Communists' League were all in a state of complete disarray and unable to function while the formerly respected party cadres were either in disgrace or too frightened to open their mouths. The police force had ceased to function in some areas and so, too, had the Public Security Branch which regulates the movement of foreigners and others from one city to another. This was due to the fact that these offices were frequently manned by veteran party cadres who had come under attack from the Red Guards and they were too frightened to venture into the street or go to their offices. To add to the problems, in many towns radical groups were still fighting one another for power, while, for the first time since the early 1950s a black market emerged in Guangzhou, Shanghai, Tianjin and Peking. Goods were stolen from shops and, in fact, in the large Xidan market in Peking there was a disturbance followed by widespread looting in which shots were fired.

It was hardly surprising that the formation of administrative Revolutionary Committees in major cities and provinces was taking so much longer than Premier Zhou had anticipated. Order, such as it was, was being maintained by the PLA whose morale had improved with the news that their Minister, Lin Biao, had moved to the right as a result of the excesses of the Red Guards and their ultra-leftist supporters.

Lin Biao, during his first two or three years at the Defence

Ministry, gave tremendous support to the radical General Political Department which decides on the political line to be propagated by the army's political commissars. Lin was then extremely anxious to publicize the 'Little Red Book' and to promote the cult of Mao's personality. The army never forgave him either for what they regarded as destructive radicalism or for his insistence on being 'red' rather than 'expert'. Nonetheless when the disorders and the breakdown of public security reached a nationwide scale Lin was convinced that a well-organized solid army was essential not only for the survival of the party but also of the state. He changed his mind, or, as some of his enemies claimed, he saw which way the wind was blowing and quickly adjusted his sails.

Outside the armed forces a majority of those elements amongst the 'broad masses' who had initially backed the Red Guards had also turned their backs on the extremists and transferred their allegiance to Premier Zhou. Meanwhile many of the local party members, who had been natural supporters of Liu Shaoqi, had followed the example of Lin Biao and, after noting the way the political wind was blowing, decided that Premier Zhou was the better bet.

Mao, when summing up the scene, reportedly concluded that while it was difficult if not downright impossible to assess party loyalties, some 90 per cent of the bureaucracy was solidly behind Premier Zhou and over 85 per cent of the armed forces supported Lin Biao. Further, reports reaching the Chairman from his intimate advisers claimed that agricultural production was increasing while the workers were warmly clad in winter and had sufficient food to eat. This he confirmed during his tour of agricultural communes. In addition, many of them were engaged on long-term projects such as the construction of dams and irrigation schemes, tunnels or additional terraces.

Like so many directives that came from the Chairman at this period, it was under pressure from Premier Zhou that he had put his chop (signature) on the final plans for the restoration of a much needed state and party administration. By the end of 1967, despite encouragement from the PLA, only five cities had established Revolutionary Committees. Indeed, little or nothing had happened in this direction since the Chairman had himself suggested provinces and cities should set up Revolutionary Committees based on those already in being in Peking and Shanghai composed of veteran party cadres, representatives from the PLA and the Red Guard in equal proportion. Party veterans were somewhat naturally reluctant to serve on committees with the wild young men who had so frequently beaten them up, while the Red Guards in turn retained their scorn for the older generation of revolutionaries. Truly the Revolutionary Committees representing the young, middle aged and veterans, which was another way the Chairman had expressed their composition, were proving extremely difficult to establish.

Thus Lin addressed senior officers on August 8th, 1967 at a rally with Premier Zhou Enlai, the radical organizers of the Cultural Revolution Group, Jiang Qing and Chen Boda, and key regional commanders, including Chen Xilian (then in Manchuria, later to command the Peking Military Region) and the ultra-leftists Wang Li and Qi Benyu (Ch'i Pen-yu). In an effort to appease both radicals and moderates Lin opened by stressing that the Wuhan 'mutiny' had been welcomed because it had made it possible to expose 'bad people and bad things'. Virtually using the same words as Chairman Mao had done, Lin suggested that the gains of the Cultural Revolution were enormous and the price people had paid for these was comparatively very small. Lin, in strange contrast to speeches he had made only ten days earlier, then urged that the army be cleansed of 'counter-revolutionaries'. Some officers had made mistakes, Lin admitted, but he blamed Xiao Hua, the head of the General Political Department (Chief Commissar), for the fact that the commissars, who had been successful initially, had failed 'to keep abreast of the situation' due to the fact that Xiao had 'made one mistake after another'.

The commanders got the message, which was that they and not the commissars would now become the main repositories of power. During the following week, the Peking military authorities publicly condemned over fifty political commissars in the army who had promoted the Cultural Revolution to the disadvantage of the professionalism of the armed forces. At the same time, a slogan was relaunched backed by a campaign, 'Support the army and cherish the people.' However, the ultra-leftist May 16th Group continued to demand a major purge in the armed forces until they themselves were purged in late September 1967 as Chairman

Mao criticized factionalism. In September, Lin issued an order authorizing the army to use force in self-defence.

Jiang Qing spoke in favour of the new line and, as a noted extremist and the wife of the Chairman, she had plenty of 'clout' with the Red Guards. Premier Zhou, who had been deeply worried by the two-pronged attack against the defence forces and himself, had successfully persuaded Chairman Mao at this point to press his wife into action. At the earlier stage in the Cultural Revolution Jiang Qing had demanded a purge of the army while urging the Red Guards to 'take up arms'. Now she claimed the army was 'the corner stone of the proletarian dictatorship' and anarchy would follow if it were allowed to disintegrate. Having in the past suggested that Red Guards should rob garrisons for weapons, Jiang Qing now stressed 'the penalty for stealing weapons is death'. The time, Jiang Qing said, was one to sit down, take stock and study documents however difficult this might be. The leader of the Cultural Revolution directorate, Chen Boda, made a similar speech calling for the 'end of civil war' and 'begging the Red Guards' not to allow their minds to get 'over-heated'.

However, despite increased assistance from the PLA only fourteen new Revolutionary Committees were formed between January and May 1968. The pace had been slowed down by the upsurge in Red Guard activity that Jiang Qing unexpectedly encouraged during March.

In the absence of an effective police force, troops were authorized to pick up young men and women who had taken part in disturbances and demonstrations if they had no obvious job and send them to agricultural communes near to the Russian border. Indeed, many thousands of young people were merely sent back to the agricultural communes they had deserted during the first heady flush of freedom that the early days of the Cultural Revolution had brought, when they travelled around their own country, free of charge and without permits, and were treated as very important people while they exchanged what were then called 'revolutionary experiences'.

In 1967 security was so lax that Chairman Mao was strongly advised by his personal bodyguard, Wang Dongxing (Wang Tunghsing), against making a tour of agricultural communes in Huxian county as the factional fighting there rendered it too risky. (Wang was later to become an important member of the Politbureau and famous for his arrest of the Gang of Four in 1976.) The Chairman went ahead with the tour and although he was treated like a superhuman being throughout, he realized the chronic state of unrest that existed in the region. The Chairman was personally horrified not so much by the factional fighting but by the reasons some of the more violent radicals gave for their actions. Translated into comparable English, many youthful leaders, after proclaiming their loyalty to Chairman Mao and the radical line, admitted in Harbin (Manchuria), Hangzhou and Chengdu, Sichuan Province, to quote but three, that there was only a limited amount of 'cake' and they were also fighting for it. The cake was good housing, the use of a car and the right to attend banquets given in honour of visitors, combined with the easier life senior cadres enjoy.

Back in Peking for a brief visit in the latter half of September 1967, the Chairman put his chop (seal) on a new series of directives that appeared as big character posters on the walls to the university and also in the main streets of the capital. The directives were carried by some newspapers but not, significantly, by the *People's Daily*, the official organ of the Chinese Communist Party, which was still in the hands of the ultra-leftists. For the uninitiated foreigner, the Chairman's message was and indeed still is difficult to understand. It read, 'The situation is excellent, everything in the world is in a state of disorder.' 'World disorder' equates with 'excellent' in the Chairman's oft-used jargon. But following this he described the troubled conditions inside China and the urgent need to re-establish order. The Chairman also claimed that the 'masses' had been mobilized in a vital political struggle against the 'revisionists' – Liu Shaoqi's name was not mentioned – and this, in turn, had raised the level of their political consciousness. In Chinese terms this means that the people had developed a greater acceptance and understanding of Marxism as taught by Chairman Mao.

Premier Zhou Enlai, who had been worried and under constant, although mostly indirect, attack for some months, had his position as the solidly entrenched Premier re-established by the publication of a large and widely distributed coloured picture which was captioned the 'Proletarian Headquarters'. The Premier was in a group that included Chairman Mao, Defence Minister Lin Biao and the leaders of the Cultural Revolution Group, Chen Boda, Jiang Qing and Kang Sheng. Shortly after this Zhou's protégé, the Foreign Minister Chen Yi, was given a place of honour at the celebrations marking the eighteenth anniversary of the People's Republic. This confirmed that he, Chen Yi, was once more in charge of his own Ministry and the ultra-leftists were expelled.

Nonetheless, the Regional Military Commanders freely admitted they were experiencing difficulties in some areas in their efforts to restore order. But they held the guns and, of almost equal importance, the means of communication. Although it took time, the army commanders had little doubt they would win in the end. It was especially significant that in a country famous for warlords there was no attempt to return to this traditional way of life. Both Premier Zhou and the Chairman were frequently worried by the ever increasing overall power of Lin Biao and the military authorities but, at that time, never about the ambitions or authority of any one individual general in the High Command, although they were secretly concerned that the hundred per cent pro Lin-ist, Zheng Weishan, commanded the 38th Army in Peking.

May 7th Cadre Schools

The Chairman, then acting on the advice of the Defence Minister, Lin Biao, agreed in May 1968 to the establishment of the first 'May 7th Cadre School' which was set up at Liuhou in Heilongjiang Province as a pilot project for the 're-education' of former Red Guards together with the hundreds of thousands of party and state officials who had become redundant during the Cultural Revolution. It was an ideal system for putting political opposition at all levels into cold storage. At first it was regarded as a punishment to go to one of the May 7th Schools, although a high proportion of those people who were sent to them were displaced in the special campaign the Chairman inspired to produce 'better officials and a simpler administration'.

The May 7th project caught on and in Guangdong (Guangzhou) Province alone some 300 such schools had been set up by the end of 1968 and were attended by over 100,000 officials and former Red Guard leaders. Despite these schools, however, the Red

Guard continued to cause trouble even in such a radical stronghold as Shanghai where intellectuals complained bitterly that they were being barred from party membership and had inadequate representation on the new Revolutionary Committees. Marx was quoted in support of the Red Guard argument: 'Old things always seek to restore and consolidate themselves in newborn forms.' An editorial in *Wen-Hui Bao* said that 'Even if, in form, they [the Revolutionary Committees] have absorbed revolutionary fresh blood, they have also done everything they could to get rid of fresh blood – like squeezing a tube of toothpaste.' (Again I have used the official translation.)

Liu's sad and sick purge

The final purge of the Head of State, Liu Shaoqi, and his dismissal from all the posts he held in the state and Communist Party came as an extraordinary anti-climax after nearly two years of political upheaval. Indeed, when it happened, Mao's 'chosen successor', who had opposed the Chairman's policies at the time of the Great Leap Forward, was a sick man in an unknown prison. Mao never forgave Liu for having attempted to 'push him upstairs' and transform him into a powerless figurehead – 'a Buddha on the shelf'.

Obviously, Liu Shaoqi and his friends knew they were facing a possible purge from the time of the Eleventh Plenum of the 8th Central Committee held in August 1966 when Lin Biao was named as the 'exclusive Vice-Chairman' of the party, replacing Liu as Mao's 'heir designate'. The Chairman had made a dramatic change in the nomination of his 'chosen successor' and Liu's stock had fallen sharply. Further, Mao's famous poster, 'Bombard the headquarters', left no doubt in the minds of all party cadres that the Chairman wanted either to purge Liu or transform him into a harmless old stooge.

Despite the fact no names were mentioned both Liu and Deng Xiaoping were well aware that they were the 'monsters' the Red Guard were urged by the Cultural Revolution Group to 'sweep away'. Although Liu set up work teams, which have already been described, of party stalwarts to oppose the radical elements, both he and Deng realized there was but little they could do to regain their lost power. For the personality cult of the Chairman was then at its height and every man, woman and child who did not want to run into trouble in the streets was wearing a large red Mao badge. Mao had become a communist god/emperor to 800 million Chinese of whom only a handful knew his real power was limited.

By January 1967, the whole nation was aware that the man constantly reviled in the press as 'China's Khrushchev' and the 'top person in authority taking the capitalist road' was Liu Shaoqi. In addition, he was denounced as the 'Head Boss' of all revisionists in the party, the Government and the army and the supreme commander of the 'bourgeois headquarters' opposed to the 'proletarian headquarters' headed by Chairman Mao and Lin Biao.

Liu Shaoqi called on Chairman Mao after the way had been prepared by Premier Zhou. During the interview Liu, as Head of State, offered 'to retire at once to the country and farm for the rest of his life with his family'. In other words to fade out and become a harmless old stooge. But the Chairman said nothing and continued to smoke. When Liu finally ran out of words the Chairman dismissed him suggesting that he should 'study hard' and 'look after his health'. It is likely that the Chairman did not want Liu to retire to his birthplace, which was only a few miles – the other side of the hill – from Shaoshan, not far from the Hunan capital of Changsha. For this was 'Mao country' and the house where the Chairman was born already received thousands of tourists and visitors every year.

This was the last time the two leaders actually met. From that moment, according to Liu's wife, they were both gradually cut off from communicating with their supporters and friends in the outside world. But with one or two notable exceptions they were left to enjoy the security and calm of living in Zhongnanhai.

It is now known that Jiang Qing, Kang Sheng and Chen Boda together with Lin Biao deliberately made many false charges against Liu Shaoqi and persuaded others to 'frame' him. But these nefarious actions of Jiang Qing and her associates, which were later disclosed during the trial of the Gang of Four (1980/1), were then only known to a few frightened people. Chinese officials insist that Chairman Mao knew nothing but if this were the case he should certainly have suspected something, for as early as August

1966 Jiang Qing and Lin Biao acting in concert began to trump up charges against Liu Shaoqi. Lin Biao's wife, Ye Qun, persuaded a senior army officer to write a letter accusing Liu Shaoqi of wanting 'to become Supreme Commander' and of 'building up' in co-operation with Deng Xiaoping the 'bourgeois headquarters'. During the subsequent trial of the Gang of Four, massive evidence was produced that indicated Jiang Qing as the instigator and leader of the group especially established to persecute Liu Shaoqi and Deng Xiaoping. Jiang also appeared to have sponsored the small extremist party of Red Guards, some of whom were admitted to Zhongnanhai and to Liu Shaoqi's bungalow in July. Chairman Mao apparently did not believe quite all he was being told about the man with whom he had worked so closely for forty-seven years, who had stood next to him in that glorious moment when he had proclaimed the establishment of the People's Republic. Mao's doubts were accounted for later by the rare and sporadic attempts he made to protect Liu Shaoqi from the worst of the indignities inflicted by the Red Guards on their victims.

The Chairman may have been influenced by what afterwards appeared as phoney charges against Liu Shaoqi made by people who had worked for him and others when they were in prison. But he was reportedly moved by Liu Tao's repudiation of her parents Wang Guangmei and Liu Shaoqi. Not only did Liu Tao criticize their bourgeois way of life but gave details of the 'splendid' food they ate and the 'leather' shoes they wore. The Chairman went to the other extreme of always wearing canvas shoes and patched clothes, as well as eating hot but simple food. He was horrified to hear Liu Shaoqi had been responsible for the construction of a beautiful villa (now a guest-house) near a palm-covered beach in the south of Hainan Island and that it had been fitted with a Japanese air-conditioning plant in 1955 as well as luxurious furniture and bathrooms. Much of what Liu Tao said was exaggerated and her motives in endangering her parents' lives were based on self-interest. However, she and her husband later tried unsuccessfully to escape to Vietnam. After the death of Chairman Mao and the arrest of the Gang of Four she renounced almost all she had said in an effort to work her way back into favour.

(It is interesting to note that the last three and the most serious of the people who opposed Mao's policies were denounced by intimate relatives. Peng Dehuai was personally damaged in the eyes of the Chairman and other members of the Politbureau by the public criticisms made by his wife, Pu Ancui, which were magnified by Jiang Qing and the radicals. They were later divorced. Lin Toutou, the daughter of Lin Biao, betrayed his escape plans to Premier Zhou Enlai, which enabled him to ground all planes. She received several public messages of gratitude at the time but nothing has been heard of her since.)

There are contradictory reports of what happened on the night of July 18th, 1967, when a large crowd gathered in the Avenue of Heavenly Peace just outside the entrance to Zhongnanhai and loudly demanded to be allowed to enter in order to question the Head of State, Liu Shaoqi, and his wife Wang Guangmei. One version is that acting on 'top level' instructions, which were later said to be from none other than Chairman Mao, the special guard refused the crowd permission to enter. After hours of waiting, during which some of the demonstrators in the crowd even erected tents, two small groups of extremists were escorted to Liu's bungalow. While one group questioned Liu and his wife, separately, in two public rooms 'for two hours and twenty minutes', the second group, mostly composed of Red Guards, ransacked and looted their apartment. However, Chinese officials told me in 1986 that Liu was actually 'struggled' by a small crowd of fanatic Maoist Red Guards who beat him up and stripped him naked. In any case, he was placed under house arrest shortly after the Red Guards left. Liu then wrote to the Chairman to say that the charges being levelled against him of 'opposing the Communist Party and attempting to restore capitalism' were false. He also added, 'I have lost my freedom.' Had Liu been 'struggled', that is spat upon and 'tried' by the Red Guard, it should have been mentioned specifically in the trial of the Gang of Four.

But it would have caused considerable trouble to the Chairman, Jiang Qing and other leaders if the sanctity of Zhongnanhai had been desecrated by crowds of Red Guards, for it was only here that the leaders were able to relax out of sight of the 'broad masses', put their feet up and sit by the lake in summer reading books or papers. They all valued this privacy. In addition to the report that Mao attempted to protect Liu Shaoqi from the mob, on at least two occasions he publicly refused to allow Liu to face a trial that would have been what the Red Guards called a 'struggle session'. The Red Guards were then most anxious to have Liu and Deng, together with their wives, face thousands in a public arena and answer questions about their way of life and right-wing activities before being subjected to a trial by the masses.

A handful of extremely brave party veterans who had access to the Chairman attempted to discover from him why he was allowing false accusations to be made against the man who was still technically Head of State, but Mao quickly changed the subject. Jiang Qing then made the party veterans' lives 'uncomfortable' and they were reminded that Kang Sheng had already described Liu's 'defections' at a public meeting in July. Despite Jiang Qing's deep personal dislike, indeed bitter hatred, of Deng Xiaoping, he gradually faded from the prominent number two position beside Liu Shaoqi that he initially held as a bourgeois capitalist roader. While Liu was being built up as a 'scab', a 'traitor' and an 'agent of imperialism' Deng's image was neglected. Certainly Premier Zhou was giving him what support he could but it is also likely that the Chairman decided the Cultural Revolution Group should not bite off more than they could chew. After all, Mao was fond of stating that a man must eat a meal 'one bite at a time'.

Mao's main complaint against Deng appears to have been that the Secretary General of the party never consulted him and that from 1949, when he was appointed to the post, until October 1955 he never came to see him or ask his advice. However, from 1952, when Deng was transferred to Peking and became a Vice Premier, although he was working with Zhou Enlai, Mao regarded him as one of 'his' men.

During the summer Liu's health began to fail, owing, according to his wife, to frustration, worry and lack of exercise. Gradually he became bedridden and was nursed by his wife and given tonics and other basic medicines but he was not visited by one of the experienced doctors who normally attend sick members of the Politbureau. Liu's state of health deteriorated as the 'false' and 'trumped-up' accusations against him mounted. Many of the charges were 'supplied' by prisoners in their confessions, which were invariably written in jail. (More on this later in the trial of the Gang of Four.) Liu was reported by them to have 'secret dealings' with an American, Leighton Stuart, who was a former ambassador, which were arranged by Liu's wife, who was herself dubbed 'an American agent'. In May 1950 a bizarre and utterly false report from prisoners also suggested that Liu sent his wife's brother Wang Guangying to Hong Kong to provide the CIA with a large amount of valuable intelligence.

The Central Committee was called upon to announce Liu's official 'disgrace' but before it actually met he was moved from his bed in the bungalow he had occupied as number two in the state and party in Zhongnanhai. Although under house arrest, Liu was then still receiving news from his Guards and listening to the radio. Liu's removal was ordered suddenly by Lin Biao as Defence Minister and soldiers carried him to an ambulance that took him in great secrecy to the military airport near Peking. He was then flown to Kaifeng, an old city to the east of Zhengzhou. According to Liu's widow, when his plane landed at the airport, specially selected medical workers climbed on board and found Liu 'lying on a stretcher, naked and wrapped in a pink coverlet, his eyes tightly shut'. 'A tube for feeding was in his nostril and his face was drained of colour.' Liu was transferred, naturally, by ambulance to a prison prepared for him that was heavily guarded and surrounded by electrified barbed wire. The *People's Daily* published a report in May 1980 that stated that Liu was imprisoned in a vault of a building which, before the Communist victory in 1949, had been a branch of the Golden City Bank.

At a special meeting of the Central Committee held in Peking from October 13th to 31st, 1968 with Mao in the chair, a resolution was passed unanimously 'purging' Liu. He was dismissed 'once and for all' from the party and state posts he held and he was described as 'a renegade, traitor and scab' as well as 'a lackey of imperialism, modern revisionism and the Guomindang reactionaries' who had 'wormed his way' into the party and 'committed innumerable crimes'. To make the effect more devastating, he was, again according to his widow, only informed of his disgrace on his birthday, November 24th. This she relates as an extra piece of mental cruelty inflicted on him by Mao. After receiving the news of his purge, Liu rarely spoke again. He died technically of pneumonia on the morning of November 12th, 1969 but the last year of his life has been described by his widow as one of 'silent protest'. After his death his corpse was taken by jeep to the crematorium with his legs hanging out of the back in an undignified manner.

Unhappily, only Liu's widow could gain some small satisfaction from the fact that at a conference called by the Central Committee in April 1979, 'after detailed and careful investigation and study, measures were taken to clear the name of the Comrade Liu Shaoqi'. And in an assessment of the Chairman it was then stated that, though he was a great Marxist, he 'made gross mistakes during the Cultural Revolution'.

It will never be possible to judge with any degree of accuracy how much political influence Jiang Qing wielded over the Chairman at that time. Certainly, her power increased greatly as he allowed her to speak on his behalf, while the co-operation between Lin Biao and Jiang Qing rendered life extremely difficult for Premier Zhou. But throughout the whole period of the Cultural Revolution, up to and after the 9th Party Congress, Chairman Mao was fit and in full command of his own office. If he was taken in by Lin Biao's overdone flattery or pressured by Jiang to support the radicals, he knew what he was doing. Although they dared not open their mouths, many party cadres were shaken by Mao's treatment of Liu. Deng Xiaoping was disgraced at the same time but, again, due in some measure to the influence of Premier Zhou he was not imprisoned, nor was he expelled from the Communist Party. This was a near miracle. Deng was sent to an agricultural commune where for a time he served meals to peasants at table as well as working in the fields.

Mao was reported to be relieved when the purge was all over. He had been extremely reluctant to impose drastic curbs on the activities of the extremist Red Guards until after Liu and Deng were disgraced. Although the resolution of the special meeting of the Central Committee was worded in the language Jiang Qing had been using about Liu for years, we now know it was Premier Zhou's threat to resign after the attack on the British Embassy and the Wuhan incident that caused Mao to act, too late, against the 'ultras', before ousting the Head of State. The Chairman's own sense of survival, combined with that of the party and state he had done so much to create, remained strong.

The Chairman knew well that the campaign against the Foreign Minister Chen Yi, who had been one of the main targets by the ultra-left throughout the summer, was indirectly aimed at Premier Zhou, who was Chen's protector. Chen had co-operated with the Red Guards even when they paraded him through the streets wearing a dunce's cap. Chen, too, had attempted to answer their more reasonable questions on Chairman Mao's thoughts, but he openly refused to accept their political creed. After Chen was ousted from the Foreign Ministry he lost 40 lb in weight. But the Chairman cheered his flagging spirits by saying that 'the ultras committed more errors in forty days [when they were in the Foreign Ministry] than Chen Yi had committed in forty years'. Further, Mao informed all his visitors that the list of accusations the May 16th Group had drawn up against the Foreign Minister were 'grossly exaggerated and basically worthless', and that Chen Yi was going to remain at the post he had occupied with such dignity and try to redeem his past mistakes by taking into account the criticisms that had been levelled against him.

No sooner had the Chairman, after his reported 'inspection tour' of agricultural communes in Central China, thrown his weight behind Premier Zhou than the campaign against the Premier ceased, and this was followed by a gradual phasing out of the attacks on Chen Yi. There is now no doubt that although the Chairman took some weeks to make up his mind to support Premier Zhou, with whom he had worked for nearly half a century, it was the plea by his right-hand man, the diplomat and administrator, that the country faced complete disintegration, anarchy and eventual famine that influenced Chairman Mao. And for a man who enjoyed political upheavals as much as the Chairman it must have been a difficult decision, because his number one enemy, Liu Shaoqi, was then still technically Head of State and living almost next door to him in the Politbureau residential compound at Zhongnahai. With hindsight there can be no doubt that Premier Zhou's threat to withdraw from active political life had shaken the Chairman, though he apparently did not admit all this until Premier Zhou was disengaging from office years later in 1975 owing to sickness.

After Liu's final purge, Premier Zhou, with the Chairman's backing, immediately ordered a mild repression to end 'the frenzied freedom' that had brought some urban areas to the brink of chaos. The extremists were dropped from the group that was organizing the Cultural Revolution and a vast new campaign was opened through the medium of big character posters to denounce the misdeeds of the May 16th Group and other left-wing extremists. The Chairman, who thoroughly enjoyed writing both political slogans and romantic poetry, composed some of them himself while resting in Behtaiho, where he, or more correctly the Politbureau, had a dozen villas in the former summer capital. Between bouts of swimming under heavy guard and talking with party leaders, Mao drafted the new political posters, but he did not, in fact, write the one saying the May 16th Group was a secret organization proclaiming ultra-leftism 'but in reality rightists in disguise' as some of his enemies suggested. The slogan, 'Cut off the Black Hand', which meant get rid of counter-revolutionaries was, however, attributed to him. Photographs of 'missing' ultra-leftists or ultra-rightists, as they had now become known, appeared on walls and 'splittists' and others taking the secret bourgeois line were arrested. Those British subjects who had encouraged, if not actually participated in, the burning of the embassy remained at large. They could hardly be termed 'rightists' for they had gone to leftist extremes with their Chinese friends in the desire to be more deeply communist, or 'holier than thou' in the Marxist sense.

The activities of foreigners then working in China, which have gradually been disclosed during the past few years, illustrate the incredible state of chaos, confusion and downright lawlessness that existed in some areas. The heart of all the troubles lay with the half million students in Peking, who were divided into two main factions known as 'earth' and 'heaven'. The earth group was extremely left and it was they who carried the petrol from the university to a nearby park in preparation for the burning of the British Embassy. After the Wuhan incident the earth group conspired in violent attacks on Premier Zhou in the summer of 1967, and, later, against certain army commanders.

Perhaps the most remarkable foreigner was a natural leader named Sidney Rittenberg, who was an American. Before the Cultural Revolution he wielded great influence on other members of the English-speaking community, most of whom were then working for the Foreign Languages Institute which is situated near the university. Rittenberg had been associated with the Chinese communists since they were in the Yenan caves, where he had gone as an interpreter. Now married to a Chinese he was understood to convey Chinese political views to the other foreigners working for the Peking Government. In addition he was an epicure who spread his influence from an apartment of considerable comfort furnished with rare Ming chairs.

In what came to be known as 'the last winter of Liu Shaoqi', November 1966, Rittenberg suddenly ceased to be the best known guide to Chinese restaurants and an erudite interpreter of classical Peking operas as he symbolically took to boiled rice and old clothes, a step that caused many foreign 'friends' – as communist sympathizers are called – to put away their silk dresses and don old and faded clothes. Rittenberg then threw his weight into organizing support for the Red Guards and gradually moved further and further to the left as the Cultural Revolution progressed until he openly gave his support to Yao Dengshen in 1967, in the confident belief that Yao would become permanent Foreign Minister. But the episode most difficult to explain is how this American managed to obtain control of Peking radio after the Cultural Revolution Group split in August 1967. He was powerful in a mysterious, armed and extremely left splinter group of the May 16th unit. *Pravda* was not the only foreign newspaper to report that China's key propaganda organ was in the hands of an American. Predictably, his power did not last long. For a time he was held virtually a prisoner by the staff of the radio station after his period of executive authority had come to an end.

Earlier, Rittenberg, together with a closely knit team of veterans from the Foreign Languages Institute, including Michael Shapiro, Israel Epstein and his British wife Elsie Fairfax-Cholmeley, who were reported to have supported the extremists in their fight against the British Embassy, became involved in what was later described semi-officially as 'a major ultra-leftist plot in Tianjin'. Modern foreign workers who supported the Cultural Revolution, including the authors Nancy and David Milton, called on Rittenberg to warn him that more than one of his associates were being denounced as ultra-leftists, 'frauds' or linked with the May 16th organization, but Rittenberg at least gave them the impression he believed his leftist friends would triumph in the end. Rittenberg's final undoing was an attempt to organize an ultra-left arts festival in Tianjin where the main attraction was to be the production of a play called *Madman of the Modern Age*, which he had been promoting for many months. This was afterwards dubbed 'a reactionary black play' and 'counter-revolutionary'.

A partial explanation was given by Premier Zhou Enlai to a group of foreign experts in the Great Hall of the People in March 1973 (a month after I became resident in Peking). In the presence of Jiang Qing, Zhang Chunqiao, Yao Wenyuan, Wang Hongwen and Qiao Guanhua (later to be Foreign Minister) the Premier blamed the ill-treatment of foreign experts working for the Chinese Government during the Cultural Revolution on the excesses of the movement caused by 'the subversive actions of Lin Biao and his anti-party clique'. The Premier half apologized to his audience by saying that it had taken a long time to sort things out but now the 'foreign friends' were free. David Crook, who was arrested at the time in the Foreign Languages Institute, almost by accident it appeared, was a different case, the Premier claimed. For some of 'the masses' believed there were genuine grounds for suspicion in view of the fact that the building in which he was taken was controlled by a rebel regiment backed by 'the notorious ultra-leftist May 16th Group'. The Premier ended by apologizing in the name of the Chinese Government to those 'foreign friends' who had spent five years in prison. Zhou did not mention the long periods they had spent in solitary confinement, perhaps because he hoped this fact would not become news.

Rittenberg was not released with them and Premier Zhou repeated that he was 'a thoroughly bad lot'. Premier Zhou did not, however, mention that since full diplomatic relations with Britain had been established in the previous year (1972) the new British Ambassador, Sir John Addis, had devoted considerable energy to obtaining the release of Elsie Fairfax-Cholmeley and other British subjects who had been held in detention since the Cultural Revolution. One or two later expressed their gratitude to the embassy while others actually suggested it was not unreasonable of the Chinese authorities to have locked them up under the circumstances, adding that they did not want to renew their British passports. They changed their minds about this, however, after a few months had elapsed.

Much to the surprise of Chinese watchers, Rittenberg was released from prison in mid-December 1977, four and a half years later than his associates and nearly two years after the death of Premier Zhou Enlai, who continued to regard him until the end as a 'bad element' who had deceived other foreigners. After his release Rittenberg was joined by his Chinese wife and for a time they occupied a small flat in the Friendship Hotel where Elsie Fairfax-Cholmeley, Israel Epstein and David Crook have also been living since their release from prison. Like them he has never discussed his imprisonment or release and despite the relaxed atmosphere today in Peking, they all still appear most reluctant to meet foreigners in China. However, Rittenberg now spends much of his time in the United States where he has undertaken several lecture tours.

13
The Fall of Lin Biao

Gun barrels and inkwells

The 'inside' people of Peking – members of the Central Committee of the Chinese Communist Party and Ministers – had first realized something was seriously wrong in the relations between Chairman Mao Zedong and his 'chosen successor', Lin Biao, when Jiang Qing circulated a picture she had taken of him without a cap. Lin was extremely sensitive about his bald head and no previous picture had ever been reproduced showing the shiny scalp of the Defence Minister. Indeed, Lin's vanity had caused him to adopt the habits of northern Chinese peasants, who rarely remove their headgear – generally caps – even at meals.

First leaks of important political developments in Peking are all too frequently revealed by such small details, for the Chinese remain the most secretive people in the world, even amongst themselves. In this particular case vital differences of opinion between Chairman Mao and 'his closest comrade in arms' predated by at least four years the snap Jiang Qing took of Lin's bald pate after he had wiped his brow on a hot summer's day in 1970. Indeed, many Chinese now feel Mao's mistrust of Lin dated back to his relationship with Gao Gang and Lin's expulsion from the Politbureau before 1955 after having been a member of that ruling body for five years. The secret Mao/Lin disagreements were a part of the intense power struggles within the communist hierarchy that flare up into the open every few years, although it now seems truly incredible that the quarrels were known only to the Chairman, Premier Zhou Enlai, their politically active wives, and two or three other intimate friends in the Politbureau.

The last and most dangerous threat to Chairman Mao's life and unique position as leader came from the second of his 'chosen successors', Lin Biao, who attempted to have the Chairman assassinated when he refused for the second time to be kicked upstairs and play the role of a powerless head of state. Despite his position as Defence Chief, Lin must have realized the risks he was taking, for he knew all too well that Mao's previous 'chosen successor', Liu Shaoqi, had been disgraced and purged largely because he had attempted to treat the Chairman 'like a Buddha on the shelf'.

There is plenty of evidence that neither Chairman Mao nor his loyal and tactful Premier Zhou were happy to see the PLA emerge as the only dominant force in China during the later part of the Cultural Revolution, quite apart from any suspicions they might have held about Lin's personal ambitions. According to a letter the Chairman wrote to his wife, Jiang Qing (which has already been mentioned), Mao had been suspicious of Lin's activities since July 1966, although he had been to immense pains to hide his true feelings from Lin and his colleagues on the Politbureau.

It will be recalled that as early as May 18th, 1966 Lin had given an extraordinary address to a group of party members overtly designed to point a finger at Liu Shaoqi and his associates. Lin did not, however, refer to the fears frequently expressed by Premier Zhou Enlai that the Soviet Union might well be attempting to stir up trouble inside China in an effort to 'take the fortress from within'. Lin opened the main part of his speech with a list of coups and attempted coups in ancient China. He then proceeded to suggest that the activities of Liu's supporters in their efforts to ferment underground troubles had not all been exposed. Lin talked of the possibility of 'a counter-revolutionary coup d'état and subversion'.

'Coups d'état had become a fad,' Lin stressed, claiming that according to 'incomplete statistics' there had been sixty-one in the capitalist countries of Asia, Africa and Latin America in the past six years. Of these, Lin stated, fifty-six were successful. Eight heads of state were beheaded, seven were kept as puppets and eleven were deposed, Lin added brightly. Chairman Mao was not present at the meeting but he admitted afterwards he was somewhat alarmed by the reports he received from Jiang Qing about it. Lin concluded by saying that 'seizure of political power depends on gun barrels and inkwells', adding 'these deserve our attention'. Reading between the lines, once the opportune time comes, as when a counter-revolutionary war breaks out or Chairman Mao dies, a political crisis will occur in this vast country of 800 million.

When he gave the address, Lin had already been Defence Minister for six years, since 1959 – and had built up a General Staff that was believed by outsiders to be 75 per cent devoted and loyal to him, but he was not certain of the support of all the eleven powerful Regional Military Commanders. However, at that time he was close to Jiang Qing who was influential with the political commissars in the PLA and she had power, too, with the Chinese media as well as the cinema and theatre.

Mao, who, despite their quarrels, never appears to have doubted Jiang Qing's utter loyalty and devotion to him, wrote her early in July a confidential letter that the Central Committee took the unusual step of releasing to senior party members shortly after Lin's downfall. When the Chairman wrote to Jiang he was 'resting up' in the country while she was working from the Cultural Centre in Shanghai. Mao expressed his 'reservations' about Lin's speech in a lengthy and deeply personal letter in which he also complained that the Politbureau 'seemed in a hurry to circulate'. Some of 'his [Lin's] ideas profoundly disturb me', the Chairman wrote, adding that 'I could never have believed that the little books I have written could have such magical power.' The letter Chairman Mao wrote on July 6th, 1966 confirms that even then he was deeply suspicious of Lin's activities but took enormous trouble not to reveal his feelings. First circulated to the Politbureau and 'certain trusted members' of the Central Committee, the letter was leaked sometime in 1970 or 1971 and has since been confirmed as authentic by senior Chinese officials.

Opening with a few words about his plans the Chairman then wrote he had 'been reading' material every day. 'The situation changes from a great upheaval to a great peace once every seven or eight years,' he observed, adding, 'Ghosts and monsters jump out by themselves.'

The Central [Committee, Mao wrote] urged me to publish the address of my friend [Lin Biao] and I have prepared to agree with it.

His address was devoted entirely to a political coup. There has never been any address like this before. I was quite uneasy at some of his thinking. I could never have believed that the several booklets I wrote could have such magical power. Now after he exaggerated them, the whole nation has exaggerated them . . . It seems I have to concur with them. It is the first time in my life that I unwillingly concur with others on major questions. I have to do these things against my will . . . I have self-confidence but also some doubts. I once said when I was in my teens that I believed I could live two hundred years and sweep three thousand li. I was haughty in appearance and attitude. But somewhat I doubt myself and always feel that when the tigers are absent from the mountain, the monkey there professes himself a king. I have become such a king. But it does not mean eclecticism. In my mind there is some air of a tiger which is primary, and also some air of a monkey which is secondary.

It is valuable to know oneself. At the Hangzhou Conference held in April this year, I expressed my opinion, which was different from that of our friend's [Lin Biao's]. I could do nothing else. In the conference held in May in Peking, he spoke in the same manner. The press spoke even more so, describing me as a god. In that situation I could only go to Liangshan [the mountains] . . . Things always go to the opposite side. The higher a thing is blown up, the more seriously it is hurt at the fall. I am now prepared to be broken to pieces. This does not bother me. For the matter can never be destroyed; I may become pieces that's all. There are more than a hundred communist parties in the world. Most of the parties no longer believe in Marxism, even Marx and Lenin have been smashed by them, much less we.

I suggest that you should pay attention to this problem and should not become dizzy with success. You should remind yourself often of your weak points, shortcomings and mistakes. On this I have talked with you numerous times, and I did so last April in Shanghai. The above seem to be black words. But don't the anti-party elements say so? I feel that some methods of their presentation are not very appropriate; I mean the effect on me.

WHAT THEY WANT TO DO IS TO OVERTHROW OUR PARTY AND MYSELF. This is the difference between me and the black gang. These words cannot be made public at the present time since all the leftists say so now. Publication of these words will mean pouring cold water on them, which will help the rightists. Our current task is to overthrow a part of (it is not possible to overthrow all) the rightists in the party and throughout the country. We shall launch another movement for sweeping up the ghosts and monsters after seven or eight years, and will launch more of this movement later.

I cannot determine when we should publish these words, for the leftists and the broad masses of people do not welcome my saying so. Maybe we should wait until I die when the rightists come to power, and let them do the publication. The rightists may attempt to use my words to hold high the black banner. By so doing they could get behind the eight ball. In China, after the emperor was overthrown in 1911, reactionaries could not hold power long. If there arises an anti-communist rightist political coup in China, I am sure it will not be peaceful and very probably would be short-lived. For all revolutionaries who represent the interest of 95 per cent of the people, would not tolerate it. At that time the rightists may prevail for some time by using my words but the leftists may also organize some of my other words to overthrow the rightists.

The Cultural Revolution this time is a large-scale and serious manoeuvre. In some areas [such as Peking Municipality] the revolutionaries were resurrected overnight. Some units [such as Peking University and Qinghua University] collapsed quickly because of their involved and complicated ingredients. As a rule, where the rightists are more rampant, the worse they will be defeated and the more vigorous the leftists will be. This is a nationwide manoeuvre in which the leftists, the rightists and the staggering fence-sitters will absorb useful lessons. The conclusion is, and still is, that the future is bright but the road before us is twisted.

I have reproduced 95 per cent of the text of Mao's letter in the authorized translation because it not only accused Lin of trying to overthrow 'the party and myself' in 1966 but contains some revealing and important sidelines on Mao, his youthful boasts and his political relations with Jiang Qing. Chairman Mao mentioned all these points to Edgar Snow at a later date when he complained that Lin was trying to isolate him from the 'broad masses'. Further, the Chairman expressed anger that on several occasions, even before the 9th Party Congress, Lin had added his own name on official documents after that of Mao's together with the words 'closest comrade in arms and chosen successor'.

The catalyst for Mao's letter to Jiang Qing was, somewhat

curiously, not mentioned. It was the military reshuffle that took place during May and July 1966 when Lin Biao, without consulting Mao, who was Chairman of MAC, moved the 38th Army, commanded by Zheng Weishan (Cheng Wei-shan), which was personally loyal to him, to garrison Peking. This provided an additional reason for Mao to remain in seclusion away from the capital when he composed the letter. But the Chairman's desire to keep up the appearance of loyalty and affection towards Lin was so great that less than a month after writing the letter the Defence Minister was elected the sole Vice Chairman of the Central Committee of the Communist Party at the Eleventh Plenum in August. Shortly after this the Red Guards emerged in all the major cities of China and Lin appeared beside Mao as his 'close comrade in arms' at no fewer than eight mass rallies in Peking from August 12th to November 26th, 1966.

Both Chairman Mao and Premier Zhou were aware that Lin was putting his own men into positions in the armed forces whenever one fell vacant, but to deploy his own special loyal troops into Peking was in Mao's view the opening of another, quite different, game. Mao was especially angry that the Peking Regional Military Commander, Yang Yong, was transferred from this key post because he was, at least in the Chairman's view, a first-class soldier who had done a good job in the capital during the run-up to the Cultural Revolution.

The role of Premier Zhou Enlai

Premier Zhou Enlai appeared perfectly content to play a low-key role as the number three man in the party. During the early days of the Cultural Revolution the Premier admitted to some members of the Central Committee he had had a series of violent disagreements with his Defence Minister when the army was backing the Red Guards. But their relationship improved slightly after August 1967, when the policy of the defence forces changed after the emergence of the ultra-leftists when additional responsibility was given to army commanders to restore law and order and ensure its maintenance. The Premier was, however, frequently apprehensive, if not downright alarmed, at intervals during 1968 and until the 9th Party Congress was called in April 1969, by the enormous power the Defence Minister was wielding. But he could do little about it for, unhappily, during the autumn of 1967 and throughout 1968, the PLA was kept extremely busy by the frequent clashes that took place between rival groups or as former Red Guards resisted orders to be transported to the countryside.

It was a rather nasty eternal triangle. The Chairman could not use his power and charisma without the support of Lin Biao and the armed forces; nor could he operate the party or administer the country without Premier Zhou Enlai. Lin and Zhou had by this time little or nothing in common and frequently jarred one another. While the Premier obviously enjoyed Mao's earthy conversation he was not amused by Lin's 'dirty jokes' but what most jarred on the Premier was Lin's backstage intrigues and unrelenting 'pushiness'. In reality there was a power struggle between them despite the fact the Premier did not aspire to become the 'chosen successor' or number two man. It never ceased to surprise Lin Biao, Kang Sheng and Jiang Qing that with all Premier Zhou's advantages and universal popularity, he did not then aspire to be in the line of succession. He appeared to support Lin Biao as the 'chosen successor' but frequently stressed that a small body of people, ideally the Standing Committee of the Politbureau, should be prepared to take over the collective leadership of the nation when the Chairman (in his own words) 'went to meet Marx'. Perhaps it was because there was no effective Standing Committee at this time that the Premier stood by Lin.

The latest unofficial theories in Peking on Lin Biao's motivation in contemplating a coup d'état against Chairman Mao years before he actually planned and mounted the '571 project' are based on the belief that he was far closer to the Russians than his colleagues or, indeed, the Chairman ever realized. 'Lin was always a Stalinist at heart,' one of his former associates told me, adding that he must have been working for the Russians for years. When it was suggested that the intense security which surrounded Lin's every movement as Defence Minister would have made secret communications virtually impossible, the official replied by stating that Kim Philby and Donald Maclean had succeeded in both Britain and the United States even when they were under suspicion and observation.

Although more and more responsible Chinese appear to believe that Lin and certain members of his staff had illicit dealings with the Russians long years before the coup, official Chinese policy still stresses that Lin only allied himself with Moscow and became a traitor shortly – a matter of months, at most a year – before his attempt on the life of the Chairman in September 1971. However, mystery still surrounds Lin's three and a half year residence in the Soviet Union as well as a second visit he made from Yenan either late in 1943 or early in 1944 after he had renewed contacts, it is now assumed, with representatives of the Soviet Union when he was in Chongqing. The strained relations between Premier Zhou and Lin began in Chongqing where Zhou was already established as the Communist Party's representative before Chiang Kai-shek invited Lin in October 1942 to take part in specific talks on military co-operation between communist and nationalist forces against the Japanese. The two men – Zhou and Lin – were there together for much of the nine months and Lin returned for further negotiations on the reorganization of the communist forces in the late spring of 1943, just before he made his second visit to Moscow.

The flattering pamphlet that was produced in Peking in June 1969, as an official biography, after Lin had been formally designated as Mao's 'chosen successor' states that he 'participated in the war of self-defence in the Soviet Union'. It was popularly believed Lin took part in the defence of Leningrad in September 1941. Certainly he won the high praise of Stalin for having performed 'immortal feats of arms' despite the fact that he was not fully recovered from his wounds. Lin, who was then only thirty-one, made valuable contacts in Russia and was influenced by all he saw and heard. That he learned to read and write Russian as well as to speak the language fluently is not mentioned in the biography.

There are, understandably, two Chinese biographies and one Russian on Lin. In the one already mentioned he was stated to be the son of a poor peasant then working in a village on the north bank of the Yangtze River in a small village to the east of Wuhan, while the information given after Lin's attempted coup d'état claimed that his father was a rich and powerful landowner or warlord who insisted that Lin was brought up in the Confucian tradition. In fact, Lin's father was a 'petty landowner' and the proprietor of a small handicraft factory that went bankrupt. After this he became a purser on a Yangtze river steamer. At some time Lin's father visited Russia but whether to admire the Revolution or sell handicrafts is not clear.

What is certain is that when Lin returned to Yenan from the Soviet Union, Mao's frequent criticisms of the Russians, on whom they were dependent for arms and ammunition, combined with the 'inward-looking' parish pump atmosphere which prevailed at that time in Baoan prevented the young Lin from airing his views on the Soviet forces or Russian communism.

Unofficial critics of Lin in China today believe he again renewed, or brushed up, his contacts with many of the same Russians when he was fighting the nationalists in the north-east – Manchuria – in 1947/8. The Chinese make no secret of the fact that they were then collaborating closely with the Soviet Union. At that time Lin was both a popular and an extremely successful general and his force, initially known as the North-east PLA, was redesignated the 4th Field Army. In addition, Lin played a political role as Secretary to the Communist Party's North-east Bureau before he prepared to move south and hand over the Manchurian command to Gao Gang, who, as already reported, was ultimately purged for his too-active co-operation with the Russians. Lin's own friendship with Gao caused him to be degraded and removed for a time from membership of the Politbureau. There can have been no other reason. Lin may then have renewed contacts with the Russians during the period when he was either ill, or out of favour and angry that he had been dropped from the Politbureau, from the opening period of the Korean War until 1956. There is a strong school of thought amongst some of his critics in Peking today that believes Lin initiated important and direct contacts with Moscow during this period. It is curious that contrary to popular belief he did not go to Korea with the 4th Field Army. Instead, he received, according to the excellent biography produced by Donald Klein and Anne Clark, 'a new assignment, scarcely compatible with wartime command responsibilities, as Chairman of the Central-South Military and Administrative Committee'. Certainly he was suffering from tuberculosis and still 'in the dog house' for his friendship with the disgraced Gao Gang. Re-elevated to the Politbureau in April 1955, Lin made his first public appearance in five years at the 8th Party Congress in September 1956. Lin, however, did meet the Soviet military leader K. E. Voroshilov in April 1957. Unhappily, although rumours abound about Lin's ill health and quarrels with Chairman Mao, Liu Shaoqi and Premier Zhou Enlai during this period, no major causes of disagreement between Gao Gang and his unattractive personal habits have come to light.

After Lin became Defence Minister he organized what appeared to be genuine intelligence operations overtly geared to obtaining information about the Russian forces as well as, quite naturally, sponsoring psychological warfare projects designed to improve relations along the border where the number of major incidents in the late 1950s was running at a score or more a week. It is assumed that any feelers Lin made towards Moscow were under excellent cover and could easily have been disowned by him. Some of these psychological warfare projects were designed to ensure Lin's contacts within the armed forces of the Soviet Union and it is likely one or two people on his personal staff were used for special communications with the Russians. There was nothing crude or risky about his methods at this time, such as using the Russian Embassy in Peking.

Mao's critics now claim that despite all the Chairman knew about Lin's past political record, he was frequently 'swept off his feet by Lin's flattery'. One witness who worked in Mao's private office said Lin treated the Chairman like a god/emperor and flattered him wildly whilst at the same time fawning on him. The same person admitted that many officials were then treating Mao as a 'superhuman' being which, at times, the Chairman appeared to enjoy. Premier Zhou, for his part, maintained what has been described as a 'deferential attitude' in public towards Mao that decreased with the number and importance of the people present until, when they were alone, they once more became 'old comrades' together. Unlike Liu Shaoqi, Premier Zhou Enlai had never attempted to establish a political following in the party or the administration. The Premier knew he could rely on the solid support of the entire bureaucracy, his only power base, together with a considerable proportion of those senior officers, especially the Regional Military Commanders, in the armed forces. In addition, in my experience, Zhou was at that time widely respected by moderate men and women in industry as well as those working on agricultural communes, who knew instinctively that he stood for law and order and a gradual improvement in living standards.

Few Chinese were aware that Zhou, who had worked hard and selflessly since the People's Republic was founded in 1949, was one of the 'returned students' who had been sympathetic to the policies of the twenty-eight Bolsheviks who were sent into China by Stalin, under the leadership of Wang Ming, to press the Moscow line on Chairman Mao in the early 1930s, before the 'Long March'. Zhou himself admitted years later that 'once he realized his mistake and made his self-criticism he never again deviated from the general line of Mao's policy'. Indeed, from the time of the Zunyi Conference (January 1935), which took place during the 'Long March' and marked Mao's ascendancy over his pro-Stalinist rivals, Zhou had been steadfastly loyal to Chairman Mao, although at times deeply critical of his actions in the privacy of Mao's study or the Politbureau.

Premier Zhou did, however, make some unostentatious efforts to reduce the power of Lin and the PLA in those spheres that caused no damage to what he described as the 'only experienced party organ' the Cultural Revolution had left intact. As order was slowly restored during the latter part of 1968 and Revolutionary Committees established, Zhou's officials in the state bureaucracy were able, once more, to function and the administration gradually – very gradually – became more effective.

Although Premier Zhou gave up the Foreign Ministry in February 1958 he retained a deep interest in world affairs; indeed, apart from the period covered by the Cultural Revolution, China's relations with the Soviet Union and the West were his main preoccupation, although he was still bogged down on a day-to-day basis with domestic decision-making. Sometime during 1968, or even earlier, he appears to have relegated the United States to second place as an enemy of China. It was at the time when communist agents in both Indo-China and North America began to claim there was some hope for a speedy end to the war in Vietnam. Whatever diplomatic and revolutionary remarks the Premier made in public, he was a 'total pragmatist' in private life, according to those near him, and he fully realized that China could not afford to remain on bad terms with both the Soviet Union and the United States. While the military threat posed by the American defence forces in Vietnam and the Far East was showing signs of receding within the next few years, the Russians were causing an alarming series of border incidents. In addition, they had begun a significant military build-up along the north-eastern border of what was formerly known as Manchuria but had become one Military Region made up of the provinces of Heilongjiang, Jilin and Liaoning with a part of the autonomous area of Inner Mongolia.

An article written by President to be Richard Nixon and published in the October 1967 issue of *Foreign Affairs* urged that China should be brought 'into the world community' and predicted that the time was coming when a dialogue with mainland China should begin. This had caught the eye not only of Premier Zhou but also of Chairman Mao, much to the delight of the former, when it was translated and reproduced in *Reference News*. (*Reference News* circulates translations of important articles on China, whether friendly or not, that appear in the western press. It is crudely duplicated and circulated amongst senior cadres, but rarely falls into the hands of a foreigner. *Reference News* was believed to have a circulation of around 3 million in 1973 and to have increased to over 6 million by 1977.)

Thus it happened that both Premier Zhou and President Nixon altered their approach and attitude towards one another at around the same time. Premier Zhou gave the new President time to settle down in the White House before making the suggestion that talks between their ambassadors in Warsaw, which was the only contact they had, should be resumed. But this took place much later, in January 1970, after a break of two years.

Naturally, Lin Biao, as Defence Minister, was fully aware of the details of the Russian build-up on the border. Some of his commanders have since suggested they felt it strange, even at the time, that, although publicly noted as an anti-Russian for much of his life, Lin refused to accept that the Soviet Union posed a far greater threat to China than the 'imperialists'. In addition to the massive but gradual Russian build-up on the border, Premier Zhou continued to draw the attention of the political commissars in the PLA to the dangers posed by Moscow's possible plans to 'take the fortress from within'. In fact the Russians mounted a most successful propaganda campaign and thousands of troops and the inhabitants of agricultural communes near to the border tuned their radios to stations on the Soviet side of the frontier when no one was looking. In addition, many pro-Russian Chinese commanders influenced the troops serving under them.

Chen Boda had produced a series of well-written papers and reports in support of the theory that the 'imperialists' with their intercontinental ballistic missiles and nuclear submarines posed a far greater threat to China than the Soviet Union with its less sophisticated nuclear arsenal. Some people believe this was the moment when renewed secret high-level approaches were made by Moscow to the man who it appeared would shortly succeed Chairman Mao as an all-powerful Chinese leader. And the Russians were not rebuffed, as Lin's supporters claim, for Lin's fear and dislike of the Chairman grew to exceed that of the pro-Russian revisionists – one senior official told me 'super secret' contacts between Lin and Moscow began in 1959 at the latest and rapidly developed into an intimate relationship.

Premier Zhou Enlai, who was exceedingly clever as well as tactful and diplomatic, may well at times have suspected Lin's contacts with the Soviet Union. In any case, he continued to receive authentic reports from his intimate friend and former Chief of Staff, Ye Jianying – later to become Defence Minister – as well as other old trusties in the armed forces that Chen Boda had been observed yet again on a long tour during which he visited military units in order to whip up political support for himself and Lin. Towards the end of the Cultural Revolution, Chen Boda had found himself still a member of the Standing Committee of the Politbureau but without a power base. Further, as the former head of the Cultural Revolution Group he was open to criticism for having at times supported the ultra-leftists in the 516 Group. Indeed, many of Chen's supporters and associates were already disgraced.

Although somewhat similar accusations could be levelled against Jiang Qing she did withdraw her support from the extremist organization before Chen and, naturally, her position as the wife of the Chairman then gave her an additional measure of security. Perhaps because of his isolation, Chen had thrown in his lot with Lin Biao and the PLA. But he also enjoyed, at least in the early days of his intimate association with Lin, the protection of Chairman Mao. Mao was fond of this intelligent man and indebted to him for having 'systematized' his political philosophy during the nine long years in the Yenan caves when Chen Boda was the Chairman's political secretary and head of the Propaganda Department. Calling on his profound knowledge of the works of Marx, Lenin and Stalin, Chen 'touched up' many of the Chairman's essays and he was the only man to accompany Mao on both his journeys to Moscow. Chen had been to Mao in many ways what Harry Hopkins was to President Roosevelt, or Ismay to Churchill during the Second World War, but, unhappily, Chen was not prepared to spend his life as Mao's powerful shadow. He wanted public acclaim as well as state and party responsibilities.

Nonetheless, despite Chen Boda's close relations with Lin Biao and the PLA, and the fact that he had supported the ultra-leftists towards the end of the Cultural Revolution, the Chairman continued to regard him as one of his most intimate personal political advisers. Indeed, Chen remained close to Mao until vital differences arose between them over the proposal to create a new post as Head of State. The issue first came to the knowledge of the Chairman's personal staff and one or two members of the Politbureau after Mao angrily refused to consider the draft keynote speech Chen had prepared for him, under Lin Biao's supervision, to make at the 9th Party Congress. Naturally, Chen proposed that the Chairman should himself occupy the new projected 'top job' as Head of State but to Mao this was just another trick to 'kick him upstairs' and turn him into 'a Buddha on the shelf' after the unhappy example of Liu Shaoqi. Chen redrafted the speech knowing he had lost yet more ground despite the fact he was still a member of the Standing Committee of the Politbureau, a powerful figure in the armed forces and number four in the pecking order after Mao, Lin and Zhou. Lin Biao was happy to have this highly experienced and talented man at his side despite the fact he had lost his easy access to the Chairman's study. For Lin was intelligent enough to realize that he lacked political flair not only because he was a poor speaker, but because he found it difficult at times to be sociable or to negotiate or enter into discussions.

In the secret minor power struggle between Lin Biao and Premier Zhou Enlai, which had developed towards the end of the

Cultural Revolution, Lin realized he could only gain assured seniority over the Premier if he outranked him in both the state and party hierarchy. Just before the opening of the 9th Party Congress he was poised to become – as indeed he did become – the Chairman's chosen successor in the party. But he had noted that on state occasions the Premier generally outranked him, as he received all the important foreign guests and he was all too obviously administering the country. Zhou had the great advantage of having lived as a student in France, Britain and Germany as well as the Soviet Union for a short period. Although he rarely spoke English, French or German for more than a few minutes he generally greeted visitors from these countries in their own language and, from time to time, corrected his interpreter in his almost flawless old-fashioned English or French. While Lin not only lacked the linguistic ability, other than Russian, to communicate with visiting Ministers and Heads of State, he had no manners and, in view of his oft-mentioned personal habits, the Chinese had the sense not to press him to the fore when entertaining important foreigners. Doubtless Lin was irritated, too, by the Premier's popularity.

Lin and Chen together revived the plan to make Mao the Head of State, despite the fact the Chairman had made such a major issue about Liu Shaoqi trying to transform him into a powerless figurehead. Indeed, Lin appeared to have believed that, as a result of the flattery he piled on to Mao whenever they met, he would eventually persuade him to become the Head of State at the 4th National People's Congress, which Lin anticipated would quickly follow the 9th Party Congress. Lin's supporters would naturally insist then that he became Deputy Head of State thus ensuring his assumption of the leadership, which would keep Premier Zhou on the side-lines should Mao die.

Chen became reckless and nervous as he lost his political flair during the build-up to the 9th Party Congress when he arranged for commando units to be deployed in certain of the Regional Military Command Headquarters where the staff were not enthusiastic supporters of Lin. Some tens of thousands of commandos had been trained during 1968/9 for this form of duty, in secrecy, using as a cover Premier Zhou's oft-expressed fear that the 'enemy' might try to take the fortress from within. So far as is known neither the training nor the presence of the commandos was queried at a high political level at the time. However, detailed accounts of the activities of the commandos were passed on to Premier Zhou by his friends, the old trusties in the army, and Chairman Mao knew what was happening.

Chen made no secret of his attempts at public banquets and official party gatherings to sound out commanders and members of the General Staff on where their sympathies lay, indeed, whether or not they were staunch supporters of Lin Biao. Although western diplomats and the few journalists and other foreigners living in Peking at the time were unaware of the intensity of the rivalry between Lin Biao and Premier Zhou, or the strain between Lin and several of the Regional Military Commanders, Warsaw Pact countries appear to have been well informed.

During the 9th Party Congress Chen Boda maintained a low profile perhaps as a result of Mao's displeasure over the draft speech. Further, there was no need for action as everything was going well for Lin Biao and Chen was relieved to be re-elected to the Standing Committee of the Politbureau maintaining his place as the number four man in the party; truly things might have been said to be looking up. The unity of the 9th Party Congress was at least in part due to serious border clashes which had taken place during the previous month (March) on Chen-pao or Damansky Island on the Ussuri River to the north of Vladivostok. In an area which was only sparsely populated the Russian soldiers took possession of the island which, according to the Chinese was on their side of the river. (Some Russian maps support this view.) This attack, which caused the death of some hundreds of Chinese soldiers, produced an atmosphere of solidarity amongst the delegates that enabled Lin to be named as 'Mao's chosen successor' without opposition. Many observers now think that Lin knew about the Russian attack or even acted in liaison with Moscow.

Lin's triumph short-lived

Immediately after the congress concluded, Lin noted a certain unidentified but strong and growing opposition to himself, Chen Boda and the men he had promoted in the armed forces. At that time various sub-committees were meeting in Peking to discuss the convening of the 4th National People's Congress, generally referred to as China's rubber stamp Parliament, in order that a new constitution could be promulgated.

After the previous troubles, of which Lin was fully aware, it is quite inexplicable that he went around frequently expressing the view, to members of the Central Committee and senior officials, that it was essential to have a Head of State and, obviously, it must be Mao. He left Chen Boda to add that as Lin Biao was already the Chairman's 'chosen successor' he should certainly be elected as the Deputy. The problem was that Chairman Mao kept repeating that he did not want the job, which included a good deal of purely ceremonial duties as well as some real power. After Lin realized the depth of Mao's personal opposition to becoming the Head of State he toyed with the idea of putting himself up for the job. Members of his family and friends discouraged this obviously stupid move, on the grounds that it might well alarm Premier Zhou Enlai and the administration or, alternatively, elevate Lin into a position in which he would 'reign but not rule', 'like the Queen of England', as one Chinese intellectual added.

Chen Boda, who knew Mao's views even better than other members of the ruling Politbureau, surprised members of the Central Committee attending the Second Plenum of the 9th Party Congress at Lushan in August 1970 when he suddenly jumped to his feet and proposed that Chairman Mao be named Head of State. In what appeared to have been an unprepared speech, Chen made many flattering statements about the Chairman and then proposed that he be unanimously elected as Head of State. This was followed by a deathly hush as almost all the members were well aware of the Chairman's views, which had been aired so often. Further, they realized that were Mao so appointed it would be difficult, if not downright impossible, to give the number two slot to anyone but Lin Biao whose popularity was all-too-obviously slumping. (I have already mentioned Lin's body odour and his odd personal habits which by this time included a fanatical desire to keep out of sunlight and, more objectionable to those near him, a reluctance at times to use a lavatory.)

Ji Dengkui (Chi Teng-k'uei), Secretary of the Henan Provincial Party Committee and a former peasant, endorsed Chen's proposal with an air of enthusiastic innocence but Mao abruptly jumped to his feet and turned it down before there was any discussion. Chen was working in close co-operation with Lin Biao and, on this occasion, acting under his orders. The proposal was to cause the end of his political career and, ultimately, his freedom for having thus bounded into the limelight. Despite the fact he still ranked as number four man in the party, his actions came up for examination. Chen then found himself facing an unexpected, full-scale attack that may well have been inspired by Premier Zhou as it was strongly supported by his friends, the regional commanders and 'Long Marchers' still serving on the General Staff in Peking. To the surprise of many, Lin supported Chen because Chen had confidential instructions in writing from him, but, in any case, the General Staff knew the two men were working closely together. From his own purely selfish viewpoint this was unfortunate for Lin as it further alerted Premier Zhou to Lin Biao's activities which were even then being dubbed as 'subversive' by many of the commanders in the PLA who passed on the titbits of anti-Lin gossip.

Chen disappeared in October 1970 but his disgrace was not announced until over a year later. Lin was warned by his friends that he, too, would find himself out of favour if he did not change his tactics promptly. Thus, after having taken possession of the documents, which could have been harmful to him, Lin jumped on to the bandwagon and denounced his former collaborator. Indeed, Lin appealed to the armed forces to criticize this extraordinarily ambitious 'little ordinary person' – otherwise translated as 'humble little commoner', which was how Chen referred to himself at one of the rallies he addressed during the Cultural Revolution.

Lin must have become increasingly uncomfortable and apprehensive at this time as hundreds of his supporters were involved in self-criticism, largely because of their association with Chen. Somehow the Defence Minister managed to remain aloof but he was well aware his stock was falling dangerously. Foreigners living in China noted that from about this time Mao's 'Little Red Book', with its introduction by Lin Biao, was thrust into the background in the official bookshops to make way for the basic works of Karl Marx, Engels, Lenin and the four complete editions of Chairman Mao's works. A month before Chen disappeared Mao wrote a

'Letter to the Whole Party' urging members to criticize Chen Boda and 'rectify their work style'. The Chairman then launched a campaign for 'Education in Ideology and the Political Line', which was backed by a press campaign designed to strengthen the 'unified leadership' of the party.

After Lushan the Party hierarchy was naturally aware of what the Chairman called 'a struggle between two headquarters'. The 'struggle' was as much concerned with foreign as domestic policy. Lin Biao was overtly anxious to improve relations with Moscow while Premier Zhou grew even keener to answer the peace feelers coming from Washington. Basically, Premier Zhou believed China must attempt to get on to better terms with one of the superpowers – the United States – on the grounds that it was politically dangerous to remain on strained terms with both of them. Further, it seemed to the Premier that there was but little chance of improving relations with Moscow after his experiences with the Soviet Prime Minister, Kosygin, who had been most abrasive when he passed through Peking on his way back from Ho Chi Minh's funeral in Hanoi in September 1959. The airport meeting between the two men was a near disaster, which is difficult to understand as Premier Zhou was always so diplomatic and successful at getting along with people. But the Russian was furious with the Chinese for not having invited him in advance to spend a few days in Peking. He adopted an unfriendly attitude throughout their conversations, during which he constantly reminded the Premier that the Soviet Union retained the military muscle to 'bomb China back to the Stone Age'. The one small result of the meeting was that border talks were re-opened and these did something to relieve the tension between the two communist powers, although they continued to drag on intermittently for years without achieving any concrete results.

Thus, despite opposition from Lin Biao, Premier Zhou, with the full backing of the Chairman, was able to respond to Washington's overtures in January and February and talks on the future establishment of diplomatic relations were resumed between American and Chinese ambassadors in Warsaw. The Chinese apparently seemed keen to invite President Nixon to Peking but the American incursion into Cambodia from South Vietnam caused a sudden halt to the meetings. Mao, for a time, appeared to feel Lin must be right after all and he resumed his denunciations of American imperialism. At this time the Chairman had already invited to Peking his old friend the American correspondent Edgar Snow, who had visited him at the guerrilla base in Yenan. Snow was entertained by the Chairman in the Great Hall of the People and had the 'supreme' honour of being invited to stand on the rostrum in Tiananmen Square on National Day beside Chairman Mao, as 'a gesture of friendship to the American people'. This made Premier Zhou's task far easier for the sight of a 'round-eyed barbarian' standing for the first time amongst the communist leaders prepared the 'broad masses' for changes and, indeed, set the tone for a reorientation in foreign policy.

Edgar Snow's appearance caused disquiet if not downright alarm amongst Lin's supporters who launched a new campaign in the army, which was incorporated into political indoctrination, that it was better to be on good diplomatic terms with an unfriendly socialist state than an amicable imperialist one. Meanwhile, Edgar Snow carried goodwill messages combined with an invitation to visit Peking, back to President Nixon, who responded by referring to China for the first time as 'the People's Republic'. Mao had but little time to study international events after 1949 but he had apparently then grasped the essence of the global balance of power. He realized he had made a mistake in 1969 when he broke away from the Soviet Union without having achieved even basic diplomatic relations with the United States. However, Mao completely failed to understand the contribution made by foreign trade to rapid economic growth and was entirely unprepared for Japan's new role in Asia. He had believed – or dreamed – during the Yenan period that decolonization would quickly lead to a second socialist revolution on a global scale as a united socialist/communist world assumed the power of the dying imperialists. The Cultural Revolution had cut Mao off from the outside world but, after it, with but few lapses, he took the advice of Premier Zhou and grasped the importance of building good relations with the 'enemies' of the Soviet Union in western Europe and the United States.

On the domestic front Mao's fundamental realistic attitude that you must get rid of your enemies, one by one, caused him to think hard during the late autumn and, yet again, estimate his own influence in the armed forces as well as in the party and state.

Towards the end of the year, with the able support of Premier Zhou, he began taking small measures designed to break up Lin's power bases which were founded on loyal senior commanders in the PLA who also served on the Central Committee, the MAC and in the Peking Military Region.

In December 1970, the Chairman called an enlarged meeting of the Politbureau – which became known as the North China Conference – at the seaside resort of Behtaiho, a town which may be visited during the summer by foreign diplomats and journalists. The 'enlarged' meeting was an old Maoist ruse, according to his enemies, to obtain a certain majority. The Chairman then proceeded to demand that five of its leading members, known as the 'five generals' – all well known for supporting Chen Boda – should come out into the open and criticize their former colleague. The generals, from the highest ranks in the PLA, were Huang Yongsheng, Chief of the General Staff of the PLA, Wu Faxian, the Deputy Chief of the General Staff who was also Commander of the Air Force of the PLA, Ye Qun (Yeh Ch'ün), Lin's wife who ran his personal office, Li Zuopeng (Li Tso-peng), one of the Deputy Chiefs of Staff and first Political Commissar of the PLA Navy and Qiu Huizuo (Ch'iu Hui-tso), another Deputy Chief of the General Staff who was also Director of the General Logistics Department of the PLA. The Chairman's insistence on their open criticism of Chen Boda brought into the light of day the deep and growing political divisions amongst the elite of the army, state and party that had arisen between Mao and his 'chosen successor'. To many members of the Central Committee, it seemed even then that they were irreconcilable.

Early in January 1971, Lin Biao, again in a poor state of health, was personally disturbed, indeed alarmed, by the fact that Mao, acting in his capacity of Chairman of the MAC, had transferred the 38th Army, which Lin had so carefully deployed in Peking a few years earlier, away from the capital together with his keen supporter, the commander, Zheng Weishan. Lin was not consulted when this happened early in January and he realized it marked the crisis and turning point in his relations with Mao. There was no way in which he could now succeed Mao by natural or normal means. Lin felt, in any case, that the Chairman would outlive him, but long before any question of the succession arose, he realized that his days as 'chosen successor' and Defence Minister were numbered and there was nothing he could do – or so Lin thought – to save himself from being disgraced and ultimately purged. Although members of the diplomatic corps knew there were some strains amongst Chinese leaders, and the 'inside' people were aware of the 'two headquarters', the broad masses still had no idea that there were any problems between their beloved Chairman and his 'chosen successor'.

Meanwhile, as a precaution, Lin and his supporters in the PLA once more reformed and re-activated the commando units on air bases. Although their role and duties were meant to be secret, doubtless the commanders could produce perfectly sound reasons for their presence in the somewhat unsettled period through which China was then passing. When the news reached the Chairman via Premier Zhou, he deplored their formation. His immediate reaction was to have the armed and trained People's Militia, which then numbered around 5 million, placed under the civilian control of the Revolutionary Committees or towns. By this time Revolutionary Committees had been formed in almost all the important agricultural communes and factories. Naturally, the PLA continued to have considerable influence with the militia as they provided the instructors.

Sick and depressed, Lin Biao then began to muse on preparations for the coup d'état against the Chairman he had frequently thought about in the past. Since Chen Boda had been involved with the ultra-leftists at the end of the Cultural Revolution Lin's former good relations with Jiang Qing had sharply deteriorated. Indeed, he rightly suspected that she was actually influencing Mao to build up Zhang Chunqiao, Chairman of the Shanghai Revolutionary Committee, as the future Defence Minister. Lin was apprehensive at intervals throughout the planning of the coup because of the Chairman's formidable charisma but he felt there was no way in which he could placate him. It was a 'him or me' situation.

Lin's absence from the Defence Ministry in Peking caused little comment as he had been away from his desk for months on end during the Cultural Revolution and now he was genuinely sick. Mao for his part was annoyed by the pushy behaviour of Lin's followers in Peking and constantly alluded, many months before the attempted coup, to, 'A certain person who was very anxious to become state Chairman, to split the party and to seize power.' Mao was also angered by Lin's lobbying for support behind closed doors before meetings of the Politbureau or Central Committee in the manner of Members of Parliament in London, Deputies in Paris and Congressmen in Washington. Mao urged that Communist Party leaders should be 'open and above board' and that they should not 'intrigue and conspire', as Lin had done at Lushan. 'Why were they not brave enough [at Lushan] to come out into the open?' Mao queried. Certainly the Lushan Conference alerted the Chairman to the fact that a new and tenth 'struggle between two lines' or two headquarters had opened in earnest and Lin was about to rank with his principal enemies Chen Duxiu, Wang Ming, Zhang Guodao, Peng Dehuai and Liu Shaoqi. But Mao apparently, unlike Lin, believed or professed to believe that there was still time to settle this dispute peacefully.

Before discussing the projected coup with his intimate friends and prospective conspirators in the PLA, Lin and his wife drew up a list of Mao's failings in readiness to combat his 'almost irresistible charm'. In the secret memorandum about Mao there were five points:

1 Lin claimed that Mao was managing the economy in a disastrous manner because his associates were 'corrupt, muddled and incompetent'. No names were mentioned but this must all too obviously have referred to Premier Zhou Enlai. No other person has ever accused Zhou of corruption.

2 Foreign policy was being mishandled with moves away from the 'sane socialists in the Soviet Union' towards the 'corrupt capitalists and imperialists' in Washington. 'Confrontation between China and the Soviet Union is giving the Soviet Union a hard time,' Lin wrote. Again Premier Zhou was the unnamed culprit.

3 The disruptive influence in both the party and state caused by Mao's 'periodic purging of cadres', especially during the Cultural Revolution.

4 Mao's theory of continuing the revolution and the class struggle was denounced by Lin as being nothing more than Trotsky's creed of permanent revolution. Lin disliked what he called the 'merry-go-round' style of engaging successive groups in political struggle. He knew he was the next for what he termed 'the meat grinder' which had become

part of the state machine of Mao's 'social fascism'. Lin, indeed, saw himself as Mao's next target and victim.

5 Lin deeply disliked Mao's style of personal leadership. Although he himself had done so much to create and build the personality cult and establish the Chairman as a 'genius', he had grown to distrust and fear Mao's power, which enabled him 'to dismiss a Minister or senior party official with a mere sentence'.

After detailed discussions on a variety of plans Lin and Ye Qun left their summer residence in Behtaiho with its bullet-proof electronically controlled shutters and moved to the warmer resort town of Suzhou, 'the Venice of the East'. At the same time their son went to Shanghai where, from the safety and security of the large air base, he made contact with the men who were to become fellow conspirators.

Naturally, Mao had no knowledge of what his Defence Minister was doing but he was free in his criticism of Lin in talks with his intimates in Peking. The Chairman frequently claimed he had given Lin 'an opportunity to rehabilitate himself' by not summing up against him at the end of the Lushan Conference. Instead he had closed the meeting without what had become the Chairman's traditional remarks allocating praise and blame to those who had made suggestions. But Mao was heard to say, 'What shall we do with these people?', adding that it was best to adopt a 'policy of education' because 'we still want to protect Lin'. The Chairman even went so far as to say he would 'seek them out to talk things over and if they won't come to me, I'll go to them'. However, hc did say significantly that, 'Some can probably be saved, some not – we must observe their actions.'

Before Lin and his conspirators met, a number of – at least twenty – contingency plans for a possible military coup were drafted by his son and one or two intimate supporters. Lin's son provided most of the code names including that for the coup itself, 'Project 571', which in Chinese is a homonym for military uprising. The Chairman was 'B-52' and Ye Qun 'the Viscountess'. From the beginning Lin was worried for fear Mao would act against him as Defence Minister suddenly and without warning. From the many documents discovered after the coup, and confessions of those who took part, there is now no doubt that Lin had been secretly sounding out those generals who were close to him about the possibility of a military take-over for months before they actually got down to planning details in February and March 1971.

Lin's principal aim remained to transform the ageing Chairman into a completely powerless figurehead in order to ensure that the 'blind faith' the masses had in their leader could be capitalized upon by his faction. It was, nonetheless, quite apparent from the beginning that Lin was perfectly prepared, with detailed plans, to assassinate the Chairman or, indeed, anyone else who actively opposed his coup.

One draft plan opened by suggesting that the current situation was one which would benefit the Chairman in the power struggle and it was stressed that the conspirators must use 'a violent, revolutionary coup to block this peacefully evolving counter-revolutionary gradual development . . . Otherwise if we cannot use "Project 571" to stop this peaceful evolution who knows how many heads will fall?' (Official translation again used.) Outlining the strength of the conspirators the plan states that, 'Through several years of preparation our organization, ideological and military level has risen considerably; we now have a definite ideological and material foundation . . . all over the country this strength of ours is emerging, rising and flourishing daily . . . What attitude will our "fleet" [this was the code name for Lin's force] take in the future political revolution in China?' No answer is given but the document then goes on to say that Lin's strength is not small when compared with the October Revolution in Russia. It is then stressed that 'It is easier for the Air Force to gain political power over the whole nation through "Project 571" than for each military district to divide up local control.'

The second section of the planned programme opens with the sentence, 'B-52 cannot enjoy good sense for long; within a few years he must hurriedly arrange for things after his death . . . He is wary of us.' It then dubs the ruling elment 'the Trotskyist Clique' and suggests that Mao is in an historical sense going backwards – actually 'he has become a contemporary Qin Shihu-ang', who was the first ruler of the Chin dynasty (221–209 B.C.) and a ruthless, ambitious but extremely able despot.

Under the third section it is stated that 'the Dictator [Mao] is losing the trust of the masses every day'. The situation is very 'unstable' and 'locking horns have almost reached a climax'. The army, the document claims, 'has been oppressed' and officers who were attacked during the Cultural Revolution are reported to be still angry but 'dare not speak'. 'The peasants lack food and are short of clothing.' The plan also claims 'the Red Guards were cheated' and they 'served as cannon fodder until the later stages when they were suppressed and made into scapegoats.' Surprisingly, it then attacks the May 7th cadre schools which, as already reported, inspired by Mao were actually opened and sponsored by Lin himself. So far as foreign policy is concerned the document states that 'contradictions abroad are intensifying' as a result of the 'confrontation between the Soviet Union and China'. The paper then proceeds to 'the difficulties', in which it is admitted that 'our strength is still not adequate', and it is stressed that, 'The blind faith of the masses in B-52 is very deep.' The fact that B-52 'lives in seclusion', rarely appears in public, 'conceals his movements with mystery, and is guarded by tight security poses certain difficulties for our actions', sponsors of the plan agreed. Under the heading of 'Timing' Lin wrote, 'Both we and the enemy are riding a tiger from which it is difficult to dismount ... This is a life or death struggle – either we devour them or they devour us.'

Strategically, the document reveals, 'there are two critical moments: one is when we have completed our preparations and are able to devour them'. The other 'is when the enemy has opened his mouth to devour us, and we are in a critical danger: at this moment we must burn our bridges behind us whether or not we are prepared'. 'Tactical Timing and Methods' deals with B-52 and his key supporters on the Central Committee. 'We should utilize high-level meetings' to get them all into the net at once. 'First cut off their teeth and paws and create a fait accompli then force B-52 to surrender.'

The use of special methods such as poison, gas, biological weapons, bombs, '534' (an unknown new weapon, possibly a missile), car accidents, assassination, poisoning, kidnapping and small urban guerrilla bands were cited. Much of this seems naïve in the extreme and I was told it was typical of Lin's son to try to impress the fellow conspirators with his superficial knowledge of and possible access to secret weapons.

Basic strength and potential strength

The document mentions the Soviet Union: 'Externally, the Soviet Union (secret negotiation)'; 'Use Soviet Forces to check various forces at home and abroad.' The united fleet – Lin's strength – in Shanghai, Peking and Guangzhou was listed; also, 'the 4th and 5th Air Force Groups (backbone strength) controlled by Wang (Weikuo, Political Commissar for the 4th Air Force Group stationed in Nanjing); Chen (Liyun, Political Commissar of the 5th Air Force Group in Zhejiang) and Jiang (Dengjiao, Political Commissar of the Air Force Union of the Nanjing Military Region); the 9th, 21st and 34th Divisions; the 21st Tank Regiment; and civilian aviation'.

In Section 5 of the draft plan many suggestions for slogans that would influence the broad masses were discussed. 'Project 571' called for army commanders to 'unite to overthrow the feudal dynasty of B-52' and stressed Lin wanted 'a prosperous people and a strong country' rather than 'a prosperous country but an impoverished people'. In an obviously Russian-inspired paragraph, the 'true Marxists and Leninists in the undeveloped countries are urged to unite'. For the Chinese the line is, 'Use Marxism–Leninism to replace B-52's social feudalism.' At the same time the proposed propaganda stressed the need to 'guarantee the safety of the personnel of various legations'. This referred to the Warsaw Pact powers. In addition, slogans were ordered to be written requiring 'workers, peasants, administrative cadres and those in various enterprises and trades' to stay at their posts to observe and maintain social order. Somewhat muddled orders are given to the conspirators about the training of ground troops, logistic preparations, including weapons to be 'allocated or self-manufactured', as well as vehicle control, location of warehouses (for specially imported Russian equipment), ammunition dumps and intelligence.

The document reflected Lin's views in that its theme song was to 'strike first and then co-ordinate' and it was stressed that 'Zhang Chunqiao must be captured'. The overall orders then were 'to consolidate our battle front' by 'exerting all efforts to hold Shanghai, occupy the radio station and telegraph office and cut off all links with the outside ... Neutralize Nanjing' and set up good defences while holding Zhejiang and Jiangxi and 'control the paratroopers and air transport'. The paper stated that military instructions for 'Project 571' were 'absolutely top secret', and there were additional warnings that 'anyone failing in their responsibilities, wavering or turning traitor will be severely punished'. The instructions were also interwoven with personal warnings about dealing with B-52, who 'uses sweet words and honeyed talk to those whom he entices and tomorrow puts to death for some fabricated crimes'. 'Those who are his [B-52's] guests today will be his prisoners tomorrow.' However, Lin himself suggests that prisoners should be used as scapegoats to make false and forced confessions and statements to incriminate anyone who stood in his way.

Serious fears were expressed that Xu Shiyu (Hsu Shih-yu), who commanded the Nanjing Military Region and was a staunch supporter of the Chairman and Premier Zhou, might interfere. To the outsider it appears a large number of people were aware that a coup was being planned, including well over a hundred men who were instructing commandos, paratroops and other special forces in their duties during the projected takeover. Written extracts of documents found in the helicopter in which a group of conspirators eventually tried to escape, together with a plan found in Lin's office, confirm they all favoured the traditional rising in the south based on Nanjing. But these badly written, confused and repetitive versions of 'Project 571' which still read like fakes or second-class fiction, were superseded by more detailed and precise plans.

A Chinese official claimed Lin had maintained secret intermittent and inconclusive negotiations with unknown Russian generals throughout the previous year (1970). He added that detailed plans for the coup were finalized in collaboration with the Soviet Union early in 1971. It is the opinion of experts that Lin not only played his cards very close to the chest, but he did not disclose the plan he most favoured to the Russians. However, after 'Project 571' was agreed by some Russian collaborators, it was put to the leading conspirators at a series of meetings held in Shanghai between March 20th and March 24th, 1971.

Some of the conspirators complained of lack of clarity in the plans, as well as too much secrecy, so far as Lin was concerned, on the details of Russian collaboration and support. They wanted to know when the Russian equipment and weapons would be received, where they would be stored and what dates the Russians favoured in the autumn for limited military action in the north. One of the surviving conspirators suggested that Lin himself was confused and, at times, so worried he appeared distraught. Nevertheless, perhaps due to the short time they were able to spend together, and despite the shortcomings voiced about the plans, all the conspirators appeared to accept Lin's assertions that the Russians would be there on the night and, with them, total success was assured. It would, of course, have been virtually impossible for any of the conspirators to back out at that stage.

Foolishly and irrationally Lin counted on having all Mao's close allies both in the Politbureau and the Central Committee deprived of their liberty. This applied especially to Premier Zhou Enlai and the older men with whom the Premier collaborated in the central and regional administration and the army, together with Zhang Chunqiao, who enjoyed the backing of the Chairman, as well as Jiang Qing and the radicals. Just how Lin planned to deprive these major national figures of their freedom and use them without putting them behind bars is not clear. Initially, Lin planned to 'get them into his power' by calling an emergency meeting of the Central Committee in the Great Hall of the People which would be surrounded by his troops. In view of the publicity given to the 'two headquarters' and the strained relations existing at the time, would Premier Zhou and others have attended an emergency meeting called by Lin? Lin must have had some idea of what was going to happen, had they all attended, though none has been disclosed. Lin had, however, more realistic and detailed plans for taking over all sections of the media and rallying the broad masses to his cause with clever propaganda based on the love of Chairman Mao, their moods and their needs. Throughout all the discussions with the conspirators, Lin kept alluding to his plan to assume control of the Government in Peking and continue to rule a united China, which, once established, would initiate closer ties with the Soviet Union. Perhaps from a desire not to hurt the feelings of a sick and desperate man, with whom they had great sympathy, the conspirators discussed this overall 'dream' plan dutifully but only for a short time.

It was the number two plan the Russians supported, the one Lin in his more pragmatic moments knew was far more likely to be successful. For reasons no one has yet fathomed, after the badly drafted plans of 'Project 571' were widely circulated in February 1971, the more precise and detailed plans drawn up at a later date by Lin were not passed on as documents to the conspirators. The final plans were concerned with the role of specific military units and their collaboration with the Russians as well as how the leading pro-Mao personalities were to be treated. The number two plan was to follow Chinese tradition by initiating the rising or revolt in the south. A breakaway Central Committee of the Communist Party was to be established and a new state set up with its capital in Nanjing. The area under Lin's projected control would include the important cities and military air bases in Shanghai, Guangzhou and Wuhan. It was, or so Lin claimed, agreed with the Russians that, while Lin's army and air force attacked Mao's forces in the south, the Soviet Union would simultaneously mount offensive operations in the north-east. According to Lin, Moscow was apparently willing to mount major operations in the industrial region of what was previously known as Manchuria where some 14–16 divisions had been deployed on the border.

It would have been extremely difficult, if not downright impossible, for Mao to have fought a war on two fronts, especially when faced with the far more sophisticated land forces the Soviet Union had massed on the border and the well-equipped air bases the Russians maintained to the north-east of their naval base at Vladivostok, which were frequently used in joint air, land and naval manoeuvres and exercises. Lin's secret agreement with the Russians had been cemented, he claimed, so far as the projected coup and its aftermath were concerned, by Moscow's deliveries of highly technical communications and listening devices together with time-bombs, mines and small arms that were especially geared to assassinations. But it must have been apparent to experienced soldiers and politicians in the plot that Moscow was not going to throw its weight into the balance against Chairman Mao while the vast majority of the Chinese people lauded him as a god.

The number three plan was for all the main conspirators, led by Lin, to escape to the Soviet Union in case of failure. It was assumed they would then encourage risings and a change of regime in the People's Republic from within Russia. Moreover Moscow, according to Lin, had promised the temporary protection of the Soviet nuclear umbrella, unlikely though this may sound. Lin ultimately went all out for the second plan.

Lin disclosed to the conspirators that Wu Faxian, who commanded the air force, had at his suggestion put the entire force under the operational command of Lin Liguo, Lin's son, so far as 'Project 571' was concerned. A special detachment of pilots and crew members had been sworn in to 'serve'. They were naturally also code-named 'the Fleet'. Throughout the spring Lin's supporters made many semi-secret visits to military bases in efforts to ascertain exactly how much support they enjoyed. On the last day of March 1971, Lin Liguo summoned a group of air force commanders to Shanghai whom he dubbed the 'secret hard core of the joint fleet' in order to establish a 'command unit' for the implementation of the coup. (This was all officially confirmed as well as being recorded in the 'Trial of the Lin Biao and Jiang Qing counter-revolutionary cliques' that took place in Peking from November to January 1981.) Plans were then finalized for the distribution of secret stores of the high level Russian communications equipment and the locality of ammunition dumps disclosed.

There is no doubt that Premier Zhou guessed there was a serious political movement afoot – if nothing more. He certainly did not realize there was a major conspiracy that involved the Chief of Staff as well as the commander of the air force and senior officers in the navy.

By May, Lin's health had improved sufficiently for him to 'smell the breezes' in Peking where he found he was received with ever-increasing coolness by Premier Zhou, his former collaborator and friend, Jiang Qing and the pro-Mao members of the Politbureau. In June, Lin made his last public appearance as the Chairman's 'chosen successor' when he received, with Mao, President Ceaucescu of Rumania. The two men kept up appearances when in the actual presence of the visiting Head of State, but there was none of the feigned friendship and intimacy that had marked earlier meetings, when, despite bad personal relations, they had put up a tremendous show of deep friendship and cordiality. Early in July Lin Biao organized a well-publicized tour of major military bases throughout China to inspect their 'war preparedness'. When the tour opened on July 23rd it became apparent that he was only 'inspecting' military installations in the south, those named, although none knew it at the time, in 'Project 571' for a southern rising.

Meanwhile, the 'Long Marchers' and other old friends of Premier Zhou still with the PLA passed on to him their suspicions about Lin's political activities which the Premier immediately turned over to Mao. As a result, the Chairman himself decided to make an 'inspection tour' of the provinces. Mao was treated everywhere as a 'god/emperor' although he made obvious efforts to cut the personality cult down to size. He began his tour in mid-August with a visit to Wuhan, a city noted in history for its risings against authority. It had, as already reported, caused the Chairman military troubles during the Cultural Revolution. Here Mao, in talks with the local party, government and army leaders, explained to them the significance of the 'struggle' against him at the Lushan meeting. The Chairman also indulged in open criticism of Lin Biao, Huang Yongsheng (the Chief of Staff), and Wu Faxian (Air Force Commander), together with Ye Qun and others. Mao then talked of the 'ten great struggles between the lines' in party history. Until that moment there had only been 'nine struggles' and Liu Shaoqi was the ninth and last-named man to have risen against Mao's policy and authority.

As the Chairman travelled on to Changsha and Nanchang on his way to Shanghai, the Chief Political Commissar of the PLA Navy, Li Zuopeng, and others, passed his critical comments on to Huang Yongsheng who, in turn, conveyed them to Ye Qun. She was then staying at the Lins' fortress home in Behtaiho which is one of Peking's nearest seaside resorts. The conspirators were scattered in Peking, Shanghai and Nanjing but by a series of telephone calls, and with the use of coded words, it was agreed that the critical moment had arrived and that the Chairman should be assassinated whilst on the tour, preferably in or near to Shanghai. An order to put 'Project 571' into effect was issued by Lin on September 8th and received by all the major conspirators on that day.

There are then two different official reports of what happened. Shortly after the 10th Party Congress in August 1973, when the Lin Biao plot was first disclosed, a senior Chinese official told a group of foreign correspondents that one of the conspirators ordered a railway maintenance engineer to set a time-bomb on the line in readiness for the special train in which the Chairman was travelling. Although the engineer was devoted to his pro-Lin boss he became frightened and, after he had laid the mine, he developed cold feet and told his wife. She was a strong-willed woman who immediately insisted that he tell the local party secretary. He, in turn, telephoned to Premier Zhou's office in Peking. Naturally, the Premier took speedy action. The train was stopped before it reached the danger point and the Chairman travelled back to Peking safely by car.

The second version, now said to be the true one, was gradually leaked to foreign visitors in Peking a year or so before the trial of the Gang of Four. It claimed that Jiang Tengjiao, who was trusted as the liaison officer between leaders of the conspiracy of Shanghai, Guangzhou, Nanjing and Hangzhou, was to direct the operation to assassinate Chairman Mao. What he said later and during the trial about his plans was, like so much in 'Project 571', almost absurd fantasy combined with inefficiency but with an element of basic truth at the end. Jiang mentioned plans to attack the train with 'flame-throwers and 40 mm rocket guns', or, with 100 mm 'reassembled anti-aircraft guns at point-blank range'. The final idea was that one of the 571 trustees would shoot Mao with a pistol at point-blank range when he was received by the Chairman on board the special train. This sounds reasonable when compared with 'dynamiting the Shuafang railway bridge near Suzhou', or 'blowing up the oil depot in Shanghai's Hongqiao airport when the train drew in and then assassinate Chairman Mao in the ensuing commotion'.

The special train arrived in Shanghai from Hangzhou on the evening of September 10th. It is now suggested the conspirators believed they had plenty of time because the Chairman would be spending several days in Shanghai. In fact, the Chairman merely slept in his coach in a siding and left the following morning for Peking where he arrived safely in the evening.

No real explanation has been offered for this gigantic failure of the conspirators which took place two days after Lin had written the order 'in red ink on a sheet of white paper' for the immediate implementation of 'Project 571'. The coup 'go ahead' command was placed by Ye Qun in a specially prepared envelope addressed to Huang Yongsheng, the Chief of Staff, and delivered in person by Lin Liguo who went to Peking on a special plane from Behtaiho to carry a mass of confidential materials and instructions to be used in support of the order. Huang Yongsheng was placed in full command of the coup from his powerful desk as Chief of Staff at the Defence Ministry. A senior Chinese officer told me that Lin, having given the all clear for the plot to go ahead, was 'let down' by nervous local commanders who got cold feet at the last moment. On each occasion when the Chairman was virtually in the hands of the conspirators the man in charge cancelled that particular attempt on his life in the name of Lin. It has already been stressed that everyone who saw Lin said he was sick and, many added, in a nervous and neurotic state.

When the assassination plan failed all the leading conspirators should have flown immediately to Shanghai or Nanjing to set up what Chairman Mao called a 'southern kingdom'. But information, at least about the conspirators going south, was passed to Premier Zhou by Lin Biao's daughter, Toutou. However, a telephone operator, disclaiming knowledge of the source, informed Lin Biao that Premier Zhou was aware of the fact that he had an aircraft standing by in readiness to fly south. Premier Zhou, after being alerted by Toutou, discovered that a Trident was standing by at Behtaiho but when he telephoned to order its immediate return to Peking he was told the aircraft was on a training flight and had become completely unserviceable.

Residents in Behtaiho later told me of the tension that was great in the areas where no foreigners were then allowed as one of the outdated Russian armoured cars rushed noisily backwards and forwards from Lin's home to the naval air-base. Of course, no one had the least idea what was happening except that there was a great deal of activity at Lin's normally heavily guarded 'head-quarters' home. Premier Zhou telephoned to Lin, according to official sources, to know what was happening but Ye Qun said he was not around. After this the Premier cancelled an official meeting with visiting members of the Japanese Diet, who were due to dine with him in the Great Hall of the People, and called an immediate, emergency meeting of ninety-nine top-level supporters of Mao from the army, party and state in the Great Hall of the People where they held discussions throughout the night.

Sometime during the late evening – after 10 P.M. – Lin Biao must have decided there was no chance of success. Those few people who saw him in Behtaiho described him as very hysterical and ill-looking. The four telephone lines to his office were in constant use throughout the evening and it was not until 'around 11 P.M. or later' that he decided against flying south. In an irrational manner Lin ordered the radio as well as friends in Guangzhou to broadcast a report that the Chinese authorities were deeply concerned because Liu Shaoqi had escaped from 'house arrest' and was believed to be making his way to Hong Kong or Tokyo. Doubtless this fictitious report, which was widely believed at the time, was designed to divert attention from Lin's own planned escape to Russia.

Premier Zhou had, indeed, already issued an order that the special Trident No 256, officially on a training mission which was originally intended to transport Lin to Nanjing, should not take off without a joint order from him (Premier Zhou Enlai) and three other commanders. But Li Zuopeng, one of Lin's supporters, who was in charge tampered with the order. There was panic at the airport and Lin or his son shot one of the guards who attempted to prevent them from entering the security zone. After the Trident was refuelled, or partially refuelled, the men in the control tower had second thoughts about the orders for the take-off. Lin lost his cap as he climbed up a maintenance ladder in his haste to board the plane and, at the last moment, a truck was driven across the runway to prevent the take-off. The pilot just managed to get the plane into the air after causing severe damage to the undercarriage and wing.

Less than half an hour after the plane took off at 12.32 A.M. on September 13th, Premier Zhou issued an order grounding all military and civil aircraft throughout the whole of China. Just before Lin left his house he made what some officials called his 'one decent gesture' in telephoning to his fellow conspirators in Peking that the coup was aborted and he was off to the Soviet Union where they should follow him with the greatest speed. A loyal member of Lin's staff, Qiu Huizuo, who was also one of the conspirators, destroyed all the up-to-date evidence on 'Project 571' in Lin's house. Neighbours noted the smoke as large quantities of letters, notes, photographs, notebooks and telex messages were burned.

Lin, his wife and son, and six other people on the Trident crashed at Undur Khan in Mongolia at 2.30 A.M. All were burned to death. The Mongolians added to the mystery by stating in the beginning that there was no one over fifty on the plane but, after a few days, they admitted this was an inaccurate statement. However, one of the members of the Japanese party due to meet Premier Zhou told me they had no idea what had happened when they heard the shattering announcement that all civil and military aircraft were grounded in China. Most diplomats were bewildered by what one of them called the 'controlled silent panic' that set in after a radio announcement cancelled all leave in the PLA as well as the annual military parade on National Day, October 1st, together with the normal festivities. All planes were grounded for fifty-six hours. In Hong Kong, as a result of the various broadcasts that had been monitored, there was a general consensus of opinion that Lin was involved in the crisis but no one knew exactly how. And the China watchers were stunned when Lin's picture appeared on the October cover of *China Pictorial*, obviously printed weeks before the coup. In Peking efforts were made to get the issue withdrawn from bookshops. Gradually, very gradually, little hints of the coup were leaked to foreign diplomats while a series of documents, later proved to be authentic, were smuggled to Taiwan and released from there.

Some distinguished western scholars and thousands of cynical Chinese cadres have suggested that Lin Biao and his wife were not on the Trident aircraft that crashed in Mongolia killing all passengers. Many reports were in circulation in the mid-1970s that Lin was shot at various places ranging from Peking to Behtaiho but when attempts were made to confirm them, they fell to the ground. In Behtaiho there are a score or so of people who recall the events of the fateful night including three or four who actually saw Lin Biao on the road to the airport. The soldiers on the ground who saw him at the naval air-base at Shanhaiguan have since been dispersed but one of them reported to me how Lin departed, losing his cap in the panic, in a manner very slightly different from the official version but still confirming that he and his wife took off.

When the details of the abortive coup were finally and officially disclosed, during the 10th Party Congress in August 1973, they caused great excitement although years before diplomats had been requested not to use Lin's name in any official toast. However, until August 1972 Lin was still officially and technically Minister of Defence and 'chosen successor'. Gradually, more details were leaked to diplomats and visiting celebrities but it was only in 1977 in Urumqi (in Xinjiang) that a senior Chinese official devoted many hours to telling a small group of foreign correspondents the full story – then without names – of the coup and its violent ending. (I was there.)

After the conspirators in Peking had received Lin's message from the Shanhaiguan naval air-base that 'all was lost' and they should proceed immediately to the Soviet Union, Zhou Yuchi, Deputy Director of Air Force Command, was told by one of his trusted men in the Signals Corps that Premier Zhou Enlai was already alerted about the planned coup. Zhou Yuchi was naturally deeply alarmed but remained calm and, pulling his rank as a senior officer in the air force, he ordered a helicopter to be prepared for an emergency flight.

Zhou then telephoned to Li Weixin, who had played a prominent role in drafting 'Project 571', and Yu Xinye, both of whom were standing by in readiness to fly south to join Lin in Shanghai. They rushed to the helicopter pad, all carrying, according to the guards on duty, enormous piles of files that they flung into the aircraft. They demanded that the pilot take off at once and despite the fact he told them the engines were still too cold they pressed him to get off the ground without a flight plan for 'the north'. Once in the air they began hectically tearing the documents into small pieces as they pressed the pilot to get ahead quickly. When the pilot warned them it would be necessary to refuel before they reached Mongolia, one of them became so hysterical the pilot 'smelt a rat', as my Chinese informant said. He then flew in circles back towards Peking while the conspirators threatened to shoot him unless he got them safely across the border. The pilot, who had heard over the intercom the order that all aircraft were to be grounded feared being shot down by a Chinese fighter plane. Eventually the three conspirators agreed on a suicide pact, to open with the murder of the pilot and then each man to blow out his own brains.

After the helicopter landed at an air-base to the north of Peking, the pilot was shot as planned and only Li Weixin failed to kill himself. He was captured alive, only slightly wounded, and, my Chinese informant added, 'has been singing like a bird ever since'. Many of the torn documents were reassembled to form the basis of the subsequent trial against the conspirators.

Lin began to plan his coup immediately after his efforts to transform the Chairman into a powerless Head of State failed, according to official information produced during the 'trial of Lin Biao and the Jiang Qing counter-revolutionary cliques', held in Peking from November 1980 until January 1981. In October 1969 Lin ordered Wu Faxian, commander of the air force, to make his son Lin Liguo the real commander. Thus on October 18th, Wu called Lin Liguo to a meeting with a group of senior officers and told them 'to report everything concerning the air force to Comrade Liguo'. In this manner, as the official document stresses, 'Wu illegally put the air force under Lin Liguo's command.' An 'investigation group' was then formed that was gradually transformed into a band of conspirators who met in the commander's office. By October 1970 they were organized as the 'joint fleet' and became the backbone of Lin's plot to assassinate the Chairman and stage an armed coup d'état. From 1970 to September 13th, 1971 Lin Liguo, aided by senior officers and political commissars, established 'secret centres' for their activities in Peking, Shanghai and Guangzhou having already obtained the co-operation of the local units and the civil air line.

'From September 1970 onwards Lin Biao stepped up his preparations for an armed counter-revolutionary coup d'état.' By February 1971 he sent Lin Liguo to Shanghai where from March 21st to 24th the 'chief members' of the 'joint fleet' mapped out the 'outline of "Project 571"'. They assessed the situation, worked out a rough plan for implementation (as already reported) and decided on slogans and tactics. 'They also plotted to "seek Soviet help to tie down domestic and foreign forces".' The names of coup leaders in Nanjing, Shanghai and Hangzhou were agreed together with a general liaison officer. In addition a 'combat detachment' was organized in Guangzhou whose members were 'made' to take an oath of allegiance to Lin Biao and Lin Liguo. A month later a 'training corps' was set up in Shanghai 'in preparation for the coup'.

Little official information is available for the next few months until the conspirators heard what Chairman Mao had said to 'leading personnel' in Changsha on September 5th. 'After receiving the secret information [about Chairman Mao's conversations] Lin Biao and Ye Qun made up their minds to assassinate Chairman Mao immediately.' On September 7th Lin Biao issued the following handwritten order for the armed coup: 'Expect you to act according to the order(s) transmitted by Comrades Liguo and Yuchi [Deputy Chief of Staff of the Air Force].' 'From September 8th to 11th at their secret centres at the Air Force Acadamy' and Peking airport Lin Biao's handwritten order was passed to all the leading conspirators. While completing 'details for assassinating Chairman Mao', which included the fantastic projects already mentioned, 'Lin Biao and Ye Qun were making preparations for fleeing south to Guangzhou to set up a separate party Central Committee, and also for defecting to another country.'

'When Lin Biao and Ye Qun learned that their plot to murder Chairman Mao had fallen through they planned to flee south to Guangzhou', taking along the chief conspirators, and 'set up a separate party Central Committee there to split the nation'. 'They also planned to "launch a pincer attack from north and south in alliance with the Soviet Union, should fighting be necessary".' Eight planes were held in readiness for the flight south and one to fly to Behtaiho for the use of Lin Biao. When Lin heard that Premier Zhou had telephoned and that he was also asking questions about the various planes assigned for the coup, the family 'hurried to Shanhaiguan airport . . . scrambled on to the plane and ordered it to start taxiing without waiting for the co-pilot, navigator and radio operator to board the plane'. This tallies with the information I obtained on the spot.

Back to foreign policy

After the sensational appearance of Edgar Snow on October 1st beside Chairman Mao on the rostrum of the Gate of Heavenly Peace, despite setbacks in Warsaw and Cambodia, Premier Zhou kept up unofficial, verbal contact with Washington through various visiting ambassadors. 'Ping-pong diplomacy' enabled foreign correspondents who had left China or been thrown out during the Cultural Revolution to return to report on matches in this sport, in which the Chinese players were extremely skilful. Then in July 1971, while the world thought Dr Henry Kissinger was suffering from an upset stomach in Islamabad, he was secretly visiting Peking. Although he stayed in a guest-house just outside the city he had several meals with Premier Zhou Enlai with whom he formed an easy relationship. Indeed, Kissinger left Peking with a written hand-carried and firm invitation to the President to visit China.

Lin Biao was well aware of Kissinger's visit which further demonstrated Premier Zhou's success in steering the Chairman towards a pro-American foreign policy. Kissinger's visit and the slight opening of the window to other foreigners at that time distracted diplomats from the purely domestic political scene and possible disagreements between Chinese leaders. A handful of well-informed resident ambassadors realized that all was not well between the Chairman and Lin Biao because the latter was so rarely in the capital, but only the Albanian Ambassador, whose country was then closer than any other to the Chinese, was aware that a major political struggle was in progress. And he knew far more than the average senior Chinese official or army commander working in the Chinese capital.

Only a few days after Lin's death in the Trident aircraft in which he was attempting to fly to the Soviet Union, the Foreign Ministry in Peking announced that Henry Kissinger would pay a second visit to China later that month. In October the People's Republic was admitted to the United Nations as Taiwan was expelled. Canada and Italy opened diplomatic relations whilst talks began towards an eventual exchange of ambassadors with China's former number-one enemy – Japan.

Premier Zhou Enlai appeared to be at the height of his power. After years of painstakingly acting as a moderator and mediator he had, at last, come into his own. Small groups of 'friends of China' who had been refused visas during the Cultural Revolution were invited to return as the Chinese adopted a friendlier attitude towards 'round-eyed barbarians'. The Premier, who was virtually running the country, even gave orders that the armed forces devote more time to weapons training while civilians and the unarmed militia were encouraged to construct air-raid shelters. In addition, Zhou pressed for the reopening of the universities, closed during the Cultural Revolution, because he realized that even a small opening to the West would require considerable numbers of linguists, scientists and economists.

The radicals only accepted Zhou's moves with reluctance and Chairman Mao allowed them to retain control of the media. Despite criticism from the Premier, Jiang Qing does appear to have influenced the Chairman significantly on the line the press, radio and television should take on political issues. In addition, Jiang Qing remained in control of cultural affairs and it was quite impossible to see anything on the stage in Peking but revolutionary operas such as *The White Haired Girl* and *The Red Detachment of Women* which she had virtually produced. The radicals inspired a press campaign against 'a political swindler like Liu Shaoqi' that caused the rarely outspoken Chinese to wonder whether it was a prelude to an announcement that the second of Mao's 'chosen successors' had fallen from grace or even been killed. Zhou realized that it was vital for China to open relations with the United States as a result of the Russian threat and he managed to prevent the radicals from interfering with the preparations he was making for the President's visit. Had Lin remained in power it is important to realize that there would have been no secret visits by Henry Kissinger and diplomatic relations with the United States would not have been established, nor would there have been the slow opening to the West.

PART THREE
The Years of Decline

14

Opposition to Mao and Zhou

When Premier Zhou Enlai visited the British industrial technology exhibition in Peking at the end of March 1973 the ambassador, Sir John Addis, the President of the Sino-British Trade Council, Sir John Keswick, and other dignitaries were astonished when he did not get out of the first car of the convoy of six. The second car that drew up also contained unknown middle-aged men with bulging pockets. Premier Zhou jumped out of the fourth of the prestigious bullet-proof black-curtained Red Flag cars and quickly made his way into the Russian-built exhibition hall.

Although a secret plan had been arranged for him to view a model of the supersonic Concorde and a selection of around twenty of the three hundred exhibits, Premier Zhou disregarded this and zigzagged about the Hall, much to the distress of many businessmen. It was quickly apparent that despite the strict security measures that had been set up, the Premier felt he was under serious threat of assassination.

Security guards in the car immediately in front and behind him were armed with light machine-guns. Naturally no member of the general public was allowed anywhere near the hall when the Premier was there. The diplomatic corps was surprised because the Premier had been very much in the limelight since the abortive coup of Lin Biao in September 1971 and he had invariably appeared relaxed when he greeted visiting Ministers at Peking Airport. The explanation was of course that the airport was extremely well guarded by the PLA and the Premier did not use the normal main road from the city but another route reserved exclusively for military vehicles and forbidden to most Chinese civilians and all foreigners. The diplomatic corps and foreign journalists had also noted the Premier was at ease in the Great Hall of the People when he acted as host for scores of banquets. However, it was known that Premier Zhou and other senior members of the Politbureau who lived in the Imperial City made their way to the Great Hall through secret underground passages.

They could even drive in the Chinese version of a jeep under 'the main drag' from their homes to semi-public offices in the Great Hall.

After Lin's coup the Premier was far from relaxed. He was seventy-five and China's population of about 800 million was dependent on him to establish some form of collective leadership to take over when he and Chairman Mao died. Indeed, one felt in December 1972 the Chinese people were far more concerned with the health of Premier Zhou Enlai than of their great leader, Chairman Mao Zedong, who was five years his senior. For while the Chairman lived the cosseted and respected life of a latter-day Churchill, in which spells of brilliant constructive thought alternated with fitful repose, the administration of the vast and complex Chinese nation was directed solely by his apparently indispensable Premier. I had then failed to appreciate the full value of the charismatic personality of the Chairman. For in a curious way it was he who held this diverse nation together.

One of the reasons for the Premier's over-heavy work load was that the former five-man Standing Committee of the ruling Politbureau, established to take day-to-day decisions and spread out some of the official 'greetings and feastings', no longer functioned. Chairman Mao was available for high level consultations but Kang Sheng, the radical Security Chief and former adviser to the Cultural Revolution Group, was frequently 'incapacitated' and he certainly looked ill and emaciated. However, he doubtless feared that the Premier knew something of his 'dirty deeds' during the Cultural Revolution and felt it wiser to adopt a low profile. The fourth member had been 'the traitor' Lin Biao, while the fifth, Chen Boda, was disgraced before Lin's attempted coup.

The most active member of the Politbureau residing in Peking was, without doubt, Jiang Qing, who made life difficult for the Premier by retaining control of the media which thus remained radical in tone and rendered the task of diplomats and other political analysts perplexing by taking a line, at times, opposed to the Premier's open-door policy in foreign affairs. In addition to the Chairman, Jiang Qing was supported by Zhang Chunqiao who divided his time between his power base in Shanghai and the capital.

The Chairman's bodyguard – Special Group 8341 – directed by

Wang Dongxing, who had saved his life on more than one occasion, was efficient but, although it was intended to protect all members of the Politbureau, it tended to concentrate on the Imperial City and the Great Hall of the People.

Premier Zhou well knew he had many desperate enemies in two of the three main sources of power – the army and the party – for, despite widespread dismissals following Lin's abortive coup, there were hundreds of officers who accepted their former leader's view that it was a grave mistake for Peking to make a gesture of friendship towards Washington whilst the rift with Moscow deepened. This applied especially to the officers who had been trained in the Soviet Union or worked with Russian experts inside China. There is no doubt extreme pro-Russian elements schemed against Premier Zhou, and friends of the late Premier claimed several plots were discovered that apparently were inspired by Moscow. In fact, attempts by these extremist groups to assassinate Premier Zhou continued until he entered hospital as this provided the surest way of overthrowing the regime.

Life was quiet and public security excellent and I recall exploring Peking and Shanghai – including the docks – by walking around alone after dinner. The Minzu Hotel was the only place in the world where valuable jewellery or gold sovereigns could, with perfect safety, be left lying around and the most serious breaches of the law amongst the staff were the illegal games of mah-jong I heard from time to time taking place in empty bedrooms. The Deputy Chairman of the Revolutionary Committee in the district where the hotel was situated, which included over 70,000 people, told me with shame that they had had a grim crime rate between January and the end of March in 1973, as there had been four cases of illegal sex – sexual intercourse between unmarried people – and six cases of stolen bicycles.

However, the good public security hid, not only from the eyes of the foreigner but also the Chinese people, the diabolical crimes taking place in the main cities, inspired by Jiang Qing, who had built up the fiendish art of obtaining false information from prisoners under torture, in co-operation with Lin Biao, during the Cultural Revolution. These atrocities were not even known to well-placed provincial party leaders. It is assumed now that Chairman Mao knew something of his wife's nefarious activities while

Premier Zhou received occasional reports on them but there was little or nothing he could do.

There were, too, other groups made up of members of the ultra-left who had managed to avoid being sent to the countryside at the end of the Cultural Revolution. They were generally engaged in unpleasant manual work and maintained their contacts with one another with some difficulty. These ultra-leftists whispered complainingly that had it not been for the opposition of Premier Zhou, Chairman Mao and Jiang Qing would have remained 'on their side'. Even more dangerous were the extremists who had actually been sent to the countryside who grew to hate the isolation, the climate and the work. Somehow or other, because it is not easy to travel in China without permission, some leaders managed to return to Peking and Shanghai where they lived without ration cards, on their wits. These young people continually plotted against authority.

The fact that until the British Exhibition few, if any, foreigners realized Premier Zhou's life was at stake, illustrates how quiet and smooth superficially life was in Peking at that time. Anti-Japanese posters were gradually disappearing from the provinces as well as the suburbs of Peking, whilst fewer anti-imperialist slogans were posted up. It seemed the significance of President Nixon's visit and the Shanghai communiqué, coupled with the exchange of ambassadors with Tokyo following Prime Minister Tanaka's official tour of China, were beginning to penetrate to the Chinese men and women in the street.

But as late as March 1973, Wang Qing, a leading member of the Shanghai Revolutionary Committee, during a rare two-hour interview over dinner, told me, 'The first task of the ruling Revolutionary Committee is to educate the workers on the right political line so that they become aware of the dangers of pro-Russian revisionism' because 'the ideas spread by Lin Biao are still very much around'. Wang admitted that even in Shanghai, which was the radical stronghold and power base, they were having trouble with former students of both extreme left and extreme right persuasions. In fact non-conformists in the party, whether they veered towards Moscow or extreme radicalism, could be and, indeed, were often dubbed 'leftist' one month and 'rightist' a few months later. This certainly happened to Lin Biao as well as many thousands of students, workers and soldiers.

Russians intensify the border threat

After the failure of the Lin Biao coup, the Russians played into the Chinese hands and aided 'unification of the party' throughout this difficult period by increasing the strength of the forces on the border as well as initiating late winter manoeuvres. Western military attachés in Peking were told by their better informed eastern colleagues in March 1973 that a division plus several units from East Germany and Czechoslovakia had taken part in a major military exercise in western Siberia for the first time. The Warsaw Pact troops were reported to have been airlifted over a period of several weeks to near Irkutsk on the western side of Lake Baikal in Siberia, but the bulk of the heavy weapons and vehicles were transported over a much longer period by the Trans-Siberian railway from Europe, according to reliable Japanese travellers.

Whilst the Chinese made no official comment, they let it be known to their foreign political friends that the Russian sabre-rattling and the series of exercises were designed to evaluate new weapons and equipment under near-combat conditions at arctic temperatures. The Russians appeared to make no great secret of their activities and aircraft more than once overflew Chinese territory. Although the Chinese did not believe war was imminent, they were alarmed by the renewed threat and the fact that the Russians were slowly and steadily building up their troops along the border. In March 1973 there were about forty divisions and a far larger proportion of them were nearer to combat readiness than in the previous year. At about the same time the Chinese learned that the Russians were installing new intercontinental and medium-range missiles near the northern Chinese border. Housed in 'hardened' silos cut into rock the missiles had and, indeed, still have the capability of reaching targets virtually anywhere in China. They were vulnerable to American but not Chinese missiles.

These missiles replaced the 'soft' silo installations that had given the Russians the limited capacity to 'take out' China's nuclear base at Lop Nor in Xinjiang and hit targets in Peking, Tianjin and the industrial areas and oil-fields of north-east China – formerly Manchuria. Until around 1974 or 1975 the Chinese were, with reason, apprehensive that the Russians would mount a pre-emptive strike designed to destroy all their nuclear installations including ranges and stock-piles in Xinjiang. This accounts for the dispersal of plant, whilst nuclear warheads were said to be stored in the safety of the Himalayas – on the northern closes of Mount Everest – and in Tibet. Certainly a network of roads was constructed to Tibet that would make this possible. The Premier, whilst accepting the border threat and supporting the redeployment of divisions, remained convinced that the Russians would still attempt to 'take the fortress from within' and took measures to increase the internal security network.

Meanwhile, as the Soviet threat united the army behind Chairman Mao and Premier Zhou, the same menace proved to be a minor blessing in uniting the civil population and keeping the broad masses purposefully active. From 1971 onwards, the population of towns and cities, communes and industrial plants were exhorted to build air-raid shelters. The population followed Chairman Mao's oft-repeated order to 'dig tunnels deep, store grain everywhere and seek no hegemony'. The young and old volunteered to dig shelters after working hours and on Sunday which still remains the Chinese communists' day of rest. Every school and factory had its own shelter and, although many of them would not have stood up to shells, still less conventional bombs, they raised the morale of the population.

In Peking visiting foreigners were frequently shown the underground shelter system in the city's centre. The entrance to the underground corridor was – still is – through a trap-door behind the counter of a shop in the old part of the city that sells uniforms within a hundred yards of the famous old Peking Duck Restaurant. The corridor is well lit and ventilated by vents from the surface and there are occasional bays containing telephones or, more rarely, toilet facilities. Every shop has its private entrance to the underground corridor and the idea is not to provide the population with shelter but to urge them on to wider and deeper corridors constructed later. These, in turn, lead to the Peking underground railway system which is still being extended.

The population could with luck be evacuated from the city to areas fifteen or sixteen miles away. In the case of a nuclear explosion the officials merely stated that the masses would be directed through the new underground railway into the safest area, that is, the one least likely to be contaminated. Here they would be fed – it is hoped – from the stores of rice belonging to the local commune before moving further into the countryside. One cynical foreign expert suggested that in the case of a conventional attack the underground system might – just might – have some use but after a nuclear attack it would become a mere mass grave and require only to be sealed up at each end.

It must be assumed that the MAC, which controls the armed forces, the Politbureau and senior members of the Government, would move from Peking to a safe hideout, perhaps in the Western Hills, when it appeared war was imminent. Certainly, the western branch of the underground is being extended, it appears, in readiness to transport the party, army and government leaders in safety and secrecy. There must, too, be more than one underground communications centre although the latest information is that in a war of knocking out satellites, radar and communications, in which both sides are attempting to block out the other's means of convening messages over land or into the air, the good old-fashioned telephone may at least be useful if insecure.

10th Party Congress

Intelligent Chinese acquaintances expressed something approaching boredom when the campaign to criticize the ancient sage Confucius was mentioned, even during the early days of the movement in the spring and early summer of 1973, before the 10th Party Congress, which took place in August 1973. Periods of 'study' or political indoctrination were devoted to the destruction of the philosophy that drew its strength from obligatory respect to the emperor (state) and family. A handful of highly intelligent cadres even then believed that the anti-Confucius campaign, as it was called, was an anti-Zhou move sponsored by Jiang Qing and her radical friends. The radicals had already harmed the Premier and his ideas with their continual stress on state, party and army officials being 'red' rather than 'expert'. They were in addition making strenuous efforts to ensure that entrants to universities were 'red'.

The *People's Daily* carried many reports coming from outlying communes stressing how the peasants had debunked the old man Confucius and all he stood for, while similar accounts over the Peking radio rendered it more monotonous and repetitive than usual. Whether Chairman Mao knew of the motives in the anti-Confucius campaign is not known. Although he was giving his wife a great deal of support, he was still dependent on Premier Zhou to administer the country and organize the 10th Party Congress which it was hoped would smooth, if not solve, the succession problem. In any case the Chairman must have read and heard the daily reports. Those few people who saw Mao and Zhou together at that time always said how well they appeared to get along and how intimate they were. But there is *now* no doubt, according to a member of the Central Committee, that the Chairman was aware of the campaign his wife was attempting to launch against the Premier.

Premier Zhou was warned by his youthful supporters, who mixed with the radicals in the course of their daily work, that he was indeed the real target for the anti-Confucian campaign and sooner or later his name would be coupled with that of Confucius. It was at this point that the Premier arranged to couple the name of Confucius in the anti-Confucian campaign with that of the 'traitor' Lin Biao. All the politically conscious people throughout China became aware that Zhou was the real target, for he came from a mandarin-type background and was extremely well educated and reported to know more Chinese characters than high level professors. At about the same time Premier Zhou was told by his doctors that he was suffering from a 'heart condition' and he was frequently observed taking those tiny pills people who have heart 'twinges' in their arms or chest take to relieve the pain. It is not yet clear whether he was also informed that he had cancer although his doctors may well have known it by then. In any case, in June 1973, having rehabilitated Vice Premier Deng Xiaoping in April and restored him to power together with scores of senior state and party officials, Premier Zhou attempted to divest himself of some of the trappings of office but not the powers he wielded as the number two man in the party. He was safe from the assassin's bullet in his home or office.

The Premier told his intimate friends in the diplomatic corps that after twenty-five years in office he felt the time had come for someone else to take over some of the handshaking and speech-making in order to allow him more time to establish a harmonious leadership to follow the policy he and Chairman Mao had begun with 'ping-pong diplomacy' in April 1971. Ji Pengfei, despite the fact that he was not to remain at the Foreign Ministry, took over much of the greeting and eating with foreigners, while Vice Premier Deng, who was, after all, a former Secretary General of the Party, substituted for Zhou in purely Chinese Communist Party gatherings.

Except perhaps for Chairman Mao, Premier Zhou's wife, Deng Yingchao and Vice Premier Deng, no one knew that one of the basic reasons for Premier Zhou's withdrawal was fear of assassination rather than sickness, a fear the campaign to criticize Confucius had increased. It was then, as later, difficult to point a finger at the radicals, now known as the disgraced 'Gang of Four', for Jiang Qing had outwardly accepted Premier Zhou's policy of opening the window on to the world that had succeeded the ping-pong line of 1971 after President Nixon's visit of 1972. Only a month before the 10th Party Congress a group of American swimmers was invited to stay on an extra day in Peking in order to watch *The Red Detachment of Women*, one of the modern revolutionary ballets sponsored by Jiang Qing. The United States Chief Liaison Officer, Ambassador David Bruce, attended the show and Jiang Qing, wearing a skirt, sat by his side in the front row.

A senior ambassador in Peking said, 'Then I knew, at once, that the radicals who had sponsored the Cultural Revolution had accepted the policy of Premier Zhou and the moderates which included opening the window on the world.' He was completely wrong, together with other experienced diplomats who stressed that it had become a tradition in the Communist Party for the minority who lost in a power struggle to 'make an irrevocable and memorable gesture which indicated their change of mind to the broad masses as well as the diplomatic corps'. It was further assumed that the Shanghai leaders, Zhang Chunqiao and Yao Wenyuan, who were the only sponsors of the Cultural Revolution to survive and serve on the Politbureau, had followed Jiang Qing's lead and accepted the moderate policy as well as the return to office of Vice Premier Deng Xiaoping and other senior cadres they had earlier thrown out of power.

As always in Peking, diplomatic reports were founded on these straws gleaned from the Chinese press and the odd outspoken Chinese Minister or official together with a handful of 'foreign friends' to whom the Chinese talked. However, for some weeks mystery hung over the projected 10th Party Congress. It was obvious from the beginning of August that extraordinary activities were expected in the Great Hall of the People as the vast building was cleaned, and the larger than life portraits of Karl Marx, Engels, Lenin and Stalin outside were touched up. Fresh plants were put into the flowerbeds and additional security guards appeared on duty to keep curious citizens well away from the car parks. By August 10th excitement in Peking was at fever pitch as a series of rumours and counter-rumours sprang from mouth to mouth across the city, as delegates arrived from Hong Kong, Macao and Taiwan. By the end of the month so many buses and cars were parked outside the Great Hall that it was apparent either the congress was in progress or a greatly enlarged meeting of the Central and other committees.

The politically minded Chinese were for once as interested as foreign observers for they believed the congress really would shape the new leadership they realized must soon take over from Chairman Mao and Premier Zhou. Further, the party required a new constitution as the one adopted at the 9th Party Congress had been tailored to the succession of Lin Biao. And, in view of the Russian threat, it was hoped a new leader in the sphere of defence would emerge.

Eventually on August 29th a firework display signalled the termination of the congress, which coincided with an official announcement over Peking radio stating the congress had taken place between August 24th and 28th. 'Chairman Mao Zedong had presided – though he did not address the meetings – which were remarkable for their "unity, victory and vigour".' The most sensational item of news was that Wang Hongwen – now one of the disgraced Gang of Four – had been elected as number three man in the party. Next day his picture was on the front page of every newspaper standing on the left of a beaming Chairman Mao with Premier Zhou Enlai on his right.

Little was then known of the new leader despite the fact a few foreigners had met him at banquets in Shanghai and, although his age was variously stated to be anything from thirty-six to forty-six he was young, good-looking and apparently vivacious. Official Chinese, who are always opposed to the disclosure of details about their leaders' past lives, admitted that he had played an important role during the Cultural Revolution as leader of a Shanghai textile factory. There was general amazement that he now outranked the Shanghai leader, Zhang Chunqiao, who had, however, also obtained a seat on the Standing Committee of the Politbureau despite the fact that Jiang Qing failed to gain a much coveted place there.

15

The Political Pendulum Swings

The sight of a relaxed, smiling Premier Zhou with the radical Jiang Qing at his side 'mingling with the broad masses' in the gardens of the Imperial City on May Day 1974 did something to assuage the fears of the diplomatic corps that a new dangerous power struggle had developed in the party leadership. In fact, the power struggle had merely been temporarily papered over. Since the 10th Party Congress – August 1973 – Zhou Enlai and his able Vice Premier Deng Xiaoping had again begun to develop their policy of increasing contacts with foreign governments while at home sponsoring the slogan 'Grasp revolution: increase production'. The internal scene was, in addition, menaced by tens of thousands of rehabilitated party officials and civil servants who had been ousted during the Cultural Revolution, with the result there were many old scores to be paid off.

During the epic visit of the British Leader of the Opposition, Edward Heath, to China during May and June of that year we all noticed big character posters in Kunming and Guangzhou that were frequently critical of regional officials. Further, official interpreters, who are normally most unwilling to undertake any task not fully sanctioned by the Diplomatic Service Bureau, were ready and willing to stand in the blazing sun and attempt to translate the difficult hand-written characters. It was claimed Chairman Mao Zedong himself had 'put his chop [seal of approval]' on these attacks launched by 'revolutionary rebels' against communist leaders in Peking and other Chinese cities. Many feared the opening of another political upheaval similar to that of the militant period of the Cultural Revolution from 1966 to 1969. Nonetheless people were initially cautious and unsigned criticisms were written of 'the boss', who was normally the Chairman of the Revolutionary Committee in a factory, dock, agricultural settlement, university or even government department. Emboldened by the fact no action was taken against the writers, who put up their posters in the early morning, the movement developed and 119 big character posters suddenly appeared all attacking the Mayor of Peking, Wu De (Wu Teh). This was most significant for everyone recalled that the Cultural Revolution had opened with an attack on the Deputy Mayor, Wu Han. Wu De was accused of 'laziness' and having failed 'to lead the masses in a vigorous manner in the campaign to criticize the ancient sage Confucius'. By that time the vast majority of those who read the posters knew this campaign was initiated originally against Premier Zhou, for the Premier had the manners of his family – impoverished Chekiang gentry – who produced a number of scholars and prominent officials during the nineteenth century.

In retrospect, quite the most important of the early summer posters were some twenty-eight that appeared on May 17th violently attacking the man who was eventually to succeed Mao as Chairman of the party, Hua Guofeng (Hua Kuo-feng). At the time Hua was just becoming known in the capital as an economist and agriculturalist. The posters accused him of having 'sabotaged' the campaign to criticize Confucius as well as having persecuted 'leftist workers' organizations' in his native Hunan when he had worked at the Chairman's birthplace of Shaoshan. In addition Hua was charged with having 'strong reactionary tendencies'. Although the original posters were torn down and replaced by more moderate ones their contents were never forgotten, and 'inside' people believed them to have been inspired by Jiang Qing. The fact that these early posters were torn down suggested that the authorities did not want the campaign to grow too violent when the victim was one of the up and coming middle-aged men recently elected to the ruling Politbureau.

Thousands of Chinese walked daily to the city centre to read the posters, which were on the walls of the Ministry of 'something or other' – in the words of my over-discreet interpreter – and the adjoining residential compound, which houses China's most prestigious 'foreign friends'. Although the municipal building next door had no brick walls the poster writers made up for this by covering the high walls of the former International Club opposite. (By a piece of good fortune I visited this excellent club with its comfortable bar, oak-panelled restaurant and fine library of European books before the Chinese took it over in 1972, offering

instead a new characterless building, without the library, to replace
it.)

A majority of the posters there attacked the 'leaders' of the
Peking Revolutionary Committee for having 'abused their position
by using the private swimming pool, luxurious rooms and gardens
solely for their own pleasure'. The writers constantly reminded the
Revolutionary Committee that Chairman Mao had said posters
were a new and useful weapon and the 'masses' might put them up
whenever they so wished. There were many sad stories of personal
suffering frequently ending in the suicide of the victim but, as the
campaign wore on, there was no doubt the Mayor, Wu De, then
fifty-one, was the main target in the capital. A miner from Henan
told me, in a burst of confidence, that although it was against the
directives to come to Peking, the capital was the only place where
people took notice of the grievances that were being aired.

Youthful male and female officials were accused of pre-marital
sex, which was and indeed still is a serious offence in China, far
worse than adultery in middle-class Victorian England. Young
couples caught after having entered into such a relationship were
damned for life. Many of the posters were signed by a mythical
character, 'Golden Monkey', whose true identity was not disclosed
though he appeared to be a former supporter of the disgraced
Chen Boda. 'Golden Monkey' is a figure in Chinese mythology
who chased evil spirits and demons out of paradise. Scores of local
leaders were attacked for their failure 'to preserve the fruits of the
Cultural Revolution' – a safe phrase as it was first employed by
Premier Zhou himself at the 10th Party Congress. The military
leaders were not exempt from the criticism but the accusations
against them were generally milder in tone than those against the
Mayor and his cronies.

Liu Guangtao, Secretary of the Heilongjiang Provincial Communist Party near the Soviet border in the north-east, was accused of
'putting production above all else', despite the fact that he was an
alternate member of the Central Committee, which places him
amongst the first 300 in the party hierarchy which then had some
36 million members. The Chairman of a Revolutionary Committee
in the timber industry was charged with having amassed an
enormous fortune of 400,000 yuan (around £125,000 at that time)
as a result of black market dealings. He was accused of selling the

workers' food and making many illegal deals in wood. But the writer, unhappily, did not state what the accused man had done with the money. As the average worker in that area earned around 60 yuan a month he can hardly have put it into his bank account without causing comment; nor could he have spent more than £50 without becoming dangerously conspicuous. Today, black marketeers have become more sophisticated and they 'deal' with relatives – generally overseas Chinese – who hide money for them and from time to time bring them presents not obtainable inside China.

In Kunming, Wuhan, Suzhou (near Shanghai), Harbin and Shenyang and other cities open to some foreigners, the posters were more controversial and radical in tone. Almost all were addressed to Chairman Mao in terms of glowing admiration, indeed, the only other name to appear in a favourable light was that of Wang Hongwen, the former factory hand from Shanghai who had become the number three man in the party. Many of the writers expressed the hope that Wang would 'lead the radical leftists and sponsor a new political upsurge bigger and better than the Cultural Revolution'. The radicals generally claimed one of the main objectives of the poster campaign in the capital was to re-establish Wang at the centre of the political stage. The supporters of Deng, however, suggested Wang had not only been a predictable disappointment to Premier Zhou but also to his chief sponsor, Chairman Mao. Officially, Wang's job was to re-organize the urban People's Militia and reactivate the trade unions after their shut-down during the Cultural Revolution. Officials now say Wang did little at that time but run around for Jiang Qing who was, in theory, very much his junior in the party hierarchy. It now seems apparent that Premier Zhou realized, even before the 10th Party Congress, that Wang had no great administrative skill; it may be that is why he chose this good-looking young man as the vehicle for splitting what had been until then a closely knit group of radicals, later to be known as the 'Gang of Four'.

At the time many middle-aged and youthful Chinese were brave enough to express their despair to foreigners about the utter hopelessness of moving up the party, army or administrative ladder. Although the names of Chairman Mao and Premier Zhou were always deliberately excluded, the critics stressed that the old men were going on too long. Amongst informed middle-aged cadres there was open disappointment about Wang's apparent lack of ability as one of the collective leaders on the Standing Committee designed to take over when the Chairman and Premier Zhou 'went to meet their gods'.

Conditions in Peking remained calm throughout an extremely hot spell but there were many reports from provincial cities of fist fighting in front of posters between rightist and leftist gangs. Curiously inside Peking two media worlds existed side by side, the official *People's Daily* and the bright outspoken posters. The former reported 'bumper' – always a favourite Chinese word – harvests and increased iron and steel production as they described the activities of happy, dedicated workers overcoming seemingly impossible odds to serve the party. On the other hand the lively, often vulgar posters portrayed reactionary, corrupt municipal and regional factory 'bosses' who abused their power and failed to preserve 'the fruits of the Cultural Revolution'.

Gradually the steam ran out in Peking and the number of and interest in the posters declined as the authorities suddenly decided they had seen enough. This happened, by chance, about the same time as Premier Zhou suffered a massive heart attack early in July. A directive was sent out by the Central Committee of the party in July that 'strongly advised' – virtually ordered – individuals or groups to register their complaints in their own towns and not in Peking. At the same time deep differences of opinion within the party on major political issues were disclosed in the campaign, which continued to flourish in the provinces months after it had died down in Peking. Kunming, in the south-west, Wuhan, in central China, and Suzhou near Shanghai were, I noted during a series of tours, choked with posters, over 80 per cent of which according to my official interpreter, were deeply critical of the Revolutionary Committees in the region, town or factory for their 'reactionary ways'. Local leaders together with army commanders were yet again accused of failing to support 'all the newly emerging things of socialism'. The posters went to greater extremes than those in Peking in chastising local leaders for having dismissed the Red Guards and other enthusiastic supporters of the Cultural Revolution and replacing them with 'capitalist roaders'.

In Harbin and Shenyang they were critical of Li Desheng who

was not only the Regional Military Commander of the whole north-eastern region but also a member of the Politbureau. In addition, he was a known friend of Jiang Qing and generally assumed to have held some radical sympathies. But it has since emerged that he did not get along with Wang Hongwen. The poster campaign was a part of the political power struggle which at the time made but little impact on the top military commanders, even when they were attacked. Each of them believed, with some reason, that he had the personal backing of Chairman Mao because one of the last major tasks he personally undertook, significantly with the help of Deng Xiaoping, was the full-scale reshuffle of Regional Military Commanders in December 1974. (This will be discussed later.)

Although Wang then appeared well out of the limelight, he became the glamorized hero – with the Chairman – of the poster campaigns everywhere. For although the other members of the Gang of Four were angry when he was promoted over their heads, they were all anxious to make use of the enormous power this young and inexperienced man had acquired in the party. They wanted to capitalize on the sop the Chairman and Premier had, in their view, given to the millions of dissatisfied former Red Guards then dispersed in agricultural communes along the border with the Soviet Union.

When Premier Zhou emerged looking hollow-eyed and ill to take part in the reception on July 31st to commemorate the forty-seventh anniversary of the founding of the Chinese Communist Party, it was apparent that the man who had administered China on a day to day basis for twenty-five years would never again be able to resume his gigantic work load. Wang still remained mysteriously in the background working for Jiang while the Premier's administrative work was carried out by Deng Xiaoping who was then seventy. As no new Defence Minister had been appointed, Ye Jianying, then seventy-six, continued in an acting capacity as he had been doing since the abortive coup of Lin Biao. Indeed, it was known he and Deng shared some of the burden of nuclear control with Premier Zhou.

After the Premier's heart attack, Jiang Qing assumed an ever-increasing role, much to the annoyance of Zhou and his deputy, because she had automatic access to the Chairman's bedroom and study. In addition, she controlled his visitors. Much has been made of a note the Chairman wrote to Jiang some time in 1973 in which he said, 'It is better not to see each other.' Obviously, it was not meant for publication and was leaked by a dissatisfied member of her staff. It was, I am told, a matrimonial quarrel – one of several – which lasted some weeks and was connected with Jiang's fondness for establishing secondary residences crammed with luxuries and serviced by excellent chefs. But her main residence and base remained the twin bungalow she shared with Mao in the Imperial City.

Many diplomats and senior Chinese officials believe that around this time Jiang Qing had a discreet affair with Wang Dongxing, who commanded the special Security Force 8341, which (as previously stated) was responsible for the safety of all members of the Politbureau. He was good-looking and, without doubt, such a liaison could have been maintained without too much fear of discovery. Senior officials were surprised later when Wang agreed that Force 8341 should be responsible for her arrest with other members of the Gang of Four after Chairman Mao's death. There were persistent reports of her love affairs but none were mentioned in the trial as having taken place after she had become Mao's wife and an important figure in her own right. It is reasonable to assume Jiang was extremely careful as she already lived in fear that one of her earlier love affairs in Shanghai would be made public. Indeed, the brutal measures she took to collect old love letters and pictures were finally disclosed at her trial.

Mao and Jiang are known to have had some political disagreements as Jiang was inclined to veer even further to the left than the Chairman. Mao knew that Jiang's long-term policy was to keep Deng 'down', or better still 'out', to enable Zhang Chunqiao to become Premier after Zhou while she gradually promoted herself to be Chairman. What Jiang had in mind for the other two members of the 'Shanghai group' Chairman Mao later dubbed 'the Gang of Four' varied from time to time. Wang Hongwen, who was already the number three man in the party, she generally saw as working under her in that sphere while she trained Yao Wenyuan to take charge of the media. Meanwhile, Jiang was the only person who could use the Chairman's chop (seal), which is more important than a signature in China. That she used it with care is surprising in view of her other reckless activities.

The relations between Mao and his wife were, in fact, the unspoken but major problem of all those Chinese Ministers responsible for both foreign and domestic policy roughly from the end of the 10th Party Conference in August 1973 until Premier Zhou's death early in January 1976. This situation became far more acute after the Premier's heart attacks forced him to take up almost permanent residence in hospital.

A sudden and unexpected lull in the power struggle occurred in January 1975 when the surprise appointment was announced of the first Vice Premier, Deng Xiaoping, as Chief of Staff of the PLA. It was stated to be yet another attempt to ensure that 'the party commands the gun', but what was more significant was that at the same time Zhang Chunqiao, the 56-year-old leader of the Shanghai radicals, was made Chief of the General Political Department of the PLA or Chief Political Commissar. Both men were then generally recognized 'inside people' as the leading contenders for the post of Chairman of the party after Mao 'went to meet his gods' – Deng the pragmatist and Zhang the radical. The Chairmanship carried with it the office of Commander-in-Chief of the PLA, just agreed at the much-delayed 4th National People's Congress held earlier in January 1975. In addition, the Chairman presided over the powerful MAC of the party's Central Committee, which until about this time had been composed of elderly generals from Red Army days.

Neither Deng nor Zhang had any recent military experience. Deng, who served with the Red Army for five years before taking part in the prestigious Long March in 1934/5, had spent much of his time in the war as a political commissar. However, in the last phases of the civil war he had become one of the commanders of the 2nd Field Army which, in a series of brilliant manoeuvres, defeated the nationalists over a wide front along the Yangtze in the spring of 1949. Although Deng remained, in theory, political commissar for the 2nd Army and the South-western Military Region and a military administrator until 1954, he was from 'liberation' (1949) onwards primarily concerned with party administration, economic affairs and state business.

Deng's appointment as Chief of Staff gave him the power to

organize for the production and release of China's nuclear weapons, together with responsibility for the state bureaucracy which he gradually took over from the ailing Premier Zhou. Chairman Mao gave his strong support to the appointment which was, however, bitterly opposed by the outraged Jiang Qing. Members of the household staff of the Chairman later talked about the quarrels that arose about this time between Mao and his wife about Deng who, Jiang Qing believed, with reason, would render it virtually impossible for Zhang to stress the benefits of 'being red' as opposed to being expert in the armed forces. By the end of the year (1974) Deng had also assumed Zhou's role in the general direction of foreign policy, which included receiving all important overseas visitors. Deng, it was noted, showed a confidence after his visit to France in the spring of 1974 that had only gradually developed following his reappearance in April 1973 after six years out of public view when he was disgraced and reviled as a 'capitalist roader', by the radicals, including Zhang Chunqiao. It is interesting and important to note that Deng never revealed what he knew of Zhang's disreputable political background when it was later disclosed during the trial of the Gang of Four and which included making completely false charges against him during the Cultural Revolution.

It is, however, extremely difficult to envisage how the two men could have worked together. A member of the Politbureau told me later that both the Chairman and Premier Zhou had 'begged' an unwilling Deng in the name of party solidarity to work with Zhang. As a result Deng agreed to let bygones be bygones and set himself to collaborate with the new political commissar. Without doubt the Premier believed Deng's presence at the desk of the Chief of Staff would place a natural brake on Zhang's pro-radical activities in the PLA. Many well-informed diplomats at the time kept repeating that once the radicals had publicly agreed to the Premier's 'open door' policy in foreign affairs they were genuinely willing to participate. How wrong they all were proved to be!

An earlier attempt to ensure that the 'gun must never be allowed to command the Party' and to deal with high-level military decisions and nuclear responsibility had been made when the Premier and acting Defence Minister, Ye Jianying, were both sick. The unlikely triumvirate, which did not last long, was composed of Wang

Hongwen, as third man in the party, Vice Premier Deng Xiaoping and the then up-and-coming commander of the vital Peking Military Region, Chen Xilian. This group was dissolved at the time of the National People's Congress when Ye was made Defence Minister and the other appointments were announced.

Major military reshuffle

There is no doubt that Mao Zedong and Zhou Enlai had been deeply shaken by the attempted coup d'état of September 1971 organized by the late Lin Biao, who was then Mao's 'chosen successor' and Defence Minister. The forced resignation of over 250 senior commanders and the cross-posting of scores of others did little to diminish the strength of the power bases that the eleven regional commanders had built up after the Cultural Revolution, enabling them to ignore or water down orders from Peking they did not like. Five of the eleven regional commanders, in Fuzhou (Foochow), Nanjing, Wuhan, Guangzhou and Shenyang, also held top posts in the Communist Party and could, without too much difficulty, have transformed themselves into 'Red Warlords', although it is most unlikely that they would have contemplated this during the Chairman's lifetime.

The scope of these regional commands was surprising. For instance, Shenyang (Manchuria) covers an area of 466,000 square miles – more than twice the size of France – and includes over 65 million inhabitants compared with 52 million in France. The region supplies China with over 16 per cent of its total coal requirements, 47.8 per cent of crude oil, 12.67 per cent of chemicals, 39 per cent of lorries and 27.6 per cent of steel. It is surrounded on three sides by the Soviet Union, which at times had deployed some 650,000 men and 8000 tanks, as well as 1500 tactical aircraft in the area, making with other troops further to the west a total of around 1 million men.

In addition to their political and military power, certain regional commanders in the industrial areas were using their authority to divert the production of trucks and lorries designed for agricultural communes to their own forces. Several Revolutionary Committees in charge of heavy industrial plant were also ordered to produce spare parts for weapons, especially outmoded Russian tanks and artillery. These interferences by the military, it was claimed, seriously disturbed the industrial targets of the current Five Year Plan, due to terminate in December 1974.

The 'Marshals', as the eleven regional commanders were known before the abolition of ranks, proved to be difficult to dislodge from their power bases. After weeks of discussions, in which both the Prime Minister and Deng took part in the autumn of 1973, Chairman Mao sent for eight of the commanders in turn – one of the last tasks personally undertaken by him. He gave them a week to decide whether or not they would accept the proposed changes and, at the same time, he informed them that they could take a maximum of three staff 'officers' with them to their new command.

When the changes were finally made public, it was stressed that no one was being dismissed or demoted and, indeed, what happened was that commanders in Guangzhou, Jinan, Lanzhou (Lanchow) and Peking changed places with their opposite numbers in Nanjing, Wuhan, Fuzhou and Shenyang. It is reasonable to add that many of the commanders had held their appointments for periods that would have been considered over-long in any European army. Thus Xu Shiyu, the new commander of the Guangdong region, was in control in Nanjing – which includes Shanghai – from 1954 to the end of 1973; Han Xianchu (Han Hsien-chu), was commander of the Fuzhou region from 1958 to 1973; and Chen Xilian held the vital Manchurian command from 1959 to 1973.

The most important of the changes announced at the beginning of 1974 appeared to be the swop of commanders between Peking and Shenyang. Li Desheng, then aged sixty-four, the former Director of the General Political Department, was a member of the nine-man Standing Committee of the ruling Politbureau, which was also, wrongly as it turned out, recognized as the body that would assume collective responsibility should Chairman Mao or Premier Zhou die. Li was also a Deputy Chairman of the Central Committee of the Party and the most senior soldier in the party hierarchy. Although he has veered with the political winds, he was considered one of the most radical of the 'Marshals'. Despite the Manchurian commands, ranking as the second most important post for a commander in the field, Li was reluctant to leave his powerful seat in Peking.

The 61-year-old Chen Xilian moved from Shenyang to take over the vital Peking Military Region. His command, which includes the ultimate responsibility for the safety and protection of China's leaders, also covers the frontier with the Mongolian Republic. This sector is particularly important since Mongolia, an Asian Soviet satellite, could (as recorded earlier) be used by the Russians to mount a Second World War-type of 'blitzkrieg' operation against the Chinese capital and the port of Tianjin. The new commander was extremely active in meeting distinguished guests and attending banquets in the Great Hall of the People. He also made a point of being seen to be on friendly terms with Jiang Qing, as well as with Deng Xiaoping, with whom he sometimes acted as a joint host at receptions. Although he was the youngest of the Regional Military Commanders, Chen has a veteran's background: as a young officer he took part in the Long March and later in the Korean War, before assuming command of the artillery.

After the reshuffle there were many reports that Li Desheng was in trouble and he was officially dropped as Vice Chairman of the Central Committee of the Party. Another commander who was criticized in big character posters after the transfers took place was Han Xianchu of the Lanzhou Military Region, who, when commander at Fuzhou, authorized the publication of a book written by his deputy in praise of Lin Biao. But it was significant that no senior military commander who had been attacked in wall posters had, so far as is known, lost his job. There was a considerable strengthening of the position of moderate officers serving on the General Staff with the rehabilitation of (General) Yang Chengwu, a former Assistant Chief of Staff, together with over a score of other 'generals' dismissed during the later phases of the Cultural Revolution.

But it was the rehabilitation of the former Chief of Staff, Luo Ruiqing (at the end of July 1975), that was then considered most likely to influence future defence policy. In addition to being a veteran of the Long March and an expert on internal security, he was Secretary General of the Party's top policy-making body, the MAC. In the early 1960s, Luo (who experienced in Korea the disastrous results of the PLA's attempts to attack well-armed

American conventional forces) began to find himself leading those professional soldiers who favoured a modern, well-equipped conventional army in opposition to his Minister of Defence, the late Lin Biao, who by that time had become the chief exponent of Maoist people's war philosophy. Indeed, in 1965 Luo published an article advocating the 'defence of the cities', a strategy that would have required land forces with sophisticated weapons. Further, as Chief of Staff, he stressed the need for a more balanced mixture of military training and political indoctrination, asserting that it was a first principle that soldiers should learn to shoot accurately. As a result, Luo was charged with 'espousing the bourgeois military line' and became the first top military leader to be purged at the beginning of the Cultural Revolution.

The PLA did not escape the in-fighting of western defence forces. There was and still is a nuclear lobby, a naval lobby, and an air force lobby. In addition, there was and again still is a powerful group of commanders who are demanding more conventional equipment, especially modern anti-tank weapons, artillery, and armoured personnel carriers. The 'conventional' lobby then argued that a pre-emptive nuclear strike by the Soviet Union was most unlikely, largely because it would have global repercussions. Moreover, experts believed the time had passed for the Soviet Union to mount a successful strike to 'take out' once and for all the Chinese nuclear installations at Lop Nor and the stores of nuclear warheads, for it was known that there had been a great deal of dispersal in western China since the initial nuclear effort was begun in Xinjiang and that warheads are now stored in the Tibetan mountains.

The conventional lobby quoted Premier Zhou Enlai's statement that the Russians might 'try to take the fortress from within' by stirring up troubles inside the country or even in the defence forces. They claimed that more armoured personnel carriers (APCs) and mobile artillery, which would be invaluable in a defensive action should the Soviet Union attempt to invade China, would have the additional advantage of serving another useful purpose in case of civil disturbances. The conventional lobby had been greatly strengthened by the rehabilitated officers, much to the annoyance of the 'Gang'.

The Chinese armed forces were geared entirely to a defensive role – they still are. Excluding minor frontier skirmishes or incidents like the takeover by the navy of the Paracel Islands from the South Vietnamese in January 1974, the PLA lacked the capability to mount a major offensive action in the conventional military sphere. In 1969 Chairman Mao had summed up both the defensive stance of the PLA and the strategy to be adopted should an invasion take place.

If the enemy should invade our country, we should refrain from invading his country. As a general rule, we do not fight outside our own borders; I say we should not be provoked into doing so, even if you send us an invitation. But if you should invade our country then we will deal with you. We would see whether you want to fight a small war or a big war. If a small war, we would fight on the border. If a big war, I propose that we make some room for that. China is a vast country . . . We want the whole world to see that in fighting such a war, we should be on logically sound grounds. As far as I can see, if he enters our country, we shall have the advantage . . . making it a good war to fight and making the enemy a victim of the quagmire of the people. As to such weapons as aircraft, tanks and armoured cars, numerous experiences have shown it is within our competence to deal with them.

Unhappily this was no longer true and a sophisticated enemy could also have challenged the small and outdated air and naval forces from the air or sea. Despite the network of air-raid shelters built in readiness for attacks from the air, the Chinese are extremely vulnerable owing to a chronic shortage of weapons to use against low-flying aircraft and they lack also modern interception aircraft.

In 1974 the campaign to criticize the ancient sage Confucius and the late Lin Biao provided various groups within the military establishment with an opportunity to comment critically on China's past and future defence strategy, in such authoritiative journals as the theoretical party monthly *Red Flag* and the more radical Shanghai magazine *Study and Criticism*. But while Chairman Mao was alive, there was continuing stress on the concept of people's war.

The main force, as opposed to the regional forces, together with the artillery and nuclear arm, came under direct command of the MAC. Main force units could be sent anywhere in the country whereas the regional forces, which were armed with more outdated equipment and were lamentably short of transport, came under the regional commander's orders and could not be moved out of his area. By 1974 the Chinese had developed missiles capable of hitting targets such as the Russian naval base at Vladivostok, the important industrial and communications centres at Irkutsk and even cities west of the Ural mountains.

There was much discussion amongst foreign experts – mostly military attachés – in Peking at the time about the drawbacks of conducting modern warfare under party control and the possible length of time it might take to reach vital and urgent decisions by consensus. But it was generally assumed that with a nod from the ageing Chairman and the sick Premier Zhou, MAC, under the chairmanship of Deng, was empowered to give the order to fire a nuclear missile if there were irrefutable evidence that Soviet (or American) missiles were already in the air targeted on China. No secret was made of the fact that in the worst possible contingency, were for example the industrial areas of central China to be overrun, the army would evacuate as much of their equipment as possible to areas in the west and south-west. According to the well-known pattern of the civil war, certain units would attempt to hold pre-selected 'mountain tops'. This sounds over-simplistic in the nuclear age, but many of the older Chinese commanders still tended to think in terms of the Yenan caves and other redoubts as bases for the initial offensive to regain their lost territory. Deng and the really active 'Generals' in MAC were already well aware that the main danger to China arose from the massive build-up of Soviet land forces on their joint border. As already described some forty-odd divisions, permanently deployed near the frontier, were augmented every autumn by squadrons of bombers and fighters flown in from the west to take part in large-scale joint manoeuvres.

The Chinese had a mere trip-wire along the frontier manned by border guards and backed by agricultural communes, and the MAC realized – though they could not admit this – that the people's war just would not work effectively in places where there were no people, such as the deserts of Xinjiang, which cover much of the distance between the Soviet border and Lop Nor. How could soldiers 'melt like fish into the sea' when there is no sea, that is, few towns or village oases in which to disperse? This was the question posed by many commanders and foreign military attachés in Peking at the time who believed that the north-east – formerly Manchuria – which contains the main oil-fields and industrial base, was also vulnerable to a sudden attack by Russian armoured forces, as were Peking and the nearby port of Tianjin.

However, the experts were widely divided on how long the Russians would be able to occupy these areas. It was generally accepted that, owing to problems of obtaining supplies from the west, it would be impossible to hold Peking or the former area of Manchuria indefinitely as the only means of transport for supplies was the Trans-Siberian railway. (Since that time the Russians have been constructing a second railway a few hundred miles to the north of the original track.) Many of the attachés tended to believe that if the Russians had been rash enough to make a dash for Peking they would merely have driven their tanks around the city and evacuated it. This gesture would have been sufficient to make the Chinese leaders lose face not only before the world but in the eyes of their own people. A few experts, however, thought the Russians would make Tianjin where they might stage a demonstration with submarines of the Soviet Navy.

Although China had managed to occupy the small, potentially oil-rich and virtually undefended Paracel Islands at the end of the war in Vietnam, there was no question of Peking attempting to occupy Taiwan by force. Despite Premier Zhou's earlier talk of the future 'blue' deep-sea navy and the issue of new uniforms to sailors, the navy was only suitable for coastal defence. The air force, with its 4000 combat aircraft, was in reality made up of 2000 outdated copies of Mig 15s and 17s, some hundreds of which were permanently grounded through lack of spare parts – especially brakes – as a result of faulty industrial planning.

The PLA chose its recruits, despite conscription, through 'selective service', for each year there were far more men and women in the right age groups anxious to join the service than were required. Thousands from the more remote agricultural communes hoped that by serving in the PLA they would acquire some technical skills that would cause them to be directed after three years to a much sought-after job in a factory. Much to their disappointment in 1975 many soldiers were still sent back to work on remote communes after completion of their service.

Zhang Chunqiao and the role of the People's Militia

Zhang Chunqiao was outwardly most careful in the instructions he gave to the political commissars in the PLA but he acted under the cover of Chairman Mao and generally had written authority from him when he pushed what Vice Premier Deng might have considered the radical line. Zhang, doubtless with the help of Jiang Qing, gradually assumed responsibility for various sections of the militia in key cities and areas. It is not clear even now whether Premier Zhou or Deng were fully aware of all that was happening as the Premier was really ill and Deng then grossly over-worked. Much later, the new constitution of January 1979 provided official status for the militia, at that time composed of 'hundreds of millions' of men and women. In fact everyone who had ever held arms appeared in 1975 to qualify for the unarmed militia which drilled with sticks. But the numbers were gradually cut down to around 30 million. This force was trained by the army and once every few years they used rifles for a week of training.

Armed and trained militia units were established in the agricultural communes sited in an irregular chain along the Russian border while in the cities militia units were trained to use automatic weapons and ack-ack guns and to control the many air-raid shelters that had been constructed at Chairman Mao's behest, quoted earlier, to 'Dig tunnels deep, store grain everywhere and seek no hegemony.' Commanders (officers) in many urban militia units were personally armed with the efficient automatic weapons – AK47s – produced in China. Zhang made it quite clear, in secret, to the urban militia of Shanghai and other cities, that, although trained and working on a daily basis in full co-operation with the PLA, they might well be required to 'keep regular soldiers in their place should they at any time grow out of hand and attempt to control the gun themselves instead of leaving this to the party'.

Early in 1975 the Chinese had taken the unique step of publishing an illustrated handbook, the ABC of military knowledge, that was intended not only for the militia but also for the 'broad masses'. Here, in 383 pages, were the details of how to carry out Chairman Mao's instructions to 'drown the enemy with people'. Amongst other things, the militiaman could learn how to destroy a tank after he had run out of ammunition by fouling its tracks with logs of wood. The preparations required to survive a nuclear attack, and to administer first aid after it, were also outlined. The book on basic guerrilla training, especially in mounting ambushes and operating secretly in the countryside, provided useful information for irregular forces throughout the world. At that time when foreigners were not allowed to buy all the daily newspapers, the manual's public appearance in the bookstalls caused a sensation. The argument for an effective militia had some force given the fact (already noted) that the Soviet Union was then suffering from logistic problems and limited transport facilities between Moscow and Siberia.

Throughout 1974 and 1975 diplomats and correspondents based in Peking realized that the media, under the direction of Jiang Qing, was voicing far more radical views than Deng, who towards the end of that time was the acting Premier, but few realized the intensity of the power struggle soon to build up again at all levels. However, the myth persisted – maybe it was fanned by the radicals themselves – that once they had agreed to accept Zhou's original 'open door' policy publicly, they were committed to it indefinitely.

It is now suggested that Chen Boda, under the direction of 'the traitor Lin Biao', opened the campaign to criticize Premier Zhou as early as October 1966 when he gave orders that, 'Everyone can be criticized except Chairman Mao, Lin Biao and Jiang Qing', which meant, 'Criticize Premier Zhou'. A poster criticizing the Premier was put up in the university in January 1967 but was taken down within two days on the express orders of the Chairman. From that time onwards, despite the great respect and popularity the Premier enjoyed with the 'broad masses', it is now known there were constant open and undercover attacks led by Jiang Qing against him. Although the healthy leaders were frequently photographed laughing and joking together, perceptive friends such as Prince Norodom Sihanouk and even the late Edgar Snow were deeply worried.

Many cadres were away for periods that varied from a few months to a few years at the May 7th Cadre Schools, already mentioned, which were established in 1968 to re-educate officials. Initially they were regarded as places of punishment for people who had sympathized with the 'capitalist roaders' during the Cultural Revolution, but gradually their role changed and, by the early 1970s, I recall a sophisticated senior official saying it was 'as necessary for a cadre to go to the May 7th School as to go to the Staff College for an ambitious British Army officer'. But despite many such statements and the fact that by the early 1970s officials even claimed to have 'enjoyed' their spells at the Cadre Schools, there was always a fear they might be forgotten while they were there or someone take over their job, or merely plot against them.

Mao's original idea that the cadres and peasants should work side by side and learn from one another was soon dropped as the latter made it abundantly clear they did not appreciate the assistance of these 'soft-handed' urban intellectuals who were both ignorant and inexperienced in the field. After a few years the pressure from the Revolutionary Committees running the agricultural communes became so great that the Chairman was reluctantly forced to accept the fact that cadres 'were more trouble than they were worth'. But Mao did not give up entirely and arrangements were made for the Cadre Schools to have their own farms and the time they spent in actual work with peasants was reduced to two or, at most, three weeks a year. The May 7th Schools I visited were reasonably comfortable – a cross between an open prison and school. The Chairman of the Revolutionary Committee in charge of one of them was willing to admit their production was 'more than fifty per cent below that of the nearby commune'.

The period 1972–4 which is now included in the Cultural Revolution was, at the time, considered well after it, for the 9th Party Congress of 1969 was then understood to have terminated that particular phase of contemporary history. I remember it as a time of whispered talk and people's fear and insistence, on meeting, even in winter, in open places where round-eyed barbarians were not too conspicuous. It surprised me, however, that so many people were willing to talk in confidence, perhaps with the hope that 'if anything happened to them' one foreigner, who had nothing to lose or gain, would be able to write about their life. A typical example, a woman, an intellectual who had travelled in Europe, told me how she and her husband somehow or other obtained a bottle of French wine and on the anniversary of their wedding, after their teenage children and all the neighbours were asleep, they took out his dinner jacket and her long evening dress, which were stored under the floorboards, and by candlelight they enjoyed a European dinner. They were taking a great risk for if they had been discovered they could certainly have been sent to different unpleasant agricultural communes on the Russian border.

16

The Power Struggle in the Open

The death of Premier Zhou Enlai on January 8th, 1976 was the catalyst for the smouldering power struggle of 1974/5 to burst into the open. Although his death at seventy-eight had long been expected the whole nation appeared grief-stricken. Jiang Qing took enormous precautions to isolate the Chairman as Premier Zhou lay dying, in an effort to prevent the anticipated, automatic promotion of Deng, who had been effectively filling the role of Premier for the past year.

Certainly the Chairman was himself ailing but the 'inside people' claimed it was Jiang Qing who personally prevented him from attending any of the sad celebrations that marked the Premier's lying in state, cremation and the scattering of his ashes 'over the country he loved'. In addition it was noted that Mao made no public tribute to his 'old comrade' despite the fact he must have seen hundreds of thousands of Chinese on his much-used television screen openly weeping with uncontrolled grief. Diplomats and foreign journalists were bewildered, too, by the fact that the only representatives of the leadership who accompanied the body to the crematorium through the Avenue of Heavenly Peace were the radical Wang Hongwen and Wang Dongxing, formerly Mao's bodyguard. However, there was general relief on January 15th when Deng Xiaoping read the eulogy, as requested by the dead Premier, who had made no secret of his desire that Deng should succeed him.

Throughout the land, in small isolated communes as well as large cities, memorial ceremonies were held but comparatively little appeared in the radical-controlled press about the man who had served the Chinese Communist Party and people for fifty-four years. Foreigners were requested not to organize any public ceremonies and, when national mourning was at its height, orders were suddenly issued prohibiting any further expressions of grief and people were told to take off their black armbands.

While foreigners living in Peking were concerned that Deng was not named as Premier and did not appear in public, they appeared to believe that in the end the Chairman would appoint him on the grounds that he had been well trained by Zhou. Before the end of January I discovered almost by accident that Deng was already in disgrace for a second time when I tried to purchase an official Xinhua News Agency press photograph of him and Deng Yingchao – Premier Zhou's widow – taken during a tea-break at the 10th Party Congress in 1973. I had the index number of the picture but the man behind the counter insisted that it did not exist and, in addition, that he had never heard of anyone called Deng Xiaoping. Although I guessed this meant Deng was being purged for the second time, I thought the man might just be being rude to a round-eyed barbarian about the way I was pronouncing the name, and I took my Chinese interpreter to the official shop and she was given the same information, that 'no one of the name of Deng Xiaoping had ever existed'. (I always hope the man was mildly reprimanded for being such a liar.) Later that day I wrote a report saying Deng would not succeed Premier Zhou and that he was already in disgrace somewhere in the countryside. (Unhappily, this important piece of information failed to attract the eye of the news editor and the piece was drastically cut and used on an inside page where it passed virtually unnoticed.)

During the last days of January Deng's disappearance was followed by that of Ye Jianying, the Defence Minister, and Li Xiannian, the 'financial wizard', both of whom were close friends of Premier Zhou. At the same time posters appeared in the university attacking 'capitalist roaders' (some of them even mentioned Deng by name) while the theoretical journal, *Red Flag*, reviled 'rightist elements'. The sensational power struggle resulted in a compromise as Hua Guofeng, Minister for Public Security, the agriculturalist from Mao's home town, was named Acting Prime Minister on February 8th by the *People's Daily* in a report on the reception of the new Venezuelan Ambassador. As Hua's promotion, from the fifth-ranking Vice Premier to the top, was announced the press and posters broke into violent criticism of Deng and Zhou's associates. Deng was accused of 'unscrupulously splitting the Central Committee' and one poster urged, 'Let us drag him off his horse, so that we can kick him.' However, the far-sighted Xu Shiyu, commander of the Guangdong Military Region, rushed Deng off by air to the comfort and safety of southern China where the former acting Premier was put up in the guest-house of the hot springs near Guangzhou. He went around to visit friends and supporters in an ambulance or police car.

Jiang Qing threw her weight around in Peking by encouraging anti-Deng posters to be put up together with reports – frequently all too true – of scathing remarks Deng had made about her radical policies and stage productions. Deng was criticized, too, for his stress on productivity and for cutting down the time workers both on agricultural communes and in factories devoted to political indoctrination, which was euphemistically called 'studies'. He was ruthlessly attacked for his reversal of the radical educational policy which stressed that it was more important for students to be 'red' than proficient and for teachers and officials to be chosen because they were good radical communists rather than 'expert'.

Although the Red Guards were no longer destroying temples or any building that looked old, few museums were then open except to visiting overseas Chinese or foreigners and no foreign books or newspapers were available; nor, indeed, were any films or plays or traditional Chinese operas produced. Jiang Qing and what was then dubbed the 'Shanghai Gang', which became the 'Gang of Four', insisted on simple, cotton clothes – Mao jackets – for the broad masses, combined with plain food and a frugal existence, relieved by the odd Chinese-made revolutionary film or opera. But they, personally, did not follow this way of life. When Jiang Qing was away from the Chairman she lived in hotels, guest-houses and flats where she indulged in exotic foods and wines, rare fruits together with western clothes and silk sheets. It was said that when she fancied some good-looking young man who appeared either in a sporting event or as an actor on the television screen, she sent for him to share her couch for the evening. But if this were the case I am astonished that such goings on were never mentioned in her trial.

However, she did insist that the Beihai Park and its famous restaurant were closed on the grounds that they overlooked the Imperial Palace where members of the Politbureau were living. She kept the restaurant open in order to serve exquisite food to the Gang and other friends. They watched, according to a young waiter who served them throughout this period, erotic films after dinner which they all obviously enjoyed. But the waiter stressed he never noted any sign of affection either between Jiang and other members of the Gang or between Jiang and the men she brought in to entertain.

At that time young Chinese couples were made to live very austere lives; they never went out alone even for a walk on Sunday unless they were officially engaged. It was frequently suggested to the broad masses that loyalty to the party provided a far better basis for marriage than affection or sex. Further, the educated elite were encouraged to marry workers or peasants. No hairdressers were allowed to work, except for foreigners, and for Jiang, who had her hair 'set' every time she appeared in public. Personal service of this kind was otherwise forbidden on the grounds that it was improper and undignified for Chinese workers to 'serve' others in this way.

Deng became the major target for all criticism in the press and on the radio and Zhang Chunqiao actually said, 'Heads will have to roll . . . it's an us or them situation . . . we haven't killed enough . . . However, first let us bring down Deng then deal with Hua.' The Gang put the blame for their lack of official power fairly and squarely on the shoulders of the late Premier whose revered memory in the eyes of the Chinese people worried them enormously.

The late Premier's widow, Deng Yingchao, passed through an extremely difficult phase because it was known she was a good friend and supporter of Deng. I recall meeting her at a reception in March to celebrate Women's Day when her friends expressed relief that she had been 'allowed out' and provided with an official car. But few Chinese dared to speak with the distinguished widow, who was to become a member of the ruling Politbureau, because they feared the Gang would punish them if they were seen to make a friendly approach.

The media remained in the hands of the Gang and the quality of news and views printed was extremely low and repetitive, even by Chinese standards. More reliable news of what was happening after Hua became acting Premier was passed by word of mouth from clerks and other servants to their friends. Through these means, I recall learning that Mao had suggested Deng should publicly admit he had gone too far in encouraging production as well as in his criticisms of the cultural productions of Jiang Qing. But despite appeals from Mao, who obviously wanted him back at the centre at this time, Deng refused to admit he had made political errors. Naturally, the Gang were delighted by this. They appeared to have a reasonable idea of their support in the country, which they claimed was from one-third to a half of the population – many experts believed they had less than a third. Their support was strong amongst those people – mostly young – who had risen to positions of power during the Cultural Revolution and feared that should Deng return to office they, like thousands before them, would be dismissed. Membership of the Communist Party then stood at 36 million but nearly half were new members, supporters of the Gang, who had been admitted during the Cultural Revolution.

Throughout the early part of the year there can be no doubt that the Chairman's health deteriorated sharply. He managed to hold a successful talk for over an hour and a half in February with a distinguished visitor but by late March he could only stand with assistance and sometimes his appearances were embarrassing. It was, however, stressed that he still had periods of alertness and the Gang insisted that the broad masses wanted to see their leader. Most outsiders during the early part of 1976 believed the broad masses were being prepared by the Gang for his death and the promotion of his widow Jiang. Behind the quiet calm exterior Peking presented to the outsider, Jiang Qing was rushing round trying to persuade or blackmail key Ministers and senior officials to come out into the open in support of the radicals. At the same time, Zhang Chunqiao, Yao Wenyuan and Wang Hongwen were sucessful in influencing various groups of left-wing writers such as 'Liang Xiao' and 'Luo Siding' to 'vilify' in the press and magazines those officials who had been reinstated in their posts at the end of the militant period of the Cultural Revolution, either by Premier Zhou, Deng Xiaoping or the PLA. In the eyes of Jiang Qing – and she quoted Mao in support of what she said – these officials were failing to 'continue the revolution' on the grounds that they had 'turned from bourgeois democrats into capitalist roaders'.

Yao Wenyuan also arranged that reporters were sent out from the *People's Daily* in Peking to the provinces to concoct material against local party leaders the Gang disliked because of their support of Deng. Meanwhile, portraits of Hua were beginning to appear and the people were showing an interest in his personality and, of course, his relations with the Chairman, to whom he only had access with Jiang Qing or when she said the Chairman was 'well enough' for a chat. Jiang Qing also acted as a matchmaker at the time as a means to increase her influence. The wife of the late Foreign Minister, Qiao Guanhua (Chiao Kuan-hua), had died. She was Kong Peng and their careers had followed similar patterns as she and her husband had both worked for Zhou Enlai in Chongqing during the war. Later they worked as journalists in Shanghai and Hong Kong before she joined the Foreign Ministry in 1949 as Head of the News Department until she became an Assistant Minister in 1964. Kong Peng was openly devoted to Premier Zhou and accompanied her husband to Geneva with him in 1954 and to Africa in 1963/4. Her death was a bitter blow to everyone except Jiang Qing who immediately introduced him to a beautiful and vivacious woman Zhang Hanzhi who at one time had attempted to teach English to Jiang and now acted as interpreter for Wang Hongwen. A speedy divorce was arranged for her and shortly after the new marriage Qiao dropped all his old friends who were associated with Premier Zhou.

The triangular power struggle continued as Hua, who held the Chair as Premier, attempted to placate the radicals without offending the right-wing 'Marshal' on whom he was also dependent.

Strangely enough it was the broad masses who brought matters to a head during the Qing Ming Festival in early April on Tiananmen Square. Obviously preparations to mourn the death of Premier Zhou during the traditional ceremonies of 'sweeping out the graves' had been made weeks in advance. On March 30th a huge wreath dedicated to Zhou was placed on the Martyrs' Memorial in the square. I lived nearby and noted that from that moment groups of people began to bring large wreaths of white artificial flowers from factories and outlying agricultural communes. Although the radio stressed that people should not waste their time in making wreaths or taking them to Tiananmen Square during a ceremony that 'was meant for ghosts', adding that commemorating the dead is an outmoded custom, by Friday April 2nd the small stream of visitors had developed into a flood. Almost all the people in the square wore black armbands and many wore buttonholes of white homemade artificial flowers. In Peking news soon gets around and by Sunday the entire population believed it was the thing to do to go to the square. Indeed, as I left the city early in the morning for a brief visit to the Western Hills, I met tens of thousands of people on foot, in buses and on bicycles converging on the city in an orderly manner. Some were singing the songs they had composed in praise of the late Premier whilst others were reciting poetry.

Later in the day, when the square appeared to hold hundreds of thousands of people – it does hold a million – wreaths were stacked over fifty feet high on all sides of the monument. Hundreds were hung on lamp-posts and others displayed on special tables and trucks with ribbons or scrolls containing verses mourning Zhou. Two volumes of poems have been produced from the poems and tributes displayed during those days of mourning. There were, too, notices criticizing Jiang Qing in slightly disguised terms such as 'Down with the Dowager Empress: down with Indira Gandhi!' while others were indirectly critical of the Chairman for failing to implement Premier Zhou's 'pragmatic and progressive policies'. Throughout the day the gates of the university had been closed in order to prevent students joining the crowds in the square but many climbed the high walls in order to take their tributes to the square.

In the early hours of Monday morning lorries belonging to the army but driven by members of the People's Militia drove into the square and a few hundred uniformed men and women tore down the wreaths and slogans and threw them into the lorries. Then shortly after dawn I watched hundreds of efficient-looking troops getting out of buses in barracks near to the square, but these regular soldiers, so far as I know, remained in reserve and were never used in the subsequent disturbances.

When the word got around that the wreaths had been removed, despite continuous warning over the radio not to go to the square again, angry crowds collected demanding of the police and the urban militiamen what had happened to the wreaths. The word got around – this time quite wrongly – that they had been taken into the Great Hall of the People. The crowd then surged towards the hall loudly demanding admission but a few hundred policemen suddenly emerged from the hall and prevented the crowd's approach. This made them even more angry. Then a young man, obviously a strong supporter of Jiang Qing, shouted from the top step of the memorial that the crowd's demands were wrong and claimed there was no need to present wreaths to the late Premier Zhou, who was 'The biggest capitalist roader in the Party!' I watched as the crowd rounded on him in fury and threw him down the steps of the monument causing him serious injuries. Groups got together as the day progressed to sing the 'Internationale' and to demand access to the Mayor or the 'boss' of the security bureau in the square. In the early afternoon, as the crowds were ordered to disperse by loudspeakers being distributed by the police and militia, one crowd in a moment of mass hysteria set fire to an empty car and then to two jeeps and a small bus that were following. Meanwhile, the crowds in other parts of the square were laying even more wreaths apparently unaware of the burning cars until they saw the smoke and smelled the burning rubber. Scores of people were injured as the crowds moved first in one direction and then in another. Little if any anti-foreign sentiment was expressed. The hurly-burly grew worse as the afternoon wore on and after the jeeps were burned the crowd burst into the head-quarters of one of the security forces, initially in an effort to discuss the problem of the missing wreaths with a senior officer. Confidential files were hurled from the windows by angry young men and women before the building was set on fire.

Soon after six in the evening the loudspeakers broadcast an appeal from the Mayor of Peking, Wu De, to disperse and not 'to fall into the trap that had been set for them'. Thousands obeyed, largely because it was time for their evening meal, they were getting tired and there seemed no hope that the original wreaths would be returned. Those who remained tended to form groups of anything from fifty to a hundred people, generally near the monument, a lamp-post or a group of trees. The groups discussed the situation between bursts of the 'Internationale' and other patriotic songs. They appeared to anticipate that sooner or later the police or the army would attempt to throw them out of the square.

I wandered round with a Japanese correspondent and we noted food and water were being brought in by friends to some of the groups who were increasingly being isolated by squads of policemen in the darkness. Suddenly at around 9.30 P.M. all the lights were turned on, the loudspeakers blared forth loud martial music as thousands of militia dashed into the square from the Imperial City, the Great Hall of the People and buildings in the southern part of the square where I was at that moment. The majority of foreign diplomats and journalists observing the scene were in the northern sector.

Large trucks were driven into the square and the people were ordered to get into them. It was not clear whether they were to be arrested or not. Several groups refused to move but as the cold plus the physical need for a toilet grew, the crowd was gradually dispersed and the square completely cleared soon after 2.30 A.M. The militia did beat people up, but I did not see any blood, although some did flow. The following morning scores of demonstrators returned and although they realized the game was up they were outspoken enough to tell foreigners that the 'Shanghai radicals' led by Jiang Qing were responsible for the wreaths being removed and the actions that followed.

At a meeting of the Politbureau the following day, called to discuss the series of incidents in the square, it was later disclosed Chairman Mao proposed – although he was not present – that Deng Xiaoping should be stripped of all his offices but remain in the party. Hua Guofeng was then promoted to be First Vice Chairman of the Party as well as acting Premier. It was clear that officially Deng was blamed for the disturbances in Tiananmen Square as well as for having initiated the massive wreath-laying ceremonies in honour of Premier Zhou. But few in Peking were taken in by this condemnation as it was already well-known that Deng was in disgrace and living somewhere in the south.

Jiang Qing had earlier led a campaign inside the Central Committee of the party to have Deng expelled 'once and for all' as a 'capitalist roader and enemy of the people'. She failed only because she lacked the full backing of the Chairman who was sporadically active although he suffered a series of minor heart attacks as a result of the Tiananmen demonstrations and the incidents that followed. On the television screen the sharp deterioration in the Chairman's state of health was visible for all the world to see. No longer could he stand unaided to greet distinguished visitors and frequently he appeared to lose track of the conversation.

Despite Jiang Qing's failure to get Deng expelled from the Communist Party, the power of the radicals increased sharply. She prefaced almost all her ·orders and suggestions with Chairman Mao 'wants' or 'has ordered' and as she was the only person with automatic and direct access to him she achieved her ends. A majority of Ministers and senior civil servants appeared then to believe she would eventually take over as Chairman and they openly rushed to do her bidding.

I was personally shocked, during the large-scale demonstrations Jiang Qing ordered to be organized against Deng two days after the Tiananmen incidents, to witness the Foreign Minister, the late Qiao Guanhua, preceded by ceremonial gongs, leading his staff of Chinese diplomats round the same square chanting 'Down with Deng Xiaoping' to a well-known rhythm from another world. (The French in Algeria had used that rhythm to chant 'Algérie Française' – three long and two short beats.) Qiao's friends tried to excuse him by saying he was acting under the influence of his lively new wife but many senior Chinese officials were deeply embarrassed by their Minister. My intelligent interpreter, who was a keen supporter of Deng, merely lay down in my bedroom/office until I gave her a certificate to say she was 'too ill to demonstrate as ordered' against Deng Xiaoping.

Shortly afterwards shots on the television screen of the Chairman receiving the Prime Ministers of New Zealand, Singapore and Pakistan made it clear to the Chinese population that their beloved leader was almost senile. However, Chairman Hua was able, after accompanying the Prime Minister of New Zealand, Mr Muldoon, on April 30th to stay behind alone with the Chairman for half an hour. During this time the Chairman reportedly wrote to him, 'With you in charge my heart is at ease.'

The first time I heard this now-famous phrase was in Peking about a year earlier when Premier Zhou was ill and Deng Xiaping had taken over almost all of his responsibilities as Premier. The Chairman had then repeated to several visitors his growing concern about the Premier's state of health, adding the now well-known words, 'With Deng in charge my heart is at ease.' The Prime Minister of Pakistan, the ill-fated Zulfikar Ali Bhutto, was the last foreigner to see the Chairman and although he said publicly he 'did not expect to see a Tarzan' in private he admitted Mao was already 'extremely frail and alarmingly senile'.

Despite the support the new Premier Hua was receiving from the Chairman who whether senile or not was still respected as a god/emperor by hundreds of millions of Chinese, the new leader from that moment came under grim and heavy pressure from radicals and pragmatists who realized Mao would shortly die and wanted to be ready to take over.

It was widely believed that only Jiang could have persuaded Mao to change his mind about Deng whom he had so publicly welcomed as one of the leaders and the successor to Premier Zhou. Although there is no hard evidence to support the view, many senior officials believe Jiang used false evidence against Deng, which her personal staff invented.

Jiang looked firm and triumphant after Deng's second public disgrace and at ceremonies it was obvious she was 'throwing her weight around'. The radicals, who had controlled the media since shortly after the end of the militant period of the Cultural Revolution in 1969, began in an all-too-obvious move to prepare the Chinese people for Jiang's succession as Chairman of the Communist Party. They ordered the press to make frequent references to Empress Lu who ruled, after the death of the Emperor Kao Tsu, from 195 to 179 B.C. Historians were unkind because in their view she 'had violated the principle of legitimacy' but apart from 'removing' members of her husband's family she now appears to have been well meaning and efficient. Even more space was given to the Empress Wu who had been a concubine of the Emperor Tai Tsung and, after his death, was forced to become a Buddhist nun. During an inspection tour of the religious house, the new emperor, Kao Tsung, fell in love with her and made her, contrary to tradition, his own concubine. By A.D. 655 he had become so dependent on her, he actually divorced the empress in order to marry and promote Wu. As empress she became extremely influential, for, in addition to being beautiful, she had a strong personality and was literate and, indeed, she wrote poetry. After the emperor died in 683 she became regent first for one and then a second of her sons until she grew tired of ruling through a third party and pronounced herself the 'son of heaven' and empress. She enjoyed scores of lovers in a world in which women were treated almost as equals with men. She was a serious ruler and insisted on revising the examinations for the civil service as well as hunting with men and enjoying a freedom that women in China were not to know again for another thousand years.

The Chinese interpreters working in embassies relished reading and translating the spicy almost sexy reports about the dead empress, because they were so obviously starved even of romantic love stories and many of the older generation had told their children of the erotic literature of the past.

Whilst the people relished details of the concubine's life, these items in the newspapers cannot have done much good in promoting the image of Jiang Qing, and, in fact, they caused scores of stories about her life to be whispered from one worker to another. The whole city suddenly seemed to be giggling and whispering tales of Jiang's past that were even reported to me by waiters in the hotel dining room.

Certainly Jiang had experienced plenty of sex in her life before she met the Chairman. It was widely stated that her mother was a prostitute in Tianjin and there is much evidence to support this. However, Shu-meng, as Jiang was then known, lived mostly with her grandfather and found her way to the Shandong Provincial Experimental Drama Academy. She was extremely flirtatious at an early age and enjoyed a series of carefree minor affairs involving sex before she fell violently in love with a young left-wing intellectual, Yu Chiwei. During the period they lived together Jiang joined the left-wing movie circle and became interested in communism. She was 'attractive but pushing' and became known as the 'Big Miss Li' before she moved to Shanghai as Lan Ping.

In common with many youthful actresses, Jiang was not above sleeping with men who could assist her to obtain parts and one of her lovers helped her to get a job as a bit part player with a salary of $25 a month. Eventually Lan (Jiang) married another lover, a scriptwriter and director named Tang Na, who helped her to obtain the leading role in a feature film. But Jiang's 'acting won no acclaim', according to one of her colleagues and a series of smaller disappointing parts followed after she believed herself to have made the break-through to semi-stardom.

Doubtless disappointment drove her to desperation and she was described by one of her colleagues as a 'despicable and ruthless young woman'. Many of the troupe were angry that she managed to get occasional pictures of herself in past film or stage shows reproduced in the local press as a result of 'sleeping around' with journalists. At one point Lan (Jiang) had no need to offer favours to journalists for publicity as her devoted husband attempted to commit suicide when he discovered she was sleeping with Chang Min in pursuit of a role in the film *The Big Thunder Storm* he was about to produce. In an enormous burst of publicity about the 'love-sick husband' she became something of a local celebrity.

(I met the man who claimed to be her husband years later, in 1950, in Paris, where he had opened a small Chinese restaurant just off the rue du Louvre. After working late in the *News Chronicle* office my husband and I enjoyed many suppers listening to the *patron*'s stories of how he had been married to the attractive but wicked woman who was now the wife of Chairman Mao Zedong. Our problem was that the troupes all changed their names far too frequently for professional and, later, political reasons, for us to be able to identify all of them. Also, we did not take notes at the time.)

The Japanese bombardment of Shanghai in 1937 caused many film and stage troupes to leave the city and Lan (Jiang) went to Wuhan where, yet again, she obtained a series of small parts. After more disappointments, Lan decided to leave Wuhan and make her way to Chongqing via Xi'an. It is reported she was seriously criticized at the time by colleagues for her promiscuous behaviour as well as her lack of ability on the stage. These reports were extremely mild when compared with the stories about her licentious behaviour in Shanghai in the 1930s then floating round Peking. And there can be no doubt together with more up to date ones of her selecting lovers from the world of sport (which I believe to be unfounded) they played a part in the destruction of Jiang's image as that of a brilliant wife destined to succeed her husband.

There were also efforts made in those months following Tiananmen by friends of the late Premier Zhou and the disgraced Deng to inform foreigners secretly of what was happening. My own view is that the followers of the late Premier were fully aware of the report on her life Jiang Qing had virtually dictated to an American scholar whom she had dubbed 'her Edgar Snow'. It then appeared extremely likely that the Gang of Four would take over after the

Chairman died – or even before this happened – and that once the radicals were in power the pragmatists would be silenced for ever. Thus a surprising number of men and women who had been tight-lipped and uncommunicative suddenly began whispering not so much about the sins of the Gang of Four, which it must be assumed were well known after the flood of gossip, but the aims and objectives of the pragmatists in both foreign and domestic policy.

One of my informants, who spoke French, was particularly anxious that the true story of Premier Zhou Enlai's devotion to the party and the people should be told. She believed that a majority of those 'foreign friends' who had spent their lives in China would, in the forthcoming crisis, support the radicals as they had done in the Cultural Revolution whilst others would be too afraid to 'give Zhou his due'. It was assumed the Premier's widow, Deng Yingchao, would be arrested with Ye Jianying, Li Xiannian and Li Desheng, together with, of course, Xu Shiyu and almost all the 'Marshals' and Regional Military Commanders. One heard frequent reports of the radicals 'building up a separate army' which really meant that they had taken over the organization of the armed urban militia in Shanghai and a few other cities. The man responsible for this was Zhang Chunqiao who was Mayor of Shanghai as well as the Chief Political Commissar in the PLA. In the latter capacity he had violently opposed the policies advocated by Deng Xiaoping when he was Chief of Staff. Zhang's position was strong as he schemed to separate the 5 million-strong armed militia from the regular army. In Shanghai he was successful and he obtained large quantities of arms and ammunition from other regions that were hidden in readiness for 'an emergency'. Zhang may well have been successful in other areas in the south where stocks of ammunition were later discovered.

All the whispers were silenced in late July by the Tangshan earthquake, which really frightened the Chinese people for natural disasters traditionally herald the end of a dynasty. According to official statistics, with nearly a quarter of a million dead and over 160,000 seriously injured, it was the worst natural disaster the world has known. The quake was followed by a period when thousands in the capital were living in tents expecting further tremors and the administration was at times ineffective. There were strikes in industrial centres including Wuhan, Luoyang and Harbin as well as widespread trouble on the railways. The political unrest was encouraged covertly by Jiang Qing's provincial supporters who claimed that Chairman Hua had fallen into the hands of the 'rightists'. Members of the urban militias began openly to raid barracks and seize stocks of small arms as well as handgrenades and mines.

A group of Ministers and scores of senior officials pretended to be ill and stayed at home or even went to hospital in order to remain silent since many were being ruthlessly pressed to come out into the open in support of Jiang Qing and the Gang of Four. The official media devoted much of its time to preparing the nation for the Chairman's death as he was already eighty-two and growing steadily more frail and senile. His poems were frequently read over the radio while his 'thoughts' were shown written in his well-known calligraphy and quoted at greater length than usual. Many people were still camping in the streets of Peking preparing for new earth tremors. At 4 P.M. on the afternoon of September 9th, 1976 those diplomats not in their swimming pools were alerted by their Chinese staff that the flag in Tiananmen was at half-mast. Within minutes Xinhua, the official Chinese news agency, put out a statement that I will repeat as it was so typical of journalism in the People's Republic at the time.

Message to the whole party, the whole army and the people of all nationalities throughout the country. Comrade Mao Zedong, the esteemed and beloved great leader of our party, our army and the people of all nationalities of our country, the great teacher of the international proletariat and the oppressed nations and oppressed people, Chairman of the Central Committee of the Communist Party of China passed away at 00.10 hours, 9 September, 1976 in Peking because of the worsening of his illness and despite all treatment, although meticulous medical treatment was given him in every way after he fell ill.

The cause of his death was never released but it was assumed to have been a combination of Parkinson's disease, from which he had been suffering since the late 1960s, and a series of heart attacks. In the streets the broad masses dutifully wept but even before the funeral ceremonies were announced people wanted to know 'what next?', 'who will take over?' There were immediate differences of opinion in the Politbureau, which were leaked to the diplomatic corps, on whether Mao's corpse should be cremated or preserved. On this issue, Hua supported the pragmatists and won the day and the famous Tiananmen Square has since been spoiled by the new Memorial Hall where the Chairman's embalmed body is now on display.

Only a week before Mao's death, the leadership had striven to present a picture of complete unity but few of the inhabitants of Peking were taken in by this although none was sure who would win the obvious struggle for the succession. Meanwhile millions, literally, walked to the square to pay their respects in a silent but uneasy manner. For days the radio played the national anthem and read Mao's obituary, all in an exaggeratedly slow rhythm. Television was difficult because all the old films and even pictures of Mao appeared to include one or more of the ten men who had risen against him whose faces were now taboo. After a time pictures were shown especially of the Long March and the early days of the Republic with the faces of Liu Shaoqi and Lin Biao deleted. Many set pieces were transmitted by television of children bursting into floods of tears as they were told of the Chairman's death. Some diplomats, who realized the outward show of grief when Premier Zhou had died was spontaneous and very sincere, thought thousands were merely acting a part expected of them while they were really worrying about their own future and that of the nation.

Meanwhile, Deng Xiaoping, with the assistance of General Xu Shiyu, issued a statement on the political scene that was an open attack on the Gang of Four: we cannot let either the party or the nation 'degenerate' and be destroyed 'by those four people'. Thus he urged his supporters to 'struggle against them as long as there is breath in our body', adding that if they won, everything could be solved and if they lost they could take to the mountain tops again. He ended by saying that at least they, the pragmatists, had the backing of three Military Regions: Guangdong, Fujian (Fuzhou) and Nanjing and urged them to avoid procrastination which would make all the risks greater.

Jiang Qing had earlier forecast that 'enemies' of the people would take action against her within a month of the Chairman's death. She was angered a few days after Mao's death by an announcement that the Central Committee had decided that Comrade Hua should edit the fifth volume of the Chairman's selected works.

The funeral rally, like Mao's death, was for China almost an anti-climax perhaps because there was no coffin and the uneasy members of the Politbureau became the centre of attraction. Indeed, as they moved from the gatehouse on to the balcony overlooking Tiananmen Square, where the Chairman had proclaimed the establishment of the People's Republic, not a word or glance passed between them as they took up their position in the prescribed pecking order. Everyone acted as though he or she were alone on the terrace though Jiang Qing gave the impression of being aloof and self-contained. On the stroke of 3 P.M. the dead Chairman was accorded a 'three minute silence' terminated by the national anthem. Wang Hongwen then called on Hua Guofeng to read the funeral address which he did with no sign of emotion. The speech contained no clue to the choice of Mao's successor and, as Hua was reading it, Wang Hongwen leaned over his shoulder as if to ascertain whether he was sticking to the text. Hua appealed for unity and repeated many of the old Mao slogans such as 'Practise Marxism but not revisionism', 'Be open and above board: do not conspire and intrigue.' As the address ended the military bands played the 'Internationale' and the crowds dispersed. As the German Ambassador wrote, 'The nation's farewell to Mao had been dignified but surprisingly brief.' There were rumours that the Politbureau feared the crowds might demonstrate in favour of one faction or another. The press, still under the command of the Gang of Four, urged the population to act, 'In accordance with the principles laid down,' but no one appeared to know exactly what this meant.

After the funeral rally, at an emergency meeting of the enlarged Politbureau, Jiang proposed that Hua should support her claim to succeed her husband as Chairman and he declined. Apart from ordering the media to 'deepen their criticism of Deng', the Gang of Four then spent their time secretly rousing the armed militia in Shanghai to be ready for drastic military action.

Suddenly on October 12th the entire nation rushed to the nearest powerful radio to hear BBC transmissions in Chinese and English that announced the arrest of the Gang of Four. Although diplomats had received leaks of the arrests two days earlier there were still long delays before an official Chinese confirmation was issued. Hua, who had become Chairman of the Communist Party as well as of the MAC, had come under heavy pressure from the generals 'to get it over quickly'. Indeed, Xu Shiyu reportedly threatened, although with a smile, 'to march north' unless 'that woman was arrested'.

The arrests were made under the direction of Wang Dongxing, Mao's personal bodyguard and commander of the Brigade Group known as the 8341 Unit which was responsible for the personal security of members of the Politbureau. Although Jiang Qing had moved around amongst the guest-houses in and around Peking since Mao's death, the 8341 unit naturally knew at any given moment exactly where she was. The troops making the arrests were, in each case, commanded by a man senior in rank to the head of the individual's bodyguard. Wang Hongwen and Zhang Chunqiao were called to an emergency meeting of the Standing Committee of the Politbureau and picked up within minutes of one another as Chairman Hua watched the scene on closed-circuit television. Jiang Qing was arrested in a guest-house in the Western Hills.

Immediately after the death of Mao, commanders of the urban militia in Shanghai under the orders of the Gang of Four had begun careful and secret preparations for a take-over. During the night loads of automatic rifles and ammunition were distributed to various commands in the city, suburbs and the areas surrounding the harbour and the airport. Orders were given for the local commanders to warn 'officers' down to platoon level to 'be on the alert' and have their uniforms at hand and sleep beside a telephone. Wang Hongwen had taken over an underground shelter which, long before Mao's death, had been deepened, strengthened and fitted with what were then in China the latest communications systems, together with radio, television and facilities to broadcast. This was used by the militia, then said to be 1 million strong – though this must have been gross, indeed, stupid exaggeration – as their local headquarters. Groups of trained young men and women reported back to the militia commander the activities of the regular PLA forces – but especially the army – in the area.

The new leaders in Peking for a brief spell played a clever game based on Chinese tradition designed to break the power of the rebels by splitting the leadership and causing delays. Within hours of the arrest of the Gang of Four, Premier Hua, acting in his capacity as Chairman of MAC, sent for Mao Tianshui, the leading party official in Shanghai and a well-known radical. Initially Mao was reluctant to go. Finally, as his attempts to make contact by telephone with members of the Gang or their supporters in Peking failed, and after arranging a code to explain over the telephone what was happening, he did. The lack of news from Mao made tension rise in the underground headquarters in Shanghai and when at last he got through to them, his coded message was not clear. He said their friends – the Gang of Four – were all well but so busy he had not had time to talk with them.

The urban militia continued their efforts with the deployment of special armed platoons at key points including stations, banks, bridges and the municipal building in Shanghai. These moves were all noted by the 'Peking' government 'spies' who had been carefully planted by the regular army – the PLA.

Officials and secretaries working personally for the Shanghai-based Gang, Zhang Chunqiao, Wang Hongwen and Yao Wenyuan, grew hysterical when they failed to make contact with their bosses in Peking, which in the past had been extremely easy. In addition, they could obtain no news of what was going on in the capital from anyone. After lengthy and desperate efforts had been made, contact was again established with Mao Tianshui which brought the bad news, in code, that Jiang Qing had been arrested.

Meanwhile, the population was becoming increasingly restive and the militia leaders decided to block the Peking radio. By this time over 30,000 armed members of the militia were reported to be deployed in key positions in the city and surrounding area. Peking then ordered two more of the Shanghai leaders to proceed immediately to the capital. After a tense meeting between party, trade union and militia officials it was decided they should obey the order. There were misgivings and, indeed, some officials felt they should launch the revolt at once. There was also a fear that the Shanghai representatives might be arrested on arrival in Peking. However, after they had arrived safely in Peking on October 10th they made a reassuring telephone call to the militia headquarters saying all was well and they would be back shortly. In the meantime they urged that the preparations (for the revolt) should continue. However, teams sent out from the militia headquarters to give pep talks to the factory workers were not as warmly received as they had been in the past as rumours had begun to circulate that the Gang of Four had been arrested.

The diplomatic distraction of the militia accounts too for the delay in the official confirmation of the news of the arrests. The basic mistake made by the Gang of Four and their senior supporters was that they trusted Wang Dongxing because Jiang Qing had told them she had been close to him when he was Mao's bodyguard in Yenan, and throughout the years in Peking their relationship had never cooled. After all, he had paid frequent visits to the Chairman's bungalow to inspect the security arrangements and pay his respects to Mao. Jiang implied to some supporters she had a 'special relationship' with Wang, naturally not involving sex in any way, which would protect them all. In addition, Wang did from time to time give other radicals to understand that he supported their cause.

Deng's restoration

The political and personal pressure on Chairman Hua after the arrest of the Gang was enormous but, perhaps mercifully, because he had so little experience of both party and state government at the centre, he failed to realize the full dangers, though not the delights, of power. To those around him at the time he appeared to be imperturbable for 90 per cent of the time but when he heard bad news he became gruff, grumpy and unapproachable. It was all too apparent that he lacked the charisma of Mao and the charm and intelligence of the late Premier Zhou. The new Chairman could never become 'the red star in the heart' of hundreds of millions of Chinese, and small children would never sing: 'Father is dear, Mother is dear/But Chairman Hua is dearest of all,' as they had of Mao.

On paper, but only on paper, Hua had become more powerful than Mao ever was for he had never been Premier as well as Chairman of the party. The dual role would have been too much for a man with far greater experience than Hua who was plagued by the two opposing factions of the party. There were the noisy 'whateverists' led by the man who had arrested the Gang, Wang Dongxing, supported by the popular commander of the Peking Military Region, Chen Xilian, who claimed that everything the Chairman had said was correct. But by far the stronger faction in the new power struggle was made up of the supporters of the still-disgraced Deng Xiaoping.

Initially Hua, who misguidedly began to foster a cult of his own personality, followed the Maoist line, especially in foreign affairs, and the comrades were urged to support the 'just struggle against imperialism, colonialism and hegemonism' – the code word for Russia. At the same time Hua called for support for 'revolutionary and progressive causes'.

Deng's followers – the pragmatists – who expected him to return immediately after the arrest of the Gang were distressed to hear Hua call for 'the masses to deepen their criticism of Deng'. The cry fell on deaf ears and by November 1976, two months after Mao's death, the anti-Deng campaign died a natural death. Many party cadres were heard to say that Hua was running into serious problems because he had so little experience with only three years in the Politbureau, whereas Deng had been a member for twenty-one years. Members of the Standing Committee of that ruling body, who were then giving their guarded support to Hua – Ye Jianying and Li Xiannian – attempted to persuade the new Chairman to call a National People's Congress in order to consolidate his position before the inevitable return to power of the forceful former Vice Premier and Party Secretary, Deng. They all feared the effects of his strong personality as well as his vast experience.

Posters began to appear in Peking, first paying homage to the late Premier Zhou and then calling for the restoration of Deng. 'We want Chairman Hua to give Comrade Deng Xiaoping a job,' was a popular short poster, together with, 'Bring back Deng,' while longer posters were pasted on walls at odd places throughout the city, in factories and, of course, in the university. These long posters, generally written by students, demanded 'a return to democracy' although it was unlikely any of them had experienced this form of government. Many writers, as in previous outbreaks of wall posters, aired personal grievances about their treatment in office, factory or commune and scores accused supporters of the Gang of Four of corruption, and grave misconduct. Many posters urged that 'the verdict be reversed on the Tiananmen demonstrations of April 5th, 1976 and that its counter-revolutionary label be removed'. The commander of the Peking Military Region, Chen Xilian, was blamed with the Mayor, Wu De, for the suppression. There were, too, scores of posters demanding that the Gang of Four be brought to trial. Posters that implied severe criticism of Chairman Hua, or his immediate supporters, were torn down during the night by the police.

Hua had the advantage of actually being in the seat of authority backed by the mass of personal and political information he had collected during his spell as Minister for Public Security. For instance, the reason Hua was able to persuade them to act quickly in arresting the Gang was that he had been on the committee that investigated the Lin Biao coup and he realized it was Lin's all too frequent hesitations at the last moment in the implementation of his plans that formed the root cause of his failure.

Many cadres were aware that the Chairman, during those last months, when he was growing ever more senile, had urged Hua and other members of the Politbureau to 'help Jiang Qing carry the Red Banner'. 'Don't let it fall and help her to avoid committing the mistakes she has made in the past.' This, combined with the well-known but little understood instructions to Hua that he should 'Act according to the principles laid down', was accepted by many Chinese as an effort by the Chairman, doubtless acting under Jiang's influence, to make her his successor. It was known even at the time that all sorts of contradictory orders were coming from Mao's office and were either suppressed or somehow sorted out by the Standing Committee of the Politbureau meeting unofficially with Jiang who was exceedingly bitter that she was not a full member of that body.

Despite the fierce cold of Peking in December, hundreds of people continued to write posters and thousands stood around in sub-zero temperatures reading them. The majority of the visitors were either young or middle-aged members of the party who wanted news of Deng's return, which they could not obtain from the press or radio. These men and women feared that, unless the policy to modernize the country outlined by Premier Zhou before his death was implemented and an immediate pragmatic economic policy introduced, a serious internal situation would arise that might well turn into a crisis. The radical supporters of the Gang were certainly maintaining a low profile but production on both the agricultural communes and in the factories was falling, largely through lack of inspiration or incentive. While the commanders of the PLA were behind Deng, many young soldiers had been influenced by the radical political commissars appointed when Zhang Chunqiao had been their Chief. News of what was written on posters on the walls of Peking sometimes took days or weeks to filter through to the provinces but, gradually, the whole nation became aware of their themes.

There were constant rumours, often based on talks between members of the Central Committee and ambassadors, that Deng would be back in all his former positions 'next week' or next month but still he did not appear. The 'whateverists' were apprehensive as more and more responsible people began to mouth open criticism of Mao and to suggest that the excesses of the Cultural Revolution were not only the diabolical inspiration of Jiang Qing but also of the Chairman. Sometimes people even dared to whisper of 'The Gang of Five including Chairman Mao'.

Hua feared a trial not only on the grounds that he was in charge of public security during the period when the Gang were making their final plans for the assumption of power, but also because he was 'a creature' of the Chairman, coming from his home town. Further, Hua had taken no action against the Foreign Minister, the late Qiao Guanhua, who had, as already reported, somewhat overdone the anti-Deng displays after the Tiananmen Square demonstrations. According to the then West German Ambassador and others, Qiao had actually approached Gromyko during a visit to the UN General Assembly in New York and requested Soviet support and goodwill if an anticipated take-over by Jiang and the Gang provoked disturbances verging on civil war. The Russian reply was masterly. Gromyko is reported to have said that 'fraternal' Russian help would take time to organize and the radicals would have to manage on their own for a week. In other words the Russians would only support the radicals when they appeared to win.

Early in February 1977, obviously inspired by the 'whateverists', the *People's Daily* published an editorial stressing that 'whatever Chairman Mao had said must be obeyed and whatever he had decided must be upheld'. This shook the ever-increasing numbers of Deng's supporters especially in Guangzhou. Here a group of senior cadres wrote urging Chairman Hua and the members of the Central Committee of the party 'to review and criticize the mistakes made by Mao'. They warned that the party would lose the respect of the people if they 'continued to paper over the mistakes of Chairman Mao'.

In March 1977 Chairman Hua called an enlarged meeting of the Politbureau to include Regional Military Commanders and a score or so of leading provincial members of the Central Committee to discuss Deng's position. There were some sharp disagreements but it was generally agreed that he should return to Peking and power. But no consensus was achieved on what Deng's new role was to be. The Standing Committee of the Politbureau, led by the Minister of Defence, Ye Jianying, finally agreed to let it be known to provincial party leaders that Deng would eventually be restored to his old posts of Vice Chairman of the party, Vice Premier and, maybe, the most important of all, Chief of Staff of the PLA.

Ye and the Generals were aprehensive – with good reason – that if there was no word about Deng's restoration there would be major disorders on a nationwide scale on the anniversary of the Tiananmen demonstrations the previous year. They quietened the 'whateverists' by saying that, in any case, he would not appear in public until his return had been agreed by the Central Committee and this would take at least three months to organize. There was growing impatience about Deng's rehabilitation and return but when it was finally announced on March 30th on radio and television at 8 P.M., 'firecrackers and rockets' shot into the air all over Peking and the next day there were massive processions throughout the country as provincial leaders happily celebrated his return to office. Deng's first public appearance was at a football match in the vast stadium in Peking where an audience of over 80,000 stood and cheered when the loudspeakers announced his arrival. Few people watched the game, as all eyes were on Deng, but the crowd noted that one of his former outspoken critics, the Mayor Wu De, accompanied him.

Deng gradually assumes power

Hua Guofeng retained the Chairmanship of the Party throughout 1977 but his power was slowly eroded by a series of major reshuffles of low-level posts in the secretariat, each one of which appeared to increase Deng Xiaoping's overall authority.

Observers in Peking believed early in 1977 the power structure fell into three groups. However, this turned out to be an over-simplification as Ye Jianying and his followers effectively threw in their lot with Deng shortly after the 11th Party Congress of August 1977. The three groups were listed as:

The Hua Group	The Ye Group	The Deng Group
Hua Guofeng	Ye Jianying	Deng Xiaoping
*Wang Dongxing	Li Xiannian	Xu Shiyu
*Chen Xilian	Xu Xiangqian	Wei Guoqing
*Wu De	Nie Rongzhen	Peng Chong
*Ji Dengkui	Su Zhenhua	Liu Bocheng (old, sick)
Li Desheng		Ulanhu
Chen Yonggui		Geng Biao
Ni Zhifu		Yu Qiuli
Zhang Tingfa		Fang Yi

Deng, despite his increased political influence, continued to main-tain a low profile at the back of the political stage. He was in fact preparing for the future by attempting to reopen schools, technical colleges and universities that had been closed since the early days of the Cultural Revolution. Those educational establishments that had remained open were only available to radical students who had been chosen on the grounds promoted by the Gang of Four that it was better to be 'red' than 'expert'. Deng did this because he realized there would be no engineers or specialists to deal with the 'Four Modernisations' programme unless intensive scientific training was begun at once.

In addition, Deng, who had always been critical of the glamour Mao had built up around the 'barefoot' doctors, suggested they should have 'a little medical training and wear straw shoes' – a typical Deng remark. Initially their role had been to distribute

* Leaders of the 'whateverists', known in China as conservatives because they believed all Mao's thoughts and directives should be followed without question.

contraceptives and cures for common colds but many of them had, without any training, begun to treat more complicated ailments. Deng continued to enlarge his power base by rehabilitating men who had suffered under the Gang. He also took an increasing firm stand against those who had opposed him during the Cultural Revolution and attempted to block his succession to Premier Zhou.

By the time Zhao Cangbi, a staunch supporter of Deng's, was promoted to be Minister of Public Security, replacing Chairman Hua in that role, Deng's group knew he was heading for supreme power. Many diplomats believe Hua and Deng then reached a private understanding that the Chairman would not interfere with Deng's efforts to raise standards in the sphere of education in readiness for the introduction of the modernizations programme, while Deng, for his part, agreed to slow down political moves towards a critical assessment of Mao as Chairman – especially his activities during the Cultural Revolution. This question of Mao's position in history was daily becoming a vital issue amongst party members in Peking, Shanghai and the politically active cities as well as in some factories and agricultural communes. Even more important, it was already a difficult and touchy subject in many units of the PLA. Although Mao's statues, pictures and posters carrying his 'thoughts' were gradually removed from their sites on stations and in the main squares of towns, Chinese families retained his photograph in their homes. Indeed, for safety some had put up a picture of Hua beside that of the dead Chairman. By the spring of 1978 therefore it was apparent the broad masses really wanted to know whether their former communist emperor/god had been discredited by the arrest of his wife and her supporters. They were aware that the Gang had been close to the Chairman and relied on him for their positions and promotions.

Many Sinologists, with the power of hindsight, now express surprise that shortly after the Tiananmen Square demonstrations no efforts were mounted to replace Mao as Chairman and promote him to a senior post without power, to make him, in the words Mao had used years before the Cultural Revolution, 'like a Buddha on a shelf'. For it was by then apparent to the nation as a whole, who had watched him on television, that their beloved leader was fading fast mentally as well as physically. The main reason for this lack of initiative was that Hua was still dependent on Mao as

Chairman for his position, as were the Gang of Four, and with Deng in disgrace none had the courage or the power to relieve Mao of the Chairmanship and the position he had created over the years.

It was during this period between April and September 1976 that Jiang Qing built up her power although few party members at grass roots level realized that she and her supporters – the Gang – had the Chairman so completely in their pockets. Unfortunately Jiang Qing failed to realize the vital importance of the defence forces and the Gang never influenced more than one or two of the important Regional Military Commanders, though they may well have been misled by the leftist views expressed by many young soldiers. The recruits were deeply influenced by radical political commissars at company or battalion level, who, in turn, were operating under the orders of Zhang Chunqiao, a member of the Gang, but the old soldiers and commanders had, on the whole, little sympathy with the radicals.

Late in 1977, Hu Yaobang (today the Party Chairman), a staunch supporter of Deng's, was appointed Director of the party's Organization Department, a key post for promotion and demotion. He organized a month-long Political Works Conference in 1978 that opened with a show of old films never before seen even by members of the Central Committee. In more than one of them the late Chairman admitted, after the Great Leap Forward, that he had made grave and serious mistakes. This paved the way for charges to be laid against the 'whateverists', otherwise known as the (leftist) conservatives including Vice Chairman Wang Dongxing, Chen Xilian, commander of the Peking Military Region, and Wu De, Mayor of Peking, who had been responsible for the dissolution of the demonstrations in favour of Zhou Enlai in Tiananmen Square. The illiterate peasant Chen Yongqui, who had been promoted by Mao to the Politbureau as a model peasant, was also charged. Xu Shiyu commander of the Guangzhou Military Region, Deng's protector after his second purge from power by the Gang, led the attack on the 'whateverists' who were not defended by Hua.

Hua 'renounced' the title of 'Supreme Leader' he had assumed when he succeeded Mao and requested that in future he be referred to as 'Comrade' instead of 'Wise Leader'. His power was fast waning amongst the 'inside people'. Deng spoke critically, but in low key, against the 'whateverists', suggesting that many new issues had come on the political horizon since the days of Marx and Lenin and the founders of communism. Engels, he said, had never travelled by air and Stalin had never worn dacron. Thus since Chairman Mao times had changed and it was not impossible 'to do or not to do' everything he had directed.

After the conference the *People's Daily*, the organ of the Communist Party, began to condemn the cult of Mao worship, the main target being 'counter-revolutionary forces who had attempted to shackle people's minds'. Hua, for his part, wrote an inscription to an anthology of poems written in honour of the late Premier Zhou Enlai and others during the demonstrations in Tiananmen Square. His supporters then claimed he was now 'at one' with 'hundreds of millions of people'.

Posters began to appear in many streets in Peking in 1977 suggesting that Deng was 'the living Zhou Enlai' whilst others questioned the role of the 'whateverists'. By November 1978 the long wall enclosing a bus station immediately to the west of the main cable office on the Avenue of Heavenly Peace suddenly became the main focal point for big character posters. As always some contained sad personal histories such as a man who was sent to prison for fifteen years for 'scratching his back with the Little Red Book' of Chairman Mao's thoughts during a study – political indoctrination – session. A railway worker posed the question, 'Would Lin Biao have achieved power without Mao's support?' while others claimed Mao must have given the nod to the activities of the Gang of Four. Indeed, one poster accused him of actual 'collusion' with the Gang. Deng Xiaoping, on the other hand, was praised for his pragmatism. Posters claimed that thousands – even tens of thousands – of industrial workers had received wage increases of up to 40 per cent. Further, material incentives had been reintroduced into factories together with bonuses. Some writers thanked Deng for allowing them to return to Peking – or other urban areas – from the countryside where they had been sent at the end of the militant period of the Cultural Revolution.

The wall became known to the world as 'Democracy Wall' as the posters, so often severely critical of the late Chairman Mao, caught the eye of the hundred-odd foreign correspondents resident at the time in Peking. Thus newsworthy big character posters that accused Mao of 'collusion', first with the 'traitor' Lin Biao and then the 'Gang of Four', were cabled immediately to London, Tokyo, New York, Rome and Paris. Within a matter of hours they could be heard all over China transmitted by the BBC Chinese service, the Japanese radio and the Voice of America. The sudden amazing notoriety achieved by the youthful or even middle-aged students amongst millions of Chinese sometimes went to their heads.

An increasing number of posters were aimed at the 'whateverists' who, it was said, had 'maintained a suppressive regime' after the death of Mao and the arrest of the Gang. The writers began to produce magazines that they sold to correspondents and the public outlining their views in greater detail and demanding similar personal and political freedoms to those taken for granted in the West.

Over 50 per cent of the posters that aired personal grievances were quickly covered over by others and the vast majority of the political ones were supportive of Deng and critical of Hua as well as Mao. Not only were the writers taking some risks when they put up the posters but in winter they often suffered acute discomfort from the severe cold in Peking. Many of the authors became friendly with foreign correspondents and even invited them to their homes. (In Peking this was truly amazing because during the three and a half years I lived there no foreigner ever visited the dwelling of a Chinese unless it was a model peasant's home on an agricultural commune or a model factory worker's flat. Chinese cadres entertained in restaurants.)

For a time Deng appeared to support the freedom Democracy Wall gave to the young, in fact, he even said, 'We should not check the demands of the masses to speak.' But wily old cadres looked at the wall from a distance or obtained information about the posters from friends. There were some interesting posters about the past and Kang Sheng, Mao's Security Chief, who introduced him to Jiang Qing in Yenan, was drawn wearing a Nazi uniform standing close to Wang Dongxing.

The man who achieved most fame and praise abroad was Wei Jingsheng who demanded 'the Fifth Modernization – Democracy', which, he said, was essential if the other four were to be successfully implemented, an argument he stressed both on posters and in the magazine he edited called *Explorations*. Comparatively little space was given to foreign policy though Mao was accused in his own words of 'leaning to one side', the side of the Soviet Union. The authors of several posters suggested there was no democracy in Russia and Mao's friendship with Moscow had prevented the development of good relations with 'other countries'. Meanwhile *Explorations*, produced by Wei Jingsheng in one room, increased its circulation and its appeal and he became friendly with a group of foreign correspondents who met him two or three times a week.

A few score of posters demanded sexual freedom and urged that the Chinese should be free to have sexual relations with anyone they liked. At this time reports were circulated among the crowds watching new posters being put up, in temperatures well below zero, that Deng felt some of the speakers had gone too far, but the habit of airing political and private views by big character posters had already spread to many provincial towns. Scores of posters appeared in city centres requesting help for certain areas where the comrades were hungry amidst the hundreds recounting injustices suffered at the hands of commune or factory managers.

The 5th National People's Congress held in June 1979 restored some of the rights of the people that had been envisaged in the constitution of 1954. Plans were announced to improve the judicial system as well as to redress past injustices inflicted by the courts. There must have been thousands of unknown and untold miscarriages of justice judging by what I was told in both Peking and Shanghai by lawyers working in the courts. They claimed that in their experience – each over ten years – they had never known a person to be charged who was not convicted. There were, my informants stated, 'no innocent people brought before the court'. In addition, an article in Wei Jingsheng's journal, *Explorations*, made more serious claims that hundreds of people were being detained indefinitely and incommunicado without being brought to trial. When brave prisoners protested saying this was contrary to the constitution they were told that 5000 policemen lived by arresting people, acting on orders from above. What was written in newspapers was, the police claimed, propaganda, adding, 'We are rail cars running on two different tracks.' Shortly after this issue, which citizens had clamoured to buy, Wei Jingsheng was arrested by Public Security guards in 1979 and later charged with having attacked Deng by insisting that democracy was essential for the achievement of the Four Modernizations. There were also far more serious unproven charges that he had 'given away' military secrets to foreign correspondents. Many of his supporters were also arrested and, for a time, foreign correspondents were shunned by dissidents and intellectuals.

At a plenum of the Central Committee, which had preceded the National People's Congress by some six months, Wang Dongxing and other 'whateverists' had made and lost their last stand on Mao's instructions and thoughts.

Mao's image had grown ever more tarnished as the big character posters became ever more critical. Scores of posters were again demanding that the Gang of Four be brought to trial for their crimes and political misdeeds. They were accused of mass murders and large-scale thefts as well as torturing their personal enemies. Other writers claimed almost all China's misfortunes were due to them and the influence they had exerted over Chairman Mao. Posters also urged that men involved in Lin Biao's coup should be tried as 'traitors'. Some writers expressed strong disapproval that no action had yet been taken in the courts against these 'enemies of the people'. Shortly after these posters appeared Democracy Wall was closed and cleaned by a battalion of municipal workers. Undoubtedly, Deng realized the posters had served their purpose.

Doubtless some well-informed writers realized no moves had been made to organize a treason trial because Chairman Hua was, at the peak period of the Gang's activities, Minister in charge of Public Security and he rightly feared some of the political dirt that would inevitably be disclosed at a trial would rub off on him. And there is no doubt that Hua fully realized he was already in a difficult enough situation without further complicating his relations with Deng and his supporters. His position nevertheless became increasingly delicate as Deng Xiaoping removed almost all the former supporters of Mao from the Politbureau and replaced them with his own trusties, including the economic planner Chen Yun, the Secretary General of the Party, Hu Yaobang and the provincial chief from Sichuan, Zhao Ziyang (Chao Tzu-yang), who had made a success of direct trade between Chengdu and Europe as well as the local free market. I had witnessed the Chengdu Market during a visit later in 1979 when no fewer than a thousand stalls were selling meat, fruit, vegetables and clothes, indeed, it was even possible to have one's hair efficiently permanently waved in the street.

Chairman Hua undertook a prolonged tour of Europe, including the United Kingdom, where it was apparent to old China hands, by the attitude of his entourage, that he lacked real authority. This certainly seemed apparent even to the workers at the Rolls-Royce factory in Derby he inspected. Although the Chinese were pleased for the sake of their own faces that he was entertained by the Queen, the most successful foreign tour of the year was Deng Xiaoping's triumphant visit to Washington. Unhappily, this preceded China's efforts to teach the Vietnamese a lesson on their southern border. The short conflict caused Peking's global popularity to slump, but on a long-term basis many profitable lessons were learned by the PLA that have made useful contributions to the defence sector of the modernization programme through combat experience.

In the social and cultural spheres there were great changes. Chinese films, which had been banned since the opening of the Cultural Revolution, were once more shown. Foreign books and magazines were imported and western music was again to be heard in public. The May 7th Cadre Schools, which were as stated earlier envisaged by Chairman Mao as places for senior cadres to mix with peasants, were quickly run down. At the same time girls began to use western make-up and wear skirts while young men appeared in bell-bottomed trousers and elaborate dark glasses. People with relatives abroad and access to foreign currency acquired TV sets, watches and cassette recorders as a black market hitherto unknown in communist China developed, together with prostitution (again all unthinkable when I was living in China from 1972 to 1976). On the other side of the coin religion was made more 'respectable' as a few churches were opened in the main cities while scores of mosques were refurbished in towns and oases, especially in Xinjiang in the extreme west. A campaign was also launched to propagate the idea of the one-child family and social penalties threatened for those parents having more than two children.

It is, however, important to stress that although many Chinese especially in the cities were enjoying a way of life that would have been unthinkable before the death of Mao, it was made clear from time to time that there were definite limits to personal freedom as the whole Democratic Wall episode demonstrates.

Hua Guofeng, who had been powerless for some months, finally resigned as Premier at the National People's Congress held in September 1980 in the first of two major shake-ups and several minor ones in the leadership of both government and party. He was succeeded by Zhao Ziyang who was already well known throughout China as the economic wizard who had brought prosperity to Sichuan through the introduction of free markets. Zhang Aiping (Chang Ai-p'ing), who was to become Defence Minister in 1982, became a Vice Premier while Deng Xiaoping, in an effort to set a good example to veterans, resigned as Vice Premier. However, it should be stressed the resignation made no difference to Deng's power although there are still cadres in China who believe Deng made a mistake and he should have taken over the number one post of the Government – if only for a short spell.

1981 opened with the long-awaited trial of the Gang of Four and the survivors of Lin Biao's attempted coup d'état (see separate chapter). Hua Guofeng managed to escape the painful possibility of having to give evidence. In March 1981 there were again changes in ministerial posts when Vice Premier Geng Biao (Keng Piao) took over as Minister of Defence. He had been doing the job for the past year or more. Four senior Ministers, all aged between seventy and eighty, accepted Deng's offer to become 'Advisers to the State Council'. As advisers they had 'face' that would last throughout their lives together with good housing and the occasional use of a car. Many senior commanders in the PLA were also persuaded to give up their posts by the granting of permission to retain their homes, the right to entertain visiting celebrities and the use of a car.

Deng was increasingly anxious to promote the 'rising young commanders of between fifty and sixty' because he was aware of discontent in some sectors of the PLA. This arose as a result of the activities of the radical political commissars and because many of the young soldiers, unlike their fathers' generation, wanted to return to the agricultural commune. Here they knew they could increase the family income substantially by helping to produce the extra pigs, chickens, vegetables and fruits they were now allowed to sell in the nearest free market. There was discontent at the other end of the scale in the PLA because the defence forces were fourth and last on the modernization programme. Further, many commanders were keen for badges of rank to be restored whilst the political commissars, who influenced the young troops, were deeply opposed to this much-discussed move.

In June 1981 Hua Guofeng finally resigned as Chairman of the Communist Party and was replaced by Hu Yaobang. Although Deng Xiaoping (eighty in 1984) remains the acknowledged leader he is always flanked by Zhao Ziyang and Hu Yaobang on all formal occasions and they are now universally recognized as the ruling triumvirate. 'Marshal' Ye Jiangying, eighty-five, stepped down as Chairman of the Standing Committee of the National People's Congress in February 1983 but he remains a member of the Politbureau, the average age of which is still 74.5. Zhang Aiping is now (1984) in charge of defence with Huang Hua at the Foreign Ministry where he is assisted by Ji Pengfei who is responsible for Hong Kong and Macao affairs. Deng has told more than one visitor that domestic issues are taking up too much of his time. He has increased wages and, like every other nation, is fighting inflation and chronic unemployment, which is new to the People's Republic.

However, relations have improved, albeit slightly, with the Soviet Union despite the military occupation of Afghanistan and the Vietnamese occupation of Cambodia. Disappointment is expressed in Peking that, since the exchange of ambassadors nearly nine years after the Shanghai Communiqué, there has been far less improvement in relations between the United States and the People's Republic than had been anticipated. Basically Deng Xiaoping is concerned that Washington continues to supply Taiwan with arms while, at the same time, problems have arisen about China's purchase of high technology from the United States. Peking believes the American conditions for the use of goods purchased in the technical field are an infringement of sovereignty – always a sensitive issue in China. However, relations between Peking, Tokyo and Washington have been maintained at a satisfactory level, despite difficulties.

Peking apears to recognize the theory voiced by Henry Kissinger that the economic and industrial centre of the globe is moving from the Atlantic to the Pacific Ocean. This they believe will benefit China on a long-term basis. But Deng is an old man in a hurry who dreams of reuniting Taiwan with the Motherland before he dies. Meanwhile, he must face the burning questions of how to acquire from the West machine-making tools, communications equipment and computers in order that the second item on the modernization programme – industry – may begin. Although none would admit that agriculture has been dropped as the number one item, it is difficult to envisage the current pragmatists in power causing hundreds of millions more peasants to be unemployed by the mass distribution of agricultural machines and equipment.

Campaigns against the radicals will continue and to make them acceptable to all members of the Politbureau liberal writers and intellectuals will be included in them. There have been so many truly dramatic changes in China since 'liberation' that only a brave man would forecast the future but for the moment Deng's successors, provided they get along with one another, stand a good chance of putting the modernization programme into effect by the turn of the century.

PART FOUR
In Perspective

17

Mao: God, Man or Monster

There is an ancient Chinese proverb, 'You may conquer a country on horseback but you cannot rule it from the saddle.' It is said to have been the advice offered to the first emperor of the Han dynasty, Han Gaozi (Han Kaotse) (202–195 B.C.) by the scholar Lu. Chairman Mao, however, spurned this counsel given to him on the day he proclaimed the People's Republic and stated that the Chinese had 'stood up'. Unhappily, the genius Mao exhibited during the years of struggle, first as an underground worker then as a guerrilla fighter and leader of the communist enclave in Yenan, was not so apparent when he became the 'first communist emperor' – de facto head of state as well as Chairman of the Communist Party.

Officials stress today that Chairman Mao Zedong was 'The Great Helmsman' and teacher to whom they are all deeply indebted, but there are serious reservations now openly expressed about his methods of government and the manner in which he treated those people who opposed him. There can be no question that Mao's name will live for ever more as that of a brilliant rebel who adapted age-old guerrilla tactics for use inside twentieth-century China while, at the same time, transforming Marxism into his own special Chinese nationalist political creed. As the man who overthrew the corrupt regime of Chiang Kai-shek and reunited the divided Chinese nation, Chairman Mao will survive as a great national hero. Indeed, until his death Mao was esteemed by the 'broad masses', as he dubbed the Chinese people, almost a god. There were, however, always reservations about his policies as Chairman even before 'liberation' and bitter opposition after and amongst the intellectuals who, sadly, were generally too frightened to talk. Mao's belief in the necessity of episodic political upheavals, such as the Great Leap Forward and, even more, the Cultural Revolution, were held against him even by what appeared at times to be a majority of those Communist Party members who were inspired by his truly enormous personality.

Mao owed his survival as a leader to his renowned charisma and the guidance he received from others, especially Liu Shaoqi and Deng Xiaoping before the Cultural Revolution and Premier Zhou Enlai after it. While supporting the Chairman 'up to a point' in his extravagant and dangerous campaigns, they had the courage and ability to argue and, generally though unfortunately not always, after a great deal of time had been lost, Mao either grasped the point of their arguments or gave in. In fact, when the Chairman was alone – away from Jiang Qing – the pragmatists were able to hold their own except at the peak point of the Great Leap Forward and, of course, during the early militant days of the Cultural Revolution.

Although Mao believed the end justified the means, he had, from time to time, bouts of conscience, for example when he suddenly protected Liu Shaoqi for a short time after his fall from harassment by Red Guard interrogators. Like the 'emperors' before him, Chairman Mao thought 'the Celestial Empire' or 'Middle Kingdom' was the centre of the civilized universe though he did admit the Chinese needed technology from abroad. Mao was not normally deeply interested in foreign policy except to a limited degree in his dealings with the Soviet Union and the Third World in the hope they would ultimately be converted to his own version of communism at the expense of the Soviet Union.

Mao concentrated on domestic – largely party – considerations when not involved in the organization of a political upheaval. It is a significant fact that after a few months in power in Peking he lost his former interest in the future of marriage and other philosophical subjects that had claimed so much time in his youth and early middle age. In many ways the Chairman's lack of curiosity about foreign affairs caused problems for the state, but it enabled Premier Zhou Enlai, long after he had ceased to be Foreign Minister, to initiate new policies when he felt the Chairman and, of far less importance, the Politbureau would accept them.

Certainly, Mao's thinking had largely been completed by the time he assumed power in Peking and he spent the next quarter of a century applying the theories he had learned in Shanghai, Jiangxi and evolved in Yenan, with the result that he became progressively out of tune with international reality. Mao entirely misunderstood the nature of decolonization. He believed it would lead to a second, socialist revolution and ultimately result in a global victory for the forces of communism over imperialism, which he thought was dying fast. Nor had the Chairman any understanding of state or global finance and the art of diplomacy, judging by the fact he constantly referred to the state budget as a 'housekeeping account' as he insisted China could only spend on imports what was earned by exports. In very grave circumstances a loan might be arranged, the Chairman admitted, but he was always depressed by any mention of money borrowed from the Soviet Union even at the time the two states called themselves 'brothers'. Neither Premier Zhou nor the financial wizard, Li Xiannian, was able to convince Mao of the vital importance of foreign trade as a contribution to both economic growth and national power. Some of Mao's colleagues on the Central Committee dubbed it all part of the people's war philosophy as Mao wanted to explain international politics and economics in terms a peasant could easily understand. Frequently Premier Zhou or a member of his intimate circle was able to persuade Mao to support a major sophisticated project such as the production of nuclear weapons. But there was always deep concern in the Politbureau about any changes from the Yenan concept of warfare and politics until Mao had actually committed himself publicly.

Mao completely failed to grasp the role of the United Nations and attempted to use its specialized agencies for attacks on the Soviet Union and its allies. Premier Zhou and the professional diplomats tended to accept Mao's directives in this particular sphere in order to obtain his support for what they considered were more important foreign policy issues. Despite his two visits to Moscow, a woman who worked for the Chairman and admired him claimed that over 90 per cent of his time was devoted to Chinese politics. He found the world beyond China a shadowy unreal place, she said, except at rare intervals such as when Premier Zhou was touring Africa or taking part in the Geneva conference on Indo-China in 1954.

Mao found it impossible to understand how the Japanese had recovered so quickly from the Second World War without a national defence force of their own. He expressed himself 'dumbfounded' that so few of the South-east Asian countries, which gradually became independent after the war, introduced socialist regimes. How and why Malaysia, Indonesia, the Philippines and Singapore retained capitalist-type governments completely bewildered the Chairman, who was not above displaying his ignorance on what had happened in these countries to distinguished foreign visitors who tended to be charmed by his naïvety.

There was one issue the Chairman fully understood: Moscow's efforts to dominate China, perhaps as a result of Russian endeavours to control the Chinese Communist Party at its formation and during the days of guerrilla warfare before the Long March. By the mid 1950s Chairman Mao, Premier Zhou and a handful of other members of the inner Politbureau came to the reluctant conclusion that Moscow did not accept Peking as an equal partner. They kept the information to themselves but the Russians made little secret of the fact they wished to use China for their own national objectives as they used the countries of eastern Europe. The Chairman suddenly realized in 1954 with shock and horror that the People's Republic was actually running the risk of losing the sovereignty he had fought so hard to regain from the western powers, to his Communist 'brothers'. Khrushchev had actually informed Chancellor Adenauer of 'his alarm' at China's growing potential as early as 1955 and openly proposed a rapprochement to the German Government 'to counter the Yellow Peril'. Unfortunately for Khrushchev some of Premier Zhou's friends gave Mao an account of the Russian leader's secret talks with the German Government and other European statesmen that were confirmed, years later, by Adenauer's memoirs. Unhappily, some members of the Chinese leadership doubted Premier Zhou's sources of information and the damaging report made but little impact on anyone but the Chairman.

Mao was likewise irritated when Khrushchev attacked Stalin's period of rule and his personality cult at the 20th Congress of the Russian Communist Party without any prior warning to his communist Allies. Mao had had his problems with Stalin and he and Premier Zhou both realized that the Russian leader had 'used' them during the Korean War. However, as reported earlier, this had enabled Mao to unite the new China against a foreign enemy during the initial crisis over Korea and later to obtain arms and equipment from the Soviet Union.

Other evidence has recently come to light from elderly members of the Chinese Politbureau that Stalin, long before Khrushchev, had initially envisaged the People's Republic as a major satellite for the Soviet Union, similar in style, though of course not in size, to Russia's only Asian satellite, the Republic of Mongolia. But Stalin had more discretion in his dealings with Mao.

Chairman Mao's decision to detach himself from the Soviet Union and take his own line in foreign policy took place, as already reported, after the disastrous meeting between Khrushchev and Premier Zhou at Peking airport when the Russian leader was returning from the funeral of the Vietnamese leader Ho Chi Minh, in 1959. In addition to the ever-growing problems of technical collaboration with Peking, Moscow appeared to be following a two-faced foreign policy. While the Russians were refusing to hand over nuclear information to the Chinese on the grounds that one day Peking, in a moment of madness, might use 'the bomb' in an effort to take over Taiwan, at the same time Moscow was demanding the right to establish intelligence listening posts in eastern China to monitor American naval and air activities in the Pacific and South-east Asia. In addition, they requested permission to establish radio transmitters on Chinese soil, which, like the listening posts, would be manned and commanded by Russian officers. Moscow also proposed the establishment of a Sino-Soviet navy in view of the increasing power of the United States fleet in the Pacific. The projected new navy would, it was envisaged, use all the facilities available in Chinese sea and air ports but be entirely under Russian command.

In a contradictory manner Khrushchev strongly advised Premier Zhou to cease the daily bombardment of Taiwan's offshore islands of Jinmen and Mazu. The Chinese gunners made a great deal of noise, used expensive ammunition and hurt no one. Hua Guofeng, who succeeded Mao as Chairman and still remains a member of the Central Committee of the Party, said 'Once we called the Russians "Big Brothers" but we dropped this when they embarked on their revisionist policy in 1956 when they attempted to restrict our sovereignty and bring us under their control in Moscow.'

Mao really understood the Sino-Soviet dispute because China – the Middle Kingdom – was involved and having 'liberated' his country from Chiang Kai-shek and the imperialists he sensed danger. The Russian bear was there ready to hug him and his people into submission. Thus the Russians hurriedly and angrily pulled out their 5000 technicians and experts in 1956 and abandoned scores of projects throughout China without leaving the blueprints behind them. This caused gigantic problems for Peking but the leadership felt they were worth the price of independence.

The Cultural Revolution had, with reason, caused a great deal of anti-Chinese sentiment to spread round the world and while the militant period was in progress it was quite impossible for any member of the Politbureau, other than Chairman Mao himself, to devote any time to thoughts beyond self-preservation and immediate domestic policy. After internal order was re-established in 1968/9, Premier Zhou began to make efforts to persuade the Chairman to adopt a somewhat more friendly attitude towards the United States. At first he made but little impact because Mao was by nature staunchly anti-imperialist and still deeply influenced by his 'chosen successor', then the Defence Minister, Lin Biao.

Zhou described his own concern about the political and military problems of having the two superpowers as 'enemies' and at first heard the Chairman grunt angrily many times that China's relations with the Soviet Union 'would not improve for ten thousand years', which in mandarin means a very long time. Although Mao continued to snarl even more when the Premier suggested they should attempt to improve their relations with the United States, gradually over months if not years the Chairman began to admit there was something in the thesis.

What moved the Chairman most was the Premier's statement that he was, at last, willing to forget, though never quite forgive, the greatest insult he had ever received in public. Mao knew the story as did everyone else in Peking at the time. When Premier Zhou attended the conference in Geneva in 1954 on Indo-China he proffered his hand to the then American Secretary of State, Foster Dulles, who rudely refused to touch it in front of a crowd of newsmen and French politicians. Zhou described it as 'one of the most humiliating moments of my life'. That he was nonetheless willing to offer his hand in friendship again to the Americans impressed the Chairman.

By chance, Edgar Snow, who had been such a good friend to the Chairman in the past, had applied for a visa to visit Peking. His application had been rudely turned down by Red Guard officials when they occupied the Foreign Ministry during the militant period of the Cultural Revolution. Premier Zhou immediately ordered that a special visa and invitation should be sent to Edgar Snow and his wife to visit Peking. The Premier then supervised the setting up of a programme for his visit that included several meetings with the Chairman who himself suggested giving a banquet in Snow's honour in the Great Hall of the People. The result was a triumph for Zhou's painstaking diplomacy as the Chairman and Edgar Snow rekindled their intimate friendship founded in Yenan. The Chairman was influenced by all Snow said about the changes that would take place in American foreign policy after the war in Vietnam. To the surprise of the broad masses and, indeed, of some members of the Central Committee of the Chinese Communist Party, Edgar Snow was invited to appear with the Chairman on the balcony in Tiananmen Square on National Day. The crowds then witnessed their beloved leader engaged in cordial conversation with a 'round-eyed barbarian' who was also an American imperialist against whom many scores of massive demonstrations had so recently been organized.

The Chairman gave Snow a message to Richard Nixon to say that he would be welcome in the People's Republic either 'as President or tourist'. According to Dennis Bloodworth, then the well-informed correspondent of the London *Observer*, the Chairman described himself to Snow as a 'monk under an umbrella'. This apparently was the first line of a Hunanese couplet of which the second ran, 'No law and no heaven.' Mao the rebel was hiding from the eye of his Marxist god the fact that he was preparing to sup with the devil.

In the same mood an American ping-pong team – one of six – was invited to China in 1971. A British team was included in the party and Reuters sent Jonathan Sharp to cover the tournament. He was the first member of their staff to enter the country since the Chinese had held Anthony Grey under house arrest. Thus a group of Anglo-Saxon journalists witnessed the change in the Peking line as a senior member of the Chinese Foreign Ministry apologized profusely for the 'burning' of the British Embassy and even attended a party to celebrate its reopening.

While ping-pong diplomacy was in progress Premier Zhou sent a note to Washington through his old friends in Pakistan saying he would be 'happy' to entertain a senior American official. It was thus most fortunate that the two great powers began making moves to improve their relations at the same time. Kissinger, as reported earlier, made his first visit to Peking in July 1971 when the world thought he was suffering from an upset stomach in Islamabad. Arrangements were initiated for President Nixon's visit to Peking in February 1972 which were later spelled out in detail by General Alexander Haig. By receiving President Nixon within four hours of his landing on Chinese soil, Mao demonstrated his overt friendliness to the American Head of State and his support for Premier Zhou's new policy. Only the beloved leader could have made so dramatic a change in his foreign policy and carried the party and state with him.

Despite his lack of information about foreign countries the Chairman appeared happy to receive Heads of State and other important foreign visitors and the Politbureau used these interviews, after television was introduced, to help him to keep in touch with the people. The last time he appeared in public was at the May Day Celebrations in 1972 and although he Chaired the 10th Party Congress in August 1973 he did not, for the first time, address the assembled delegates.

Just as Premier Zhou realized he was suffering from 'a heart condition' about this time so Mao felt the first real discomforts of Parkinson's disease. However, when Edward Heath, then leader of the British opposition, saw him in 1974 he was still in fine fettle and the two men got along extremely well together. One of the interpreters gave a vivid account of the interview as the Chairman, after the initial pleasantries, enquired whether Mr Heath had been satisfied with the reception arranged on his arrival at the airport. After the former Prime Minister assured the Chairman that he was 'more than satisfied', Mao said, 'Well I wasn't. Do you hear, Enlai, I watched it on television and would like to know why Mr Heath was not treated as a Head of State?'

The Premier replied that the Queen was Head of State in England and the Prime Minister was Mr Harold Wilson who would be deeply offended were Mr Heath to be given elaborate receptions. The Chairman then grew excited and said he did not give a Chinese four-letter word what Mr Wilson said or thought but that throughout Mr Heath's tour of China he would be given full honours as a Head of State. Premier Zhou nodded and when Mr Heath left Peking for Shanghai and throughout his tour he was 'treated like an emperor' with honour guards from the three services as well as graceful dancing girls, dragon dancers and singers. When he finally pulled out of Guangzhou station there were over 500 dancing girls in long dresses swaying to some music we could not hear.

It was sad to note that after 1975 the Chairman's memory began to slip badly and he fell more and more under the influence of Jiang Qing.

Mao is severely criticized for the deaths and acute suffering he caused as a result of his too speedy efforts to establish People's Agricultural Communes. No sooner had the landlords' property been divided amongst the peasants than they were forced into co-operatives largely because they lacked agricultural implements. Then the peasants were pressed into vast agricultural communes which caused the death of hundreds of thousands of sheep and cattle. Since Mao's death these units, which frequently contained up to 35,000 people, have been broken up again without loss of life. This has done something to assuage the bitter disappointment of the children of those millions, who after having achieved their lifelong ambition to own a strip of land, were forced into communes. They now have a secure private plot on which they can grow vegetables and produce pigs or chickens for the market.

Mao was no administrator, indeed, no good even at looking after himself as his frequent misadventures in early manhood, caused by lack of money when he needed to buy a railway ticket or the loss of a vital address where the Communist Party was meeting, indicate. He was fortunate in having a group of extremely able men with him, including the outstanding state administrator Zhou Enlai, who gradually re-established the civil service, and Liu Shaoqi, who with Deng Ziaoping, organized the Communist Party.

As the first communist 'emperor' Mao sometimes reminded the 'inside' people that in his youth and middle age he already realized he was going to be the third man to rise from nothing to rule China. The first was, or so Mao said, Han Gaozi (already mentioned earlier in the chapter) who as Liu Bang, an untrained soldier, rose to be ruler of all China after operating first as a rebel from a 'hill top'. The second was Sun Yat-sen, the first President of the Chinese Republic in 1911, who had trained to be a doctor. Nonetheless after having become 'ruler', Mao was deeply embarrassed initially by the crowds who wanted to kowtow to him. But the homage he received at the time Lin Biao was building up the cult of his personality during the Cultural Revolution was far worse than the kowtow. Mao recognized this when he told Edgar Snow that the cult of his personality had gone much too far. Following this realization Mao requested the first group of young people he saw in the Great Hall of the People to 'Give me back my aeroplanes', adding that metal used in making millions of Mao badges could have been far more effectively employed in aircraft to defend the Motherland.

Lin Biao's treachery was the most bitter blow Mao ever suffered and it caused a sharp deterioration in his health and spirits. That 'comrades' had in the past taken the Russian side and teamed up with them politically was grim but nothing to the horror experienced when his 'chosen successor' actually organized a coup with the help and connivance of Moscow. The Chairman would not, at first, believe the reports from Premier Zhou that Lin Biao's men were actually trying to assassinate him, although his relations with Lin were badly strained. That he, Mao, had defeated or pushed aside the men who had opposed him was one thing but Mao repeatedly stressed in his talks with visiting foreigners that he had never attempted to kill them. Hurt though he was, Lin's abortive coup provided Mao with a 'golden period' towards the end of his life when his mind was still clear and he could sit back and enjoy his role as leader. The Cultural Revolution was over (although today it is still deemed to have been in progress at this time) and Premier Zhou was administering the country as well as bringing China close to the United States and the West.

Unfortunately, neither Premier Zhou nor his deputy Deng Xiaoping seriously thought of transforming Mao into an almost powerless Head of State. This was not because earlier attempts to 'kick him upstairs had failed' but they felt they needed his authority especially in their dealings with the extremely powerful and, at times, difficult defence force Lin had left behind. Further, even Premier Zhou, when he was fit and powerful, suffered at the hands of Jiang Qing, and Deng far more so. Although the Chairman complained about her and said she would make trouble when he died, he nonetheless trusted her and allowed the media to remain in her hands. The 'golden period' gradually faded as the Premier grew sick and the Gang of Four more powerful in their opposition to Deng and the pragmatists. Mao remained anxious to end his life as the state and party leader – Chairman/emperor – but also as a rebel. He managed to remain a radical, noting most men move to the right in middle age. Despite his power Mao lived a simple life, leading a minor revolt, whenever he deemed one to be necessary, against a new communist elite, when he saw one developing. He was ever-critical of the class structure that had grown in the Soviet Union and determined China should remain free of a privileged bureaucracy and an officer class. Unhappily, sickness prevented him from realizing his last great ambition.

During his last year the pathetic almost speechless Chairman was ruthlessly used as a tool of Jiang Qing and the Gang whose actions during and after the April demonstrations in Tiananmen Square in memory of Premier Zhou caused Mao to suffer a series of strokes from which he never recovered. By this time Mao was a living corpse without the ability to think, allowing contradictory directives to leave his study. It is difficult, even with the power of hindsight, to say when he should have handed over power to the collective leadership he claimed he wanted to succeed him when he 'went to meet Marx'. This would not, however, have averted the power struggle between the radicals and the pragmatists – left and right wings of the Chinese Communist Party – which is unlikely to be resolved by the end of this century.

18

The Trial of the Gang of Four

The trial of 'the Lin Biao and Jiang Qing cliques' which opened on November 19th, 1980 has frequently been compared with that of the German war criminals in Nuremberg at the end of the Second World War – a trial of the vanquished by the victors – and there was an element of truth in this. But to be fair it was reasonable to disclose to the Chinese public at least some of the diabolical acts committed by Lin Biao and the Gang of Four in the efforts to assume power.

Apart from the period of their close co-operation before and during the Cultural Revolution, Jiang Qing's deeds were of a different blend from those of Lin Biao, both wily and wild, but nonetheless evil. That they should all have stood trial for the scores of murders they committed, the lies they told and the physical and mental torture they inflicted on thousands of innocent people was reasonable. Had all the proceedings been open to the public the international legal image of the trial would have been improved but the Chinese authorities claim this was impossible as state secrets were involved.

The public evidence released at the trial renders it apparent that during the Cultural Revolution Lin Biao and Jiang Qing first got together to trump up false charges against the Head of State, Liu Shaoqi. It is interesting to note Chairman Mao was not then in Peking but he was aware that his wife 'directly controlled' the group investigating 'the special case of Liu Shaoqi and his wife Wang Guangmei'. Mao may have been ignorant of the diabolical methods she employed, especially in the 'framing and arrest of Liu Shaoqi's wife Wang Guangmei' as an agent of the United States' strategic intelligence service. The Lius' cook was badly treated in jail and tortured intermittently for six years in order to obtain evidence against the couple. Wang's elderly professor, Yang Cheng-zuo, who had been her tutor at college, was chronically ill when taken to prison, yet Jiang Qing ordered her special group 'to squeeze what we need out of Yang before he dies'.

Jiang Qing's defence at the trial was that all her truly evil deeds were accomplished 'on behalf of Chairman Mao' or 'according to his instructions'. 'Arresting me,' she said, 'and bringing me to trial is a defamation of Chairman Mao [because] I have implemented and defended Chairman Mao's proletarian revolutionary line.' On another occasion Jiang said, 'I was the Chairman's dog. When he said bark, I barked, and when he said bite, I bit.'

However, Chairman Mao was most unlikely to have ordered her to collaborate with Lin Biao's wife, Ye Qun, to destroy letters, pictures and other relics of Jiang's past sex life when a film actress in Shanghai in the 1930s in order that she might rewrite her life story. But there can be no doubt that these two women ordered three senior officers in the PLA to have the homes of five elderly Shanghai 'personalities' of the film world searched. Over forty 'young people and soldiers' dressed up in disguise as Red Guards and in the early hours of the morning of October 9th they simultaneously ransacked the house of all five elderly film actors, actresses and producers who had been close to Jiang when she was in Shanghai. Diaries, letters, notebooks and pictures taken before 1949 were all seized. The wife of an actor, who had been taken away to prison because of his youthful affair with Jiang, told the court that her husband had been twice summoned before Zhang Chunqiao and told to hand over the 'relevant material' and this he had done. Apparently a letter Jiang remembered having written to him was missing – hence his arrest and ultimate death. A maid was arrested, framed and jailed because she knew too much about Jiang's past sex life. The author of an opera, *Red Lantern*, was also framed and persecuted because Jiang wanted to include his play among the eight model operas she claimed she had created herself.

Jiang Qing asserted that, when she was not acting under the orders of the Chairman, she was working with her old supporter, the Security Chief, Kang Sheng. Again there are conflicting reports of how much the Chairman knew of her activities but it is interesting to note that many of Jiang's wilder speeches were secretly recorded by her enemies and they were used in evidence against her at the trial. It is even said that some of Jiang's speeches were played back to the Chairman at the request of Premier Zhou but Mao took no public action. It is interesting that anyone actually dared to record her talks because at that time the Chinese were extremely sensitive about tape-recorders and, for example, it was forbidden to take one into the Great Hall of the People. Further, it was extremely difficult to obtain permission to tape a public statement for film purposes. Jiang had her brave as well as her frightened enemies.

In September 1968 she said, 'Let me tell you, Liu Shaoqi is a big counter-revolutionary, a big hidden traitor, a big renegade and big enemy agent, full of evil . . . I think he deserves a slow death by a thousand cuts, ten thousand cuts.' Her style was normally strident and repetitive. Jiang frightened people by having them arrested and put in prison if they failed to provide the false evidence she had requested them to obtain for her frame-ups. And I know how really frightened people became in China because they knew if they got into the bad books of Jiang or 'one of her minions' they might never see the outside of a prison again. (Frankly even at the time I realized she was power-hungry and unscrupulous but I had no idea how evil she really was, although many people secretly tried to present to me a true picture of her.)

It was assumed the Chairman closed his eyes and ears in March 1966 when Jiang had summoned leading party and state officials to a meeting where she called Deng Xiaoping 'a fascist', 'a big quisling' and a 'counter-revolutionary double-dealer'. When Jiang and Kang were collaborating with Lin Biao's supporters in the PLA during the militant period of the Cultural Revolution they certainly appeared to have Chairman Mao in their pocket. Anyone critical of either Jiang or Lin was liable to be framed. Thus in July 1968 no fewer than eighty-eight members of the Central Committee of the Chinese Communist Party were dubbed 'enemy agents', 'renegades', 'elements having illicit relations with foreign countries' or 'anti-party elements'. Indeed, almost anyone Jiang disliked was dubbed 'a vicious enemy agent' and a former Vice Mayor of Peking, two Ministers and Liao Mosha, a famous writer, were imprisoned for eight years and subjected to mental and physical persecution. 'One word of theirs' – Jiang Qing, Kang Sheng or Xie Fuchi – 'led to my arrrest and seven year imprisonment', according to Wang Kunlun who is now Vice Chairman of the National Committee of the Chinese People's Political Consultative Assembly. Zhang Chunqiao had, at the time of the collaboration with the Lin Biao group, a great influence on Jiang Qing although he never impressed the broad masses as a leader but rather as a 'cold fish' administrator. Zhang repeatedly urged the need for a 'change of dynasty' and stressed that, 'Our aim in the Great Proletarian Cultural Revolution has always been to seize power from the grass roots to the central organizations, including the powers of the party, the Government as well as the financial, cultural and other fields.' In fact, his speeches frequently opened with the words, 'We must seize power everywhere.'

Veteran cadres were serious obstacles to the usurpation of party and state power, Zhang claimed, saying, 'All of them are bad and none shall be spared.' The Chairman might have agreed that elderly officials frequently stood in the way of progress during the Cultural Revolution but he would not have urged their liquidation, merely that they should be pressed to retire. It is, in retrospect, somewhat surprising that the Chairman himself was not worried by Zhang's speeches. For Zhang administered one of China's most sinister organizations for the Gang of Four, a special espionage group code-named 224. The group, which had well-organized branches in Peking, Shanghai, Tianjin and Hangzhou – to name only those mentioned by officials – had the power to take anyone into custody. The victims were then secretly interrogated and torture was frequently used to obtain the confession the Gang was demanding.

The numbers of people involved are horrific as, for example, Chen Boda instigated the arrest and persecution of 84,000 people causing no fewer than 2955 to die as a result of the treatment they received. When the Judge asked Chen what grounds he had for making the charges against these men in the party organization in eastern Hebei Province, he answered, 'None at all. I spoke without any foundation. I plead guilty.'

Some people who then worked with Mao believed 'he just did not want to know of these unpleasantnesses going on in the background'. Those who speak of the 'Gang of Five', to include Mao, argue that he must have known something if not all of this as supporters of Premier Zhou were anxious to pass information on to him that was harmful to Jiang through sympathetic interpreters. Chen Boda, as is well known, had been close to Mao until he became the tool first of Lin and then Jiang through the lack of a power base of his own. After successfully fabricating evidence on scores of important people, the radicals went too far and in 1974 attempted to frame Premier Zhou. This was when the Chairman had, again according to evidence produced at the trial, proposed in 1974 that Deng Xiaoping be made First Vice Premier. Jiang regarded him as her most bitter enemy and she persuaded the Gang of Four to send Wang Hongwen to Changsha, where the Chairman was staying, to tell him that although Premier Zhou was in hospital he and Deng Xiaoping with others were 'colluding to usurp power', as Lin had done at the Lushan Conference after the 9th Party Congress. On this occasion the Chairman was irritated by the Gang and showed it to those visitors who were members of the Politbureau.

The Qing Ming demonstrations in Tiananmen Square in April 1976 mourning the death of Premier Zhou and praising his work obviously upset the radicals even more than diplomats and journalists realized at the time. As reported earlier, when Zhang falsely accused Deng of organizing them, he had been in disgrace and away from Peking since the end of January. Zhang dubbed him 'China's Nagy' – the Hungarian revisionist. After the demonstrations, the Gang of Four instigated the persecution of the Mayor and Vice Mayor of Shanghai together with scores of others who died as a result of their treatment in prison.

Mao rarely opposed anyone from the left of the Communist Party despite his obsession with the 'ten men who rose against him'. Although the Chairman mentioned the 'ten' to almost all his foreign visitors, some of them later admitted they had but little idea what he was talking about. All but one, Zhang Guodao, had in Mao's mind taken a pro-Russian line. In the early days of the formation of the Chinese Communist Party they had accepted Moscow's view that the party and future revolution should be based on the urban worker and trade unions rather than the peasants favoured by Mao.

Before the Long March and later in Yenan it was a question of whether Mao and his following should support guerrilla tactics based on the peasants or positional warfare. Just before independence the Russians wanted to impose their form of management and administration on the 'liberated' areas. Although Liu was not pro-Russian after independence, Mao frequently recalled Liu's youthful days when he formed illegal trade unions in Shanghai and other cities, while Lin Biao was relying for help in his coup from the Soviet Union. Thus Mao, especially during the later part of his life, tended to over-simplify the situation. He saw his support coming from the population, 85 per cent of whom were peasants, and of these he believed erroneously that the vast majority were left of centre while he saw the urban population as right of centre and, possibly, sympathetic to the Soviet Union.

Mao believed in continual moves towards true communism where there would be no money and whatever jobs people had they would receive food, clothes, housing and entertainment, 'Each according to his or her needs.' Basically, Mao opposed the establishment of a communist elite which the Russians had produced. To prevent this developing he believed it was necessary to organize episodic upheavals, such as the Cultural Revolution, every seven years or so to stop the formation of an upper class. While other members of the Central Committee wore leather shoes and new clothes and enjoyed special food from shops normally open only to foreign diplomats, Mao's own jacket was always patched and darned and his felt shoes repaired. He consumed any kind of food so long as there were plenty of red peppers in it. After the failure of his two chosen successors – Liu and Lin – Mao was unable to establish a satisfactory and reliable collective leadership to follow him and Premier Zhou. By the time Premier Zhou died he lacked the energy to do more than say or write, 'With you in charge my heart is at ease.' Much of the time he operated under the strong personal and radical influence of Jiang Qing.

19

Notes on the Ten Men Who Rose against Chairman Mao

Mao was obsessed in his later years by the ten men who led campaigns designed, he believed, to destroy his political and personal power. He constantly alluded to the 'ten bitter struggles on the question of our line' – the party line – that were, in fact, nothing but major disputes over policy and the leadership. It is most significant that the Soviet Union, the Comintern or the Russian Communist Party were intimately involved in nine out of ten of the cases.

Mao quarrelled with *Chen Duxiu*, the intellectual founder of the Chinese Communist Party, because he refused to allow any discussions on Mao's report on 'an investigation into the Peasant Movement in Hunan', at the 5th Party Congress in Wuhan in 1927. Chen, who was already on bad terms with Moscow for having opposed the Comintern policy of collaboration with Chiang Kai-shek and the nationalists, felt the future Chairman's radical thesis on land reform would provide the last straw for the Chinese Communist Party which was then financially dependent on Moscow. Mao claimed later to Edgar Snow that Chen had been guilty of 'wavering opportunism which deprived the Party of decisive leadership'. 'Chen was really frightened of the workers and especially of the armed peasants,' Mao said, adding that, 'Confronted at last with the reality of armed insurrection he completely lost his senses.' Chen resigned and joined the Trotskyists for a short time before he was caught and imprisoned by the nationalists. After his release he reverted to the classical studies of his youth.

Zhu Zhubai became the first communist martyr when he was executed at the age of thirty-six after having been left behind because of chronic tuberculosis at the opening of the Long March. He was a translator of Tolstoy and generally on excellent terms with the pro-Russian faction of the Chinese Communist Party. Like Chen he opposed peasant insurrections and believed in the revolutionary superiority of the urban worker. However, sometimes Mao claimed he forgave all Zhu's political errors because he was imprisoned and shot as a Marxist.

Li Lisan is still the best known of the early leaders in China to oppose Mao actively. After training in France he spent some time in Moscow before returning to China to become a trade union organizer in Guangzhou.

He developed what became known as the Li Lisan line and acquired great influence amongst the workers. He was described by a colleague as, 'A good labour leader and an unusually convincing agitator, influencing nearly everyone who heard him speak.' Li was one of the principal organizers of the Nanchang uprising of August 1st, 1927, which, although it only lasted five days, gave the Comintern a false idea of what could be accomplished in Chinese cities. Li was, to be fair, trying to work in the midst of a difficult triangle made up of Moscow, the Communist Party Headquarters in Shanghai and the ever-increasing number of Red guerrilla forces fighting in liberated areas, generally on hill tops. Maybe he was over-optimistic in the advice he gave Moscow about the urban support the communists could muster and the likelihood that Red Army units would provide military assistance. In fact, the masses failed to respond and the Red Army withdrew. The hoped-for insurrections in Changsha and Wuhan never materialized and Li forfeited his authority with Moscow and the Chinese Trade Union Movement. Mao condemned Li who, however, between visits to Moscow continued to play a minor role in the Chinese political scene until the mid-1930s.

Although *Luo Zhanglong* was far less important to the Party than Li, Mao disliked him with bitter personal passion because he had initially responded to Mao's newspaper advertisement in Changsha for 'youths who were hardened and ready to make sacrifices for the country'. Luo was one who responded and joined the Communist Party, which, Mao told Edgar Snow, he 'afterwards betrayed'. He, too, believed the revolution lay in the hands of the urban workers rather than the peasants and he was one of the members of the powerful pro-Soviet intellectual 'returned students group'. Mao accused him of being a 'counter-revolutionary'. He was arrested by the KMT but escaped and fled to Hong Kong and, later, North Vietnam where he is believed to have died in prison.

Unlike some other men who opposed Mao before 'liberation', Luo did not sit around in a humble capacity to salute and irritate the Chairman.

Wang Ming's name is still a household word in the People's Republic. After receiving his university education in Moscow he returned to China as the leader of the 'returned student group' and triumphed over Li Lisan in a personal power struggle during 1930/1. But although Wang won the leadership of the urban section of the party he failed to obtain the allegiance of the guerrillas. According to Mao, Wang Ming's erroneous leadership enabled the nationalists to destroy almost all the underground organizations in the areas they controlled, which, ultimately, rendered the rural bases untenable in the face of continued KMT attacks. Thus the communist guerrillas were forced to undertake the Long March.

When the Red Army – guerrillas – reached Zunyi in January 1935 on the Long March they were able to discuss their problems for the first time without being too pressed by the enemy. Wang Ming, the titular leader, was in Moscow while Liu Shaoqi was organizing resistance against the KMT, possibly in Shanghai, using a false passport. Mao who had left Jiangxi almost in disgrace called a meeting of an enlarged Politbureau and the returned students. The Red 'Generals' – guerrilla leaders – all supported Mao as did Zhou Enlai who had been until then, as a returned student, sympathetic to Moscow. Mao was thus able to secure a vital victory over the pro-Russian element in the party. Wang Ming was out of the running for the leadership but he stayed around in a minor and humiliating role.

Zhang Guodao is the only high-ranking Chinese Communist Party member who defected to the nationalists and, since then, he has been the butt of many scathing remarks by Chairman Mao and other members of the Politbureau. Basically the dispute between the two men arose out of different ideas of where the Long March should terminate. In 1935, Zhang wanted to retreat further to the west towards Xinjiang where the Red Army would be able to receive support from the Russians. Mao wanted to move north and after days of acrimonious argument each went his own way. Zhang's force was virtually annihilated but he managed to survive and he eventually joined Mao in Yenan.

Although he was no longer a rival violent disagreements between Zhang and Mao continued. Mao claimed that Zhang had pretended to agree with him while making preparations for 'his final betrayal of the party' and stated, 'He threw himself into the arms of the KMT.' Zhang did make his way to Chongqing where he took some part in nationalist affairs until the end of the civil war when he moved to Hong Kong. When he feared the Red Guards might take over Hong Kong during the Cultural Revolution he went to Canada, where abuse from Mao followed him.

The purge of *Peng Dehuai* in August 1959 has been described as one of Mao's 'greatest mistakes'. As Minister of Defence, Peng was extremely popular with the troops at grass roots level; he got along well with the Russians and, although he was critical of the Great Leap Forward, he was still basically extremely loyal to Mao. Men with his wide and distinguished military background are rare even in the People's Republic and the PLA could ill afford to lose him. For Peng had been a member of the Communist Party since 1928 and a guerrilla fighter long before that. After distinguishing himself on the Long March, Peng was put in command of the 1st Front Army in Shaanxi where he spent much of his time moving back and forth from the communist capital at Yenan to the battlefront. After the Hundred Regiments offensive in 1945 he was listed amongst those senior officers in charge of overall strategy. Although he did not go to Peking to take part in the establishment of the Central government, he was appointed to a series of top military committees.

When the 'People's Volunteers' (CPV) crossed the Yalu River in Korea, Peng was put in command of the army and remained in that position throughout the war with the rank of Marshal. After Korea he worked in Peking where he was appointed Minister of the newly created Ministry of National Defence. Peng assisted Premier Zhou Enlai in negotiations with Khrushchev concerned with obtaining large-scale Soviet economic aid and he became de facto head of the newly created MAC. Although Zhu De was the 'grand old man' of the PLA, Peng was recognized as the most important active military leader and he was constantly in the limelight. Peng led an expert delegation to Moscow to discuss Sino-Soviet military affairs and strategy at the same time as the fortieth anniversary of the Russian Revolution was being celebrated.

The Russians were 'full of themselves', Peng said later, having just tested an ICBM and launched their first sputnik. After the discussions, which Peng suggested were not entirely satisfactory, and a tour of Soviet military installations, Peng decided China would have to rely more and more on its own industrial base.

Khrushchev was alarmed by Peking's aggressive attitude towards Taiwan which a four-day visit did little to assuage. Indeed, a few weeks later Peking began a bombardment of the offshore island of Jinmen, which inflicted no damage and was, thanks largely to Peng, soon discontinued. In April 1959 Peng led yet another Chinese military delegation to eastern Europe, spending about a week in each capital, including Tirana (Albania), as well as visiting Moscow and Mongolia before returning to Peking in mid-June.

Meanwhile, differences of opinion between the Chairman and Peng which had been considered 'healthy' a few years earlier were growing acute on such issues as whether a soldier should be 'red' or 'expert' and on the policy to be adopted towards Taiwan. Many of the 'inside' people regard this period as the beginning of Jiang Qing's real political influence over the Chairman. In any case, Peng was openly critical of the shortcomings and wasted effort of the Great Leap and he passed on to the Politbureau the bitter criticisms he had heard in Warsaw, which he visited at the time members of the Warsaw Pact were gathered for a meeting. Later Peng discussed the Great Leap with Khrushchev in Tirana.

After the final break with Moscow, which took place only a week after Peng's return, he was unwise enough to question the efficiency of Mao's concept of a people's war in view of his own experiences in Korea. Peng also advocated the need for 'inter-dependence amongst socialist states'. Mao, jealous of Peng's enormous popularity with the PLA and angered by his criticism, replaced him as Defence Minister by Lin Biao at the Lushan Conference of August 1959 and Peng faded from the scene. But the soldiers and the 'inside' people never forgot him and there was frequently a movement afoot to restore Peng to power. None except Mao and Jiang Qing ever questioned Peng's absolute loyalty.

Gao Gang played a key role in the development of the communist base that served as a haven for Mao and his exhausted troops at the end of the Long March. The two men got along well together and during the late 1940s Gao became the senior official in

Manchuria when others of the top brass moved south with Lin Biao's military forces. In July 1949 Gao went to Moscow to negotiate a barter agreement providing the Soviet Union with soy beans, vegetable oils and grain in exchange for industrial equipment, petroleum, automobiles, paper and medicines. At the time the Russians still retained diplomatic relations with the nationalists. Gao went to Peking soon after his return from Russia and was appointed to several party and state committees that had special reference to Manchuria. Gao then made Shenyang 'the capital' and he dominated the political scene from there for the next three years. As the first 'liberated' major region of China key party politics were first tested under his leadership. The Russians and Chinese were then jointly administering the Chinese Changchun Railway as well as the naval facilities at Luda. Gao's work was considered so outstandingly successful that he was brought to Peking to become the first Chairman of the State Planning Commission but he retained all his posts in Manchuria.

Further, Gao was accorded that most prized accolade, that of being officially described as Chairman Mao's 'close comrade in arms'. Gao had never made any secret of his view that it was impossible to run an efficient factory, mine or indeed any industrial enterprise by means of collective leadership. He believed every factory should have a manager who was completely in charge and dismissed as 'absurd' the idea that Party Secretaries should be supreme. These ideas gradually brought him into conflict with Chairman Mao, Liu Shaoqi and Deng Xiaoping and their disagreements were exasperated by Gao's friendly relations with Moscow which he sought to establish ostensibly for commercial reasons. Gao felt Moscow had, largely through experience, developed a sounder economic policy based on giving priority to heavy industry together with a superior administration, which he had witnessed in Manchuria, and better party control. The old issue re-emerged as to whether to concentrate on the peasants and agriculture or on industry – especially heavy industry.

After attending a meeting to commemorate the thirtieth anniversary of the death of Lenin in September 1953, Gao was never seen again. At first he was merely attacked indirectly by Liu who claimed that 'certain high-ranking' officials regarded their 'region or the department under them' as their 'personal property or independent kingdom'. It took over a year before details of the 'anti-party plot' were disclosed. That this was done by Deng Xiaoping adds credence in the minds of many senior party officials today. Deng claimed that Gao's 'conspiratorial activities' to seize power went back to 1949 when he regarded Manchuria as his own independent kingdom and he had then sought support for establishing what amounted to a separate country from senior party members in the army and the local administration. At the time the ordinary party member in central China saw Gao's purge as a major personality clash in which the top man from Manchuria was trying to usurp the place of Premier Zhou Enlai as Premier or Liu Shaoqi as the Secretary General of the Communist Party. But there were strong elements of pro-Russian activities including those of Rao Shushi (Jao Shu-shih), head of the party's Organization Department, and seven important officials who allegedly had participated in the 'plot' and who were purged at the same time. They all openly shared Gao's belief in the urgent need to co-operate with the Soviet Union as well as promote heavy industry in China.

Gao Gang was 'on the point of success in his activities aimed at seizing power' when the 'plot' was discovered, according to Deng Xiaoping. But as neither he nor his fellow conspirators have been called 'traitors' it would suggest there is no evidence available that the Russians were actually involved or collaborating then in efforts to overthrow Mao. Much was made of Gao's suicide 'as an ultimate expression of his betrayal of the Party' combined with the fact that he never admitted his guilt. However, there is no doubt both the party and state administration in the north-east where the Gao accomplices held most of the key positions felt the reactions for the following year or so.

Mao's first 'chosen successor'

Liu Shaoqi died in squalor in the cellar of a prison in the ancient market town of Kaifeng after being Head of State and second only to Chairman Mao in the party. Liu, who came from Hunan where he attended the same college as Mao, was one of the first Chinese communists to study in Moscow. This influenced him to believe that the root of socialist power lay with the urban workers and he spent many years organizing underground communist parties during the Japanese occupation of China's cities. Liu took part in the Long March but after this he devoted himself once more to secret underground work, setting up trade unions amongst industrial workers in cities, whilst spending some time in Yenan where his title was 'Commissioner of Labour'. Liu lectured there while he wrote and produced his best-known work, *How to Be a Good Communist*. Liu gradually assumed a place amongst the leaders and at the 7th Party Congress in April 1945 three major speeches were delivered: the Chairman's political report, Zhu De's statement on the military scene and Liu's speech on the revised party constitution. When Mao went to Chongqing, Liu became acting Chairman. During Tito's feud with Stalin, Liu supported Moscow and poured scorn on 'Tito's bourgeois nationalism'. However, Liu had three or four wives (so too had Mao) and, when not risking his life as an underground worker, enjoyed a higher standard of living than the peasants and soldiers in Yenan. From the early 1930s Liu was a member of the Politbureau and it was generally thought that with his knowledge of the urban worker he complemented Chairman Mao who had concentrated so much on the peasant. Liu advocated that 'armed struggle' should become the base for the 'liberation' of the peoples of South-east Asia, a doctrine that made him profoundly unpopular in the West.

Liu stood beside the Chairman when the new People's Republic was declared and took over from him when Mao went to Moscow 'begging bowl in hand'. In fact he was recognized as Mao's successor long before he became the official 'chosen successor'. Liu was an enthusiastic supporter of the Great Leap in its early days but changed his attitude after making an intensive tour of the country when Mao was, as it were, behind his back rushing almost wildly ahead with the establishment of People's Agricultural Communes. This led eventually to Mao being eased out of the post of Chairman of the NPC or Head of State and his replacement by Liu who played an increasingly important role receiving scores of visiting foreigners. That Liu dared to criticize Mao for his rash behaviour in setting up the communes without doubt caused political strains to develop between them, but the real bitterness arose as a result of Jiang Qing's violent jealousy of Liu's fifth wife, the attractive and well-educated Wang Guangmei. While Jiang was still not allowed to play a political role, Wang travelled with her husband and appeared with him at most public functions. Despite the quarrels the Chairman had with his wife and her propensity to raise her voice when angered, those who worked with them suggest she had far more political influence with Mao than was generally recognized at the time. He had taught her that it pays to rebel and she took advantage of the teachings on the teacher!

Jiang's warnings about Wang certainly added fuel to the fire Mao felt burning within him against his 'chosen successor' who was, in his view, beginning to take the 'capitalist road'.

Despite his apparently colourless character, Liu was described as a 'towering figure' in the Chinese Communist Party but unlike Mao, Premier Zhou or even Zhu De, the 'soldiers' soldier', he remained a shadowy personality. Indeed, Liu was generally seen as the dour, unemotional man who implemented Mao's wishes within the party with intelligence and speed. Liu was also known as a hard worker – a man who rose early and worked until late in the evening. Most Chinese communist leaders are hard-working and Premier Zhou normally worked until three in the morning and was to be found in the office before eleven.

There is no doubt whatever that Mao launched the Cultural Revolution with the object of getting rid of Liu and his supporters but it is hard to believe he would wittingly have treated him so badly. However, when Liu volunteered to return to the countryside near to where he was born and live the life of a peasant the Chairman said 'NO'. He was obviously not wanted near the birthplace of Mao which had already become a National Shrine.

Mao's second 'chosen successor'

Lin Biao, one of the greatest of the revolutionary military commanders China produced, died as a traitor when the Trident in which he was attempting to escape to the Soviet Union crashed in Mongolia killing everyone on board.

After Lin's attempted coup designed to overthrow Chairman Mao had aborted, Premier Zhou Enlai ordered Chinese fighter aircraft to chase the plane. It is still not known whether they succeeded in shooting him down or whether the Trident ran out of fuel. The Mongolians later claimed there was evidence of shots fired inside the cabin before the crash. In either case Lin and his immediate family are dead but many of his fellow conspirators lived to give evidence at their trial which took place with members of the Gang of Four.

Lin was born in 1907 near Wuhan in a village on the north bank of the Yangtze where he became involved in radical and nationalist movements at school. In his early twenties he joined the KMT and was sent to the Whampoa Military Academy in Guangzhou where he met Zhou Enlai. Lin told Edgar Snow that in 1925 Chiang Kai-shek ordered all cadets who were members of both the KMT and the CCP to renounce one or the other. Lin chose communism. Shortly after the Nanchang Uprising Lin joined the 20th Army under He Long and in August 1927 took part in peasant uprisings in Hunan Province under Zhu De. Lin's reputation as an officer grew as a result of the successful battles and skirmishes he fought against the KMT and in 1932 he was named commander of the 1st Red Army.

During the Long March, Lin was assigned the dangerous and difficult task of covering the rearguard. On reaching the haven of Shaanxi, Lin immediately set up a military academy for training young officers. Lin's fame as a commander then grew significantly as he fought the Japanese until he was wounded and sent to Russia for treatment. There, according to Soviet sources, he took part in the defence of Leningrad and he attended courses on modern warfare. Before he left for Moscow in 1937 he was already attending meetings of the Politbureau but he did not return until 1942 when he went to Chongqing to confer with the nationalist government. But during his nine months' sojourn Chiang Kai-shek only received him three times.

Americans then in Yenan were 'impressed' by Lin who at thirty-seven was a military veteran of two decades. As the final defeat of Japan appeared imminent, the communists began moving troops into Manchuria; thus at the time of the surrender Lin had some 30,000 men serving under him. As the numbers grew dramatically so too did the amount of captured Japanese military equipment, until by the spring of 1946 Lin was believed to have nearly a quarter of a million armed troops. After an initial organizational period, this force began to occupy Manchurian cities. Chiang tried to intervene and by mid-1946 the ineffective KMT–CCP truce had given way to a nationwide civil war.

Lin dubbed his military movements as 'strategic withdrawal and mobile warfare abandoning the towns for the country'. The communist forces gathered momentum and after capturing a series of small towns, Lin opened what Mao said was 'one of the three greatest campaigns of the civil war'. Within two months all Manchuria was in communist hands; then, leaving the north-east in charge of Gao Gang, Lin moved south, passed beyond the Great Hall and with 800,000 troops he took Tianjin while the KMT General in Peking, Fu Tso-i, surrendered without a fight.

The three Field Armies crossed the Yangtze during the latter part of April. Wuhan fell and Lin was then appointed commander and secretary of the Central China Military Region. Within a few weeks, Lin's armies began advancing again to the south and occupied Guangzhou by mid-October as, once more, the leading KMT commanders surrendered. By December only Hainan Island remained in KMT hands.

Lin did not attend the ceremonies in Peking establishing the new state but retained an active role in central and southern China until overtaken by tuberculosis. Sickness, it must be assumed, kept him out of the Korean War in which large numbers of his 4th Field Army took part. Although holding, in theory, a series of important posts Lin remained ill and out of the limelight until the 8th Party Congress in September 1956 when he made his first public appearance in five years. Then, although listed seventh in the pecking order of the party, he remained in the background until the spring of 1958 when he was appointed to the Standing Committee of the Politbureau.

However, in August 1959 Lin took over the Ministry of Defence from Peng Dehuai. Here he made an immediate impact and upset many of the senior officers by stressing the vital importance of political indoctrination. His now famous article published to celebrate the tenth anniversary of the founding of the People's Republic, 'March Ahead under the Red Flag of the Party's General Line and Mao Zedong's Military Thinking', caused major problems amongst those commanders who gave military training priority over political work. Significantly, it was at the time the Soviet Union withdrew their aid and their experts from the PLA. Although Lin well knew the importance of military training he assumed a political role in line with the radicals.

In 1965 Lin caused a worldwide sensation by the publication of an article, 'Long Live the Victory of the People's War', in which he likened North America and Europe to the 'cities of the world' and Asia, Africa and South America to the 'rural areas of the globe'. In it he urged revolutionary forces to form People's Armies and rely on their own resources and not foreign aid in order to surround and crush 'the cities'.

The 'inside' people accepted the fact that Lin was close to Chairman Mao who realized the need for PLA backing in his frequent quarrels with Liu Shaoqi and the party. Lin, in turn, with the strong support of his wife grasped the power wielded by Jiang Qing and took advantage of this by being extremely cordial to the former actress who was still coldly, albeit correctly, received by many of the other older Chinese communist leaders and their wives. Their close relationship was officially based on Jiang Qing's responsibilty for 'culture and entertainment' in the PLA. One woman who knew the leadership well at this period said Jiang Qing could not always disguise her stupidity and basic lack of education at social gatherings but Lin and Ye Qun protected her, especially when Chairman Mao was not around.

Lin enjoyed a few years after the militant period of the Cultural Revolution when he realized he was the number two man, after Mao, as the army was extremely powerful. But he, in turn, grew jealous of the power exerted by Premier Zhou and the Premier's influence on foreign policy, especially the still-secret moves to develop closer relations with the United States and the West whilst regarding the Russians as the more menacing superpower. It was curious that Lin's unpopularity with the Chairman and Jiang Qing should have become so apparent so soon after he had been officially appointed as the 'chosen successor'. However, it is not difficult to understand that Lin, knowing he could not count on the support of all the Regional Military Commanders in the PLA, sought help and assistance from his old friends in the Soviet Union since, as a result of his behaviour during the early part of the Cultural Revolution, Lin realized he had no influence with Premier Zhou and even less with Deng Xiaoping. Many of those people who saw Lin during the period when he was mounting the coup against Mao frequently thought he had gone out of his mind and would soon be sent to some suitable sea-side or mountain resort for he was both sick, distrait and, at times, irrational.

Bibliography

Arai, Takao. *Rin Hyo jidai* (The Era of Lin Piao). Tokyo: Ajai hyoron-sha, 1970.

Arai, Takao. *The Practice of a Revolutionary, Zhou Enlai*. Tokyo: Cho Shuppansha, 1979.

Asian Yearbook. Far Eastern Economic Review, Hong Kong.

Barnett, A. Doak. *Uncertain Passage*. Washington, DC: The Brookings Institution, 1974.

Biographic Dictionary of Chinese Communism 1921–1965. Klein and Clark, Harvard University Press, 1971.

Bloodworth, Dennis. *Heirs Apparent*. London: Secker & Warburg, 1973.

Bloodworth, Dennis. *The Messiah and the Mandarins*. London: Weidenfeld, 1982.

Bonavia, David. *The Chinese – A Portrait*. London: Penguin, 1981.

Bonavia, David. *Verdict in Peking*. London: Burnett, 1984.

Braun, Otto. *A Comintern Agent in China*. London: Hurst, 1982.

Butterfield, Fox. *China: Alive in a Bitter Sea*. London: Hodder, 1983.

Chen, Jack. *Inside the Cultural Revolution*. London: Sheldon, 1975.

Chen, Jerome. *Mao Papers*. London: O.U.P., 1970.

Domes, Jurgen. *The Internal Politics of China, 1949–1972*. New York: Praeger, 1973.

Domes, Jurgen. *China – After the Cultural Revolution*. London: Hurst, 1976.

Elegant, Robert S. *Mao's Great Revolution*. New York: World, 1971.

Floyd, David. *Mao against Khrushchev*. New York: Praeger, 1964.

Fouman, Harrison. *Report from Red China*. New York: Holt, 1945.

Garside, Roger. *Coming Alive, China After Mao*. London: Deutsch, 1981.

Gittings, John. *The Role of the Chinese Army*. London: O.U.P., 1967.

Goodstadt, Lee. *Mao Tse-tung. The Search for Plenty.* Hong Kong: Longman, 1972.

Greene, Felix. *The Wall has Two Sides.* London: Cape, 1964.

Grey, Anthony. *Hostage in Peking.* London: Michael Joseph, 1970.

Griffith, Samuel B. *The Chinese People's Liberation Army.* London: Weidenfeld, 1968.

Han Suyin. *A Mortal Flower.* London: Cape, 1966.

Han Suyin. *China in the Year 2001.* London: Watts, 1967.

Han Suyin. *Birdless Summer.* London: Cape, 1968.

Han Suyin. *The Morning Deluge. Mao Tse-tung and the Chinese Revolution.* London: Cape, 1972.

Han Suyin. *Wind in the Tower.* London: Cape, 1976.

Han Suyin. *My House Has Two Doors.* London: Cape, 1980.

Harris, Richard. Articles in *The Times* of London.

Hierarchies of the People's Republic of China. Hong Kong: Union Research Institute, March 1975.

Hinton, Harold, C. *Communist China in World Politics.* London: Macmillan, 1966.

Howe, Christopher. *China's Economy. A Basic Guide.* London: Paul Elek, 1978.

Hsieh, Alice L. *Communist China's Military Doctrine and Strategy.* Santa Monica, Calif.: Rand Corporation, 1963.

Hughes, Richard. *Foreign Devils.* London: Deutsch, 1972.

Illustrated Atlas of China. Rand McNally, 1972. Prepared for the US Government.

Important Documents on the Great Proletarian Cultural Revolution in China. Peking: Foreign Languages Press, 1970.

Karnow, Stanley. *Mao and China.* New York: The Viking Press, 1972.

Karol, K. S. *The Second Chinese Revolution.* London: Cape, 1975.

Karol, K. S. *China, The Other Communism.* London: Heinemann, 1976.

Khruschev. *Khruschev Remembers.* (Translated by Strobe Talbott. 2 vols.) London, 1971, 1974.

Kissinger, Henry. *The White House Years.* London: Weidenfeld, 1979.

'Lin Piao and the Cultural Revolution.' *Current Scene,* VIII: 14 (August 1, 1970).

MacFarquhar, Roderick. *The Hundred Flowers Campaign and the Chinese Intellectuals.* New York: Praeger, 1960.

MacFarquhar, Roderick. *The Origins of the Cultural Revolution.* London: O.U.P., 1974.

Mao Tsetung. *The Selected Works of Mao Tse-tung.* 4 vols. Peking: Foreign Languages Press, 1961–5.

Mao Tsetung. *Selected Military Writings.* Peking: Foreign Languages Press, 1963.

Mao Tsetung. *Little Red Book.* (With preface by Lin Piao.)

The Military Balance. Annual publication of the I.I.S.S., London.

Milton, David and Nancy. *The Wind Will not Subside. Years in Revolutionary China 1964–1969.* New York: Pantheon, 1976.

Nelson, Harvey. *The Chinese Military System: an Organisational Study of the People's Liberation Army.* Boulder, Colorado: Westview Press, 1977.

Nixon, Richard. *The Memoirs of Richard Nixon.* London: Sidgwick & Jackson, 1978.

Pye, Lucian, W. *Mao Tse-tung. The Man in the Leader.* New York: Basic Books, 1976.

Rice, Edward E. *Mao's Way.* Berkeley: University of California Press, 1972.

Robinson, Thomas W. *Zhou Enlai and the Cultural Revolution in China.* Berkeley: University of California Press, 1971.

Robinson, Thomas W. *The Cultural Revolution in China.* Berkeley: University of California Press, 1971.

Schram, Stuart. *Mao Tse-tung Unrehearsed.* Harmondsworth: Penguin Books, 1974.

Schram, Stuart. *Mao Tse-tung: A Biography.* New York: Pelican Books, 1966.

Service, John, S. *Lost Chance in China.* New York: Vintage, 1974.

Siao-Yu. *Mao Tse-tung and I were Beggars.* London: Souvenir Press, 1959.

Smedley, Agnes. *The Great Road.* New York: Monthly Review Press, 1956.

Snow, Edgar. *Red Star Over China.* London: Gollancz, 1937.

Snow, Edgar. *Random Notes on Red China.* Cambridge: Harvard, 1957.

Snow, Edgar. *Journey to the Beginning.* New York: Random House, 1958.

Snow, Edgar. *The Other Side of the River*. London: Gollancz, 1963.

Snow, Edgar. *The Long Revolution*. London: Hutchinson, 1973.

Snow, Helen Foster. *Women in Modern China*. The Hague: Moulon, 1967.

Snow, Helen Foster. *The Chinese Communists*. Westport: Greenwood, 1972.

Snow, Lois Wheeler. *Edgar Snow's China*. London: Orbis Publishing, 1981.

Strong, Anna Louise. *Letters from China, 1962–1964*. 2 vols. Peking: New World Press, 1963 and 1964.

Terrill, Ross. *800,000,000: The Real China*. London: Penguin, 1975.

Terrill, Ross. *The China Difference*. New York: Harper & Row, 1979.

Terrill, Ross. *The Future of China After Mao*. London: Deutsch, 1979.

Terrill, Ross. *Mao: A Biography*. New York: Harper & Row, 1980.

Terrill, Ross. *The White-boned Demon. A Biography of Madame Mao Zedong*. London: Heinemann, 1984.

Topping, Seymour. *Journey Between Two Chinas*. New York: Harper, 1978.

Trevelyan, Humphrey. *Worlds Apart*. London: Macmillan, 1971.

Trotsky. *Problems of the Chinese Revolution*. New York: Piovers, 1932.

van Ginneken, Jaap. *The Rise and Fall of Lin Piao*. London: Penguin, 1976.

Wang Ming. *Mao's Betrayal*. London: Central, 1979.

Whitson, William. *The Chinese High Command: A History of Communist Military Politics, 1927–1971*. New York: Praeger, 1973.

Who's Who in the People's Republic of China. Wolfgang Bartke, Harvester Press, 1981.

Wilson, Dick. *The Long March, 1935*. London: Hamish Hamilton, 1971.

Wilson, Dick. *Mao. The People's Emperor*. London: Hutchinson, 1979.

Wilson, Dick. *Chou. The Story of Zhou Enlai, 1898–1976*. London: Hutchinson, 1984.

Witke, Roxane. *Comrade Chiang Ching*. London: Weidenfeld, 1977.

Yao Ming-le. *The Conspiracy and Murder of Mao's Heir.* London: Collins, 1983.

Zhou Enlai. *Selected Works of Zhou Enlai.* Vol 1. Peking: Foreign Languages Press, 1981.

Index

300–303; Mao in, 26–8, 33; and
Northern Expedition, 35–6;
People's Commune, 153–4;
unrest (1966–7), 150–53;
Workers' Revolutionary General
Headquarters (WGHQ), 150,
151, 152, 153, 162
Shanghai Communiqué, 317
Shaoshan, 15
Shapiro, Michael, 206
Sharp, Jonathan, 327
Shenyang, 268, 273–4
Shu-meng: *see* Jiang Qing
Sihanouk, Prince Norodom, 281
silk trade, 2, 3
Smedley, Agnes, 41
Snow, Edgar, 15, 17, 18, 32, 35, 57,
102, 213, 228, 247, 281, 326–7,
330, 338, 339
Socialist Education Movement, 102,
106
Song dynasty, 5
Soong Ching Ling, 11, 24, 37, 59,
140–41
Soong Meiling (Soong Mei-ling), 34
'Soviets', 35, 39–41, 48, 49, 50, 64
Soviet Union: aid from, 12, 46, 76,
93–4, 100, 341–2, 345; barter
agreement (1949), 343; breach
with (1959), 31, 93–9, 100, 113,
342; nuclear weapons, 111–12,
257–8, 325; resumed relations,
317; threat from, 184, 220, 221,
224, 238, 257–8, 276, 278, 324–6
Spain, trade with, 6
Special Economic Zones, 172
Spratly Islands, 6, 89
Stalin, Joseph, 42, 47, 69, 76, 78,
93, 216, 324, 345
Strong, Anna Louise, 116
Stuart, Leighton, 201
Study and Criticism, 277
Sun Tzu, 1, 39, 43, 179
Sun Yat-sen, President, 10–12, 19,
24, 33, 34, 329
surveillance methods, 185–6, 215

Taiping Revolt, 8–9, 19
Taiwan, 87, 89, 93, 279, 317, 325,
342

Tang dynasty, 4–5
Tang, Nancy, 122
Tang-ku Truce (1933), 50
Tang Na, 295
Tangshan earthquake, 297
Taoism, 2
tape-recordings, 121, 333–4
technological education, 110
Ting Ling: *see* Ding Ling
Tito, Marshal, 345
torture, 255, 332, 334, 335
trade unions, 267
Tseng Szu-yü: *see* Zeng Siyu
Tsu-hsi: *see* Cixi
'28 Bolsheviks', 47, 48, 49, 50, 52,
62, 145, 219
224 Group, 335

unemployment, 317
United Front, 58–9, 74
United League, 11, 12, 24
United Nations, 88, 248
United States, 77, 87, 113, 185, 220,
227–8, 248, 249, 261, 317, 326–8

Versailles Peace Conference (1919),
22, 27, 28
Vietnam War, 104, 113–14
Voitinsky, Gregory, 32
Voroshilov, K.E., 218

wall posters: *see* propaganda
campaigns
Wang Dabin (Wang Ta-pin), 177
Wang Dongxing (Wang Tung-
hsing), 194–5, 255, 270, 284,
301, 303, 304, 310, 312, 314
Wang Guangmei, 107, 126, 147,
156, 175, 199, 200, 202, 332, 346
Wang Guangying, 202
Wang Hairong, 122
Wang Hongwen, 150, 152, 207, 262,
267–8, 269, 272–3, 284, 300; in
Gang of Four, 262, 267, 269, 288,
300, 301, 302, 336; and Jiang
Qing, 267, 269, 270
Wang Kunlun, 334
Wang Li, 160, 161, 162, 193
Wang Ming, 47–8, 49, 55, 62–3,
66, 67, 219, 231, 340

The best in biography from Grafton Books

To order direct from the publisher just tick the titles you want
and fill in the order form.

GB381

The best in biography from Grafton Books

J Bryan III and Charles J V Murphy
The Windsor Story (illustrated)   £2.95 □

Margaret Forster
The Rash Adventurer (illustrated)   £3.50 □

Antonia Fraser
Mary Queen of Scots (illustrated)   £3.95 □
Cromwell: Our Chief of Men   £3.95 □

Eric Linklater
The Prince in the Heather (illustrated)   £2.50 □

Henri Troyat
Catherine the Great   £2.95 □

Sir Arthur Bryant
Samuel Pepys: The Man in the Making   £3.95 □
Samuel Pepys: The Years of Peril   £3.95 □
Samuel Pepys: Saviour of the Navy   £3.95 □

Sara Bradford
Princess Grace (illustrated)   £2.50 □

Ann Morrow
The Queen (illustrated)   £2.50 □
The Queen Mother (illustrated)   £2.95 □

To order direct from the publisher just tick the titles you want
and fill in the order form.   **GB181**

All these books are available at your local bookshop or newsagent, or can be ordered direct from the publisher.

To order direct from the publishers just tick the titles you want and fill in the form below.

Name _____

Address _____

_____

Send to:
Grafton Cash Sales
PO Box 11, Falmouth, Cornwall TR10 9EN.

Please enclose remittance to the value of the cover price plus:

UK 55p for the first book, 22p for the second book plus 14p per copy for each additional book ordered to a maximum charge of £1.75.

BFPO and Eire 55p for the first book, 22p for the second book plus 14p per copy for the next 7 books, thereafter 8p per book.

Overseas £1.25 for the first book and 31p for each additional book.

Grafton Books reserve the right to show new retail prices on covers, which may differ from those previously advertised in the text or elsewhere.